Love Me,
Love Me Not

8

IO SAKISAKA

AUG 2021

Contents

Piece 29..........3

Piece 30..........45

Piece 31..........91

Piece 32..........137

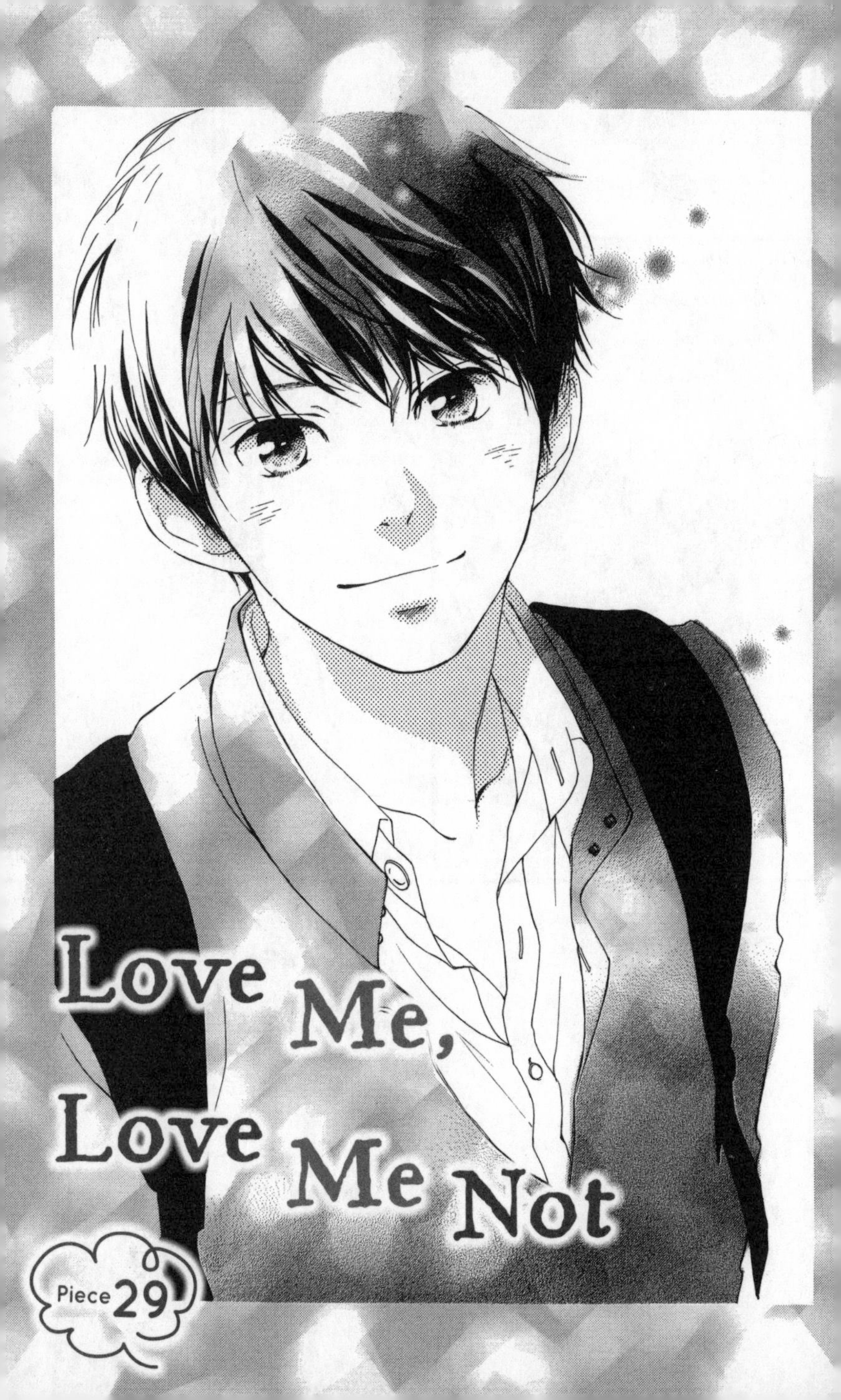
Love Me, Love Me Not
Piece 29

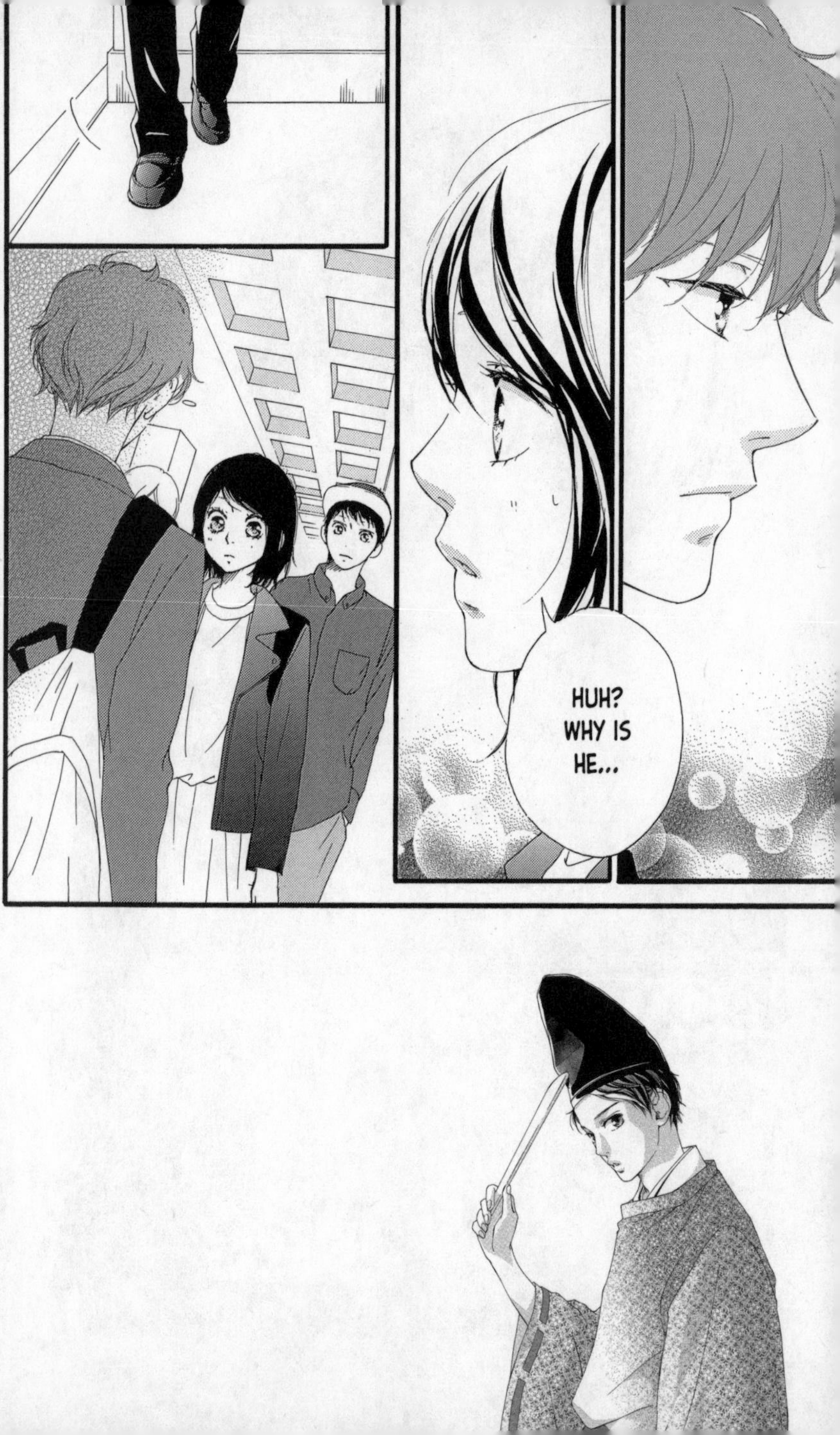
HUH? WHY IS HE...

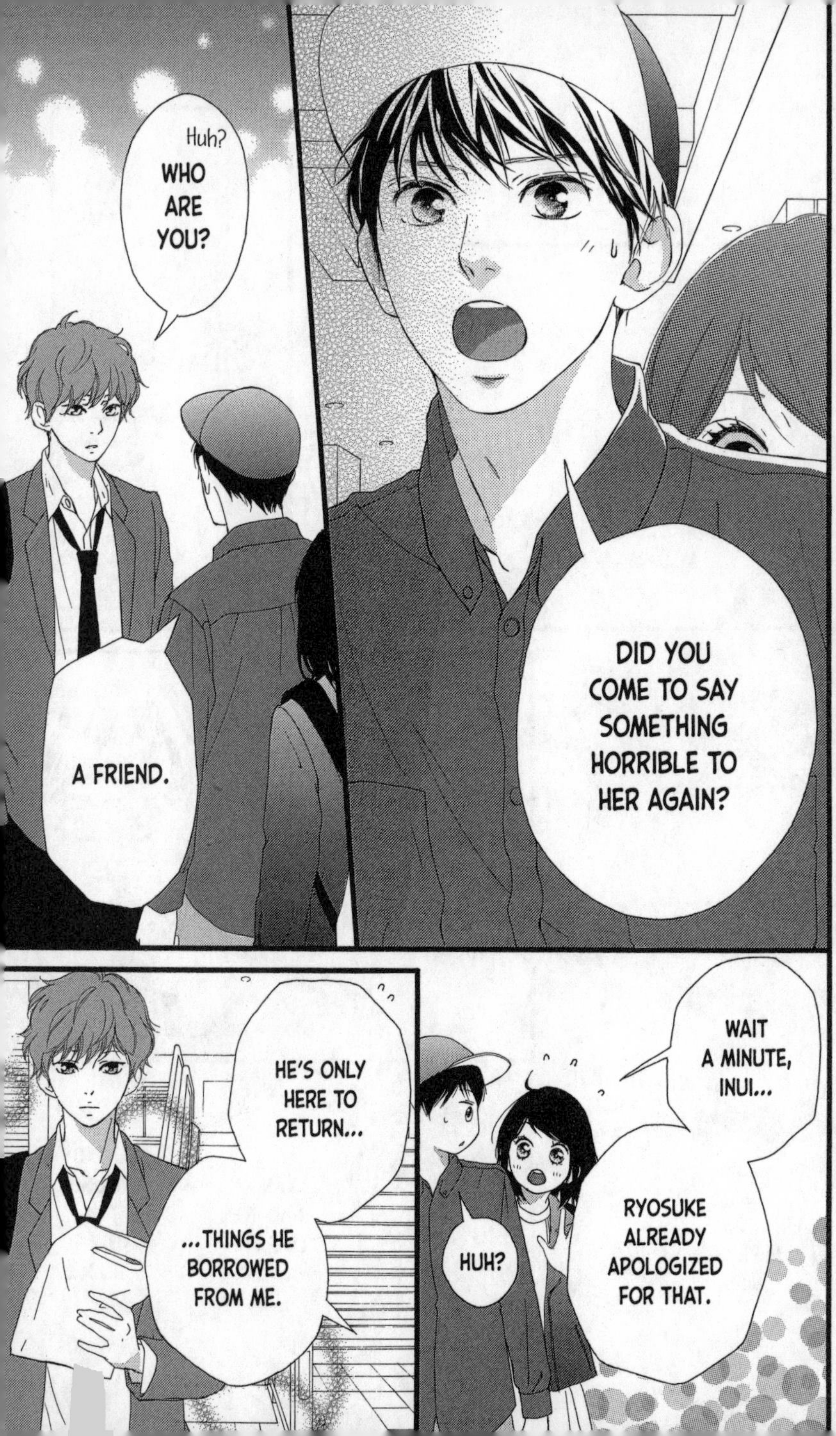
DID YOU COME TO SAY SOMETHING HORRIBLE TO HER AGAIN?
Huh? WHO ARE YOU?
A FRIEND.
WAIT A MINUTE, INUI...
RYOSUKE ALREADY APOLOGIZED FOR THAT.
HUH?
HE'S ONLY HERE TO RETURN...
...THINGS HE BORROWED FROM ME.

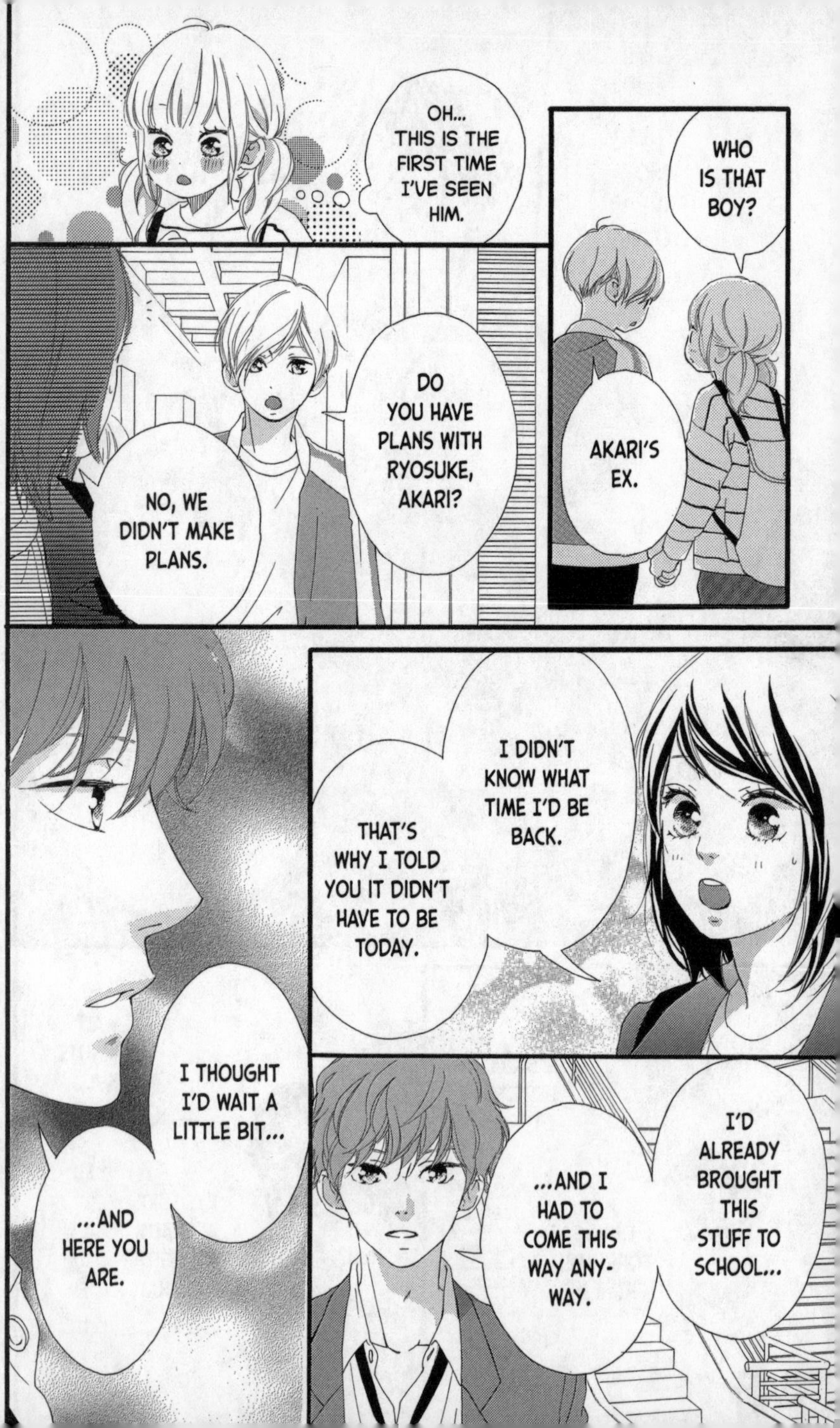
WHO IS THAT BOY?
AKARI'S EX.
OH... THIS IS THE FIRST TIME I'VE SEEN HIM.
DO YOU HAVE PLANS WITH RYOSUKE, AKARI?
NO, WE DIDN'T MAKE PLANS.
I DIDN'T KNOW WHAT TIME I'D BE BACK.
THAT'S WHY I TOLD YOU IT DIDN'T HAVE TO BE TODAY.
I'D ALREADY BROUGHT THIS STUFF TO SCHOOL...
...AND I HAD TO COME THIS WAY ANY-WAY.
I THOUGHT I'D WAIT A LITTLE BIT...
...AND HERE YOU ARE.

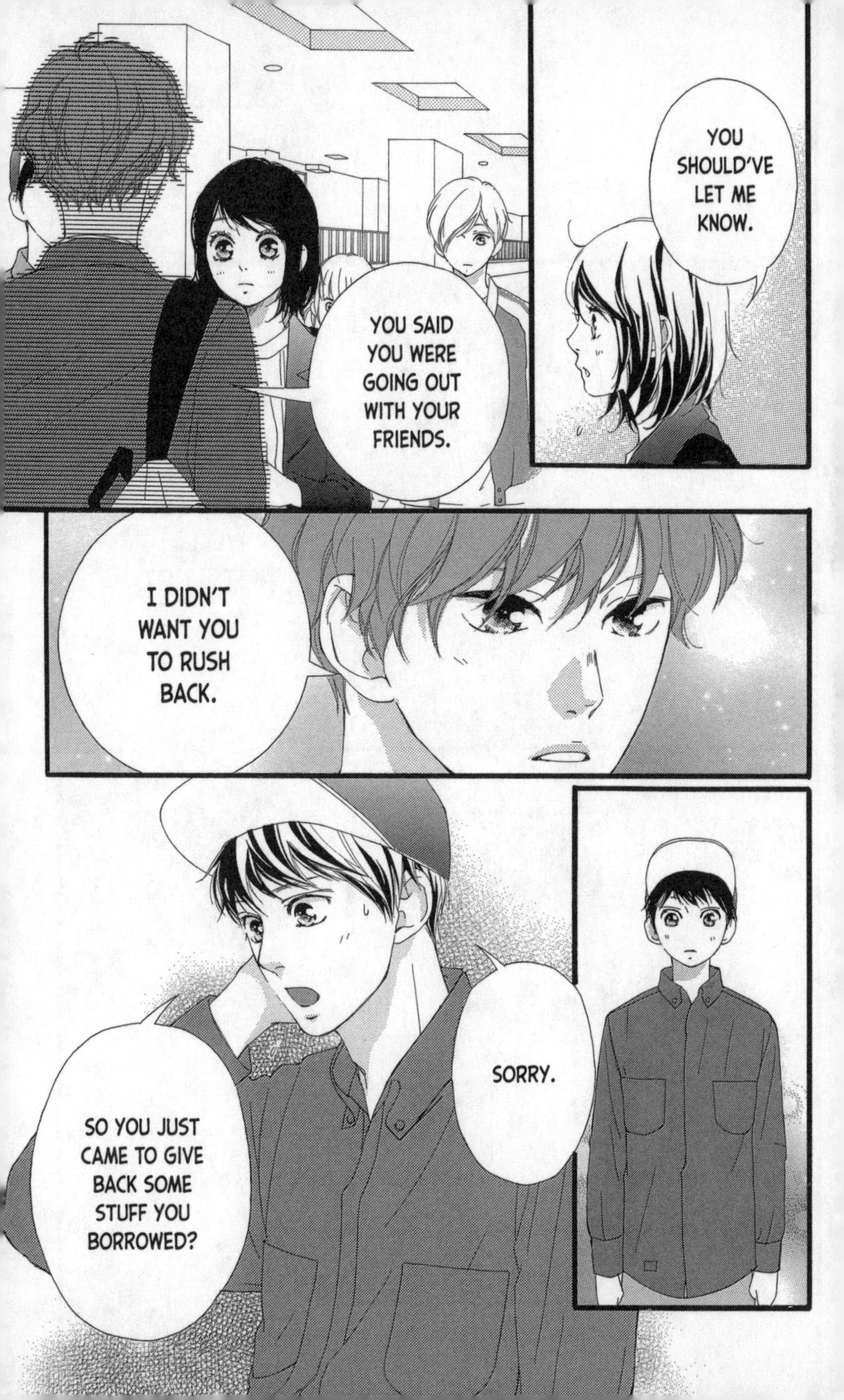
YOU SHOULD'VE LET ME KNOW.
YOU SAID YOU WERE GOING OUT WITH YOUR FRIENDS.
I DIDN'T WANT YOU TO RUSH BACK.
SORRY.
SO YOU JUST CAME TO GIVE BACK SOME STUFF YOU BORROWED?

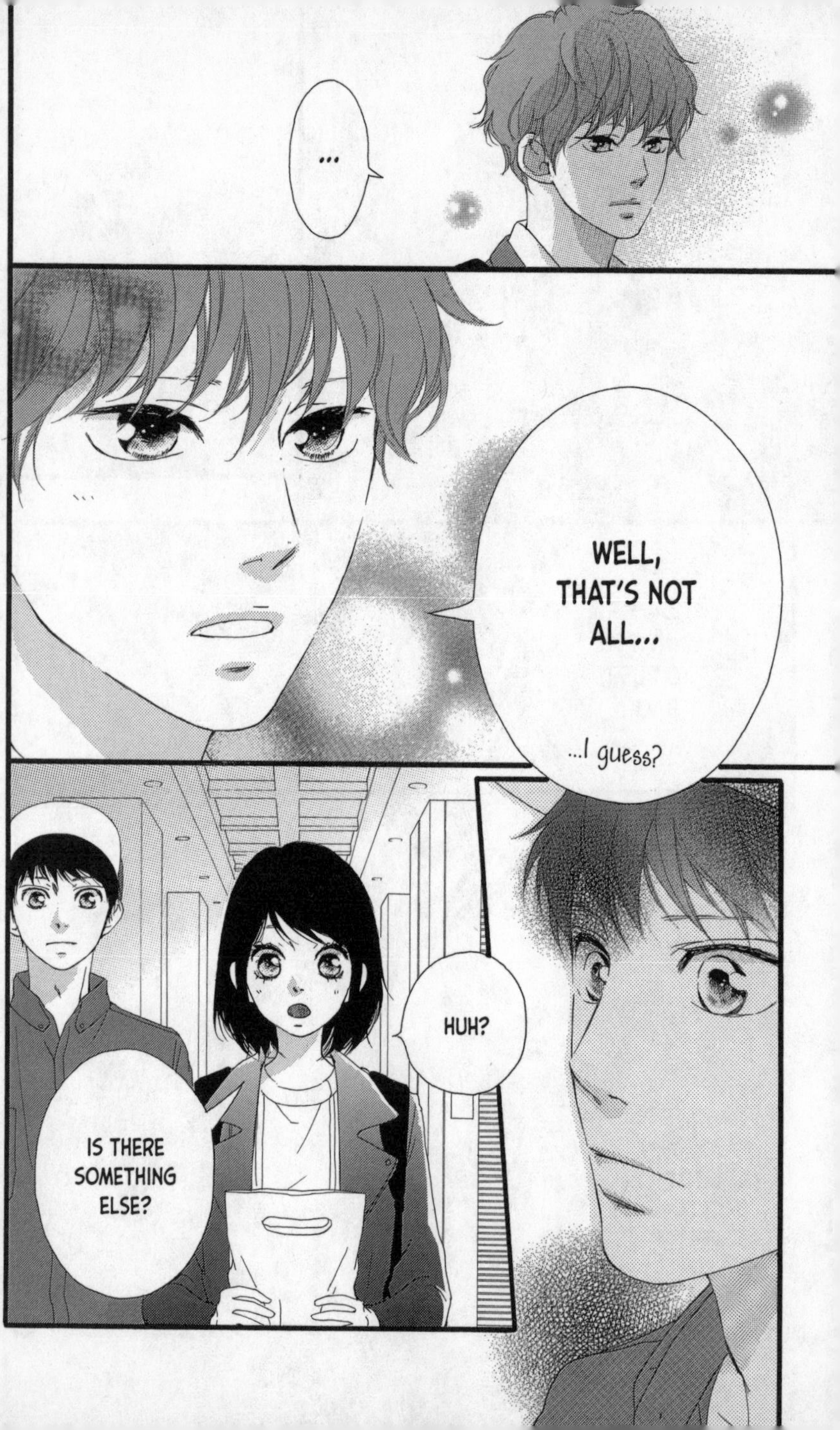
...
...
WELL, THAT'S NOT ALL...
...I guess?
HUH?
IS THERE SOMETHING ELSE?

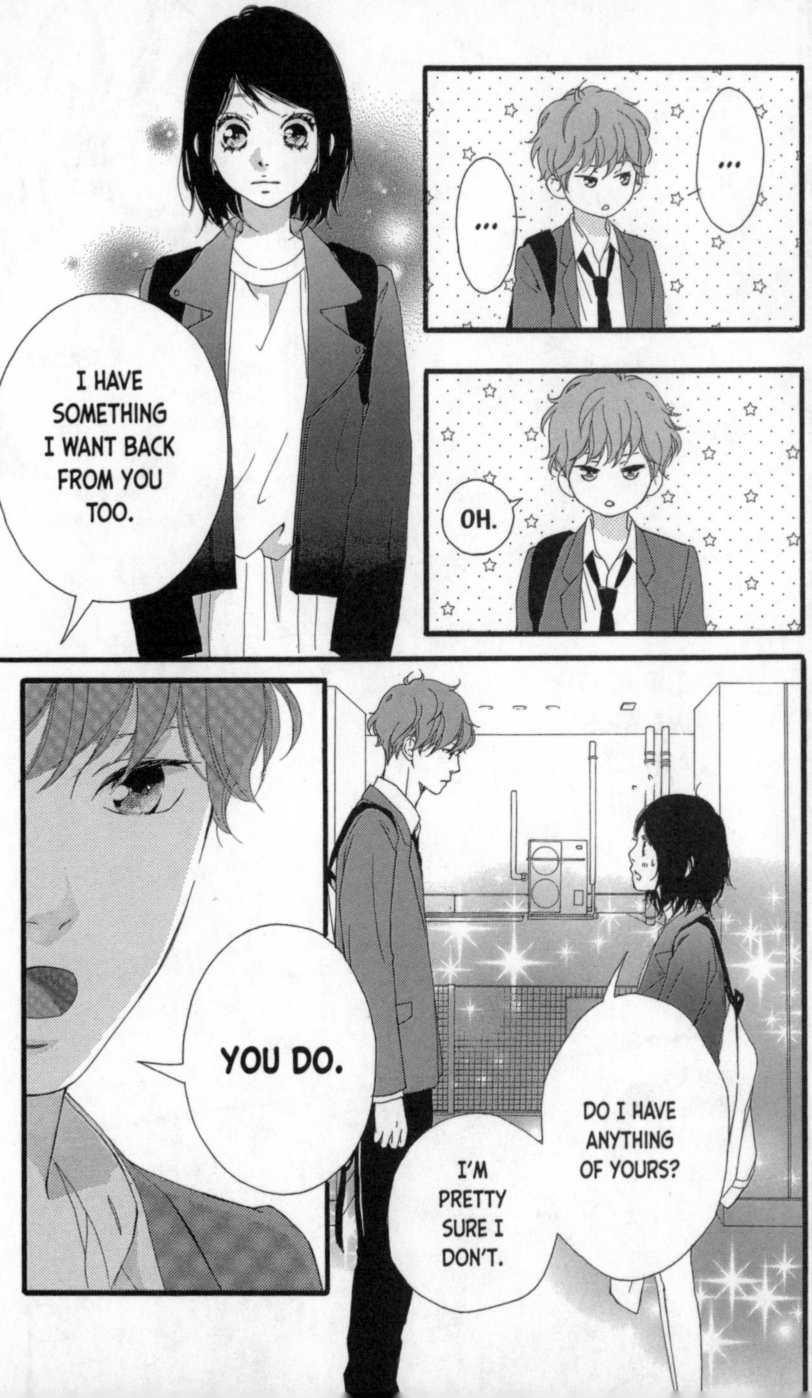
...
...
OH.
I HAVE SOMETHING I WANT BACK FROM YOU TOO.
DO I HAVE ANYTHING OF YOURS?
I'M PRETTY SURE I DON'T.
YOU DO.

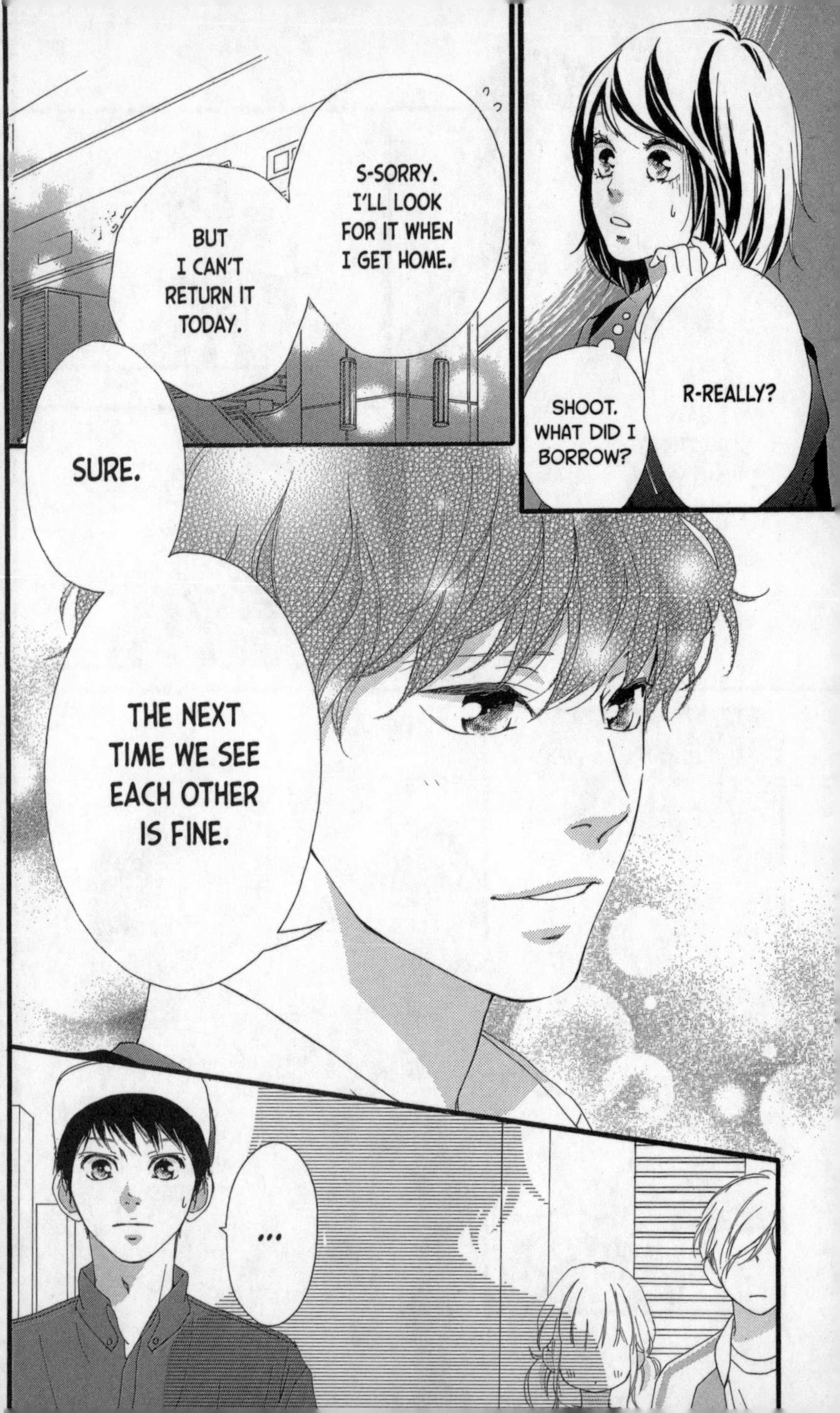
R-REALLY?
SHOOT. WHAT DID I BORROW?
S-SORRY. I'LL LOOK FOR IT WHEN I GET HOME.
BUT I CAN'T RETURN IT TODAY.
SURE.
THE NEXT TIME WE SEE EACH OTHER IS FINE.
...

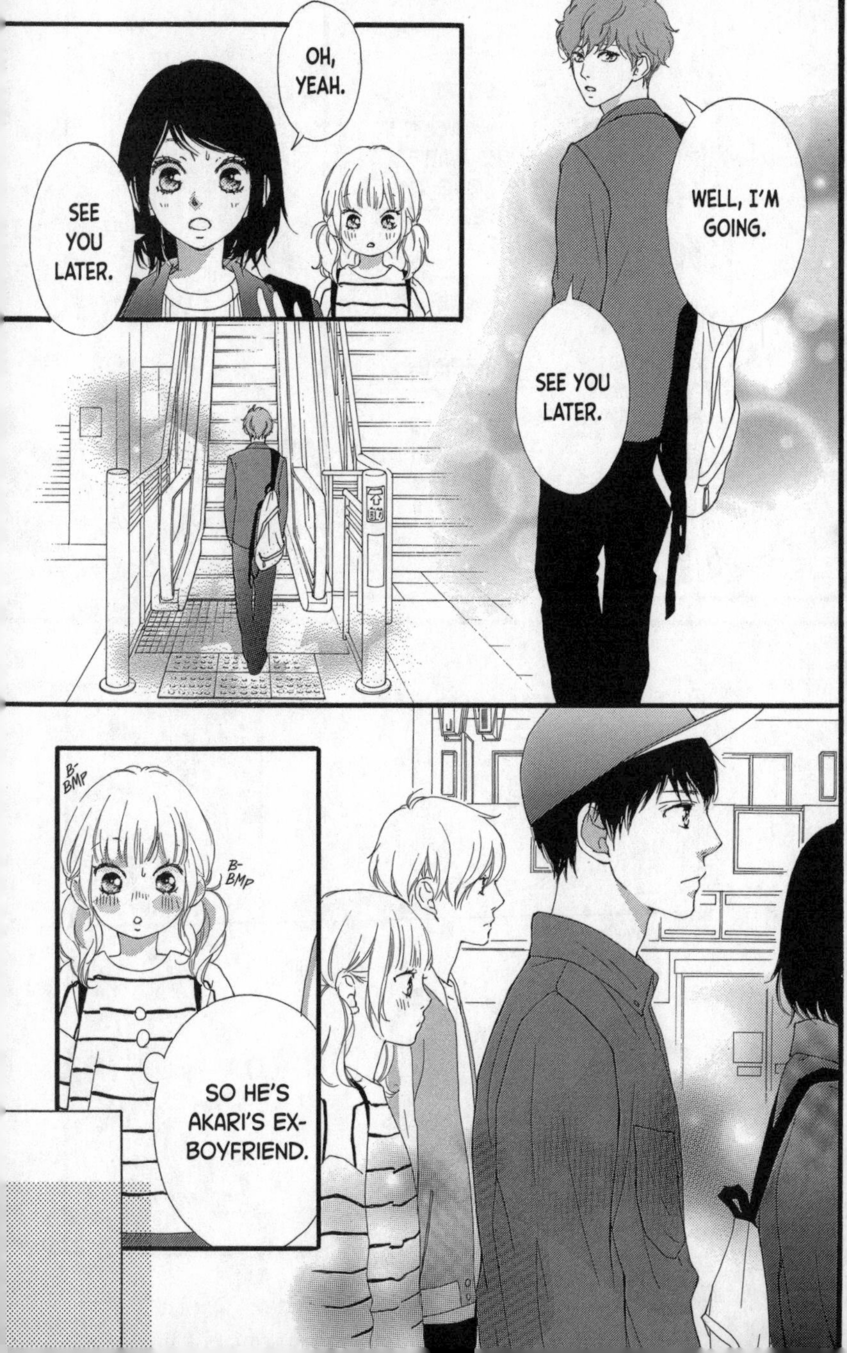
WELL, I'M GOING.
SEE YOU LATER.
OH, YEAH.
SEE YOU LATER.
B-BMP
B-BMP
SO HE'S AKARI'S EX-BOYFRIEND.

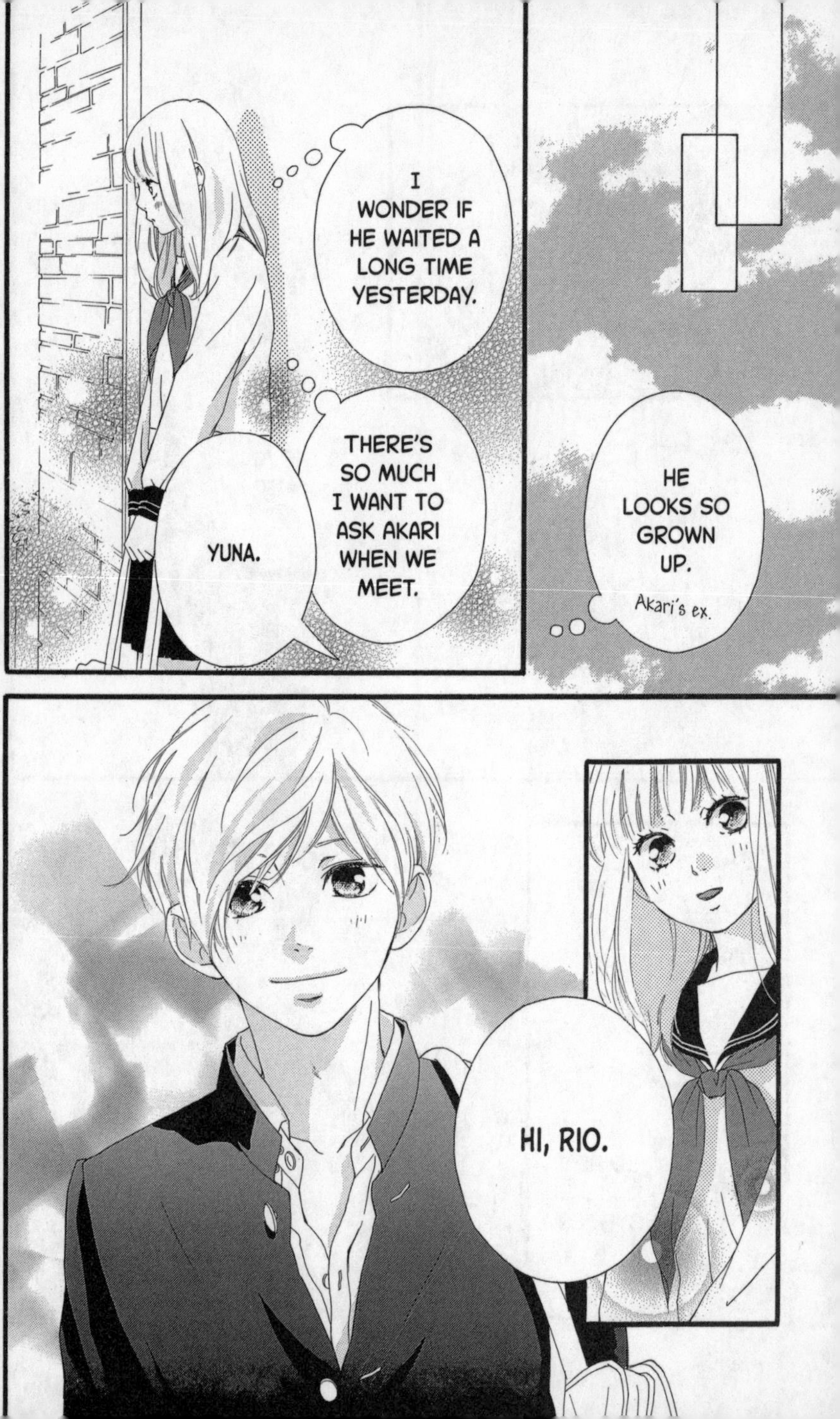
HE LOOKS SO GROWN UP.
Akari's ex.
I WONDER IF HE WAITED A LONG TIME YESTERDAY.
THERE'S SO MUCH I WANT TO ASK AKARI WHEN WE MEET.
YUNA.
HI, RIO.

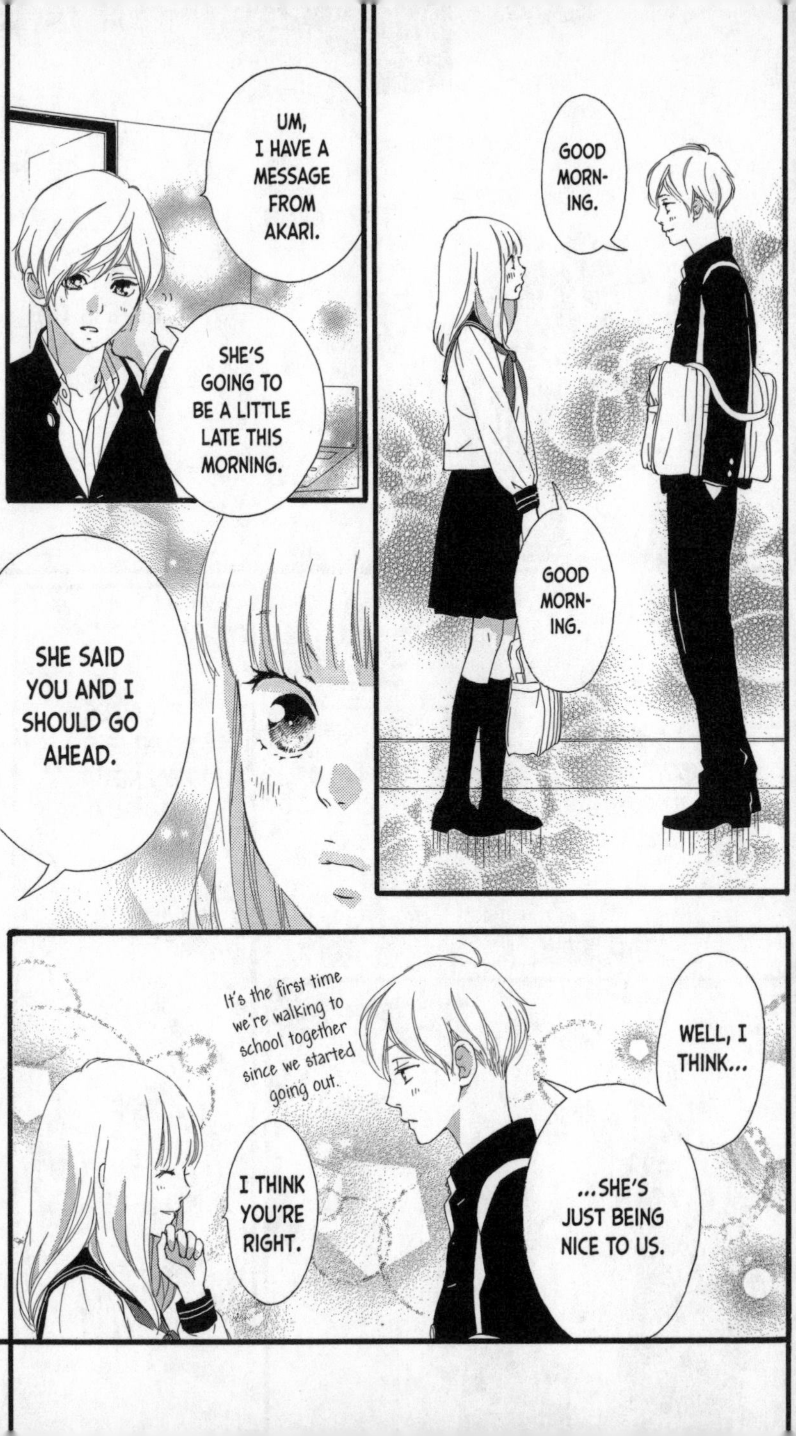
GOOD MORN-ING.
GOOD MORN-ING.
UM, I HAVE A MESSAGE FROM AKARI.
SHE'S GOING TO BE A LITTLE LATE THIS MORNING.
SHE SAID YOU AND I SHOULD GO AHEAD.
WELL, I THINK...
...SHE'S JUST BEING NICE TO US.
It's the first time we're walking to school together since we started going out.
I THINK YOU'RE RIGHT.

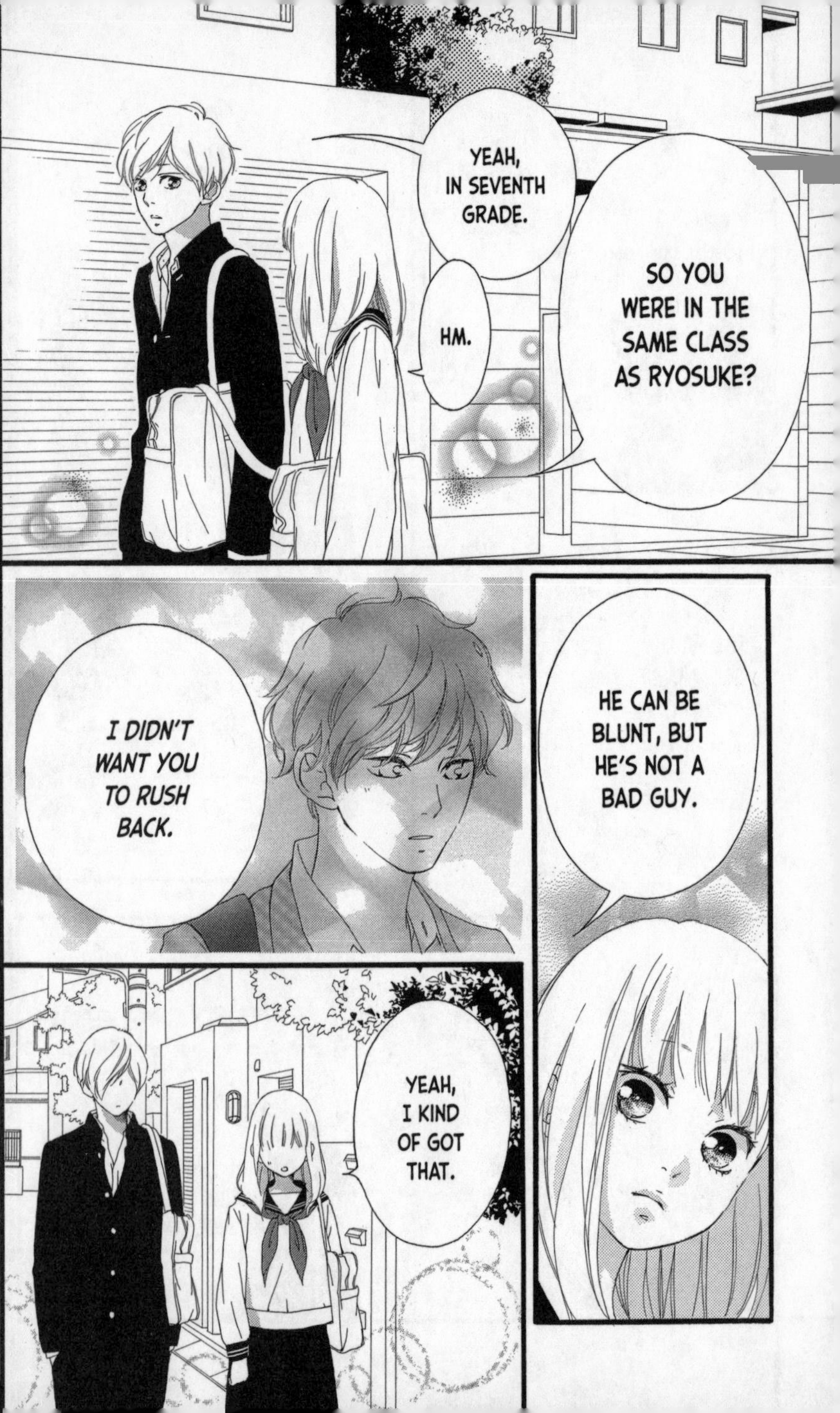
SO YOU WERE IN THE SAME CLASS AS RYOSUKE?
YEAH, IN SEVENTH GRADE.
HM.
HE CAN BE BLUNT, BUT HE'S NOT A BAD GUY.
I DIDN'T WANT YOU TO RUSH BACK.
YEAH, I KIND OF GOT THAT.

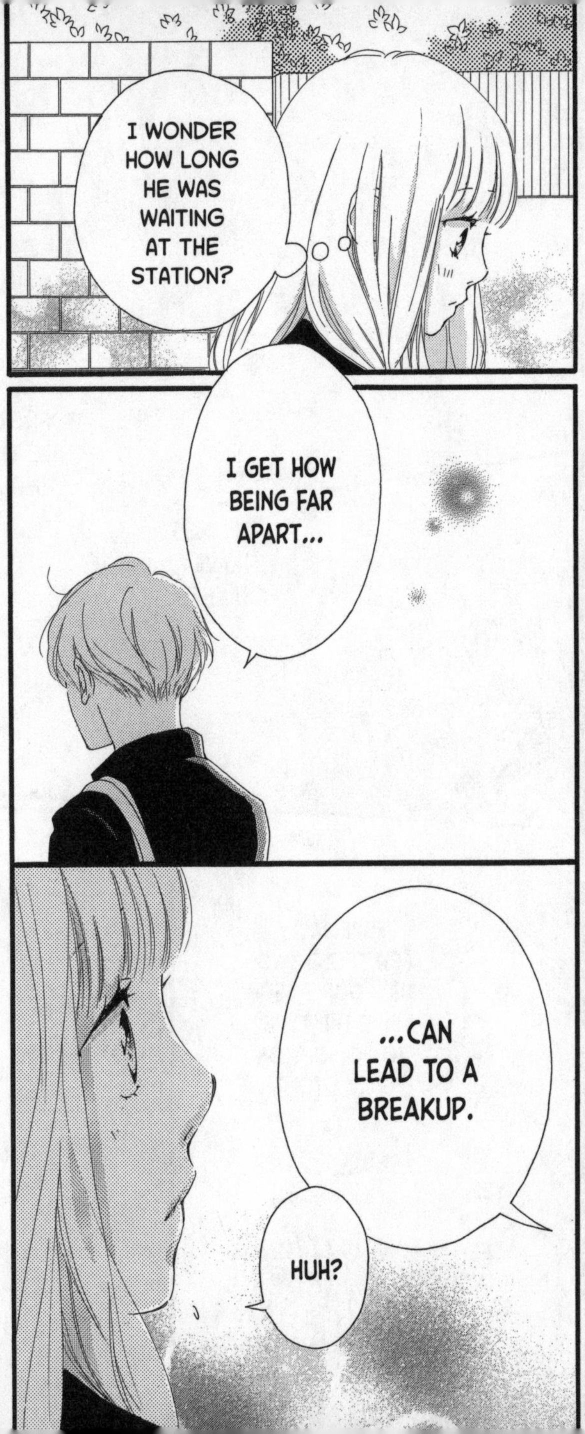
I WONDER HOW LONG HE WAS WAITING AT THE STATION?
I GET HOW BEING FAR APART...
...CAN LEAD TO A BREAKUP.
HUH?

Have you ever used the little eraser that's attached to the end of a mechanical pencil? There are people who never use it, but I use it pretty frequently. I checked all the mechanical pencils that I have around, and pretty much all of them show signs that I've used the eraser. Whenever I use one of these erasers, I think, "Why is it made out of a material that makes it so hard to erase?" The lack of evolution in the eraser at the end of the mechanical pencil has always baffled me. But I was sure there was a reason for that, so I googled it, and sure enough, there is. The material used in regular erasers has a tendency to melt plastic when exposed for a long time. So it's not suitable for an eraser at the end of a mechanical pencil. Then I remembered that eraser crumbs have actually melted my pencil case, so it all makes sense now. I feel so much better.

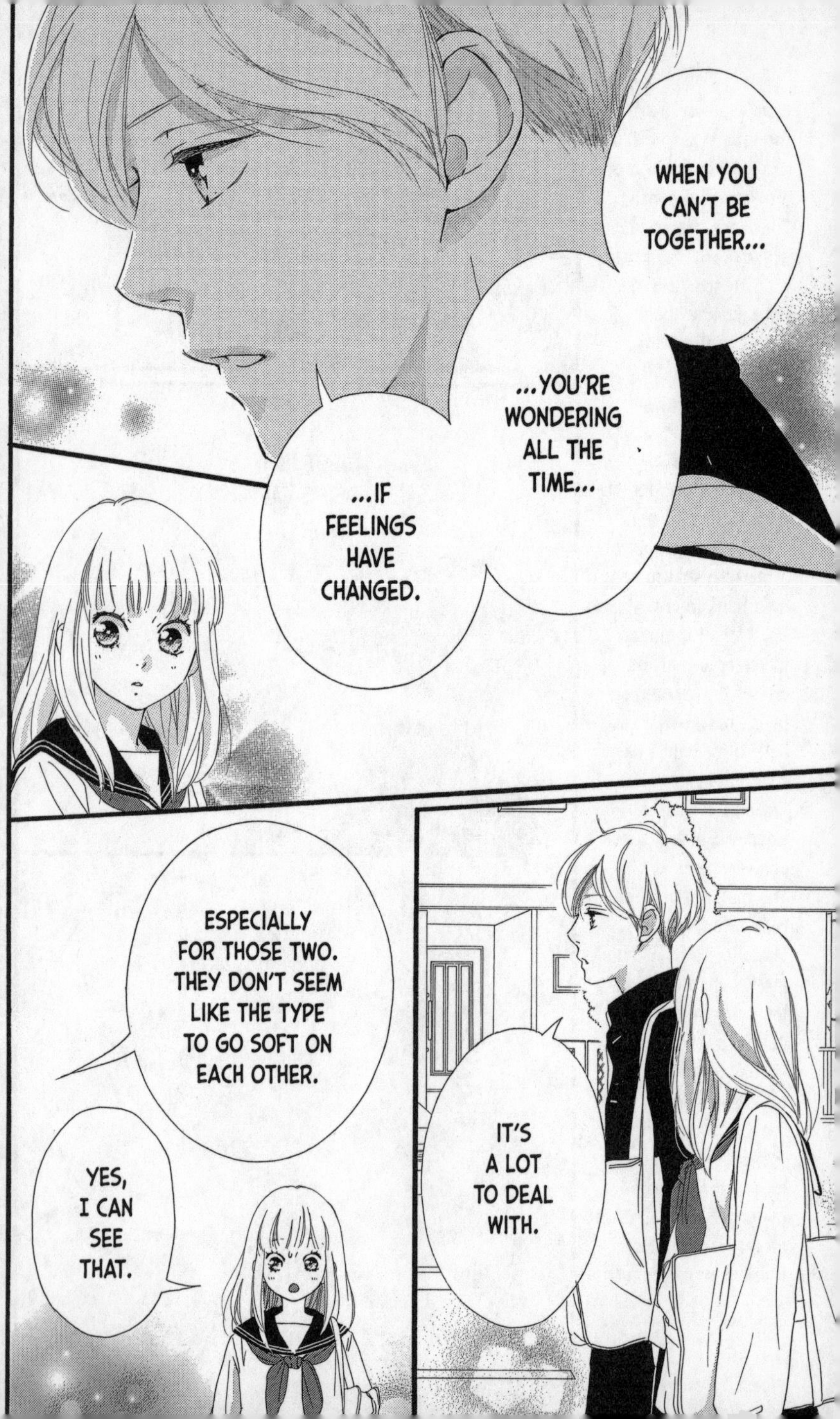
WHEN YOU CAN'T BE TOGETHER...
...YOU'RE WONDERING ALL THE TIME...
...IF FEELINGS HAVE CHANGED.
IT'S A LOT TO DEAL WITH.
ESPECIALLY FOR THOSE TWO. THEY DON'T SEEM LIKE THE TYPE TO GO SOFT ON EACH OTHER.
YES, I CAN SEE THAT.

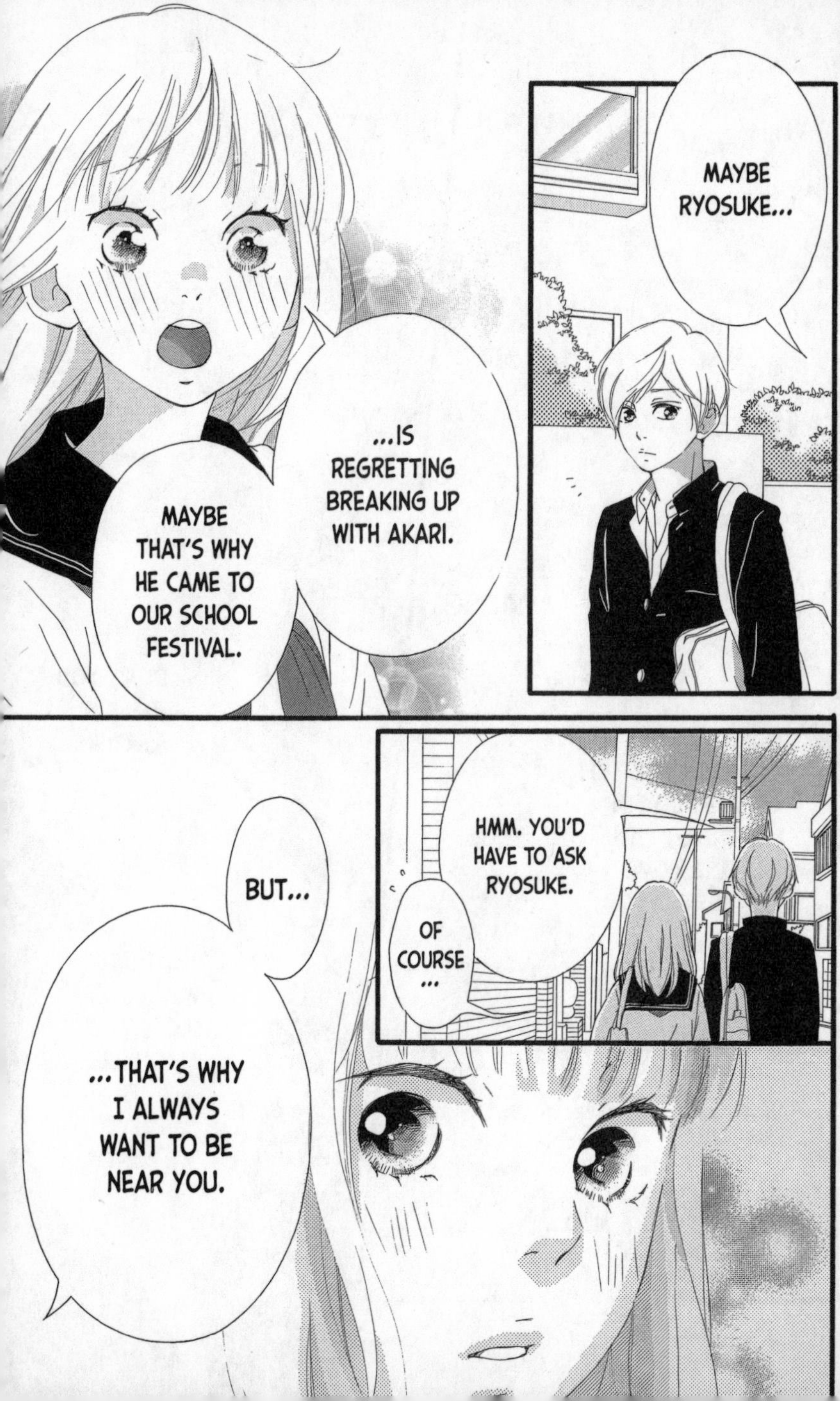
MAYBE RYOSUKE...
...IS REGRETTING BREAKING UP WITH AKARI.
MAYBE THAT'S WHY HE CAME TO OUR SCHOOL FESTIVAL.
HMM. YOU'D HAVE TO ASK RYOSUKE.
OF COURSE ...
BUT...
...THAT'S WHY I ALWAYS WANT TO BE NEAR YOU.

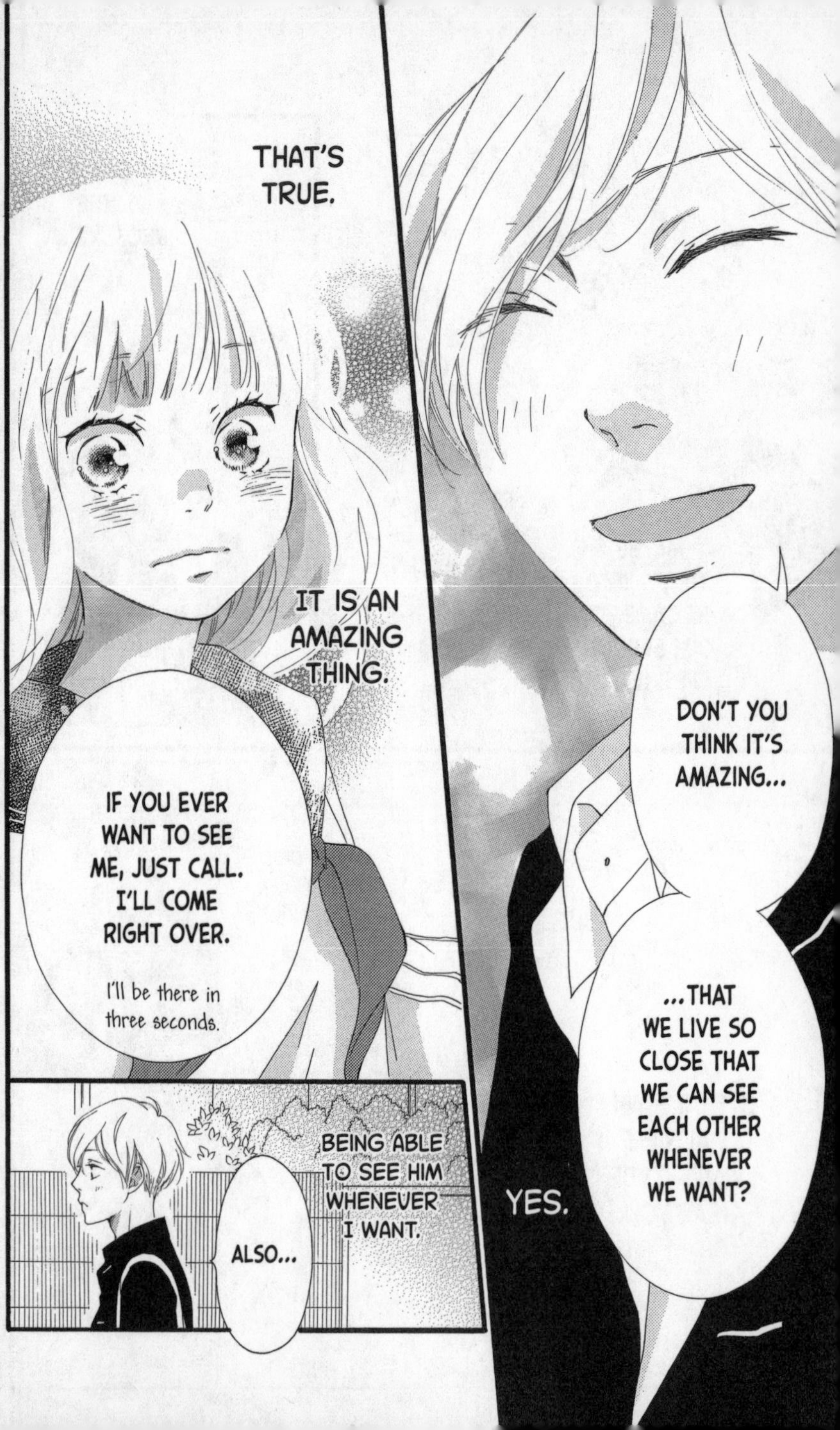
DON'T YOU THINK IT'S AMAZING...
...THAT WE LIVE SO CLOSE THAT WE CAN SEE EACH OTHER WHENEVER WE WANT?
YES.
THAT'S TRUE.
IT IS AN AMAZING THING.
IF YOU EVER WANT TO SEE ME, JUST CALL. I'LL COME RIGHT OVER.
I'll be there in three seconds.
BEING ABLE TO SEE HIM WHENEVER I WANT.
ALSO...

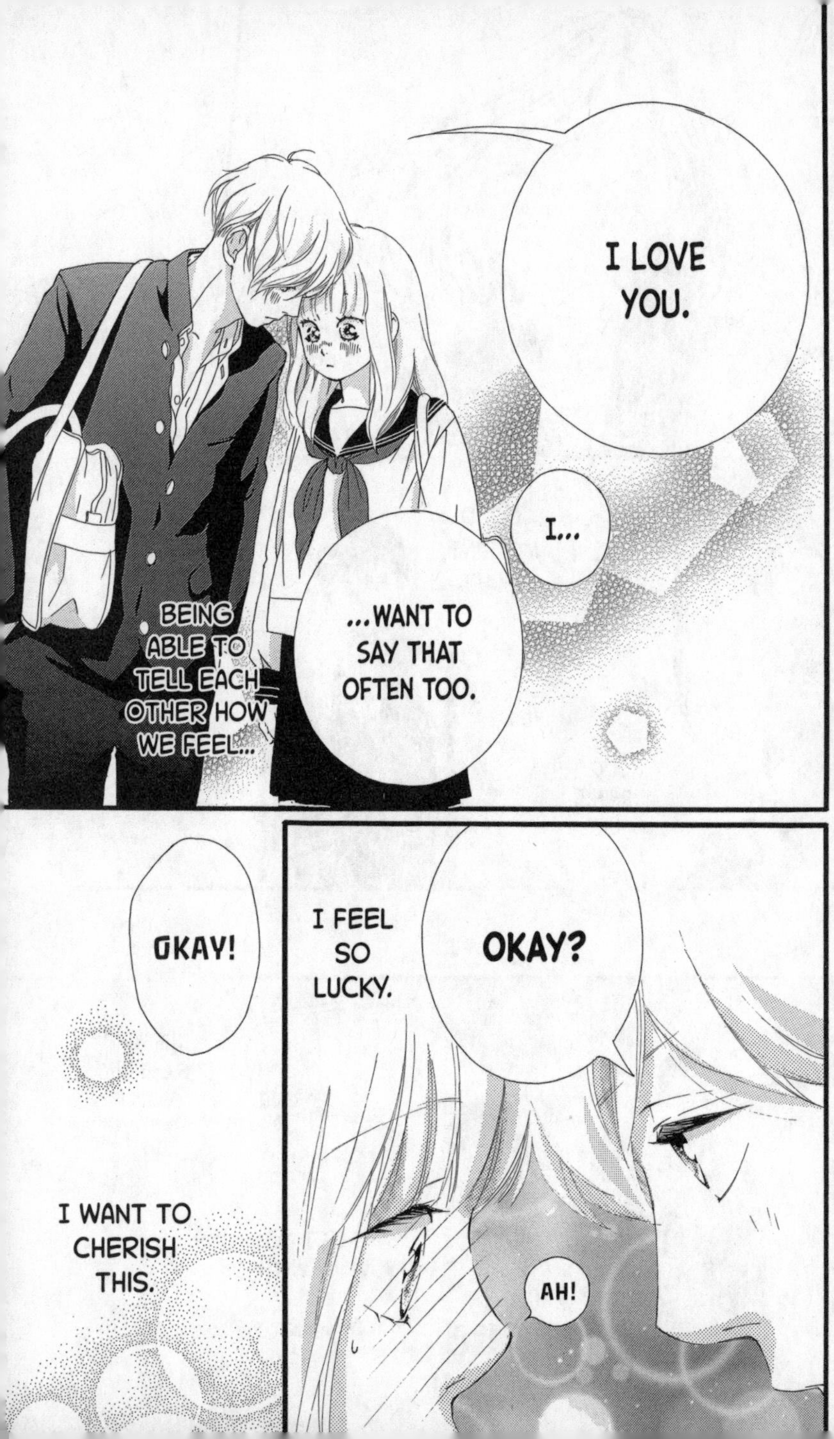
I LOVE YOU.
I...
...WANT TO SAY THAT OFTEN TOO.
BEING ABLE TO TELL EACH OTHER HOW WE FEEL...
OKAY?
I FEEL SO LUCKY.
AH!
OKAY!
I WANT TO CHERISH THIS.

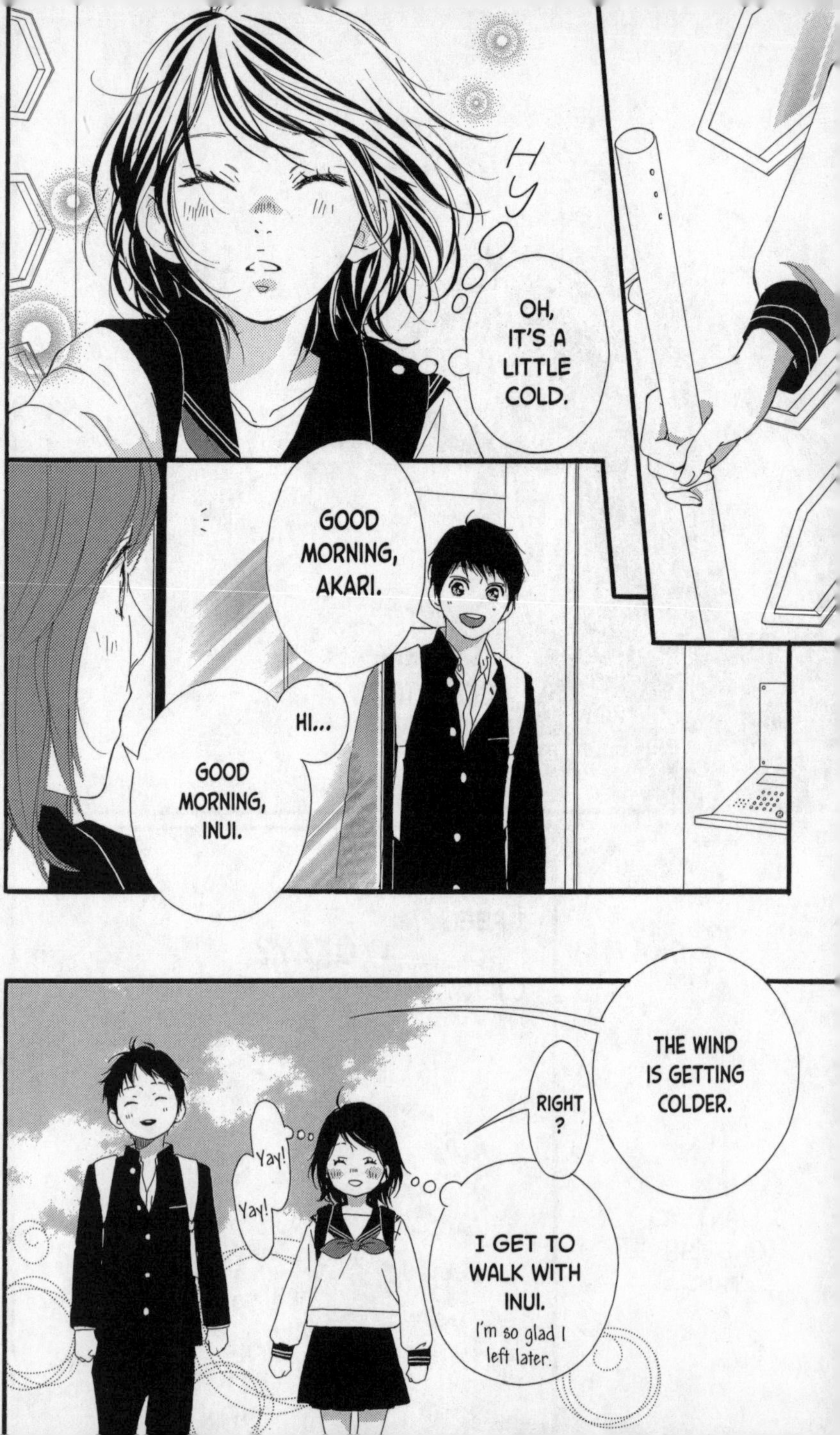
HYO
OH, IT'S A LITTLE COLD.
GOOD MORNING, AKARI.
HI...
GOOD MORNING, INUI.
THE WIND IS GETTING COLDER.
RIGHT?
I GET TO WALK WITH INUI.
I'm so glad I left later.
Yay!
Yay!

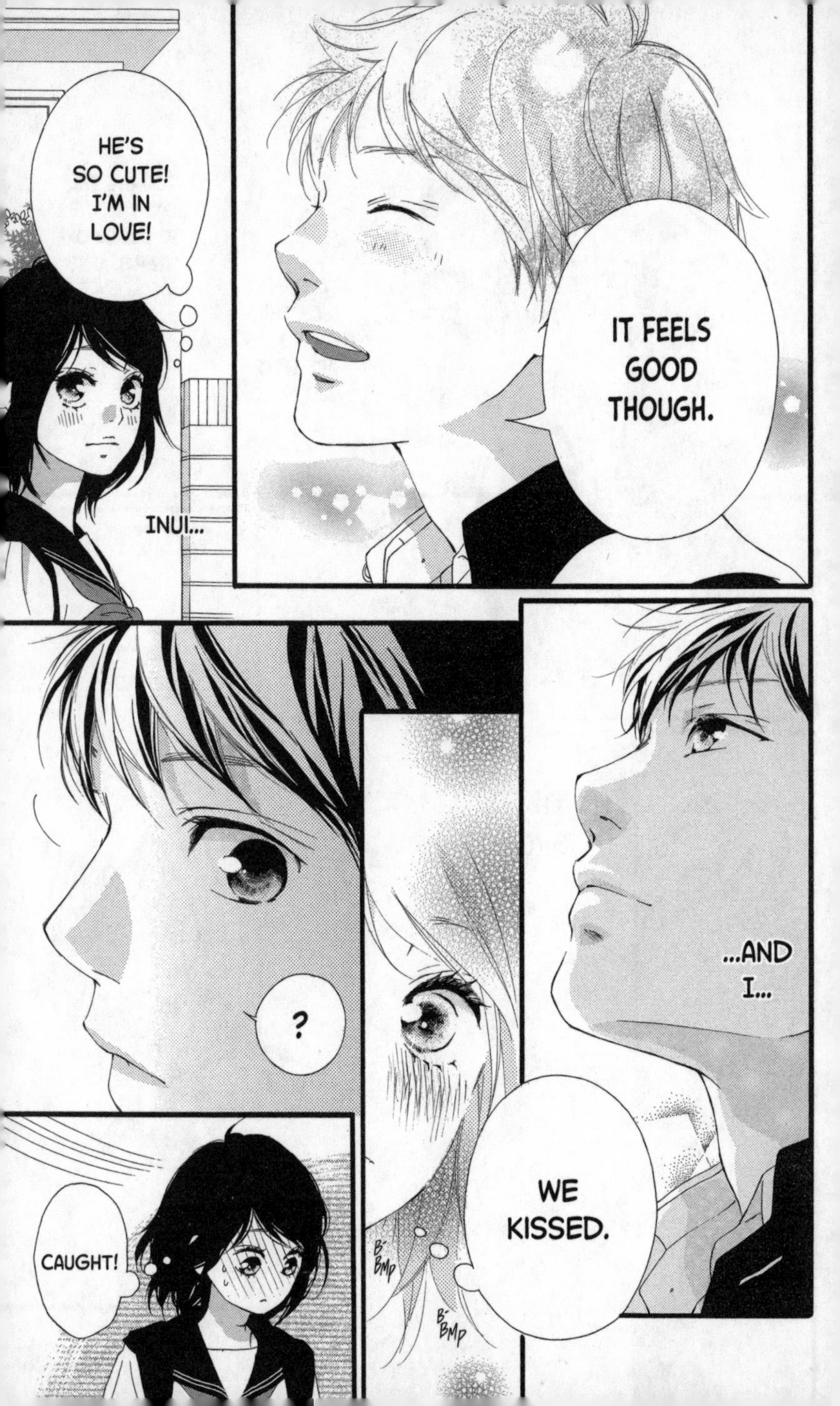
IT FEELS GOOD THOUGH.
HE'S SO CUTE! I'M IN LOVE!
INUI...
...AND I...
WE KISSED.
B-BMP
B-BMP
?
CAUGHT!

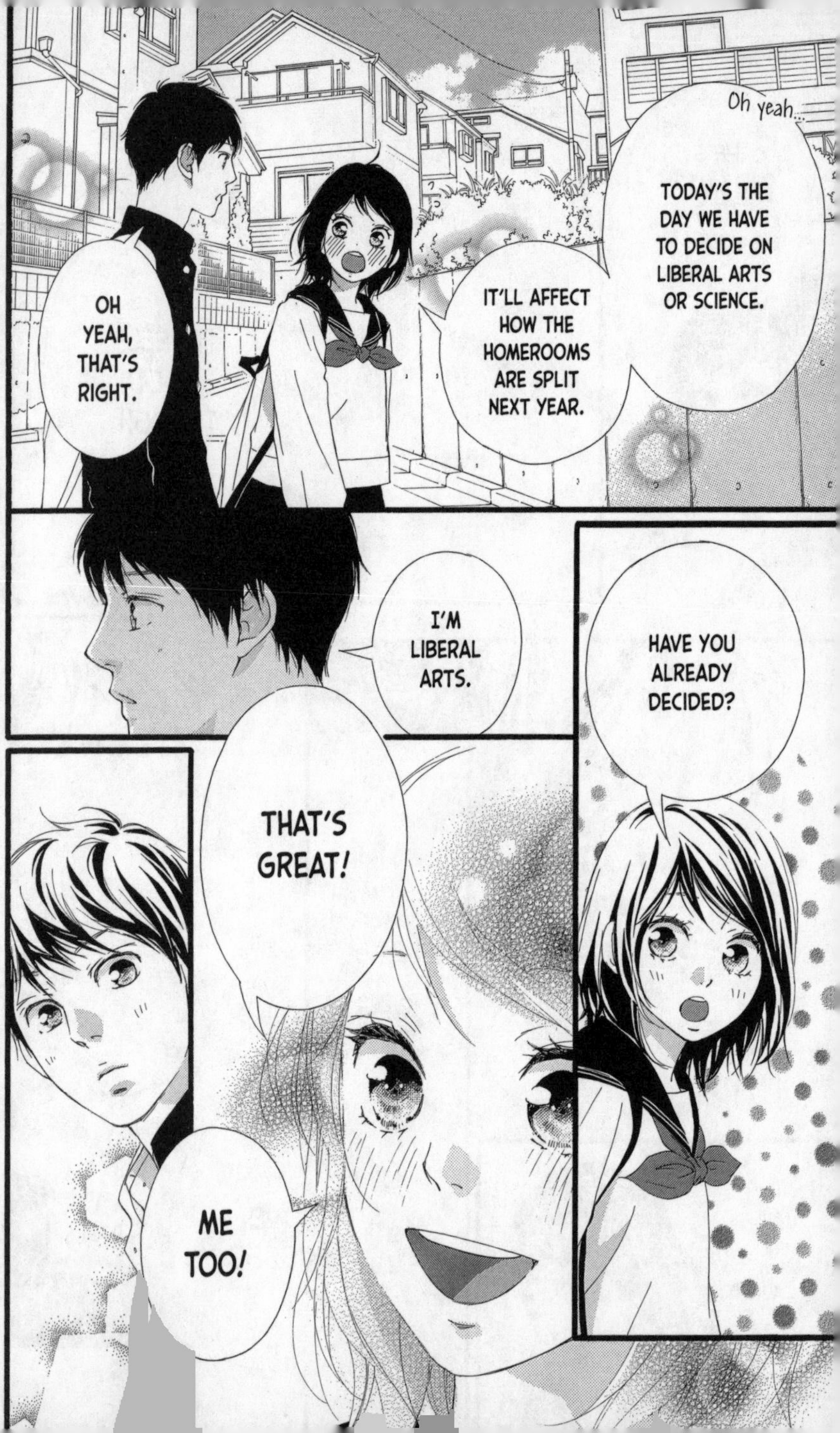
Oh yeah...
TODAY'S THE DAY WE HAVE TO DECIDE ON LIBERAL ARTS OR SCIENCE.
IT'LL AFFECT HOW THE HOMEROOMS ARE SPLIT NEXT YEAR.
OH YEAH, THAT'S RIGHT.
HAVE YOU ALREADY DECIDED?
I'M LIBERAL ARTS.
THAT'S GREAT!
ME TOO!

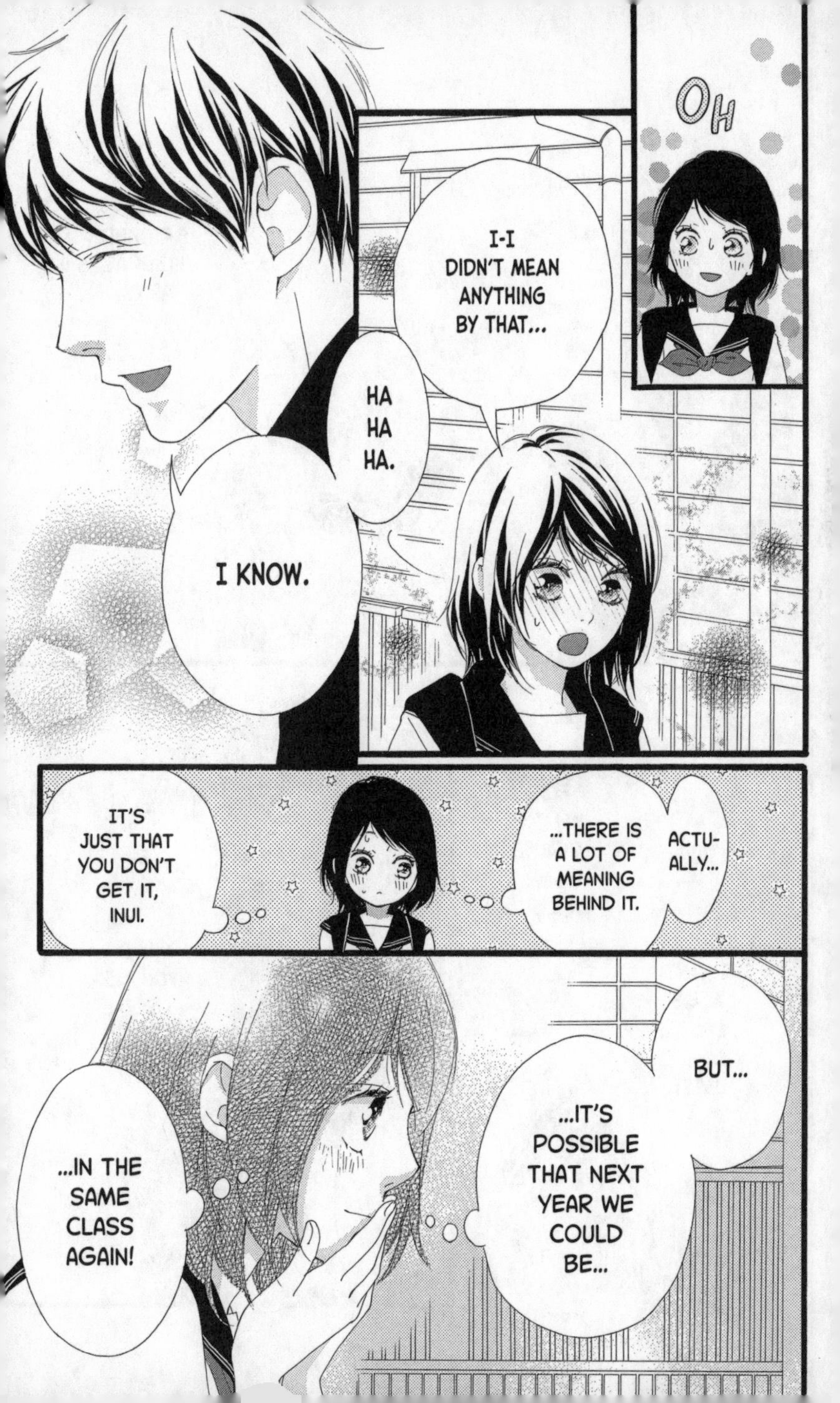
OH
I-I DIDN'T MEAN ANYTHING BY THAT...
HA HA HA.
I KNOW.
ACTU-ALLY...
...THERE IS A LOT OF MEANING BEHIND IT.
IT'S JUST THAT YOU DON'T GET IT, INUI.
BUT...
...IT'S POSSIBLE THAT NEXT YEAR WE COULD BE...
...IN THE SAME CLASS AGAIN!

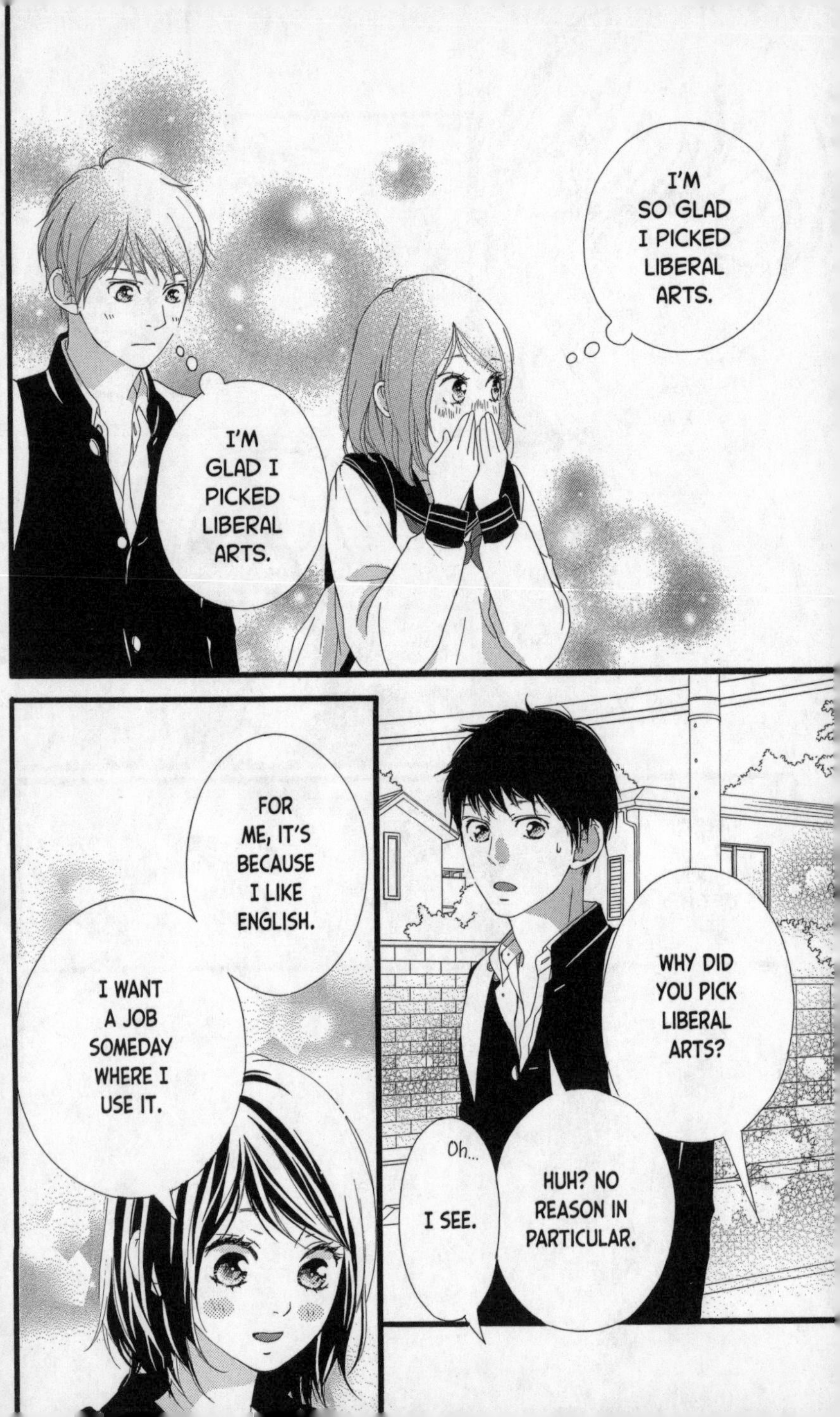
I'M SO GLAD I PICKED LIBERAL ARTS.
I'M GLAD I PICKED LIBERAL ARTS.
WHY DID YOU PICK LIBERAL ARTS?
HUH? NO REASON IN PARTICULAR.
Oh...
I SEE.
FOR ME, IT'S BECAUSE I LIKE ENGLISH.
I WANT A JOB SOMEDAY WHERE I USE IT.

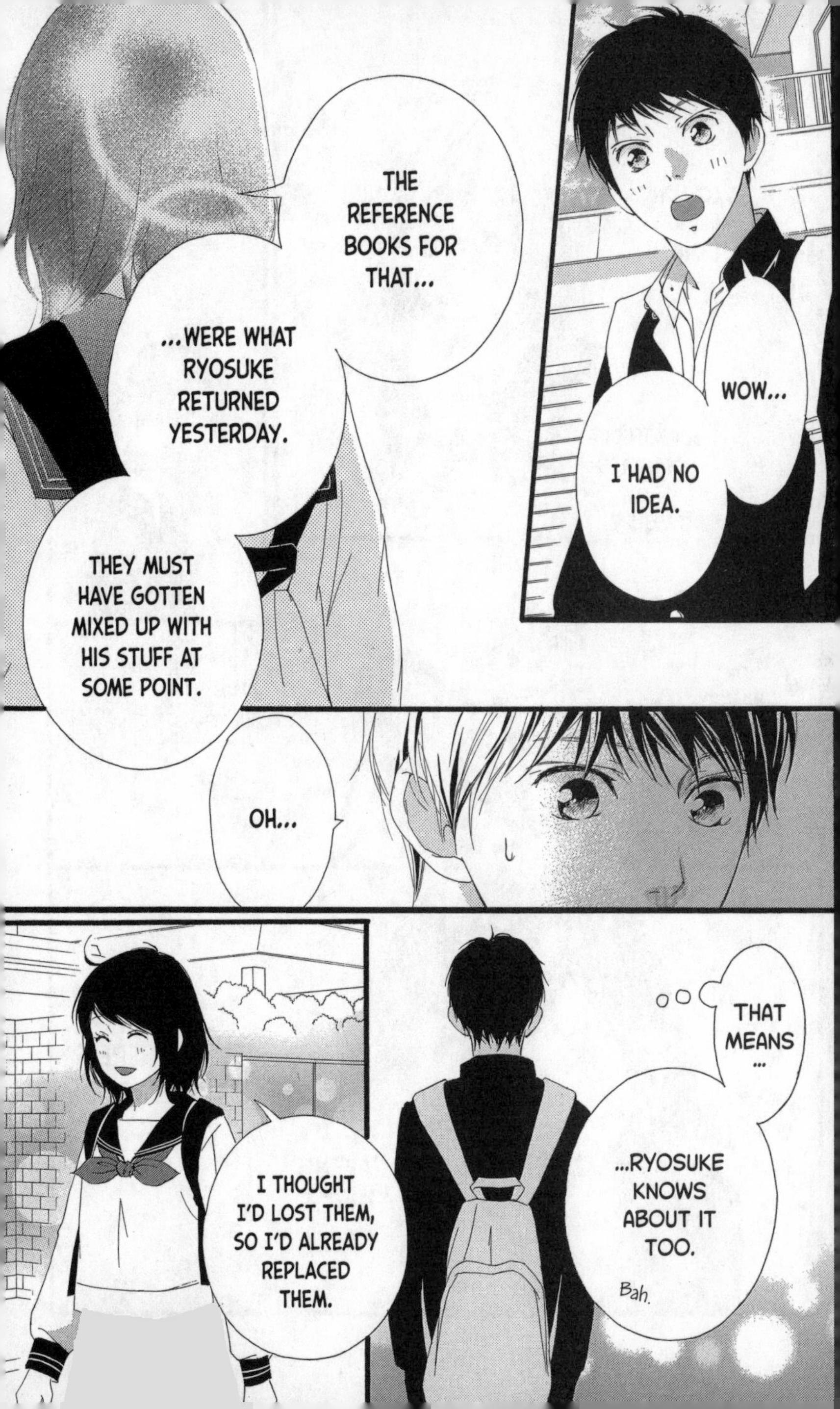
WOW...
I HAD NO IDEA.
THE REFERENCE BOOKS FOR THAT...
...WERE WHAT RYOSUKE RETURNED YESTERDAY.
THEY MUST HAVE GOTTEN MIXED UP WITH HIS STUFF AT SOME POINT.
OH...
THAT MEANS ...
...RYOSUKE KNOWS ABOUT IT TOO.
Bah.
I THOUGHT I'D LOST THEM, SO I'D ALREADY REPLACED THEM.

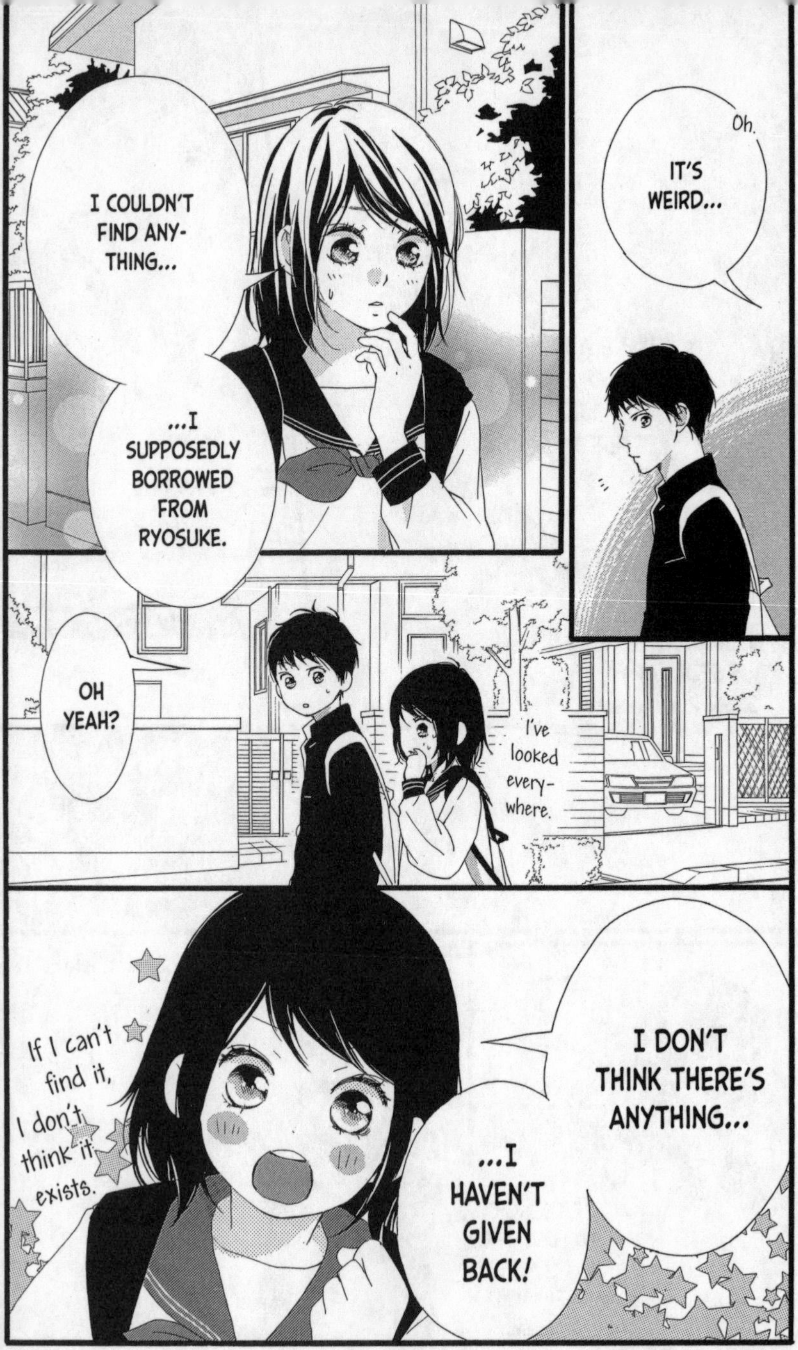
Oh.
IT'S WEIRD...
I COULDN'T FIND ANY-THING...
...I SUPPOSEDLY BORROWED FROM RYOSUKE.
I've looked every-where.
OH YEAH?
I DON'T THINK THERE'S ANYTHING...
...I HAVEN'T GIVEN BACK!
If I can't find it, I don't think it exists.

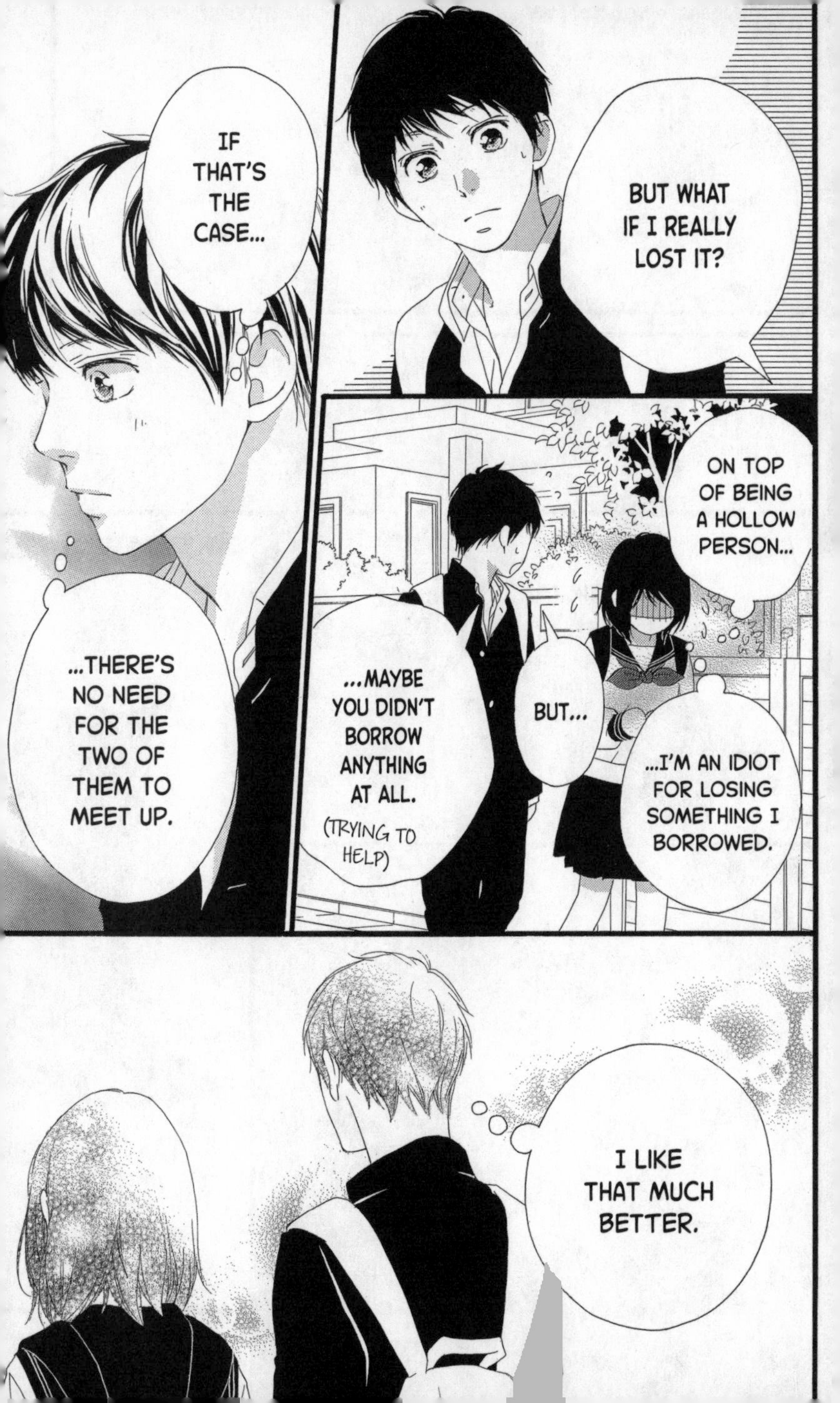
BUT WHAT IF I REALLY LOST IT?
ON TOP OF BEING A HOLLOW PERSON...
...I'M AN IDIOT FOR LOSING SOMETHING I BORROWED.
BUT...
...MAYBE YOU DIDN'T BORROW ANYTHING AT ALL.
(TRYING TO HELP)
IF THAT'S THE CASE...
...THERE'S NO NEED FOR THE TWO OF THEM TO MEET UP.
I LIKE THAT MUCH BETTER.

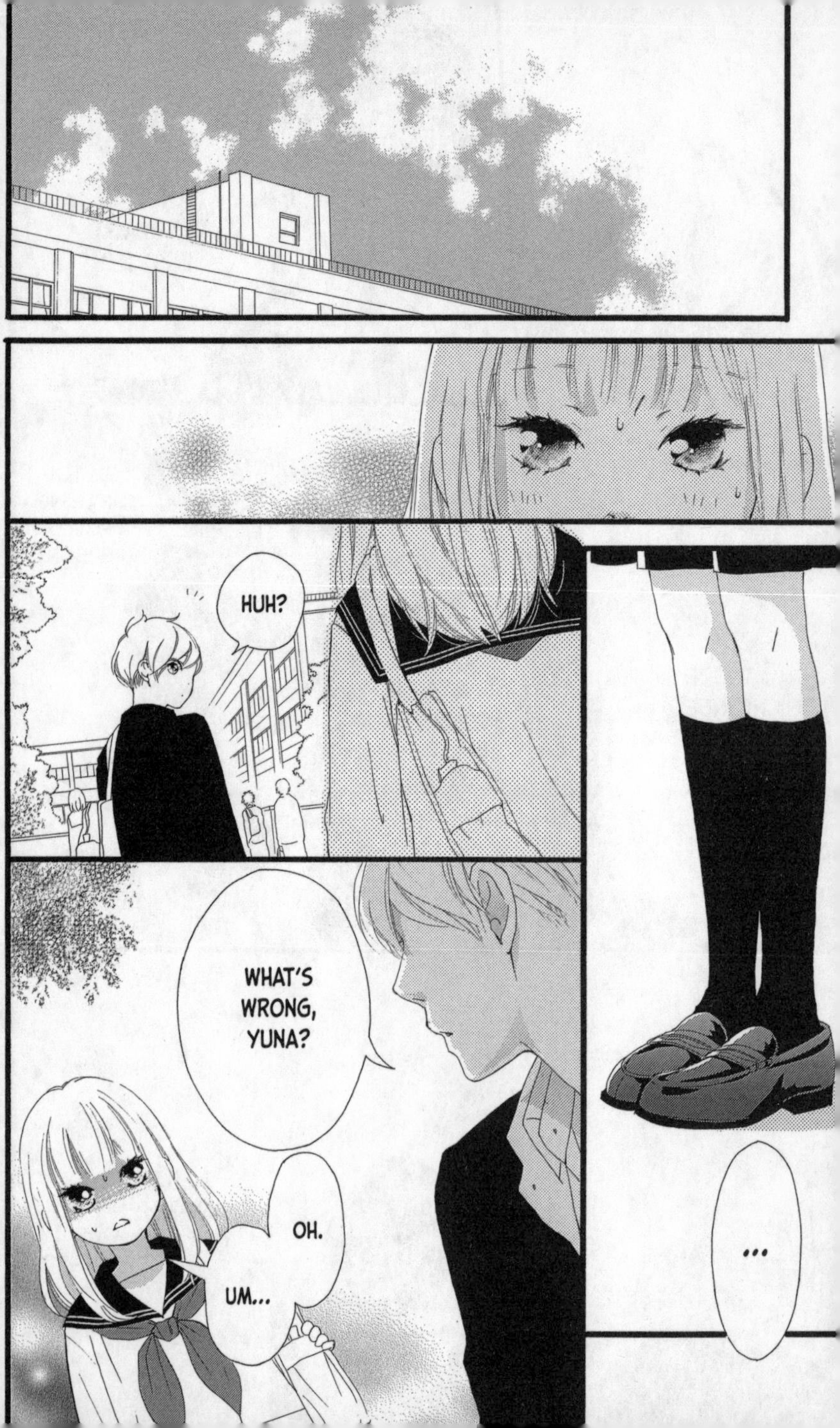
...
HUH?
WHAT'S WRONG, YUNA?
OH.
UM...

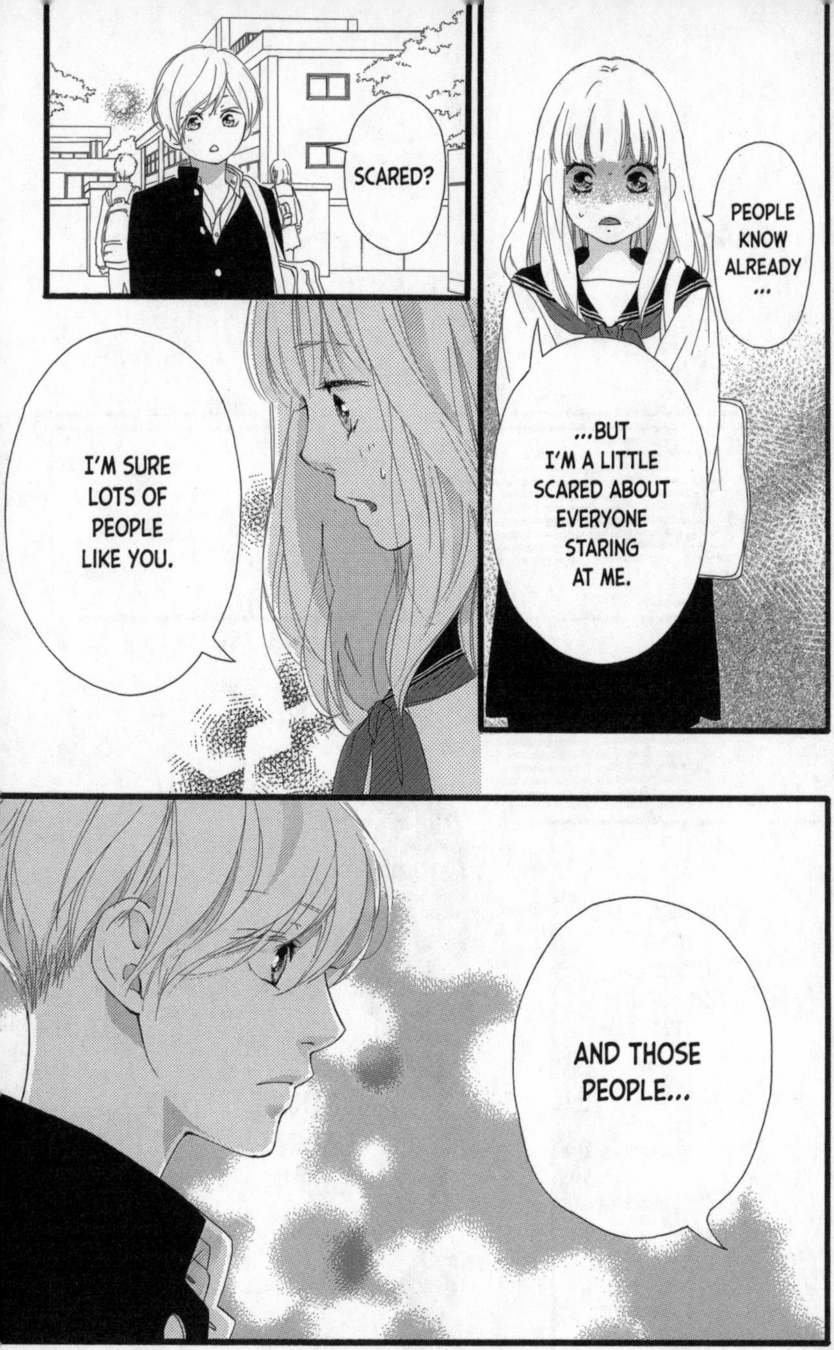
PEOPLE KNOW ALREADY ...
...BUT I'M A LITTLE SCARED ABOUT EVERYONE STARING AT ME.
SCARED?
I'M SURE LOTS OF PEOPLE LIKE YOU.
AND THOSE PEOPLE...

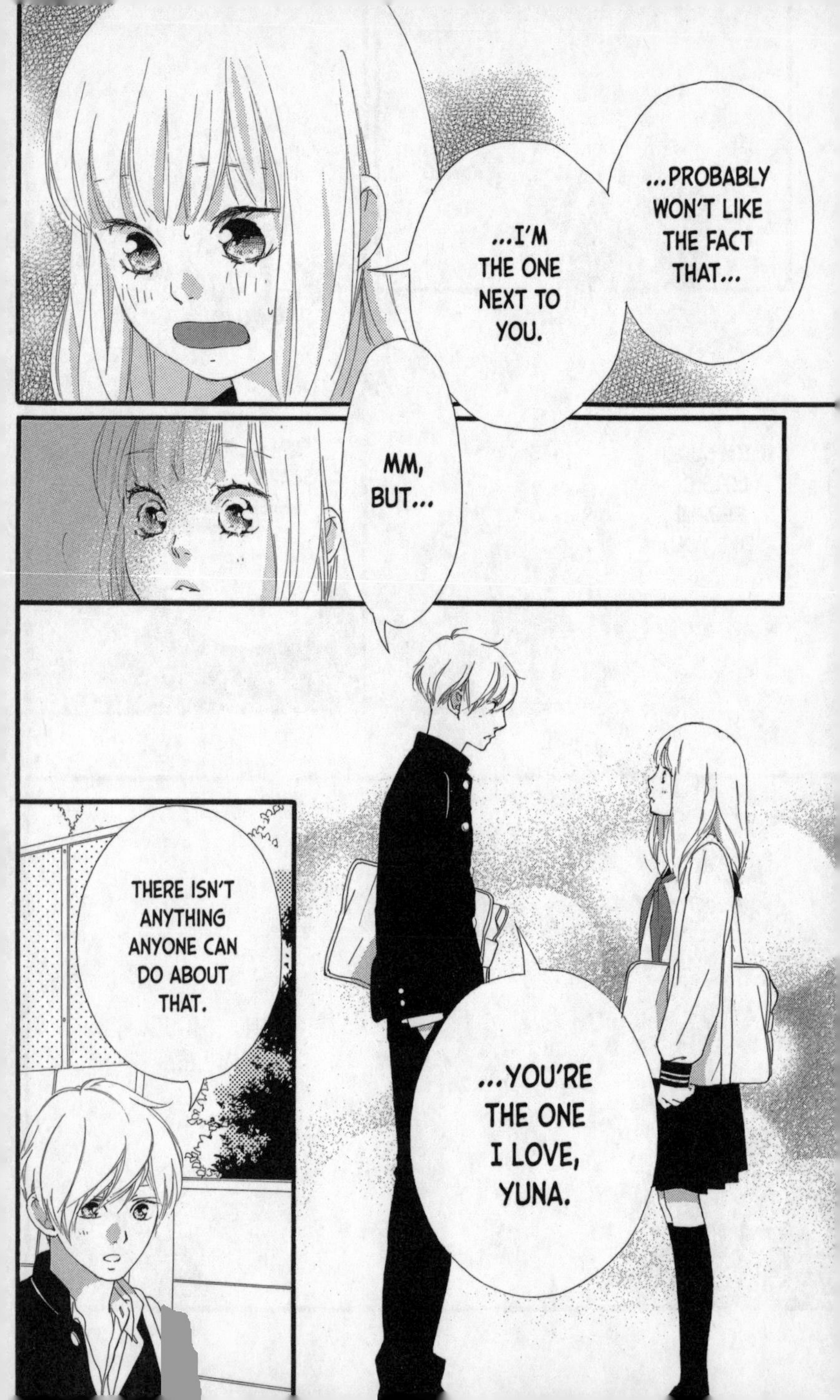
...PROBABLY WON'T LIKE THE FACT THAT...
...I'M THE ONE NEXT TO YOU.
MM, BUT...
...YOU'RE THE ONE I LOVE, YUNA.
THERE ISN'T ANYTHING ANYONE CAN DO ABOUT THAT.

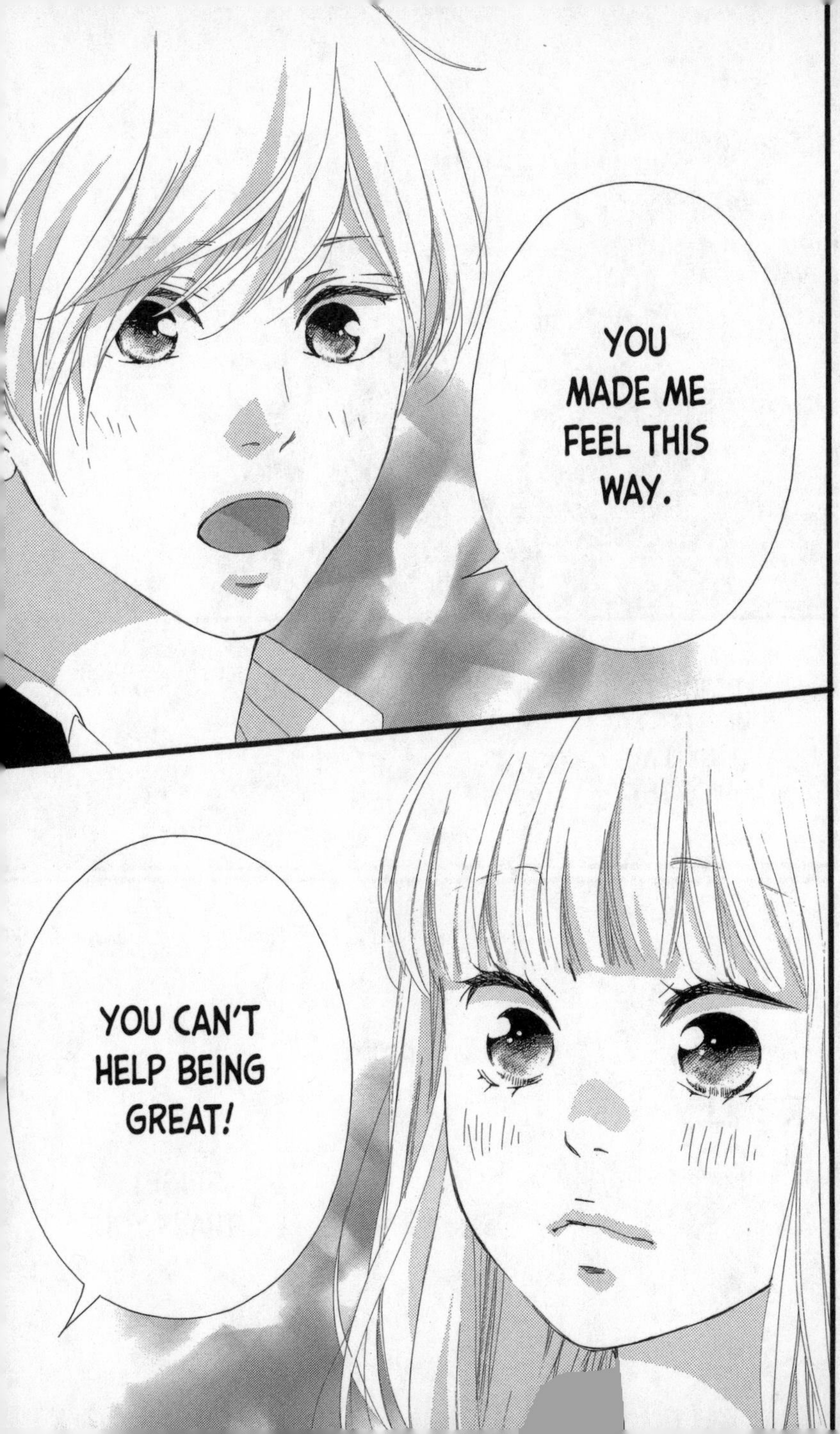
YOU MADE ME FEEL THIS WAY.
YOU CAN'T HELP BEING GREAT!

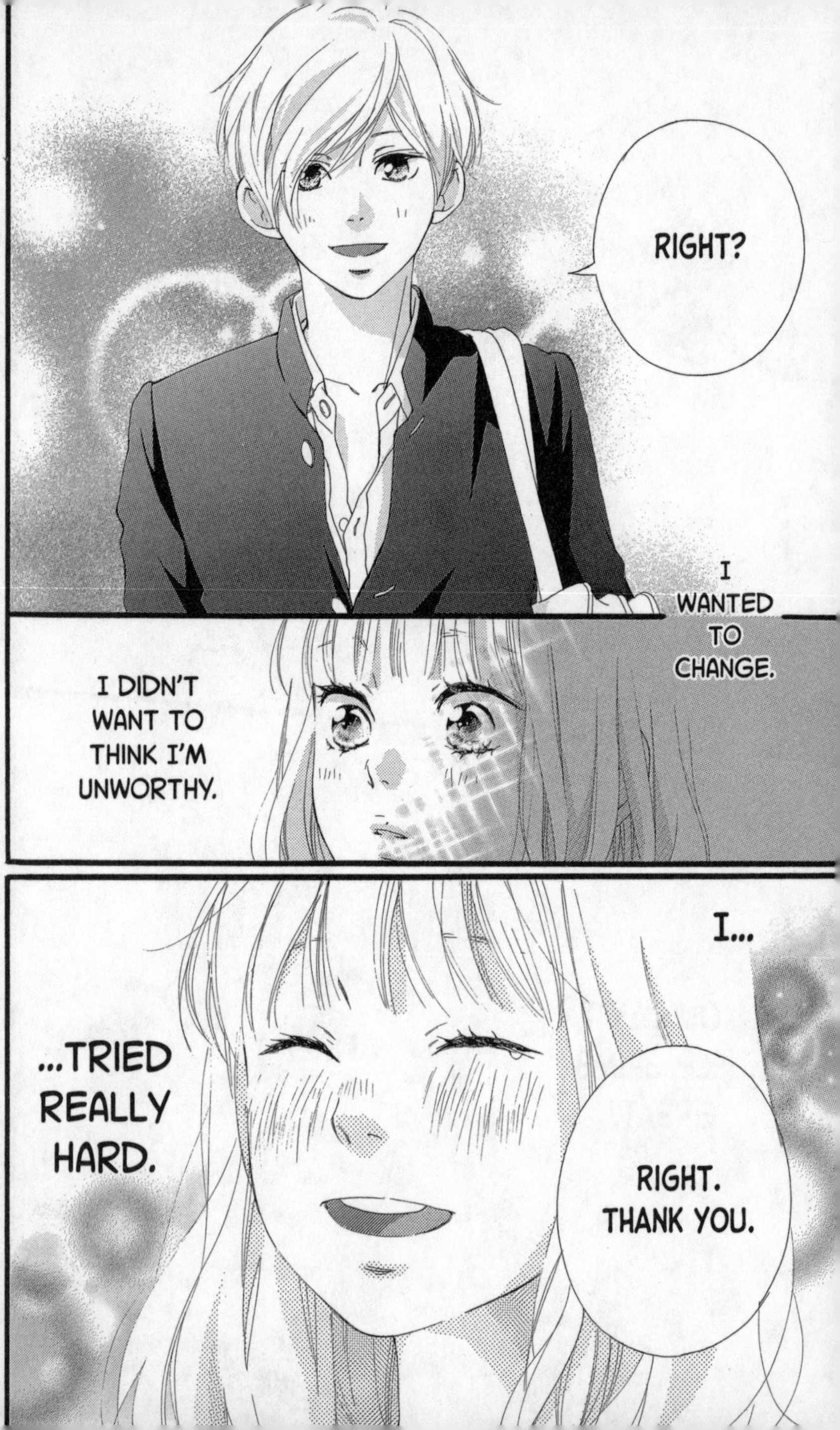
RIGHT?
I WANTED TO CHANGE.
I DIDN'T WANT TO THINK I'M UNWORTHY.
I...
...TRIED REALLY HARD.
RIGHT. THANK YOU.

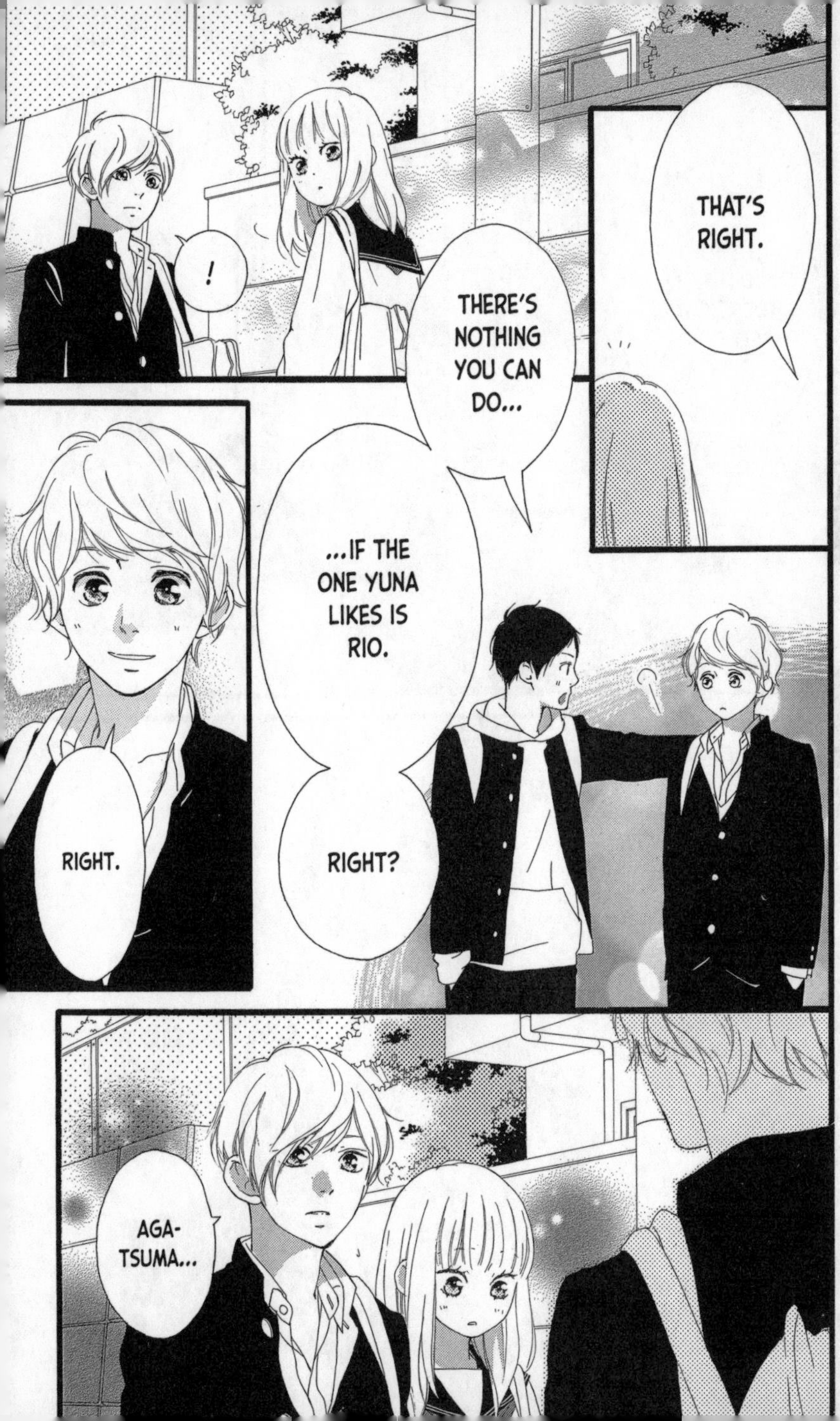
!
THERE'S NOTHING YOU CAN DO...
...IF THE ONE YUNA LIKES IS RIO.
RIGHT?
THAT'S RIGHT.
RIGHT.
AGA-TSUMA...

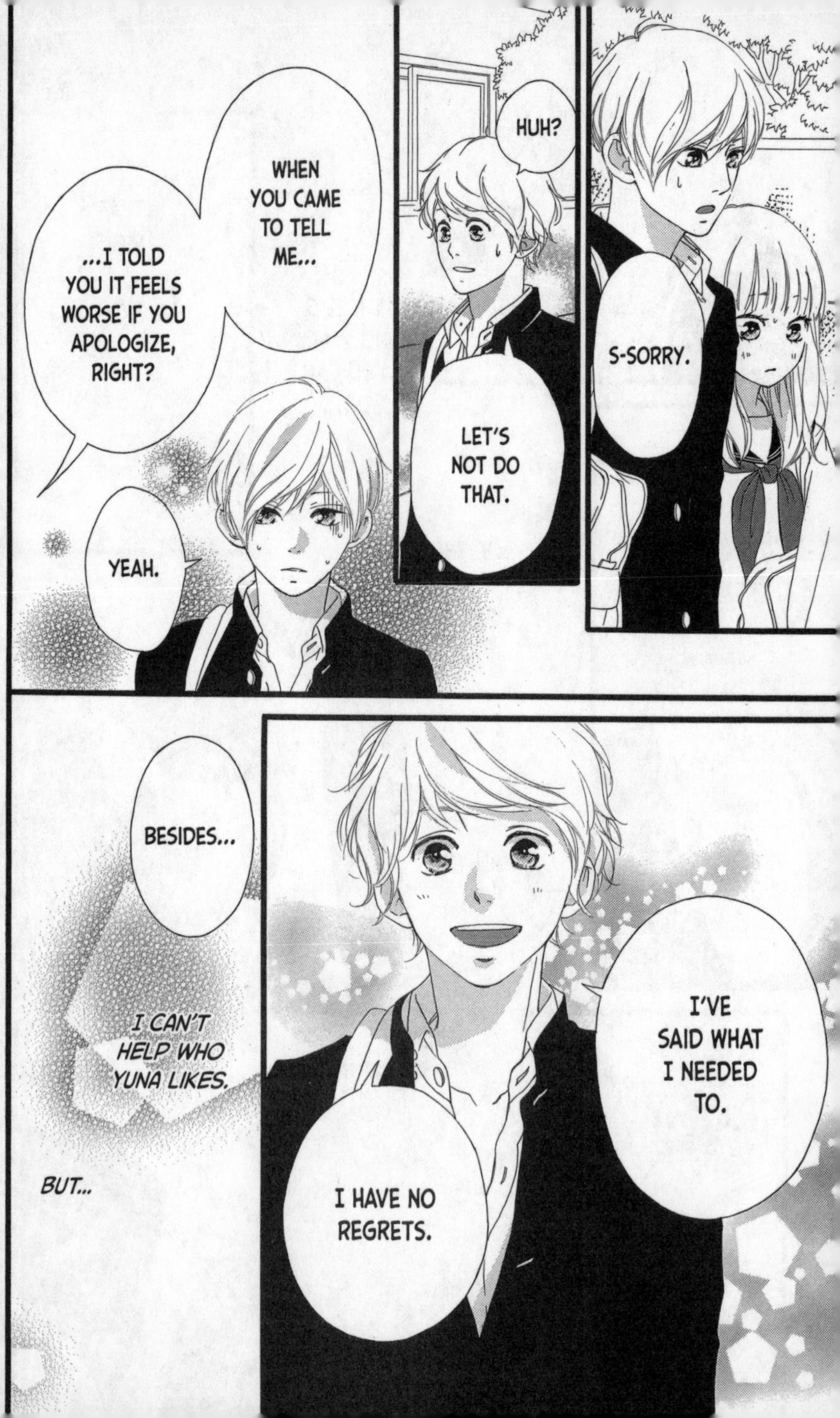
S-SORRY.
HUH?
LET'S NOT DO THAT.
WHEN YOU CAME TO TELL ME...
...I TOLD YOU IT FEELS WORSE IF YOU APOLOGIZE, RIGHT?
YEAH.
BESIDES...
I'VE SAID WHAT I NEEDED TO.
I HAVE NO REGRETS.
I CAN'T HELP WHO YUNA LIKES.
BUT...

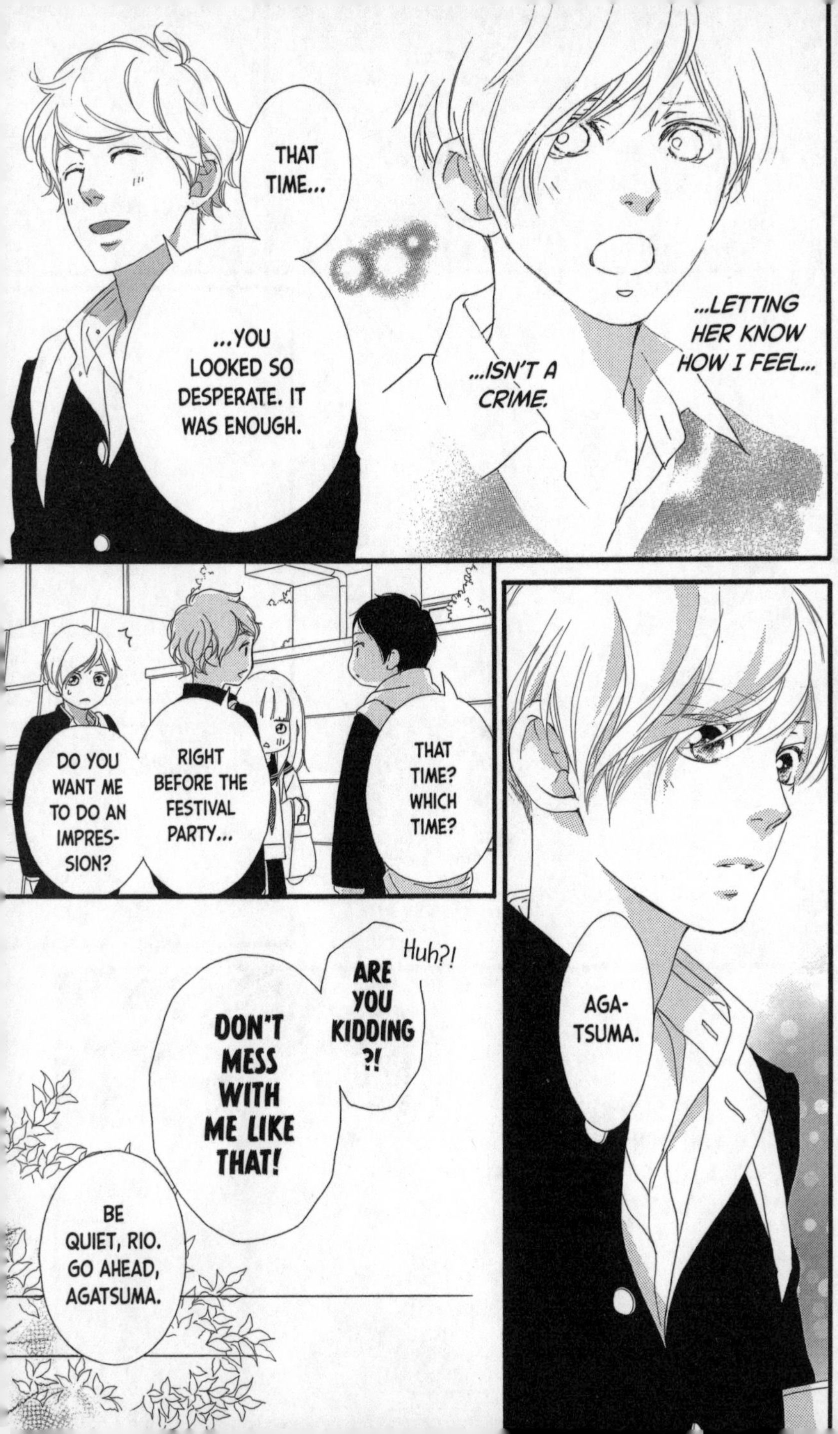
...LETTING HER KNOW HOW I FEEL...
...ISN'T A CRIME.
THAT TIME...
...YOU LOOKED SO DESPERATE. IT WAS ENOUGH.
AGA-TSUMA.
THAT TIME? WHICH TIME?
RIGHT BEFORE THE FESTIVAL PARTY...
DO YOU WANT ME TO DO AN IMPRES-SION?
Huh?!
ARE YOU KIDDING?!
DON'T MESS WITH ME LIKE THAT!
BE QUIET, RIO. GO AHEAD, AGATSUMA.

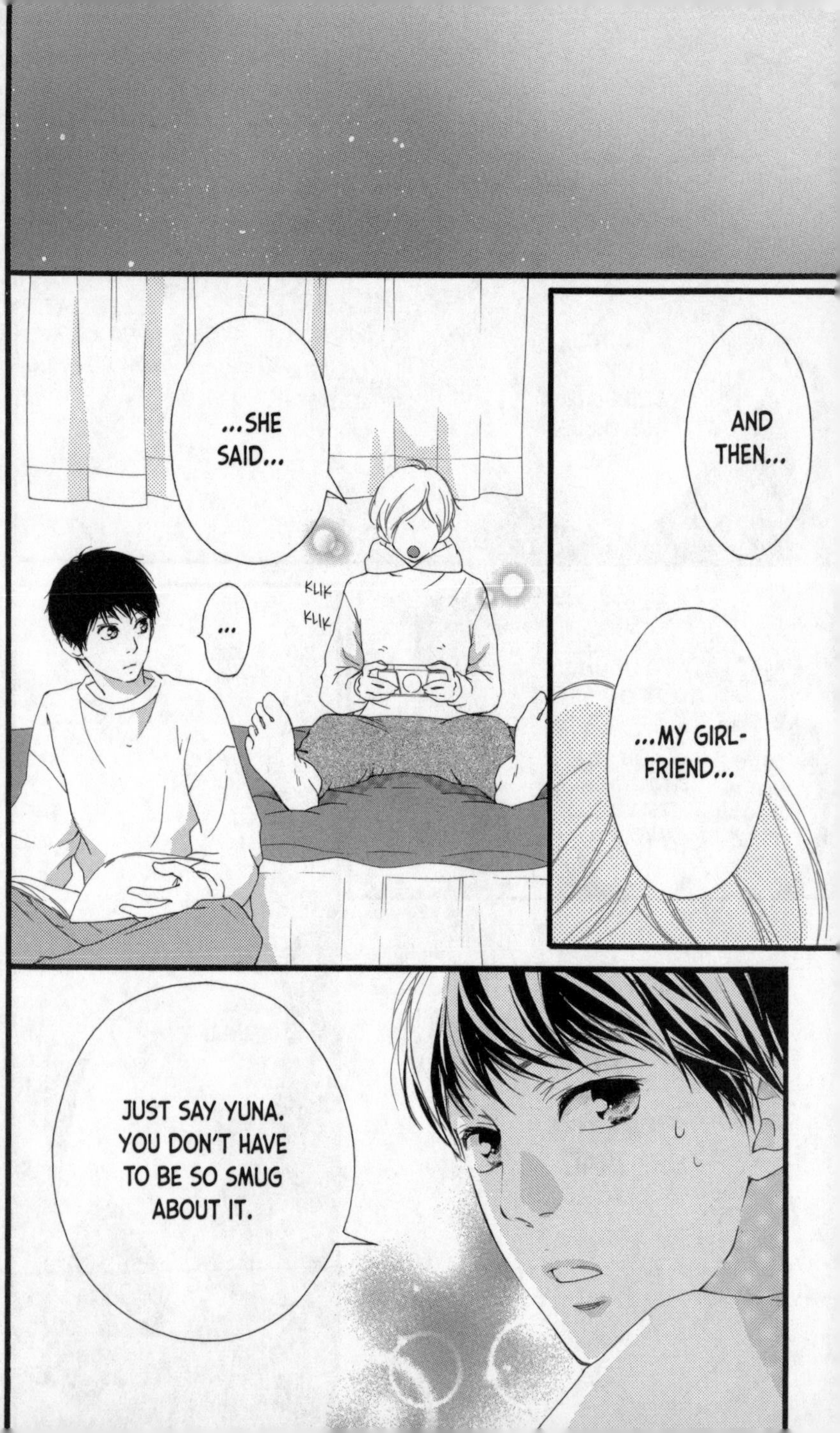
AND THEN...
...MY GIRL-FRIEND...
...SHE SAID...
KLIK
KLIK
...
JUST SAY YUNA. YOU DON'T HAVE TO BE SO SMUG ABOUT IT.

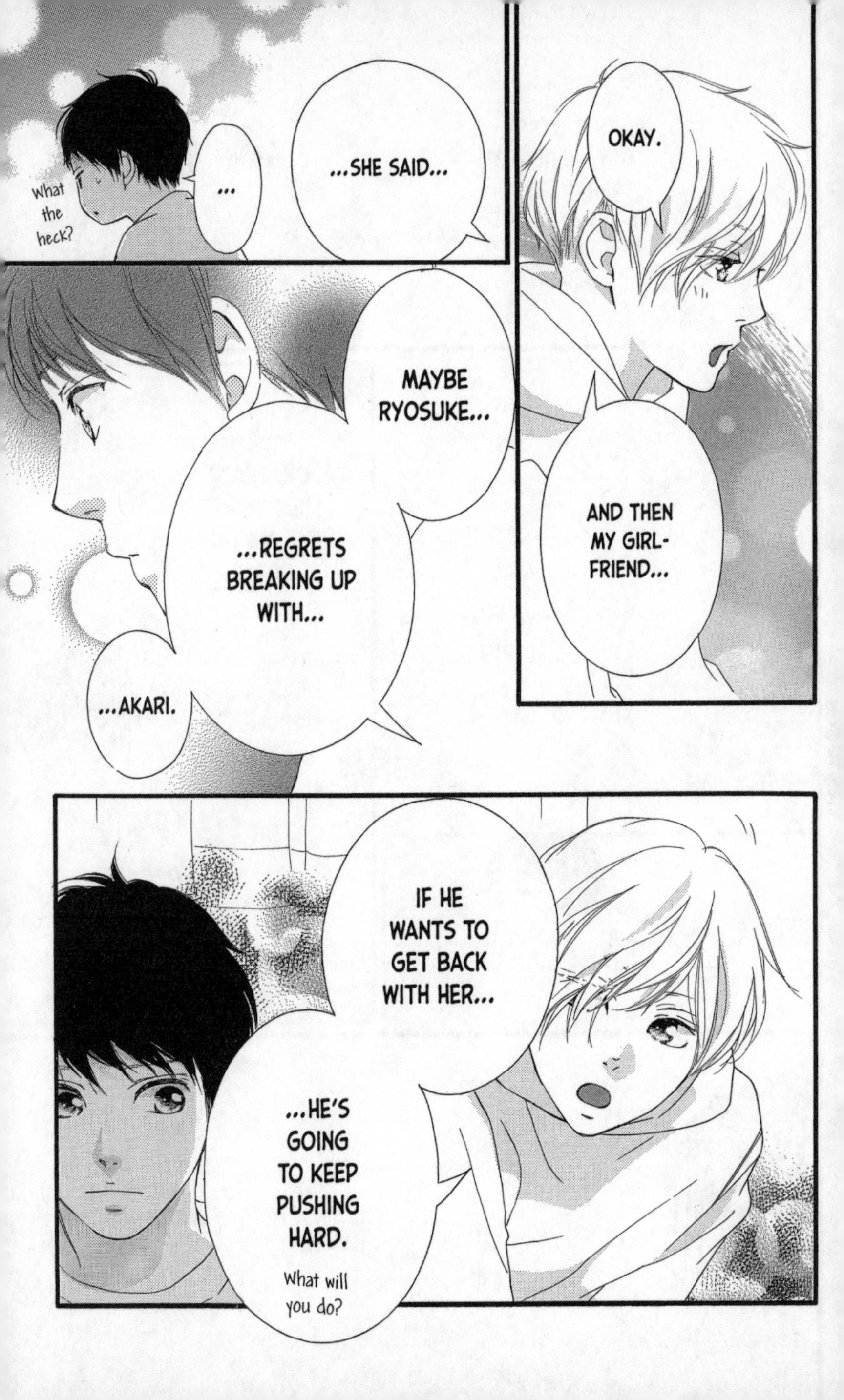
OKAY.
AND THEN MY GIRL-FRIEND...
...SHE SAID...
...
What the heck?
MAYBE RYOSUKE...
...REGRETS BREAKING UP WITH...
...AKARI.
IF HE WANTS TO GET BACK WITH HER...
...HE'S GOING TO KEEP PUSHING HARD.
What will you do?

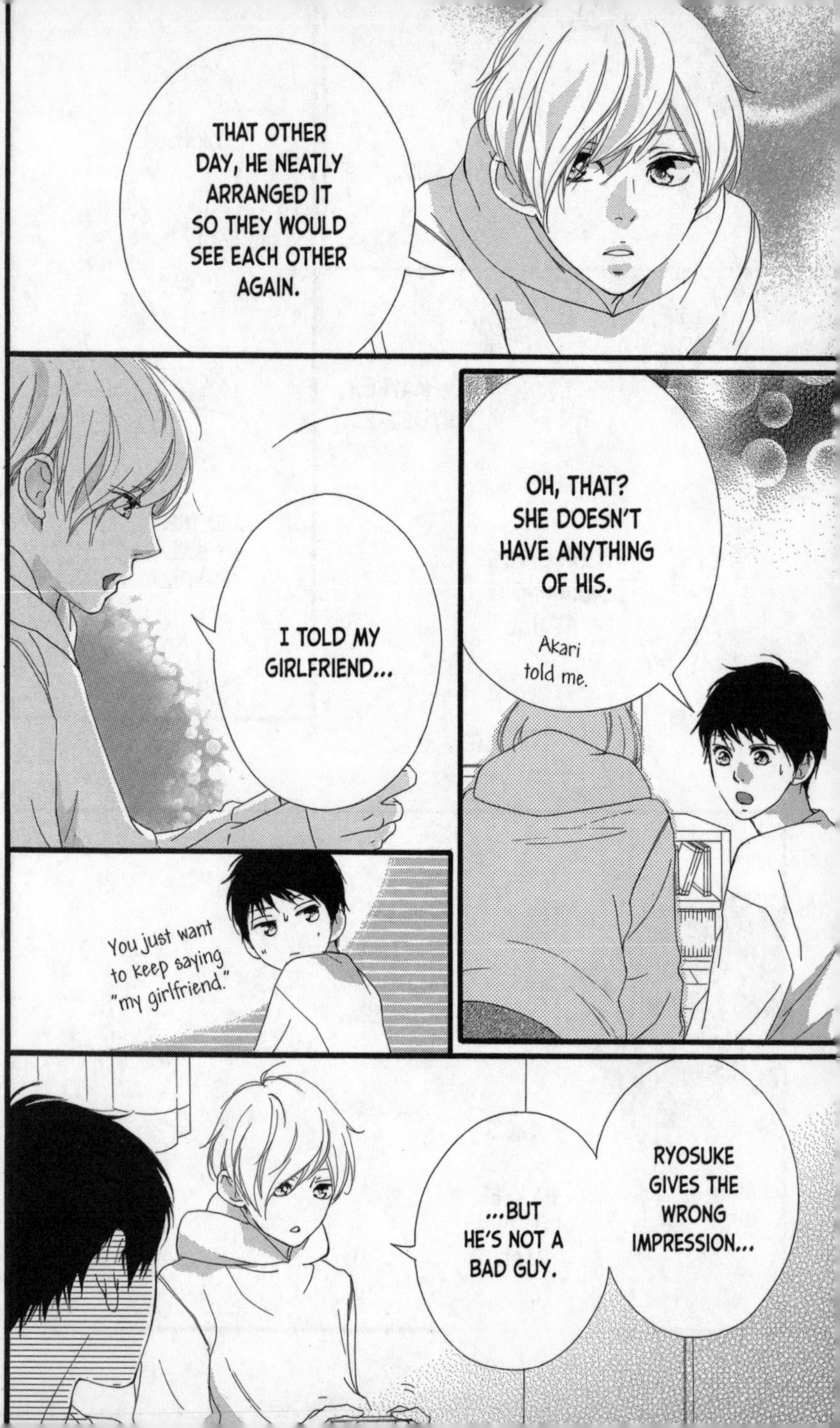
THAT OTHER DAY, HE NEATLY ARRANGED IT SO THEY WOULD SEE EACH OTHER AGAIN.
OH, THAT? SHE DOESN'T HAVE ANYTHING OF HIS.
Akari told me.
I TOLD MY GIRLFRIEND...
You just want to keep saying "my girlfriend."
RYOSUKE GIVES THE WRONG IMPRESSION...
...BUT HE'S NOT A BAD GUY.

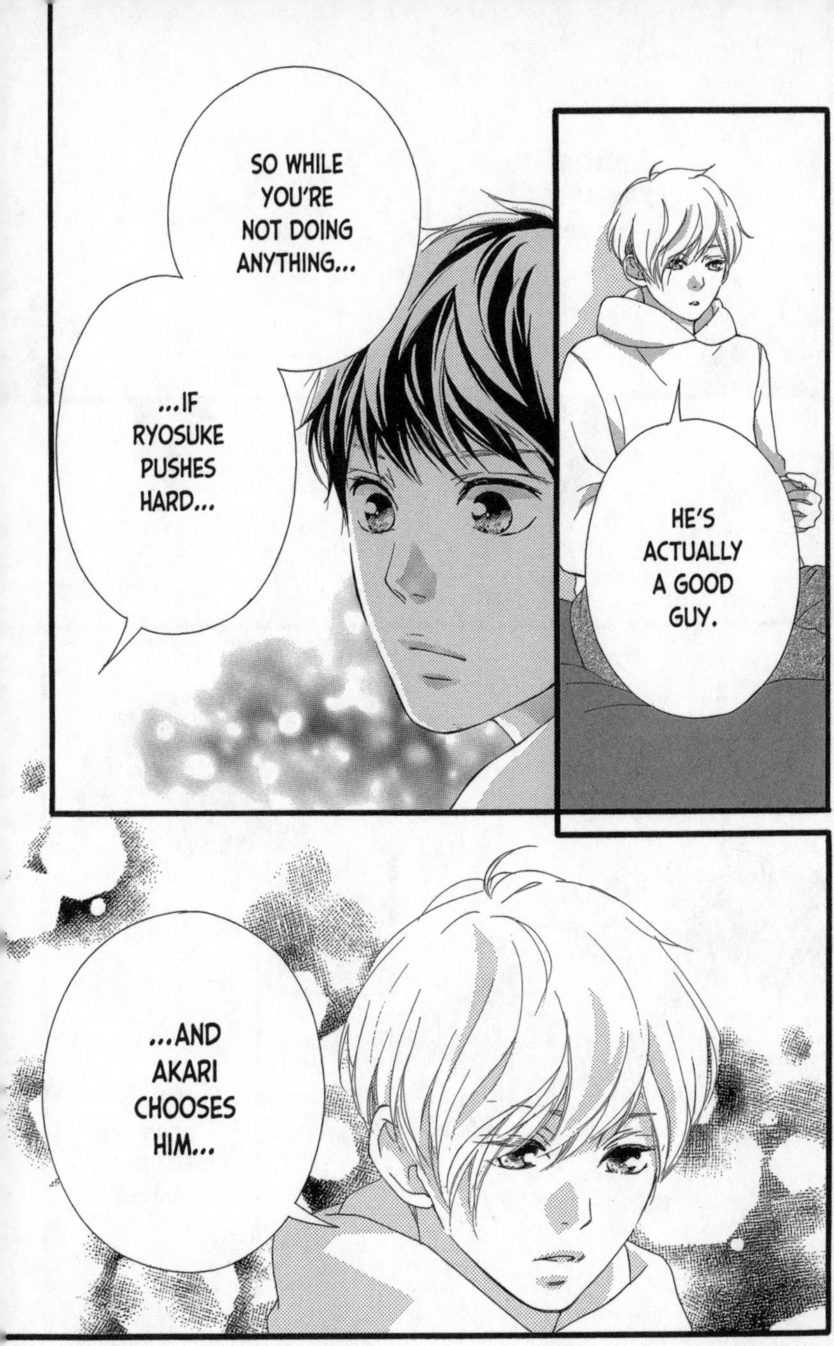
HE'S ACTUALLY A GOOD GUY.
SO WHILE YOU'RE NOT DOING ANYTHING...
...IF RYOSUKE PUSHES HARD...
...AND AKARI CHOOSES HIM...

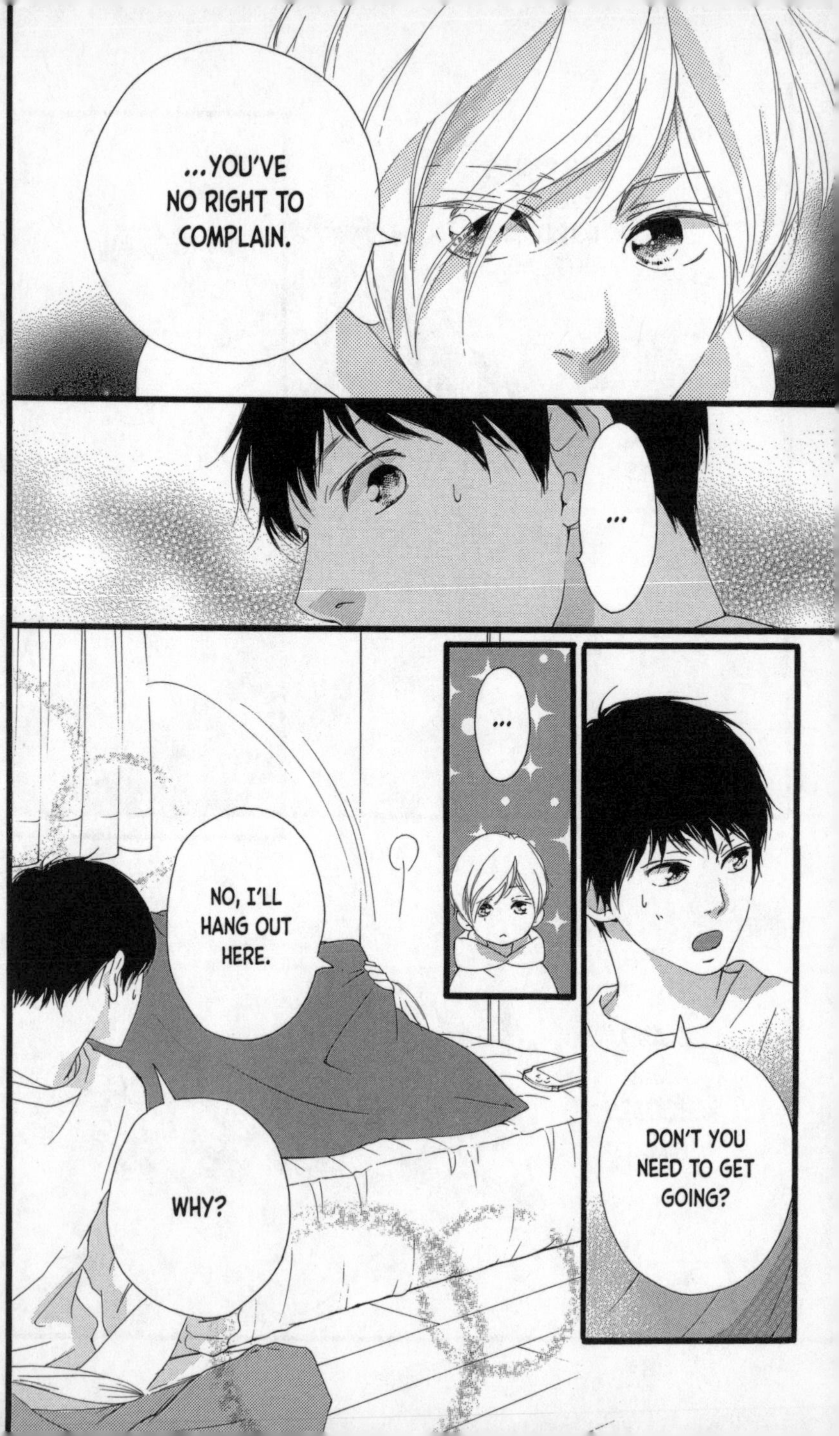
...YOU'VE NO RIGHT TO COMPLAIN.
...
DON'T YOU NEED TO GET GOING?
...
NO, I'LL HANG OUT HERE.
WHY?

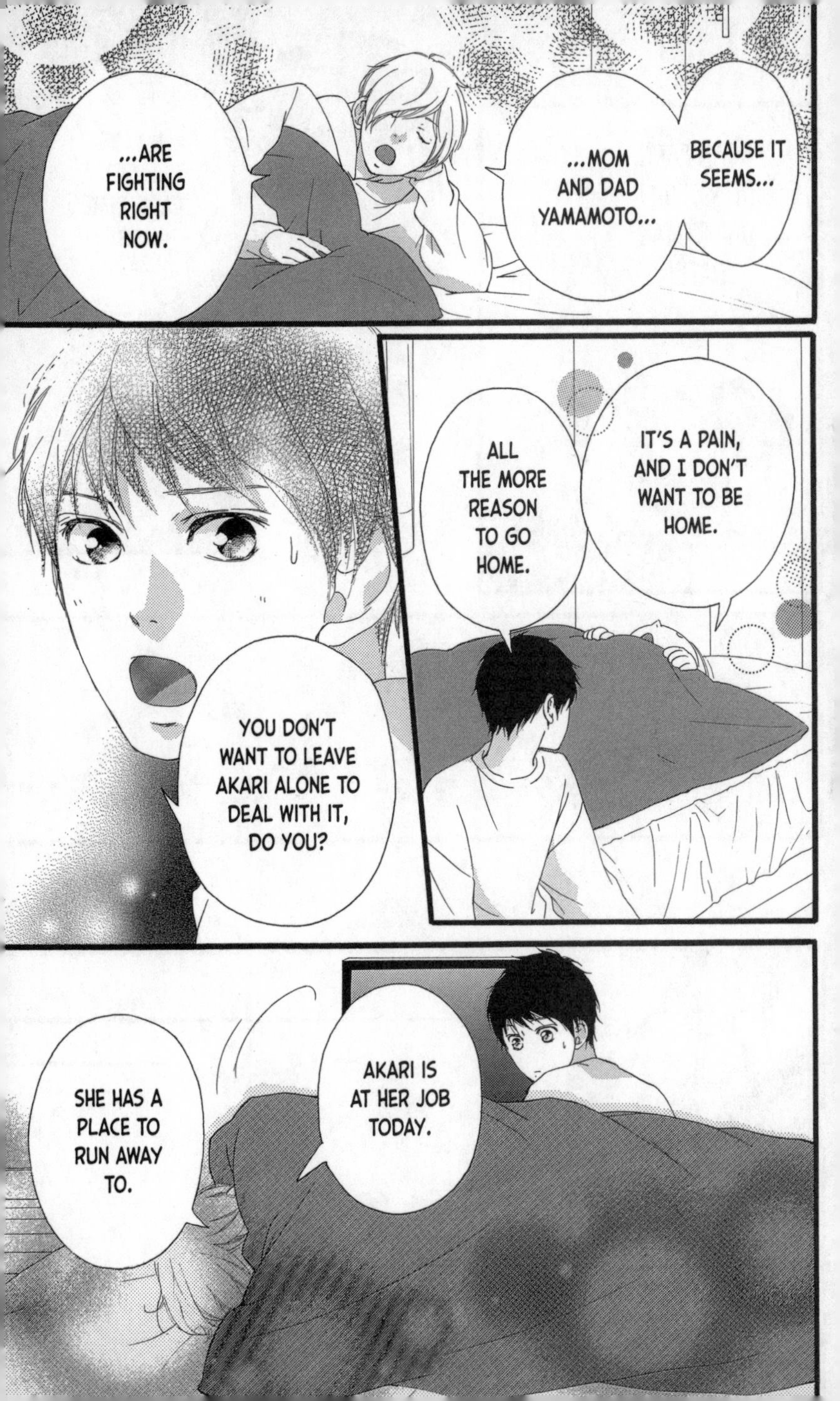
BECAUSE IT SEEMS...
...MOM AND DAD YAMAMOTO...
...ARE FIGHTING RIGHT NOW.
IT'S A PAIN, AND I DON'T WANT TO BE HOME.
ALL THE MORE REASON TO GO HOME.
YOU DON'T WANT TO LEAVE AKARI ALONE TO DEAL WITH IT, DO YOU?
AKARI IS AT HER JOB TODAY.
SHE HAS A PLACE TO RUN AWAY TO.

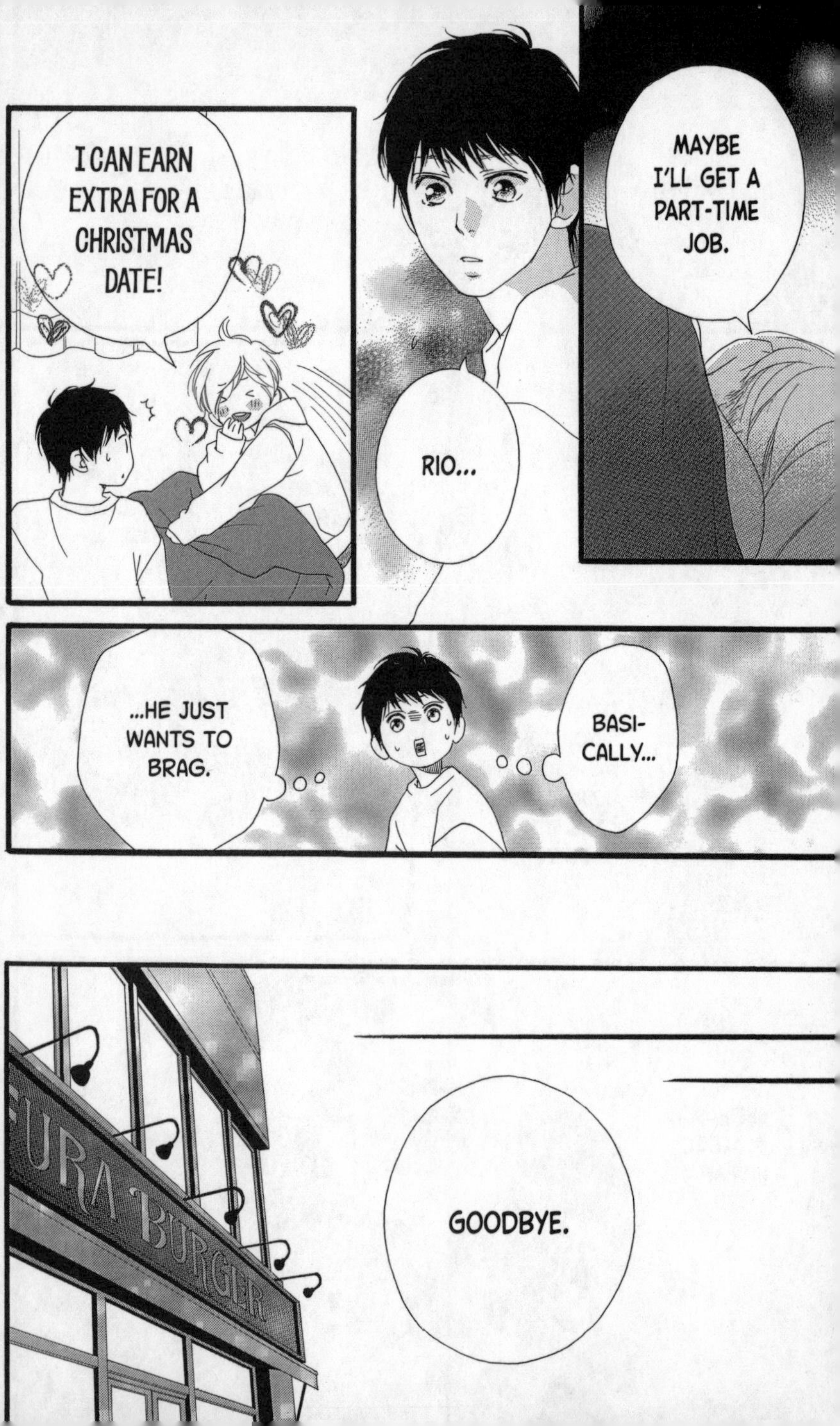
MAYBE I'LL GET A PART-TIME JOB.
RIO...
I CAN EARN EXTRA FOR A CHRISTMAS DATE!
BASI-CALLY...
...HE JUST WANTS TO BRAG.
GOODBYE.

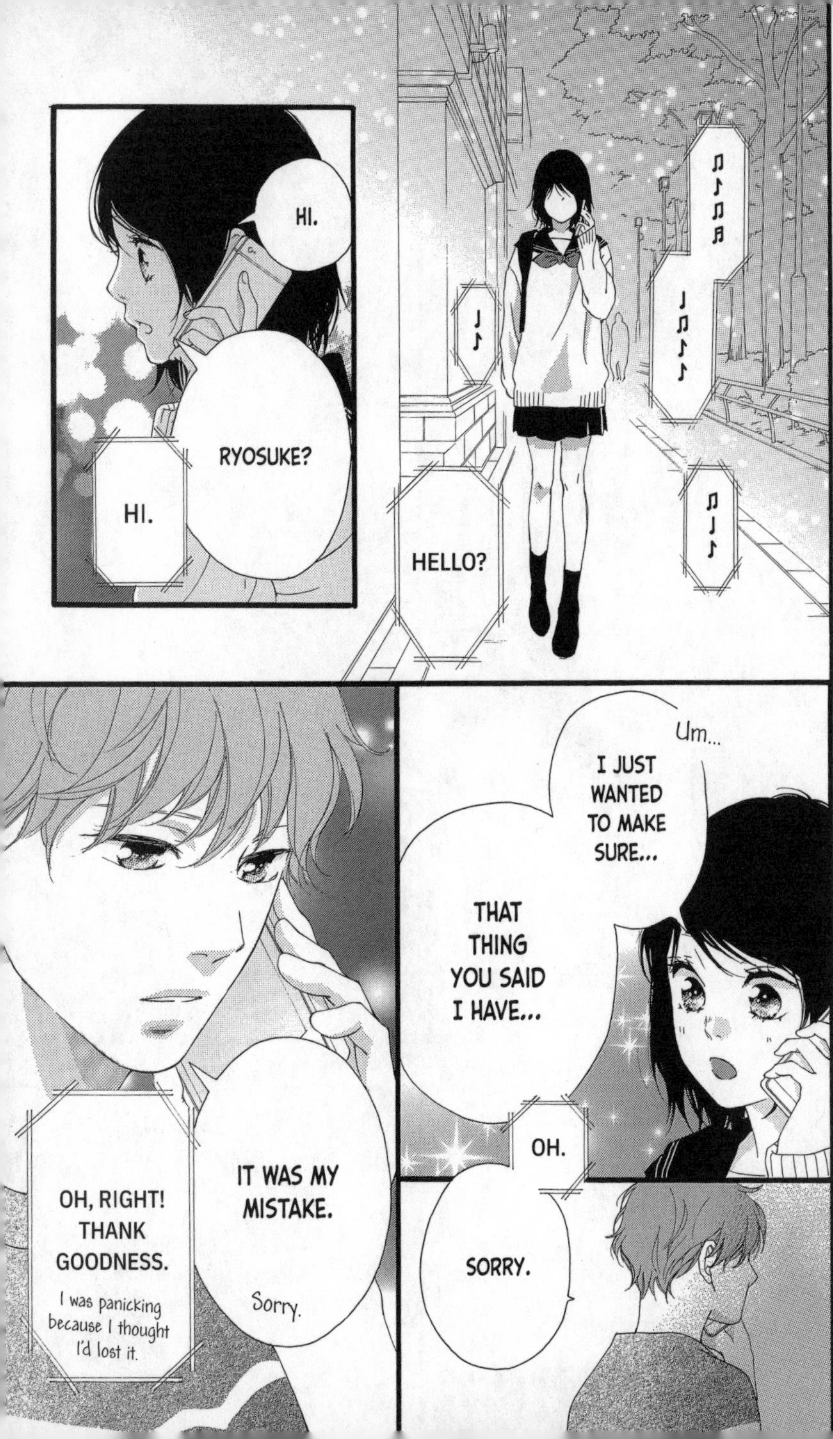
HELLO?
HI.
RYOSUKE?
HI.
Um...
I JUST WANTED TO MAKE SURE...
THAT THING YOU SAID I HAVE...
OH.
SORRY.
IT WAS MY MISTAKE.
Sorry.
OH, RIGHT! THANK GOODNESS.
I was panicking because I thought I'd lost it.

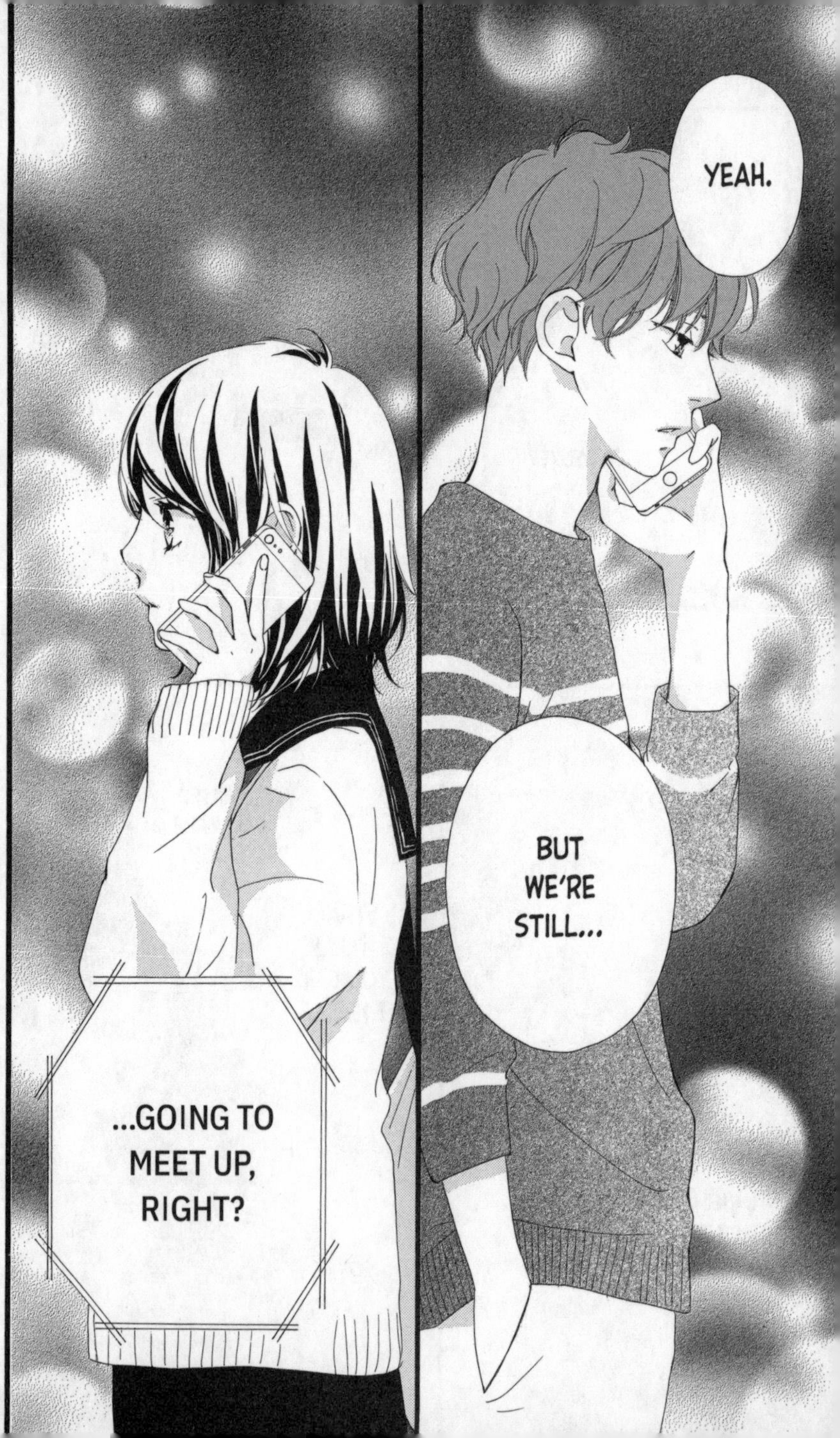
YEAH.
BUT WE'RE STILL...
...GOING TO MEET UP, RIGHT?

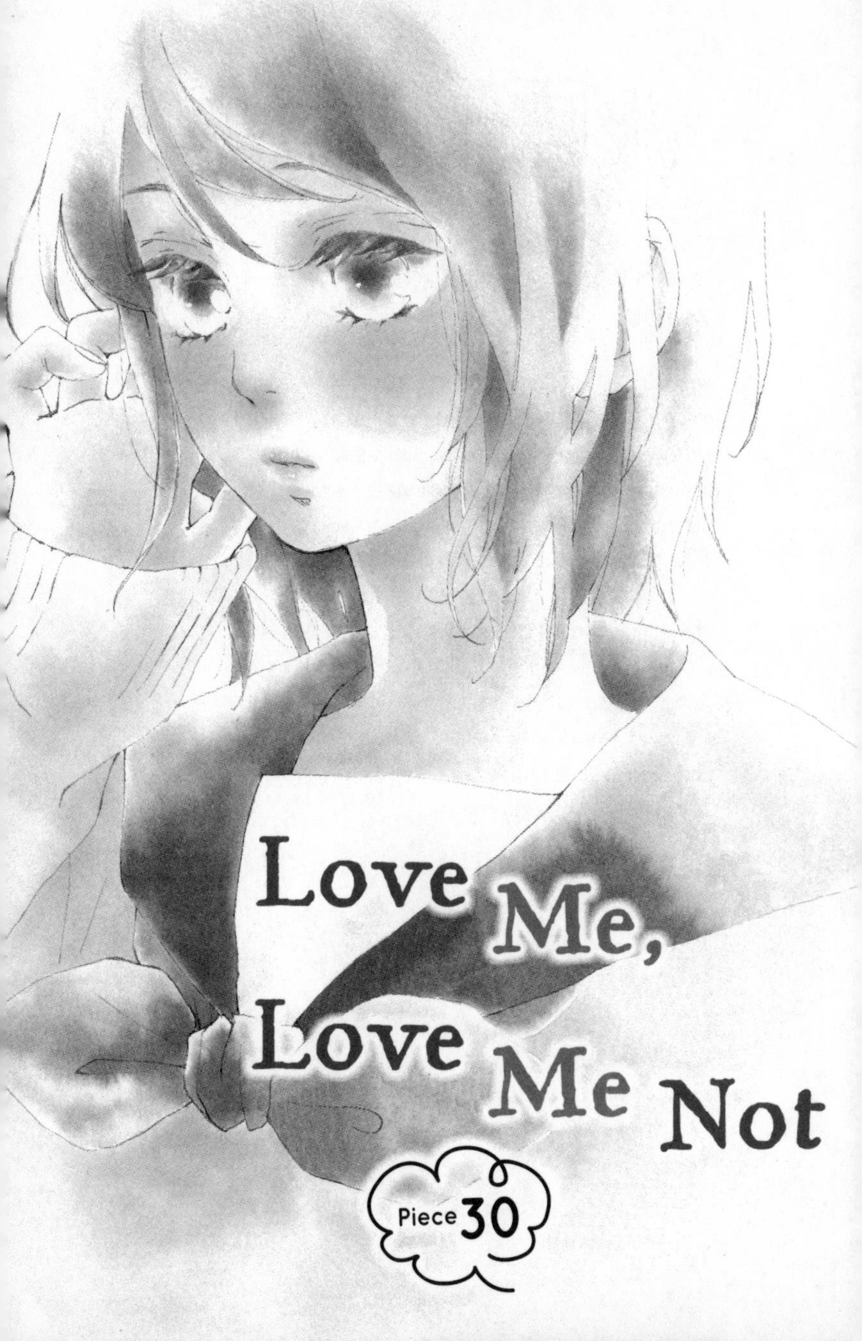
Love Me, Love Me Not
Piece 30

GREETINGS

Hello. I'm Io Sakisaka. Thank you so much for picking up volume 8 of *Love Me, Love Me Not*.

Motivation is very important to create a work over a long period with constant deadlines. "I don't feel like it right now..." is not an excuse, so I try to maintain motivation in everyday life. Even when it's not related to work, I actively make contact with people or go to events that excite me. I feel energized doing those things, and that is what turns into motivation for me. I get really excited when someone is doing something very challenging. Even though it has nothing to do with me, I think, "I'm going to work hard too!" I know that's a very simple outlook, but I also think I'm lucky I don't view other people's challenges with detachment.

Io Sakisaka

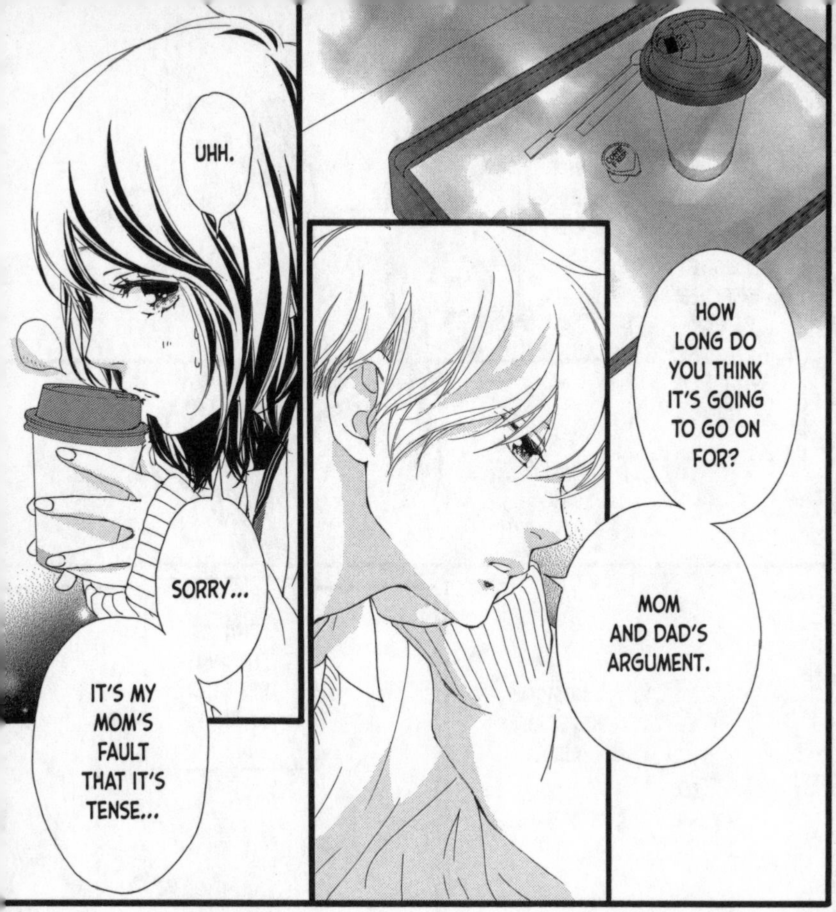
HOW LONG DO YOU THINK IT'S GOING TO GO ON FOR?
MOM AND DAD'S ARGUMENT.
UHH.
SORRY...
IT'S MY MOM'S FAULT THAT IT'S TENSE...

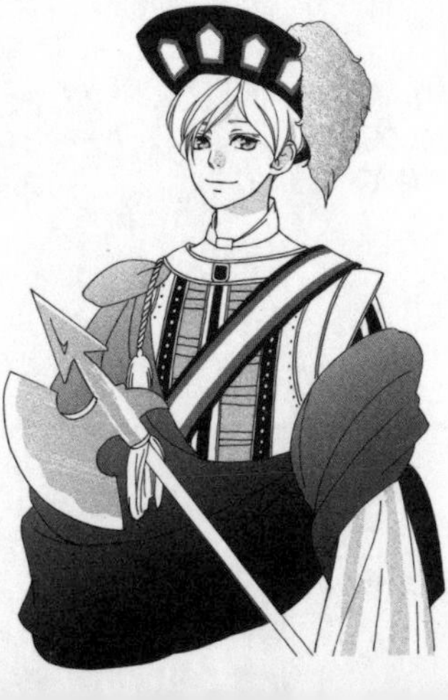

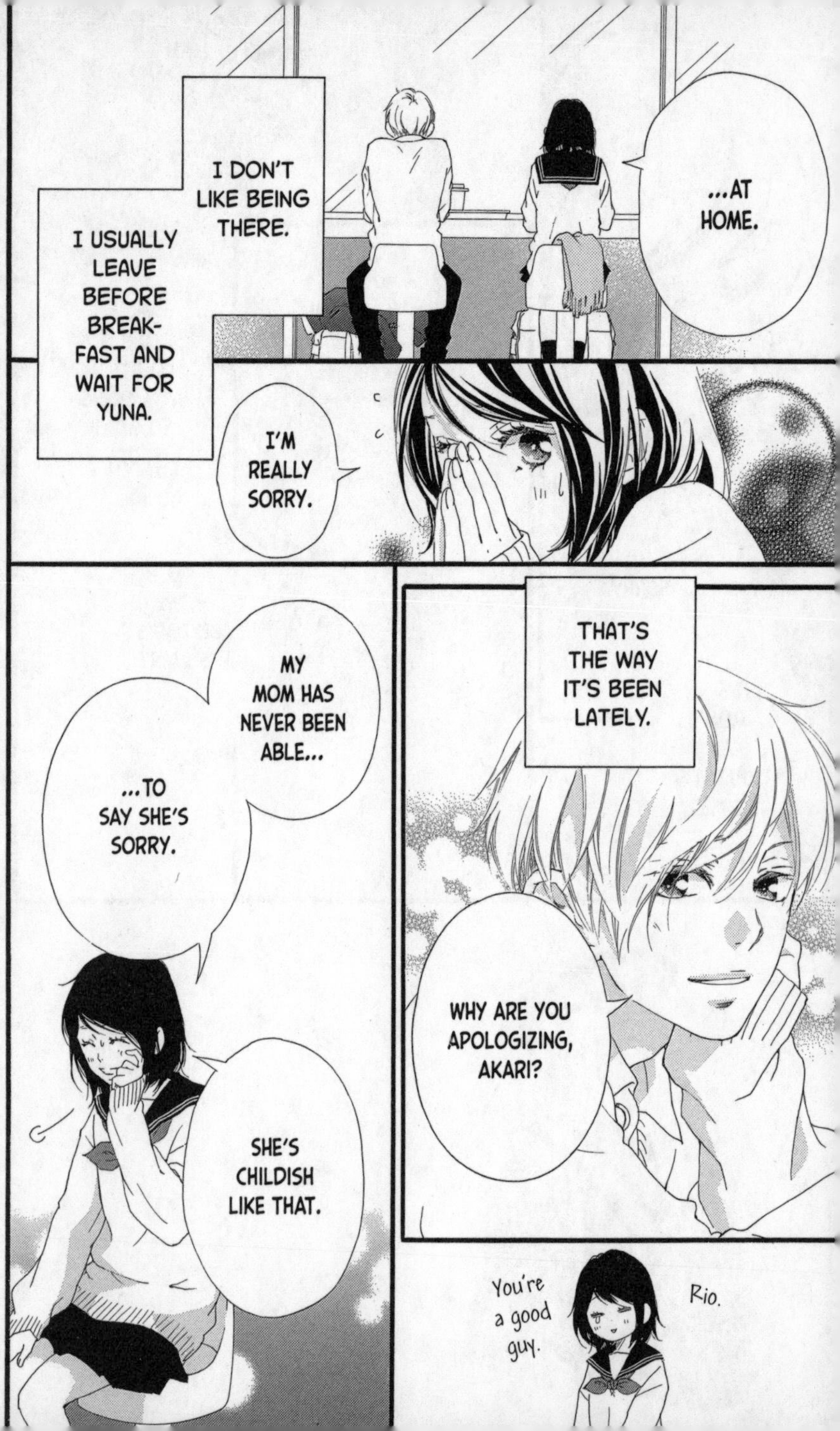
...AT HOME.
I DON'T LIKE BEING THERE.
I USUALLY LEAVE BEFORE BREAKFAST AND WAIT FOR YUNA.
I'M REALLY SORRY.
THAT'S THE WAY IT'S BEEN LATELY.
WHY ARE YOU APOLOGIZING, AKARI?
Rio.
You're a good guy.
MY MOM HAS NEVER BEEN ABLE...
...TO SAY SHE'S SORRY.
SHE'S CHILDISH LIKE THAT.

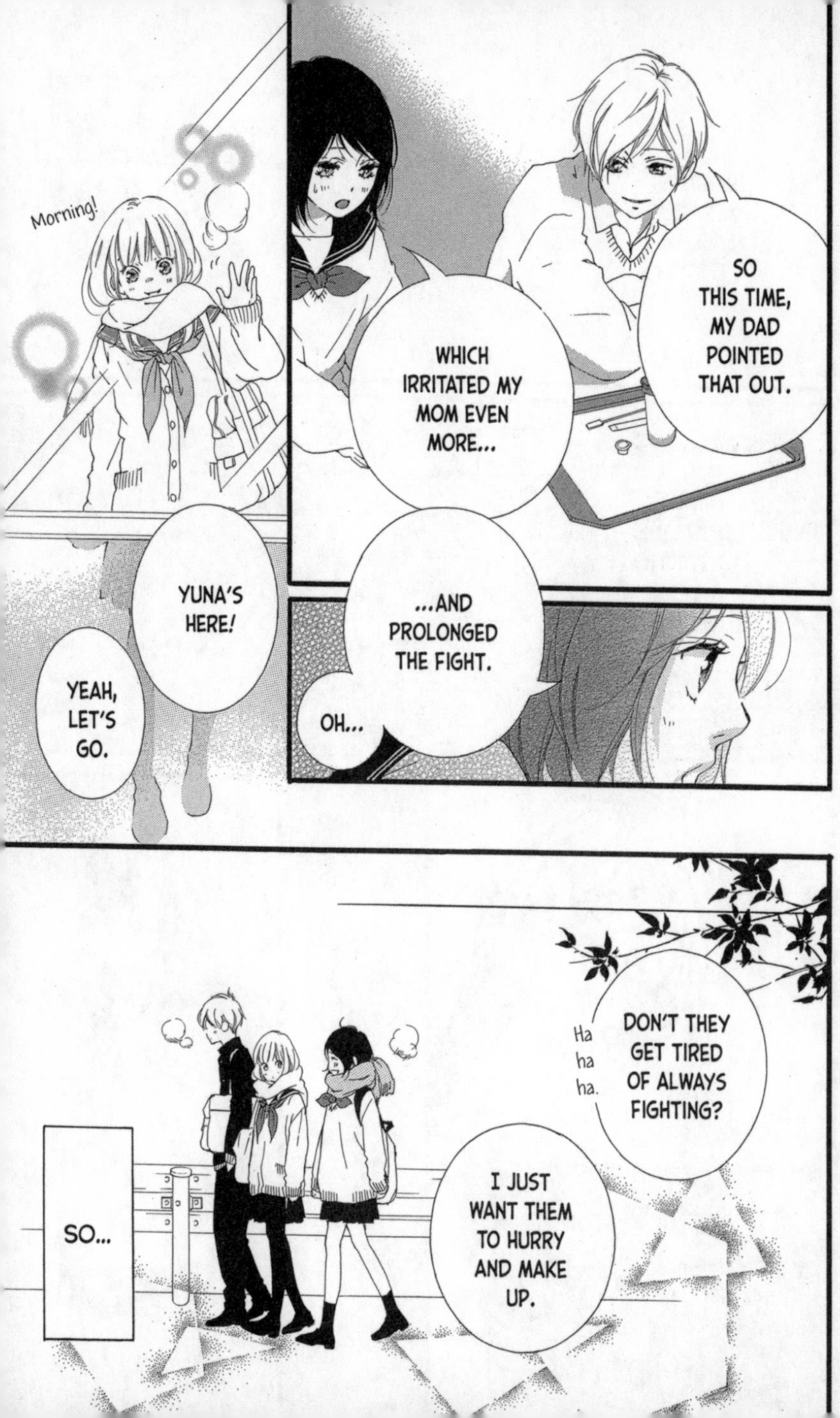
SO THIS TIME, MY DAD POINTED THAT OUT.
WHICH IRRITATED MY MOM EVEN MORE...
...AND PROLONGED THE FIGHT.
OH...
Morning!
YUNA'S HERE!
YEAH, LET'S GO.
DON'T THEY GET TIRED OF ALWAYS FIGHTING?
Ha ha ha.
I JUST WANT THEM TO HURRY AND MAKE UP.
SO...

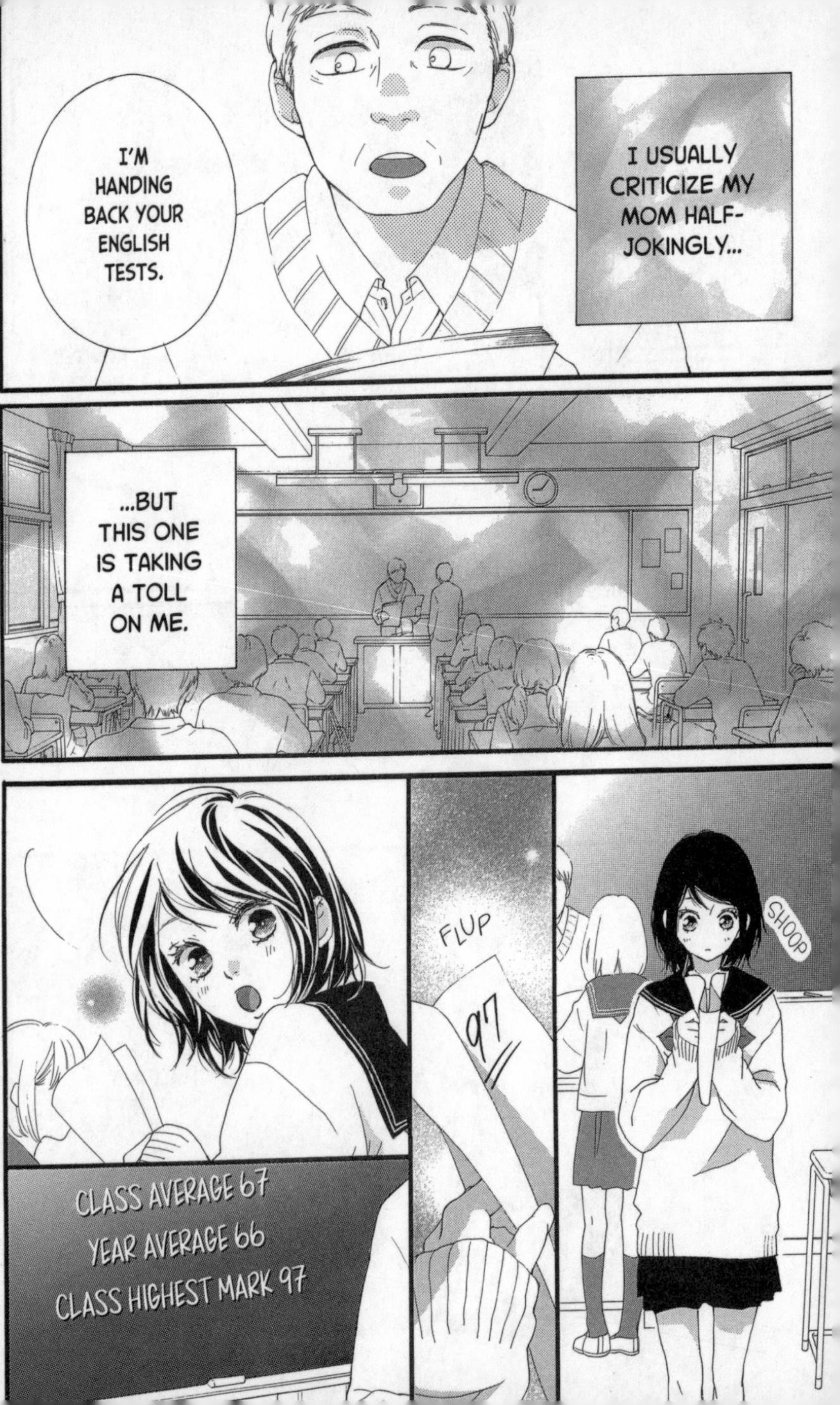
I USUALLY CRITICIZE MY MOM HALF-JOKINGLY...
I'M HANDING BACK YOUR ENGLISH TESTS.
...BUT THIS ONE IS TAKING A TOLL ON ME.
SHOOP
FLUP
97
CLASS AVERAGE 67
YEAR AVERAGE 66
CLASS HIGHEST MARK 97

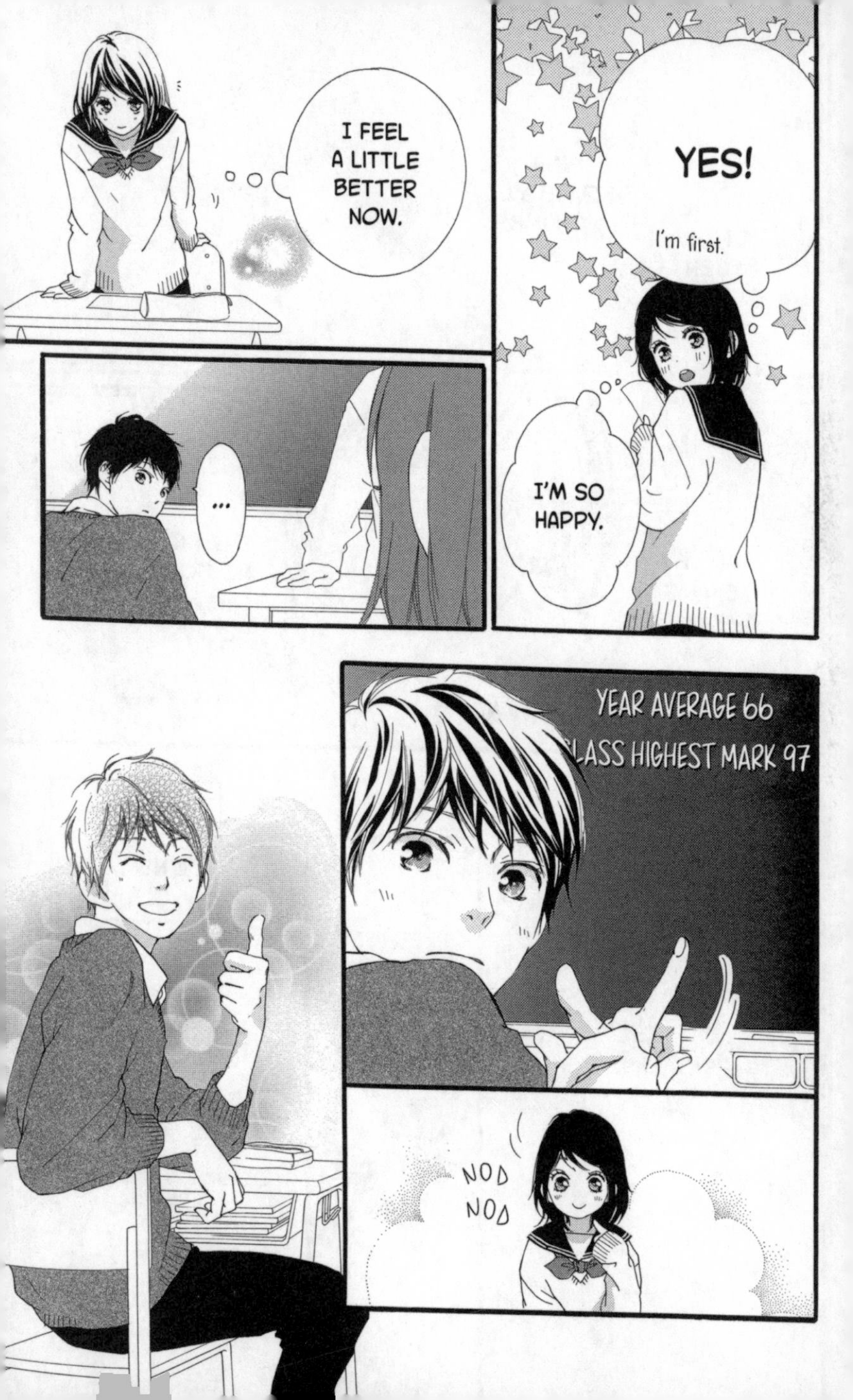
YES!
I'm first.
I'M SO HAPPY.
I FEEL A LITTLE BETTER NOW.
...
YEAR AVERAGE 66
LASS HIGHEST MARK 97
NOD NOD

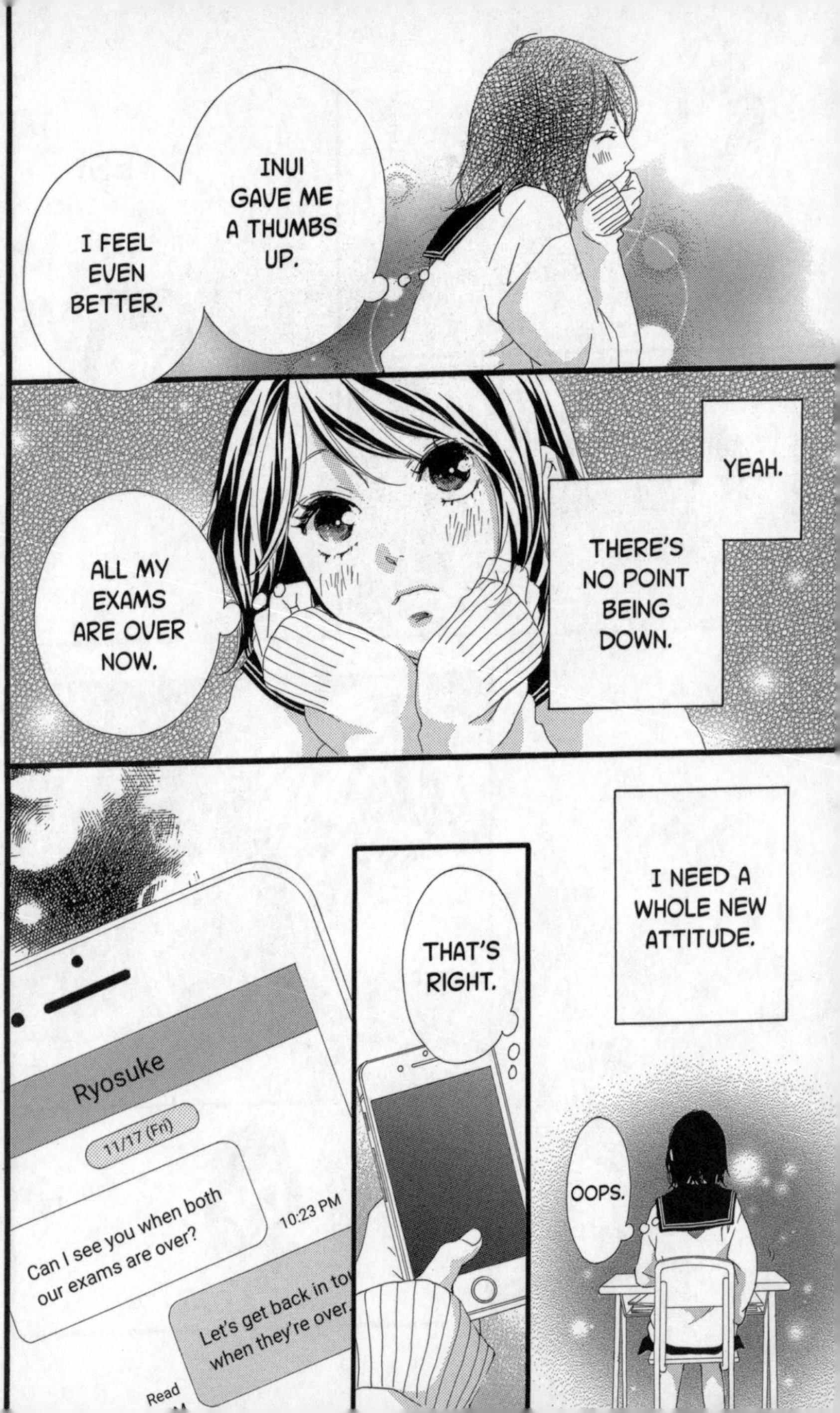
INUI GAVE ME A THUMBS UP.
I FEEL EVEN BETTER.
YEAH.
THERE'S NO POINT BEING DOWN.
ALL MY EXAMS ARE OVER NOW.
I NEED A WHOLE NEW ATTITUDE.
OOPS.
THAT'S RIGHT.
Ryosuke
11/17 (Fri)
Can I see you when both our exams are over?
10:23 PM
Let's get back in to when they're over.
Read

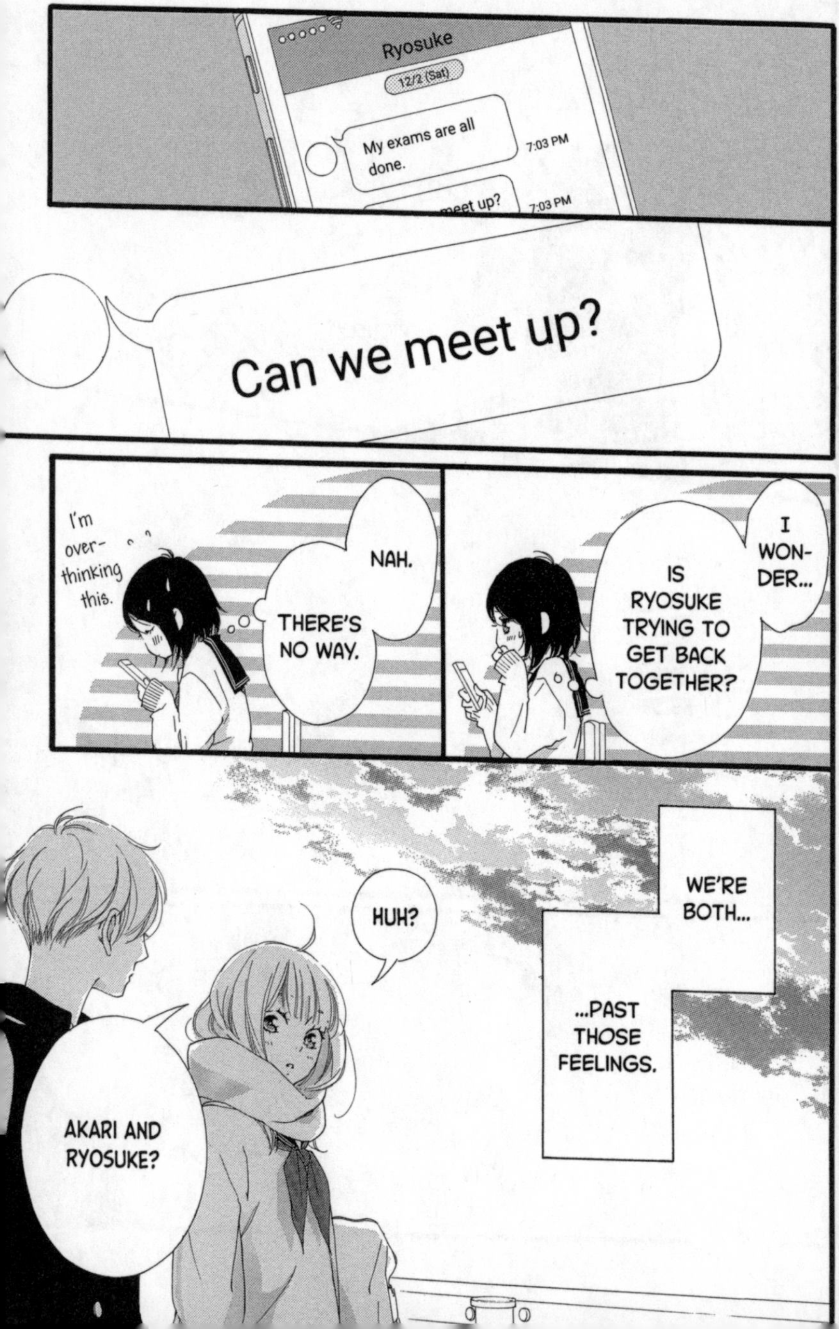
Ryosuke
12/2 (Sat)
My exams are all done.
7:03 PM
meet up?
7:03 PM
Can we meet up?
I WONDER...
IS RYOSUKE TRYING TO GET BACK TOGETHER?
NAH.
THERE'S NO WAY.
I'm over-thinking this.
WE'RE BOTH...
...PAST THOSE FEELINGS.
HUH?
AKARI AND RYOSUKE?

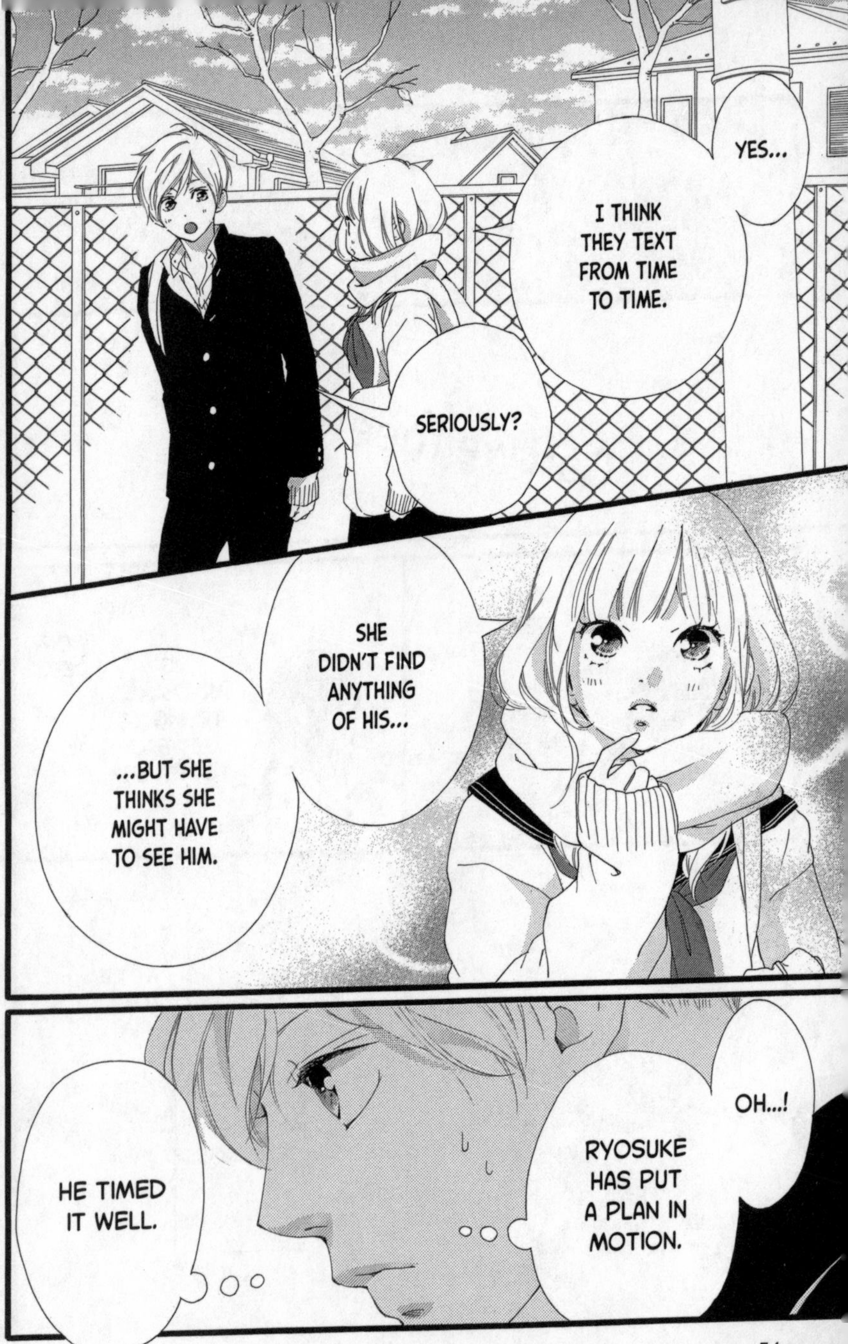
YES...
I THINK THEY TEXT FROM TIME TO TIME.
SERIOUSLY?
SHE DIDN'T FIND ANYTHING OF HIS...
...BUT SHE THINKS SHE MIGHT HAVE TO SEE HIM.
OH...!
RYOSUKE HAS PUT A PLAN IN MOTION.
HE TIMED IT WELL.

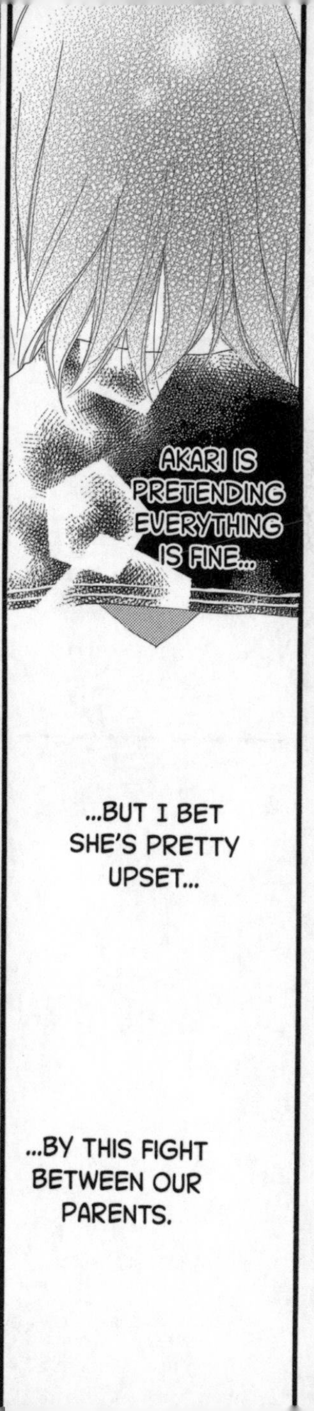
AKARI IS PRETENDING EVERYTHING IS FINE...
...BUT I BET SHE'S PRETTY UPSET...
...BY THIS FIGHT BETWEEN OUR PARENTS.

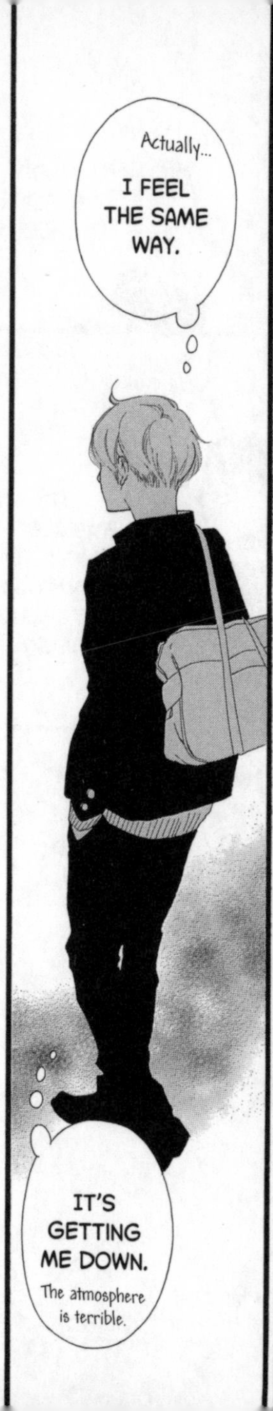
Actually...
I FEEL THE SAME WAY.
IT'S GETTING ME DOWN.
The atmosphere is terrible.

Looking at my hoodies and sweatshirts, a high percentage of them are gray. I buy them for the different fabrics, designs and shades. My favorite one is a distressed gray sweatshirt. The sleeves and collar are worn through, and there are little holes here and there, but it's a nice shape. I can wear it with anything. I really liked it and wore it a lot. But one day someone said, "That's really ratty—I'm amazed you've worn it to that point." I'm the type of person who people think if I'm wearing something distressed, it's not on purpose. They believe the garment has gotten that way through wear and tear. So, if people tend to perceive you as someone who might wear something that's beaten-up, then you need to be careful like me. Now I wear it far less often.

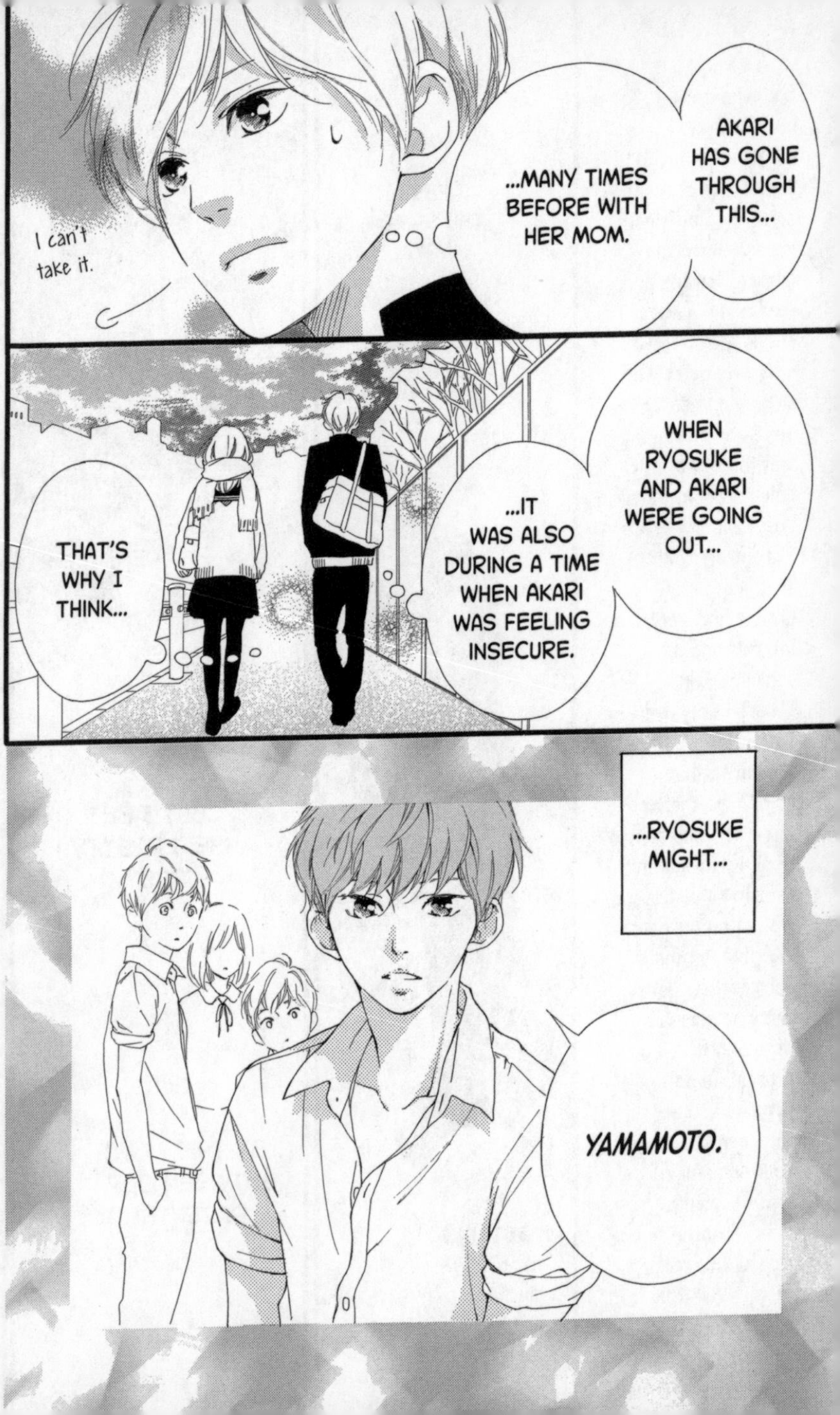
AKARI HAS GONE THROUGH THIS...
...MANY TIMES BEFORE WITH HER MOM.
I can't take it.
WHEN RYOSUKE AND AKARI WERE GOING OUT...
...IT WAS ALSO DURING A TIME WHEN AKARI WAS FEELING INSECURE.
THAT'S WHY I THINK...
...RYOSUKE MIGHT...
YAMAMOTO.

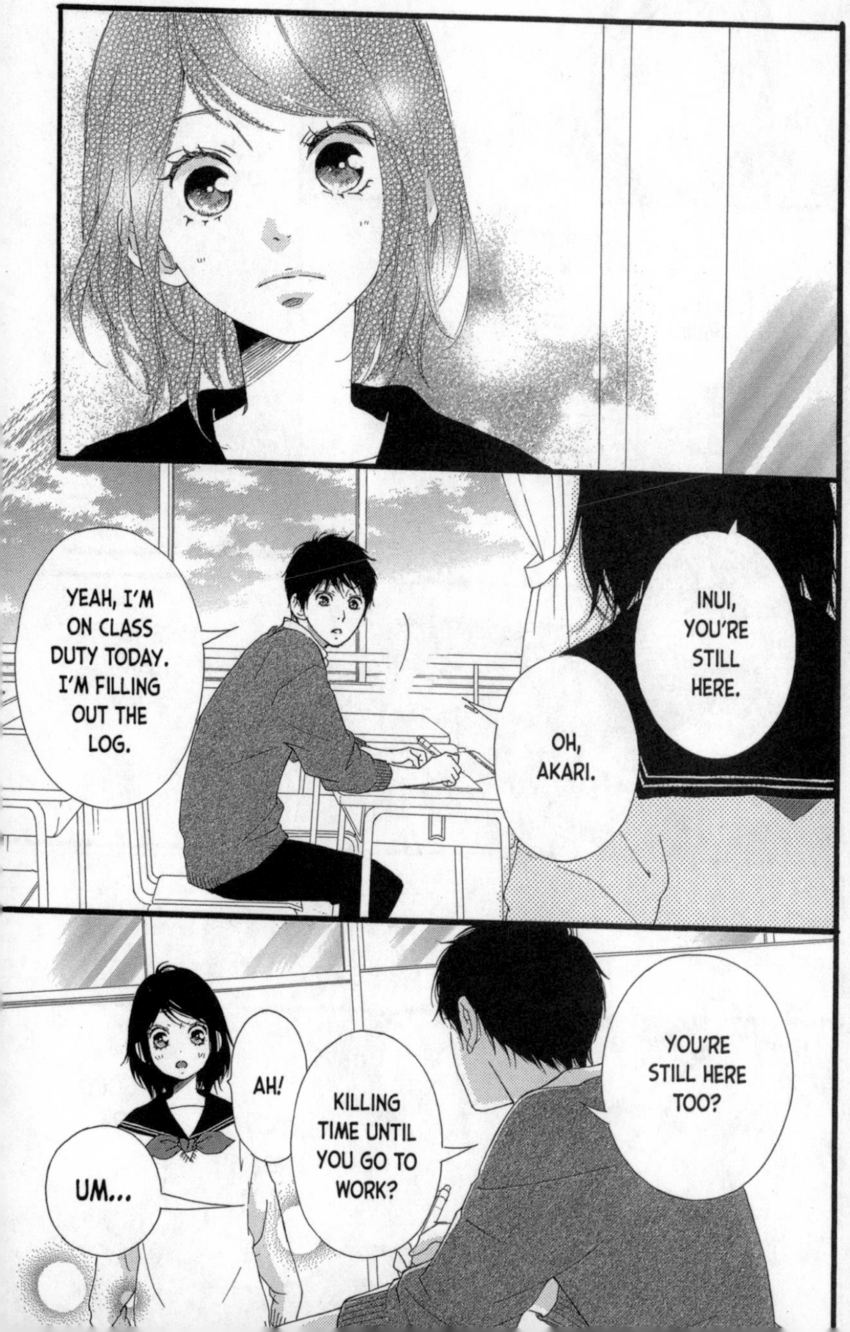
INUI, YOU'RE STILL HERE.
OH, AKARI.
YEAH, I'M ON CLASS DUTY TODAY. I'M FILLING OUT THE LOG.
YOU'RE STILL HERE TOO?
KILLING TIME UNTIL YOU GO TO WORK?
AH!
UM...

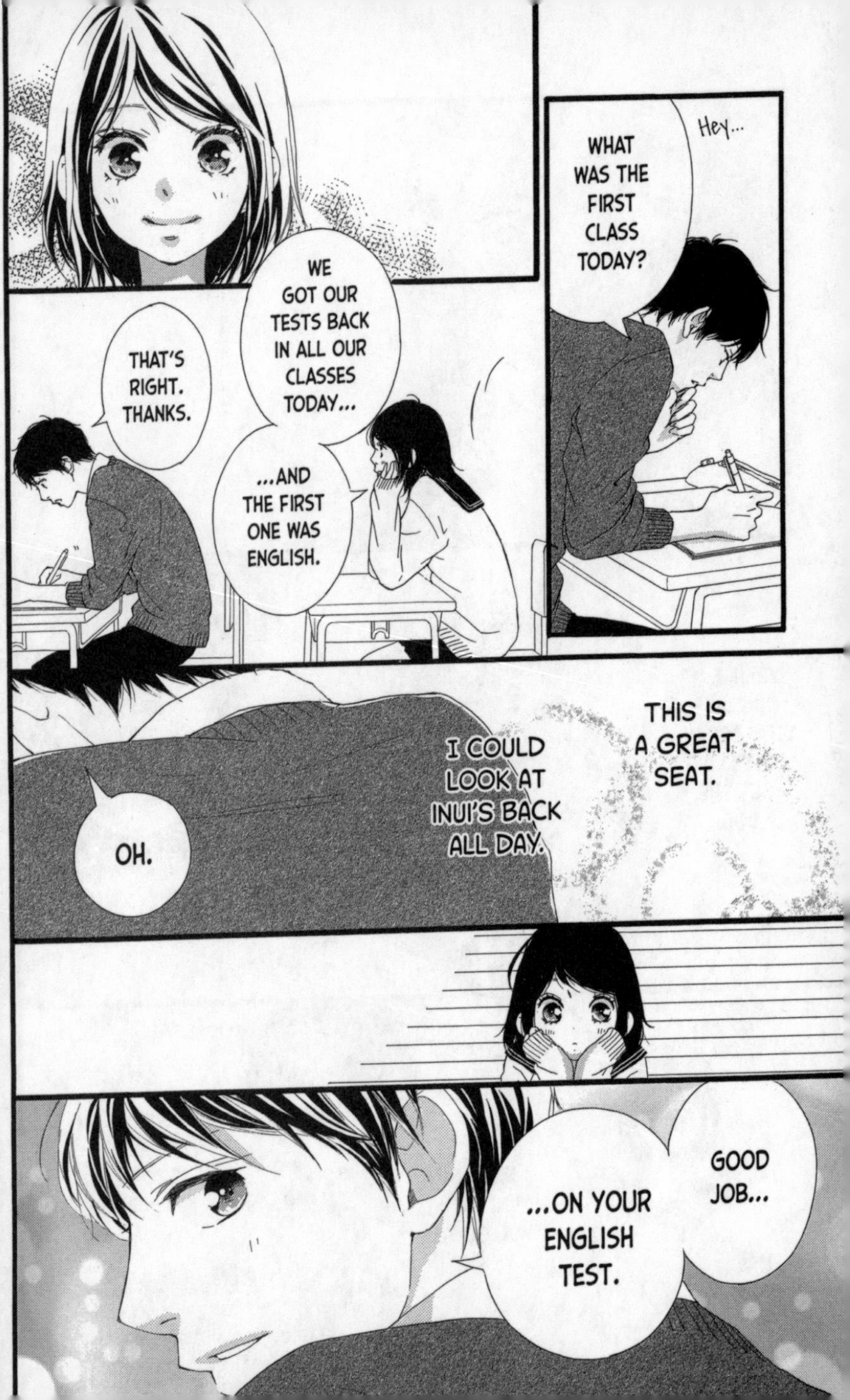
Hey...
WHAT WAS THE FIRST CLASS TODAY?
WE GOT OUR TESTS BACK IN ALL OUR CLASSES TODAY...
...AND THE FIRST ONE WAS ENGLISH.
THAT'S RIGHT. THANKS.
THIS IS A GREAT SEAT.
I COULD LOOK AT INUI'S BACK ALL DAY.
OH.
GOOD JOB...
...ON YOUR ENGLISH TEST.

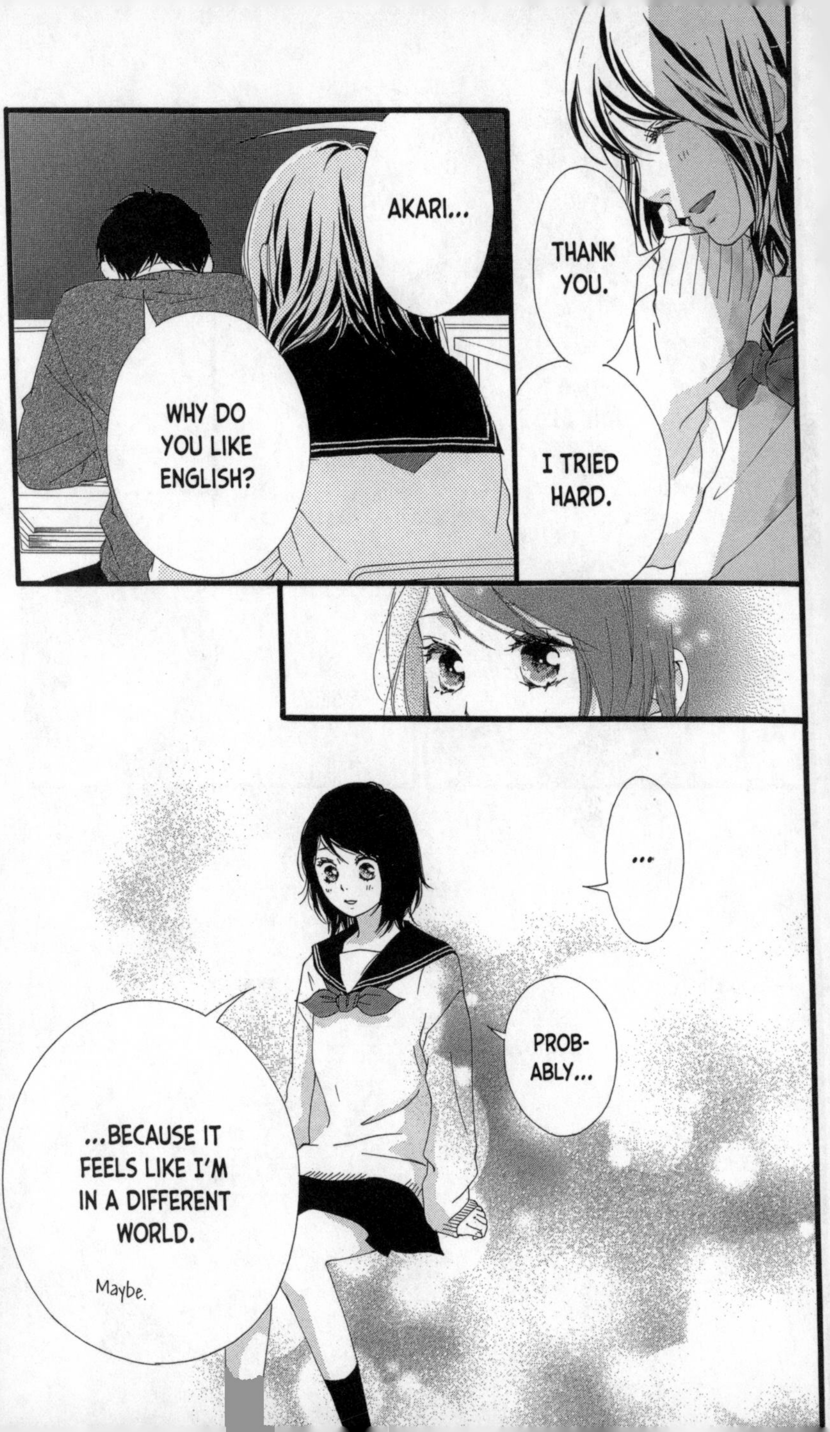
THANK YOU.
I TRIED HARD.
AKARI...
WHY DO YOU LIKE ENGLISH?
...
PROB-ABLY...
...BECAUSE IT FEELS LIKE I'M IN A DIFFERENT WORLD.
Maybe.

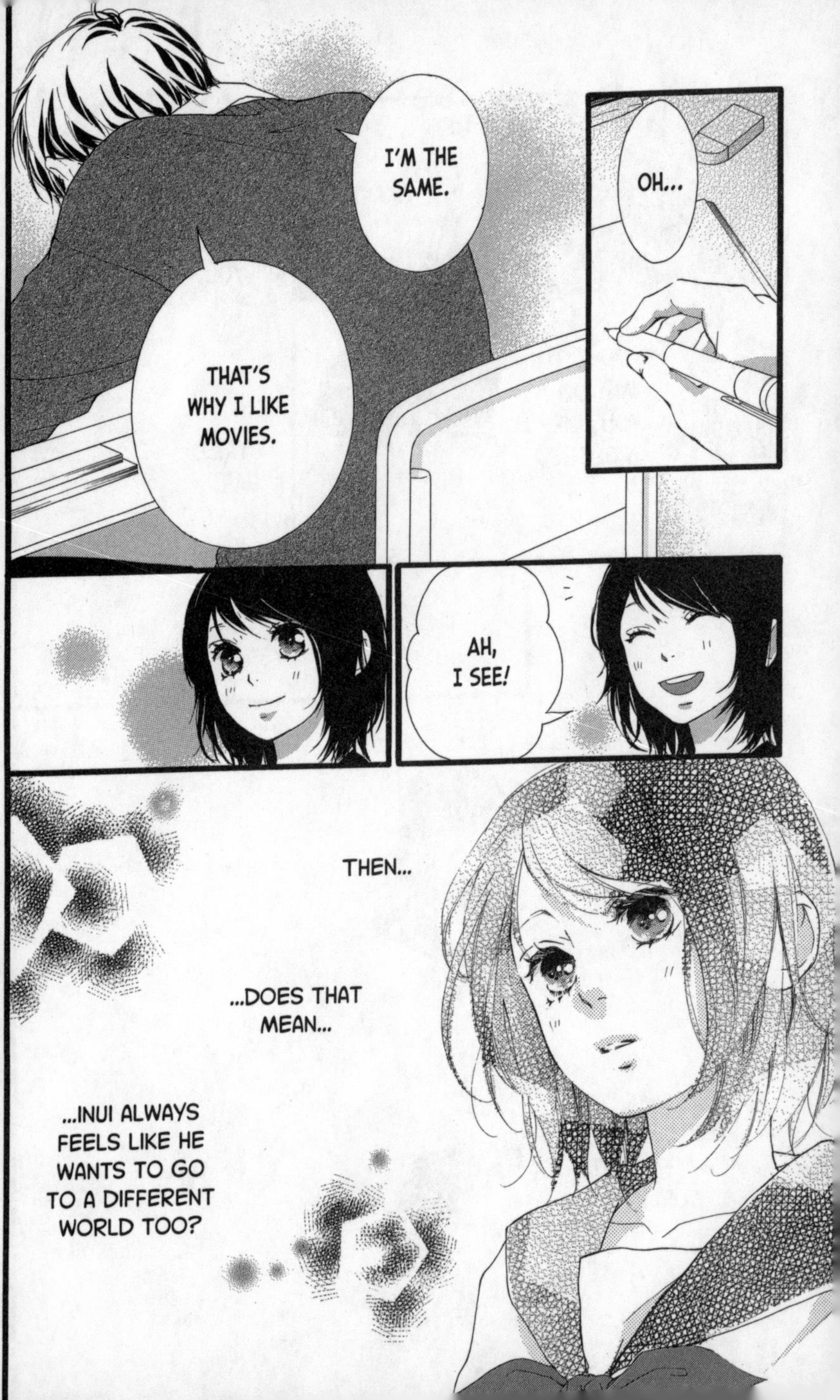
OH...
I'M THE SAME.
THAT'S WHY I LIKE MOVIES.
AH, I SEE!
THEN...
...DOES THAT MEAN...
...INUI ALWAYS FEELS LIKE HE WANTS TO GO TO A DIFFERENT WORLD TOO?

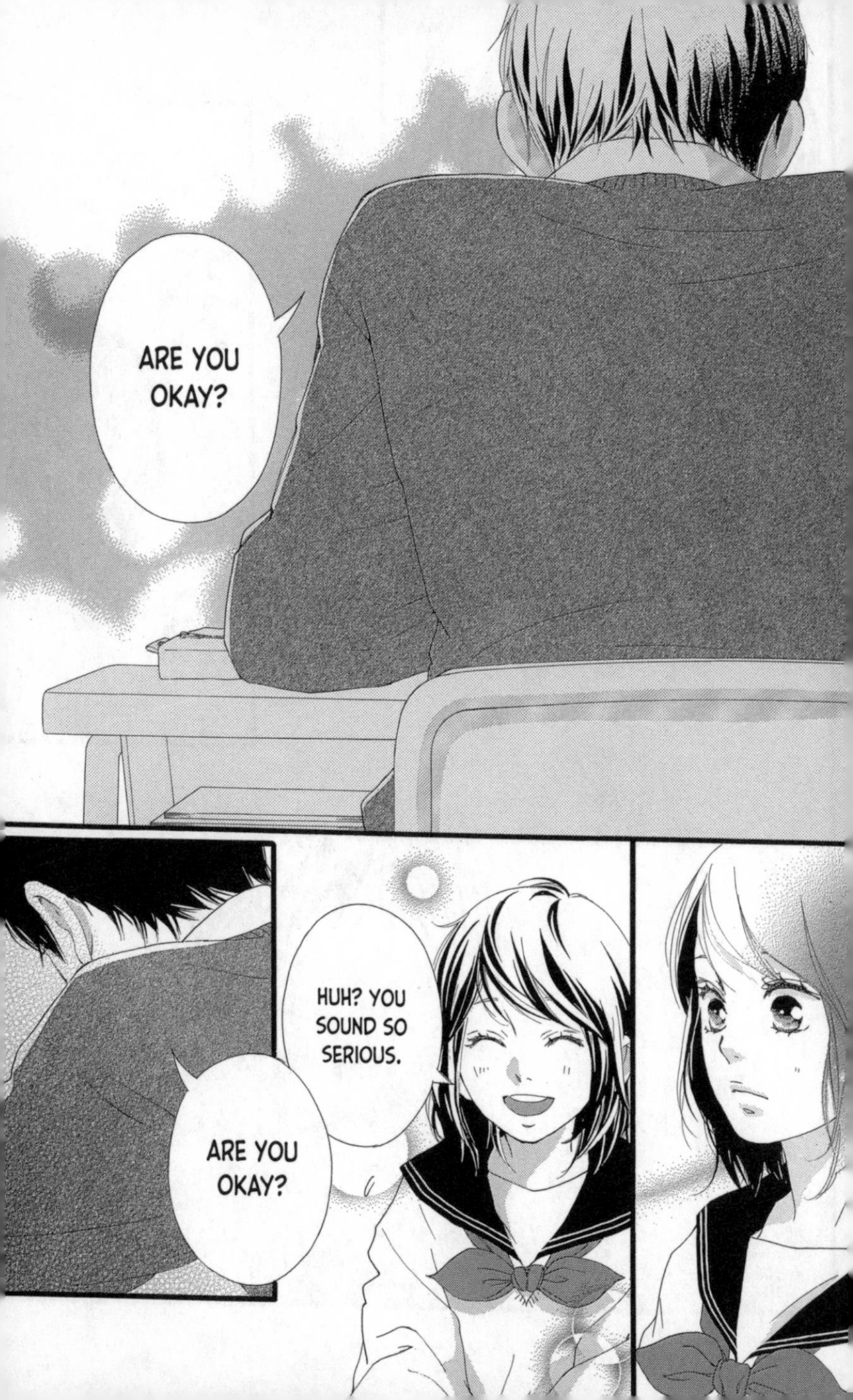
ARE YOU OKAY?
HUH? YOU SOUND SO SERIOUS.
ARE YOU OKAY?

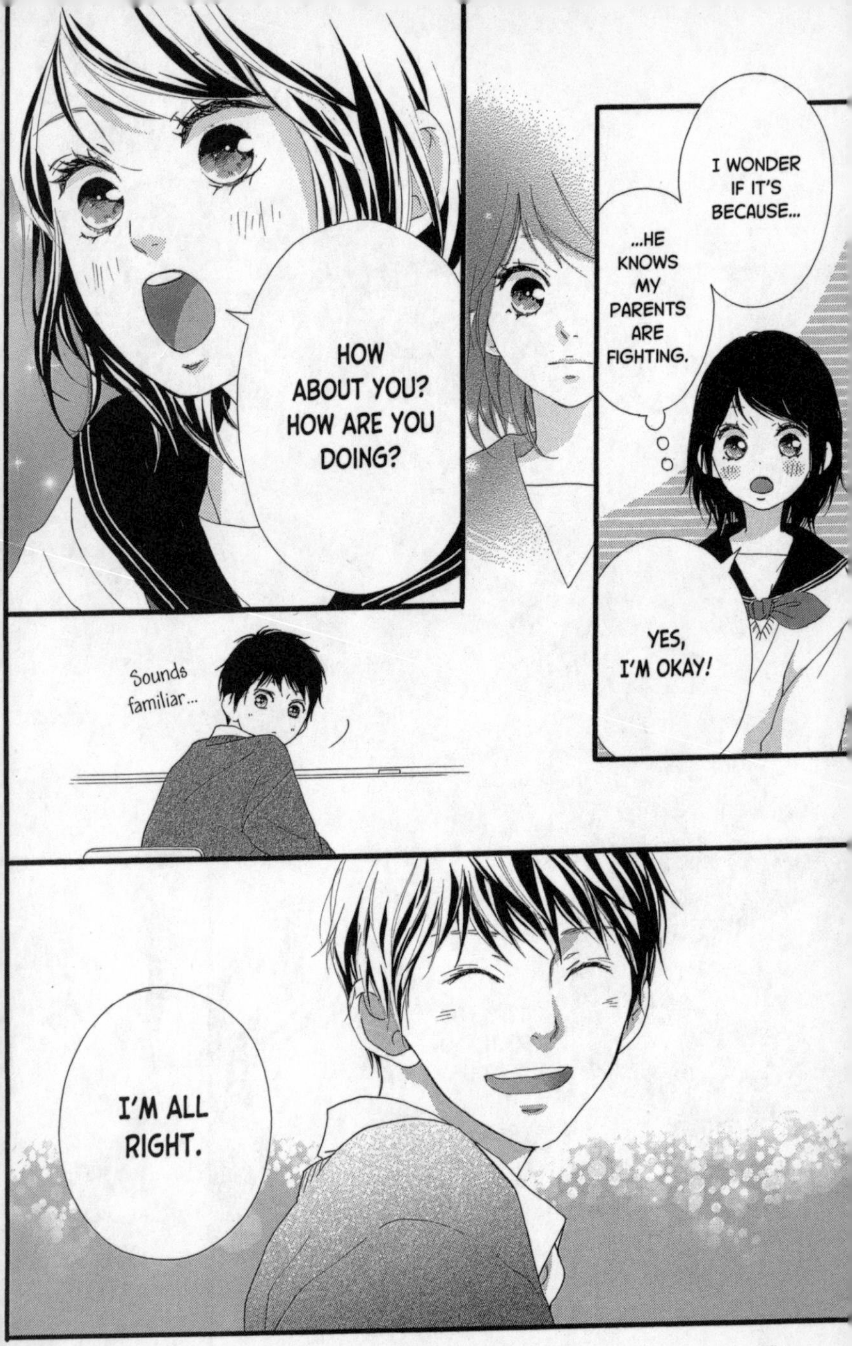
I WONDER IF IT'S BECAUSE...
...HE KNOWS MY PARENTS ARE FIGHTING.
YES, I'M OKAY!
HOW ABOUT YOU? HOW ARE YOU DOING?
Sounds familiar...
I'M ALL RIGHT.

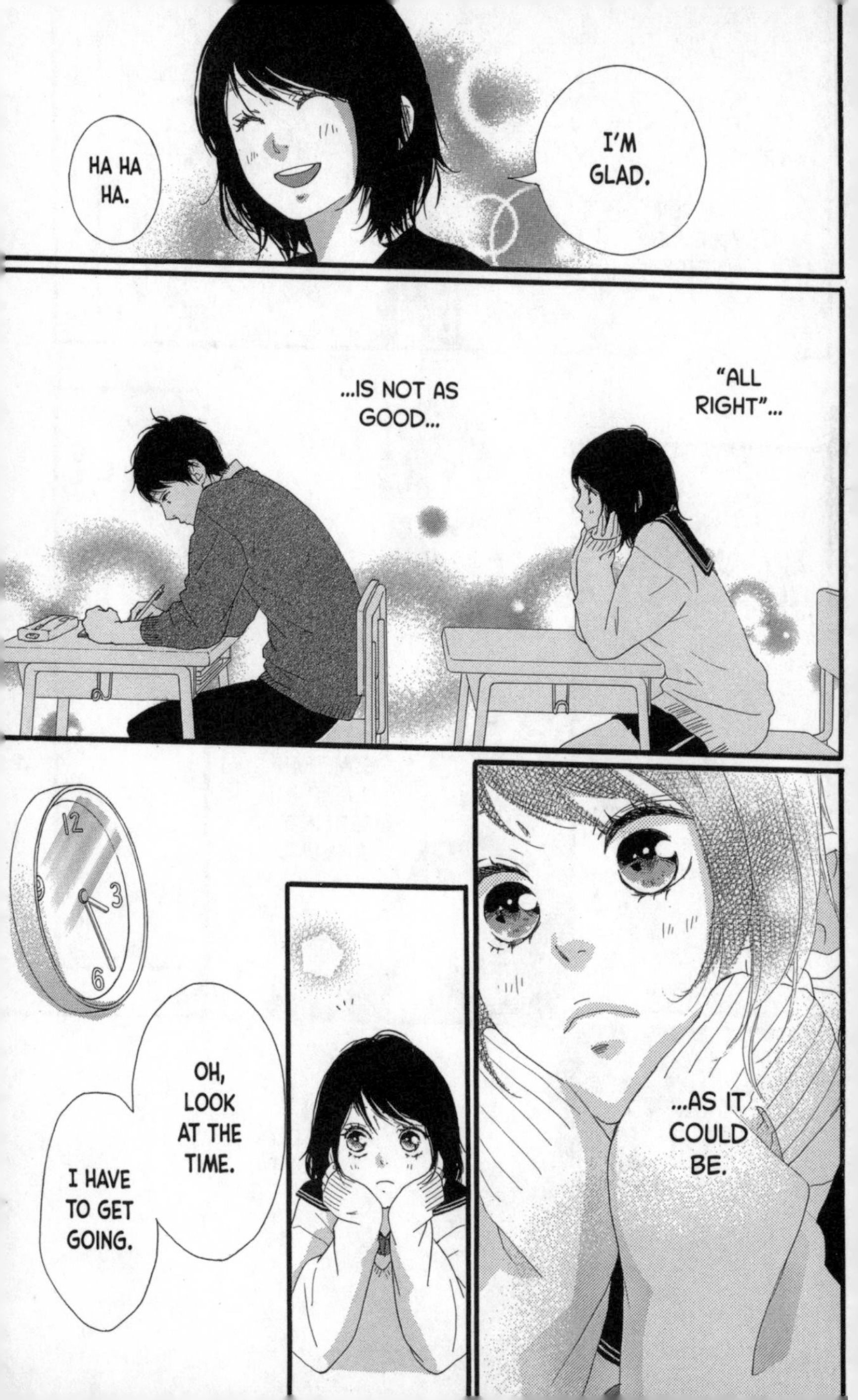
I'M GLAD.
HA HA HA.
"ALL RIGHT"...
...IS NOT AS GOOD...
...AS IT COULD BE.
OH, LOOK AT THE TIME.
I HAVE TO GET GOING.

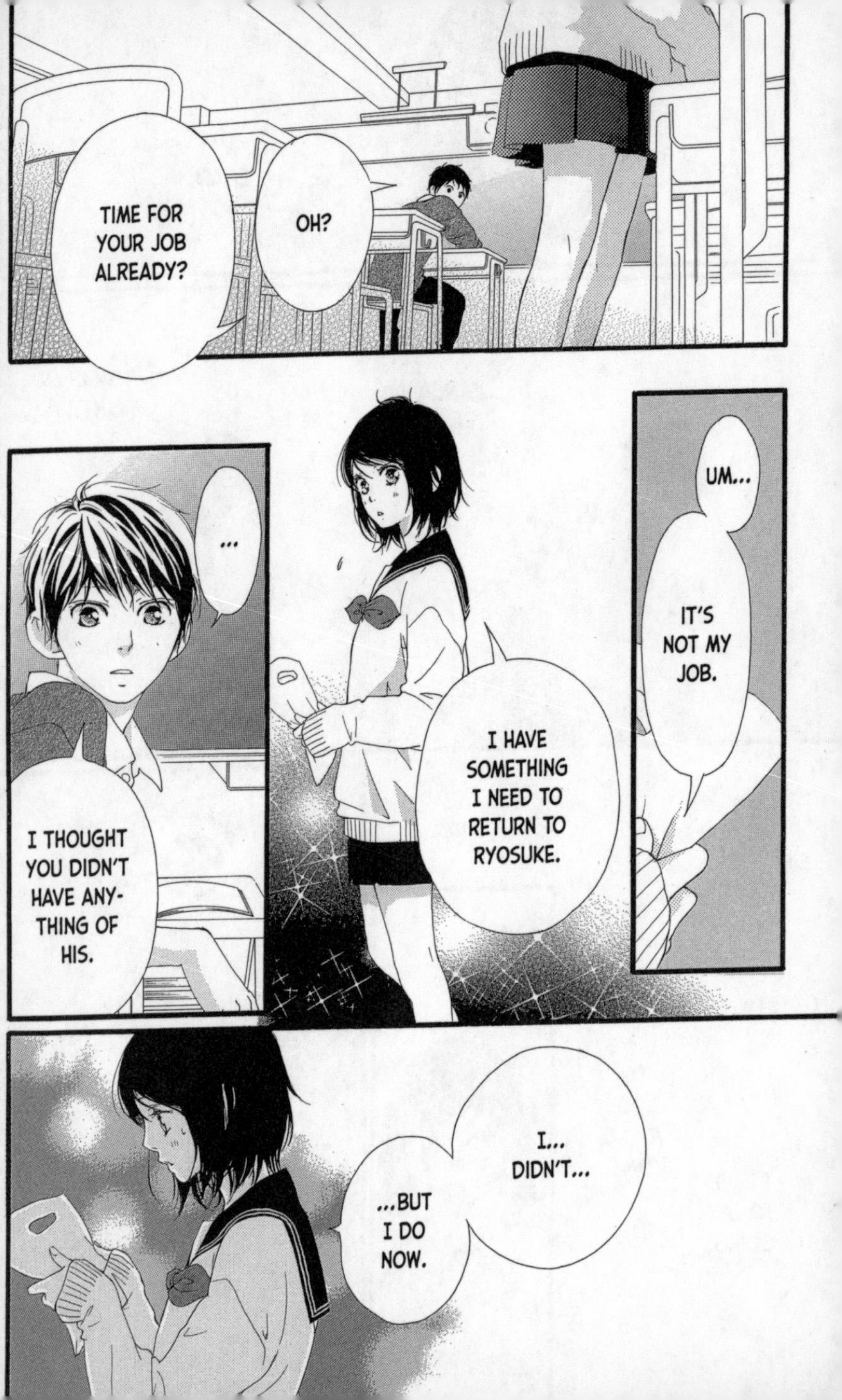
OH?
TIME FOR YOUR JOB ALREADY?
UM...
IT'S NOT MY JOB.
I HAVE SOMETHING I NEED TO RETURN TO RYOSUKE.
...
I THOUGHT YOU DIDN'T HAVE ANY-THING OF HIS.
I... DIDN'T...
...BUT I DO NOW.

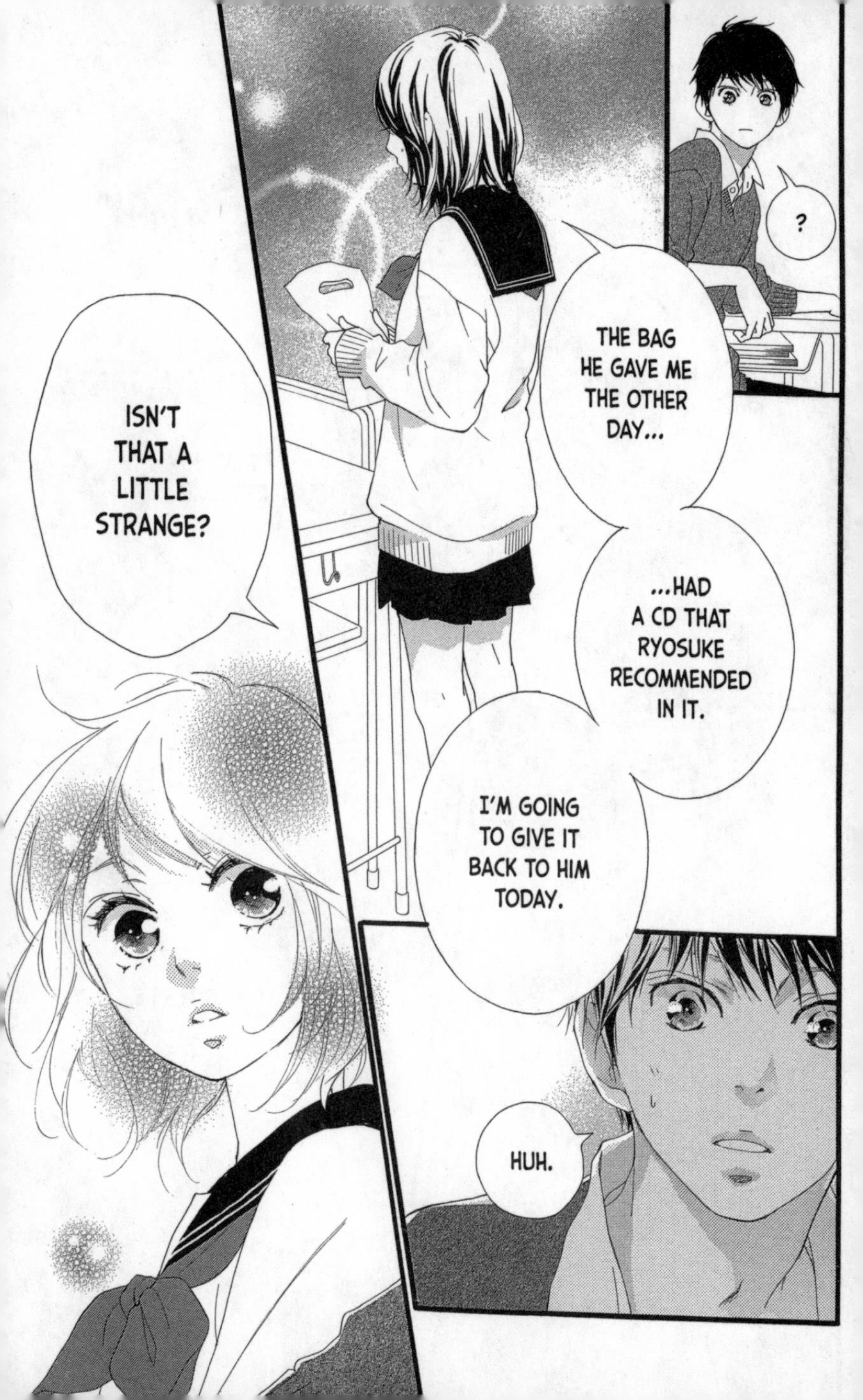
?
THE BAG HE GAVE ME THE OTHER DAY...
...HAD A CD THAT RYOSUKE RECOMMENDED IN IT.
I'M GOING TO GIVE IT BACK TO HIM TODAY.
HUH.
ISN'T THAT A LITTLE STRANGE?

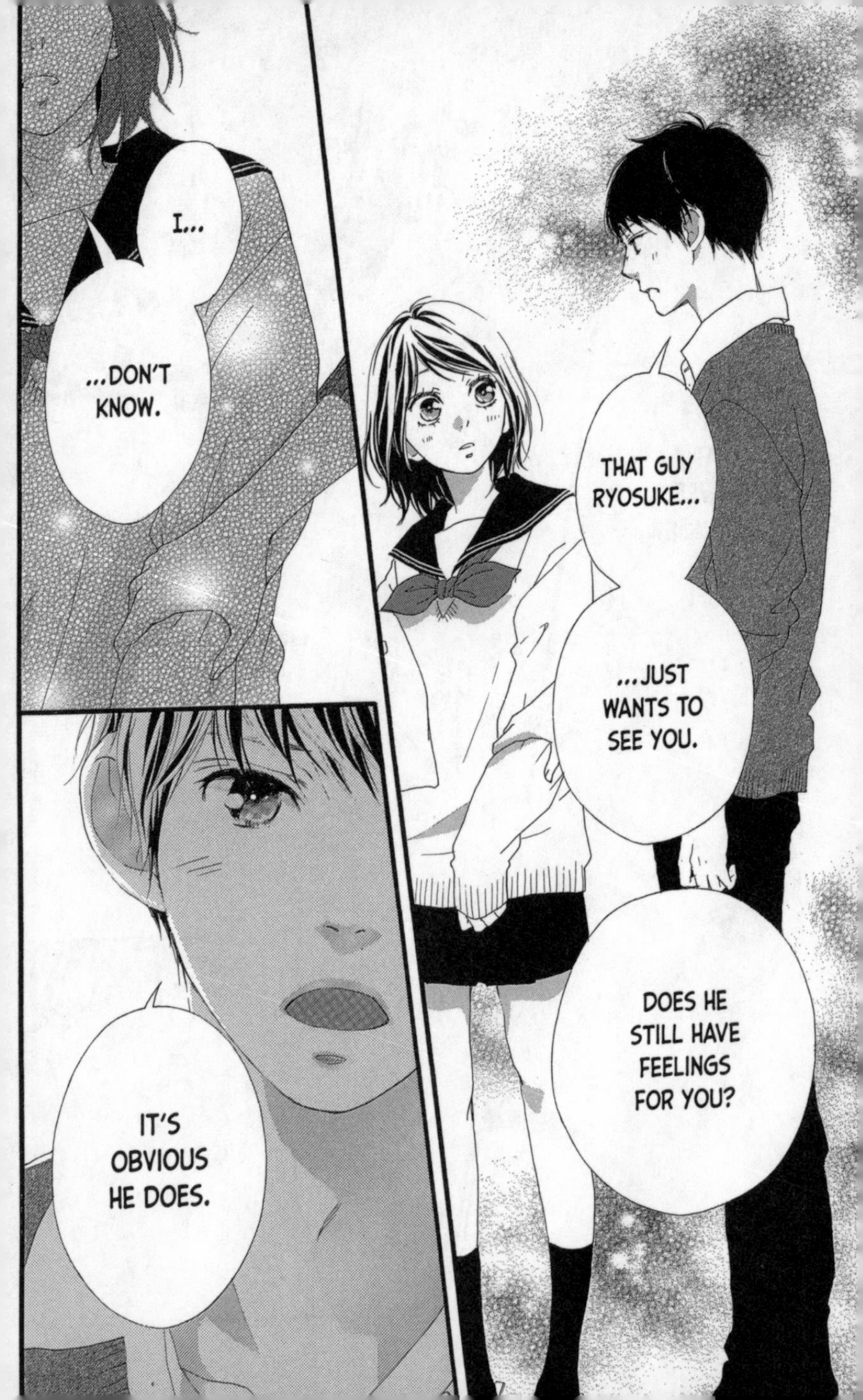
THAT GUY RYOSUKE...
...JUST WANTS TO SEE YOU.
DOES HE STILL HAVE FEELINGS FOR YOU?
I...
...DON'T KNOW.
IT'S OBVIOUS HE DOES.

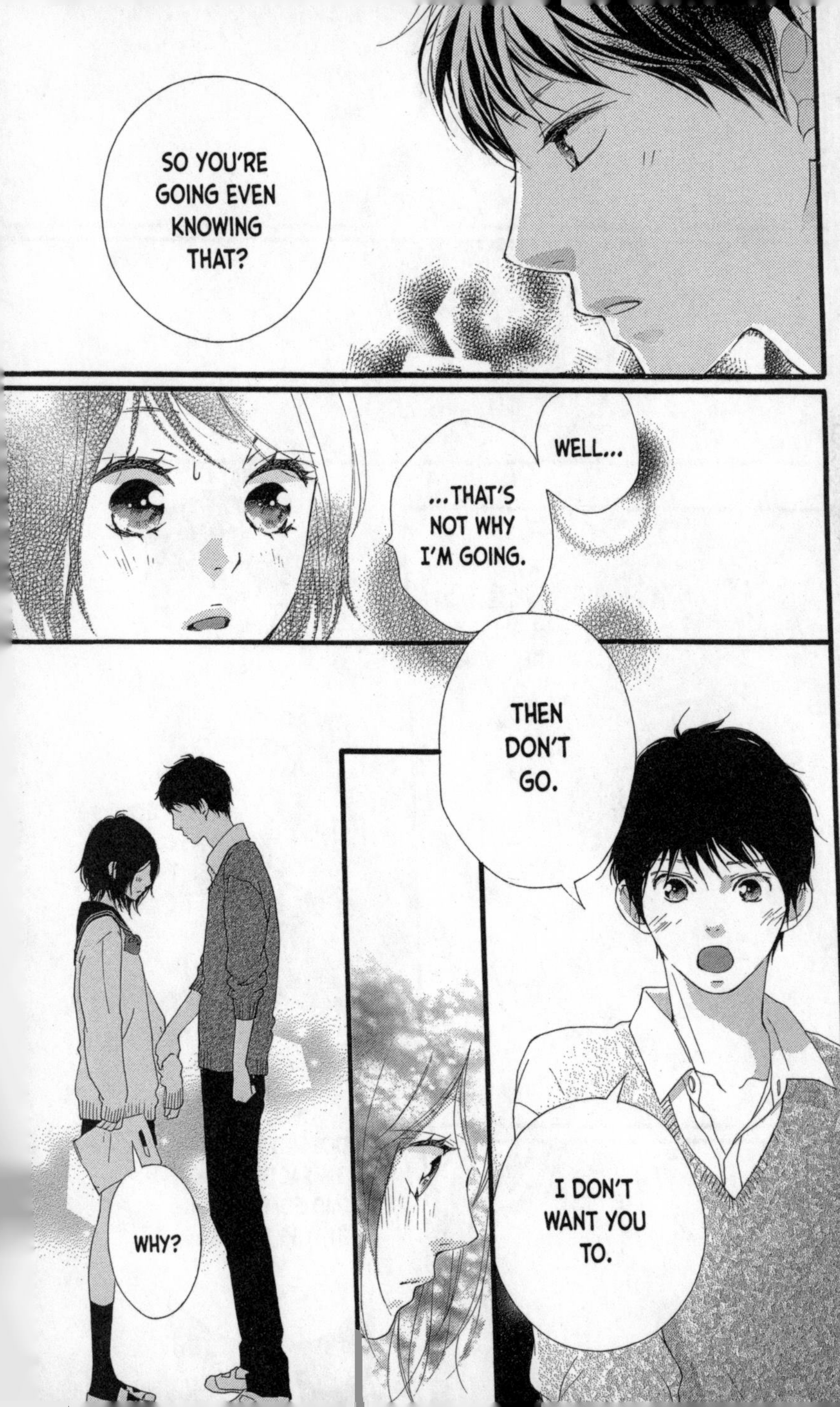
SO YOU'RE GOING EVEN KNOWING THAT?
WELL...
...THAT'S NOT WHY I'M GOING.
THEN DON'T GO.
I DON'T WANT YOU TO.
WHY?

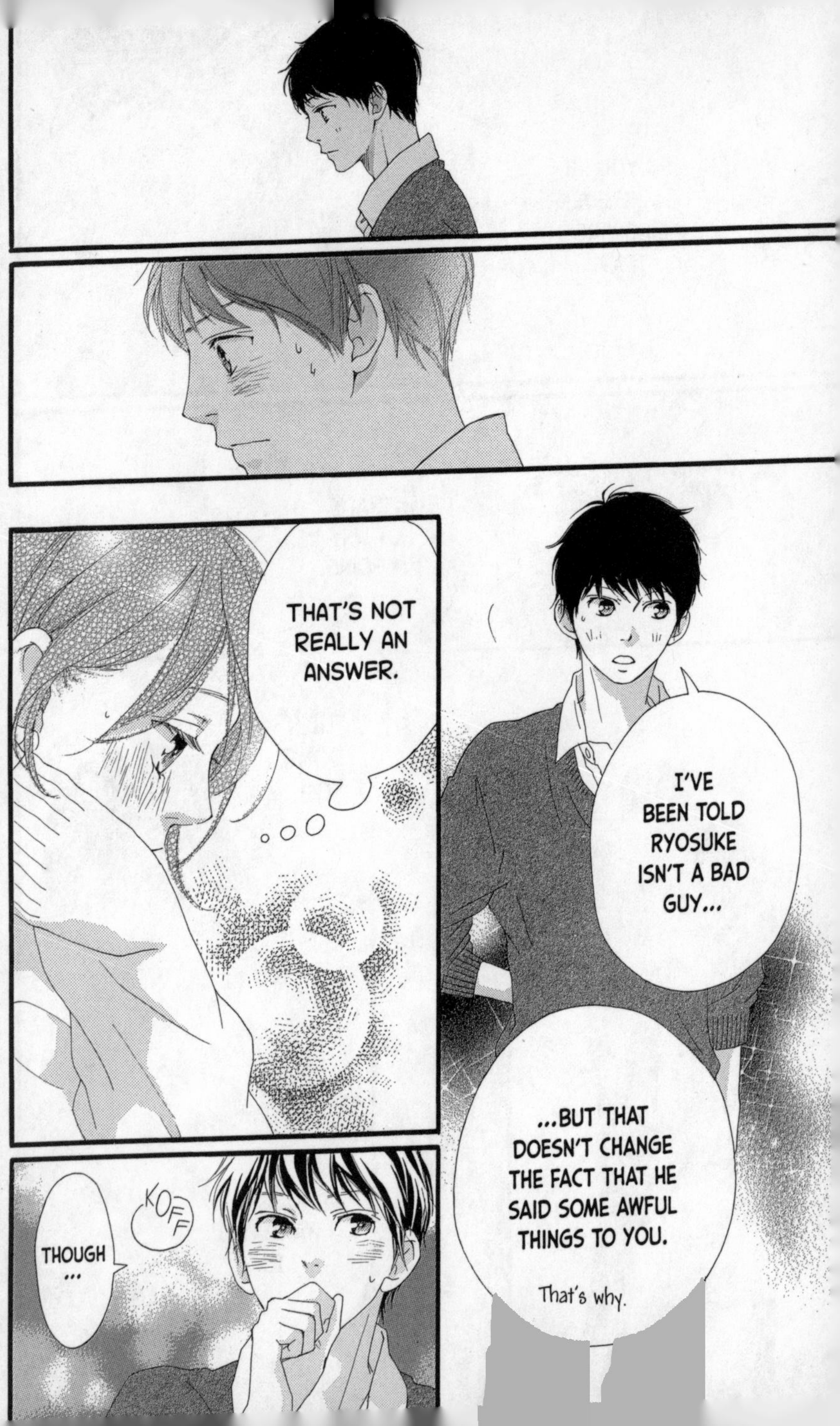
I'VE BEEN TOLD RYOSUKE ISN'T A BAD GUY...
...BUT THAT DOESN'T CHANGE THE FACT THAT HE SAID SOME AWFUL THINGS TO YOU.
That's why.
THAT'S NOT REALLY AN ANSWER.
KOFF
THOUGH...

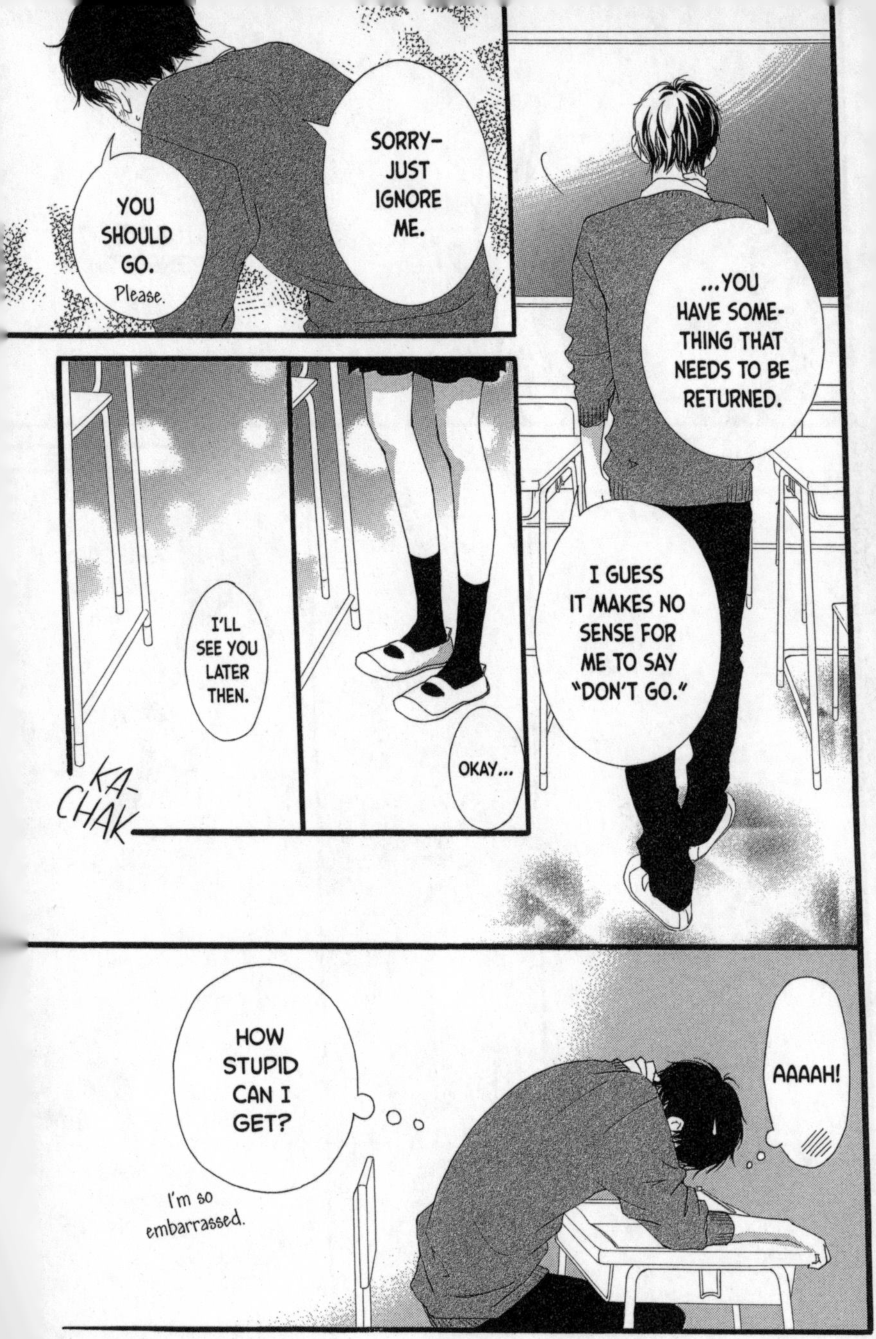
...YOU HAVE SOMETHING THAT NEEDS TO BE RETURNED.
I GUESS IT MAKES NO SENSE FOR ME TO SAY "DON'T GO."
SORRY— JUST IGNORE ME.
YOU SHOULD GO.
Please.
OKAY...
I'LL SEE YOU LATER THEN.
KA-CHAK
AAAAH!
HOW STUPID CAN I GET?
I'm so embarrassed.

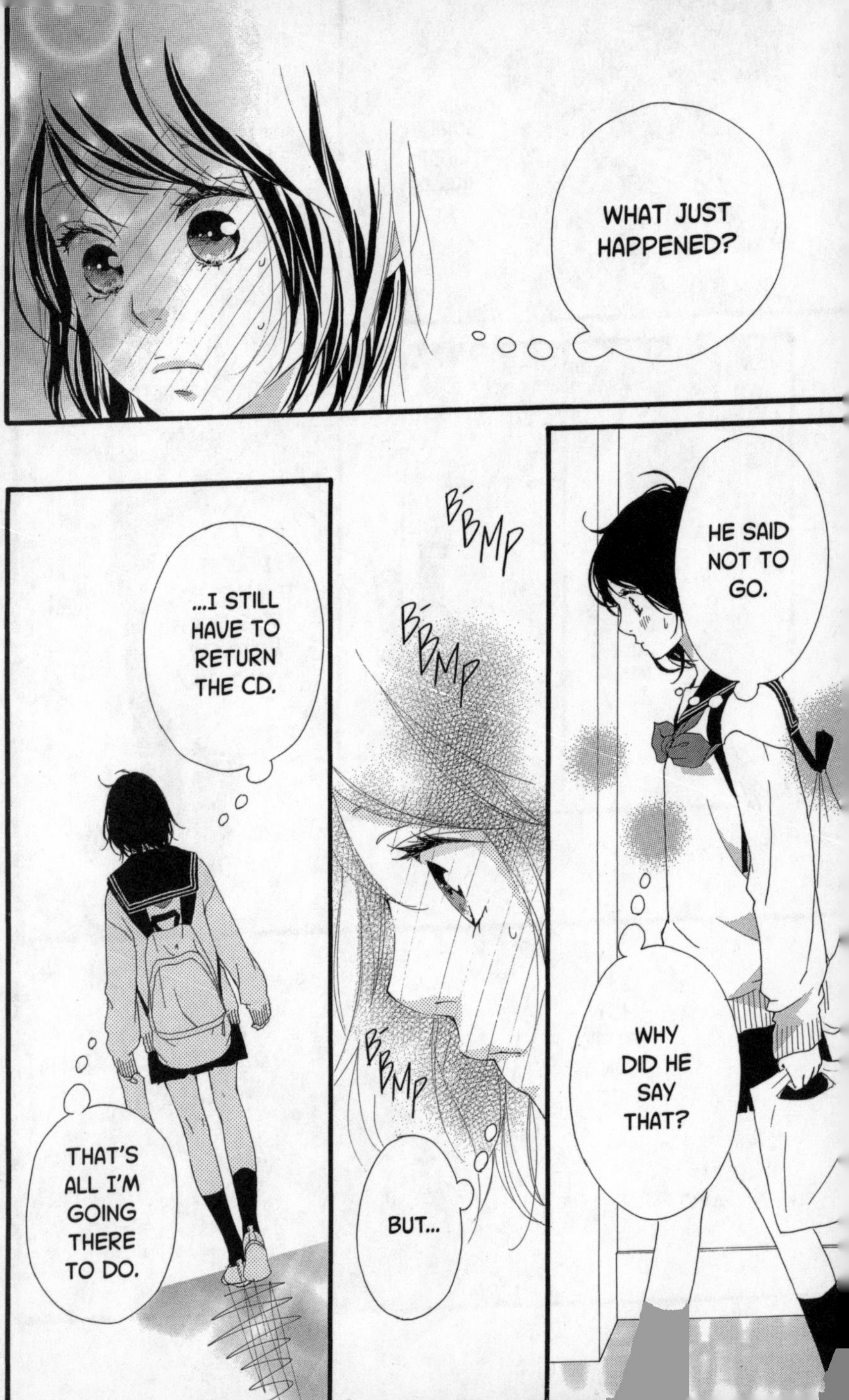
WHAT JUST HAPPENED?
HE SAID NOT TO GO.
WHY DID HE SAY THAT?
B'BMP
B'BMP
B'BMP
BUT...
...I STILL HAVE TO RETURN THE CD.
THAT'S ALL I'M GOING THERE TO DO.

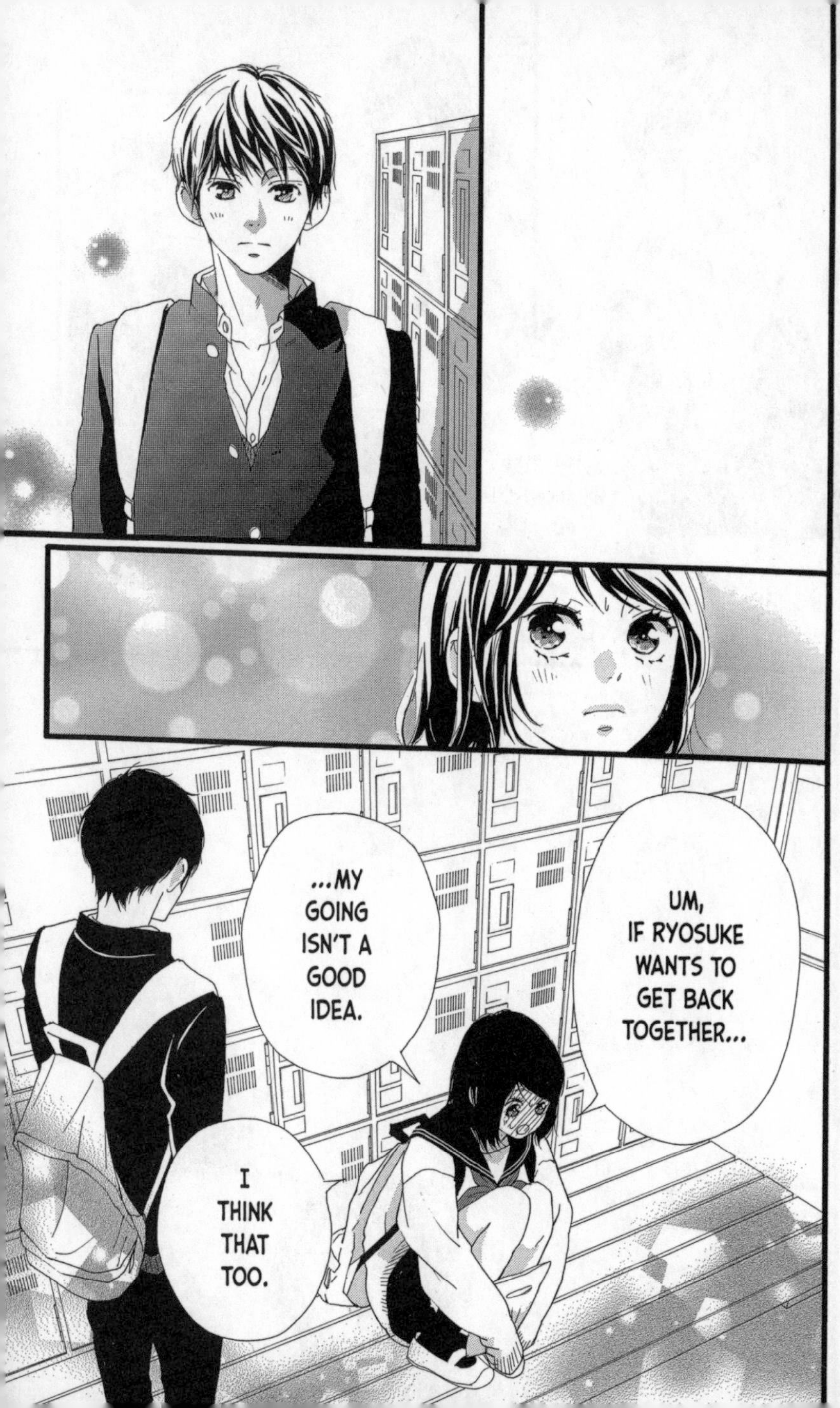
UM, IF RYOSUKE WANTS TO GET BACK TOGETHER...
...MY GOING ISN'T A GOOD IDEA.
I THINK THAT TOO.

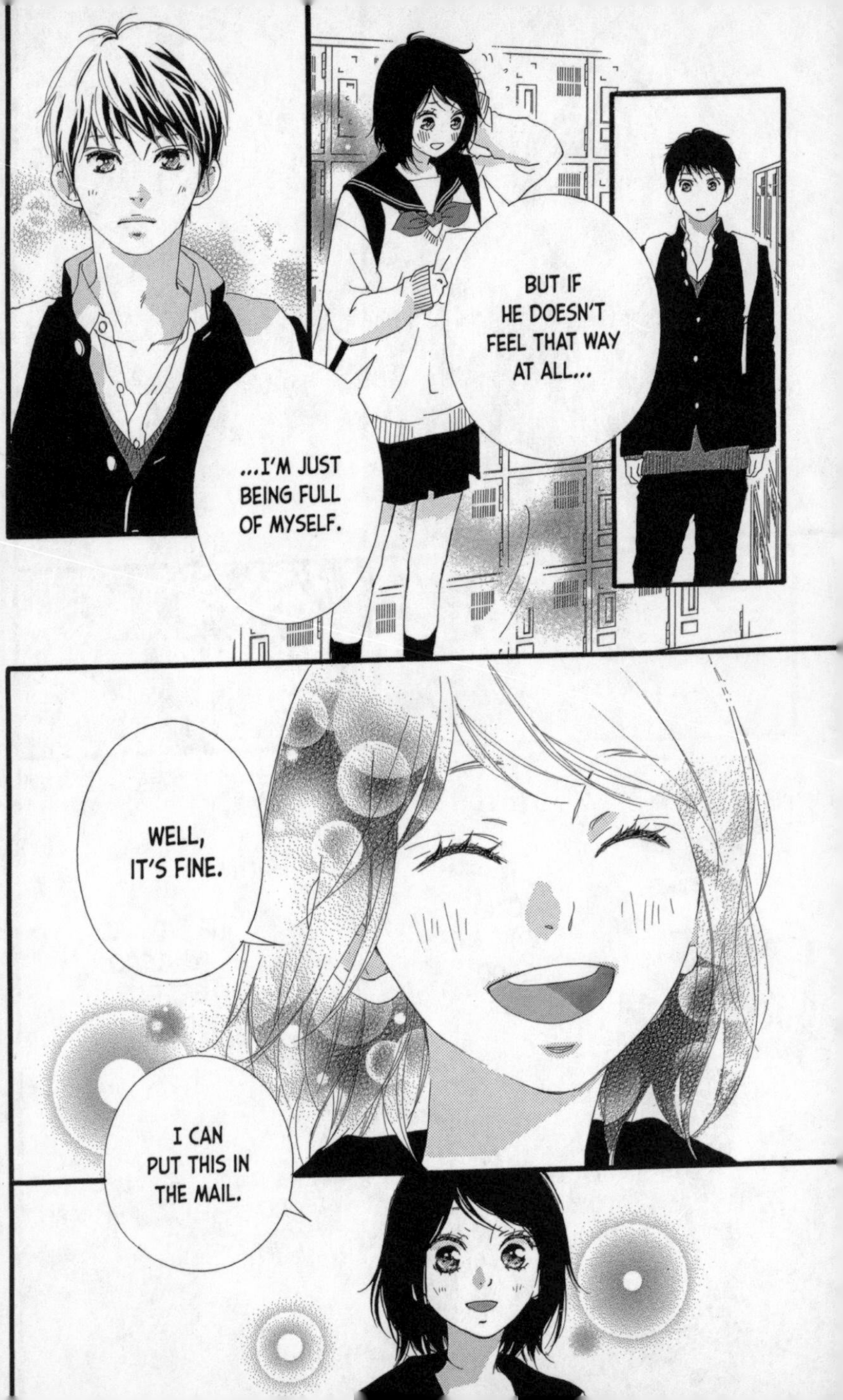
BUT IF HE DOESN'T FEEL THAT WAY AT ALL...
...I'M JUST BEING FULL OF MYSELF.
WELL, IT'S FINE.
I CAN PUT THIS IN THE MAIL.

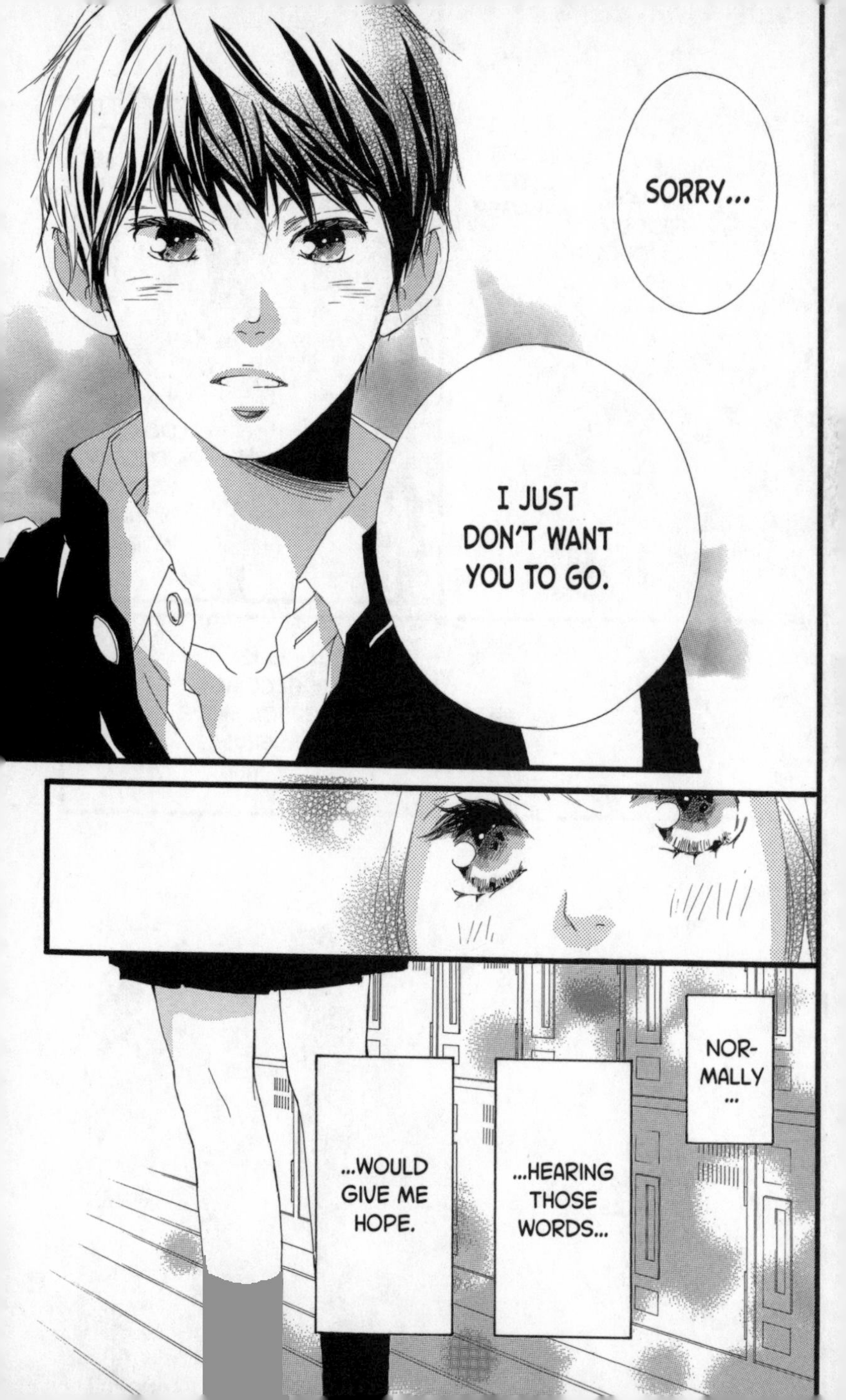
SORRY...
I JUST DON'T WANT YOU TO GO.
NOR-MALLY ...
...HEARING THOSE WORDS...
...WOULD GIVE ME HOPE.

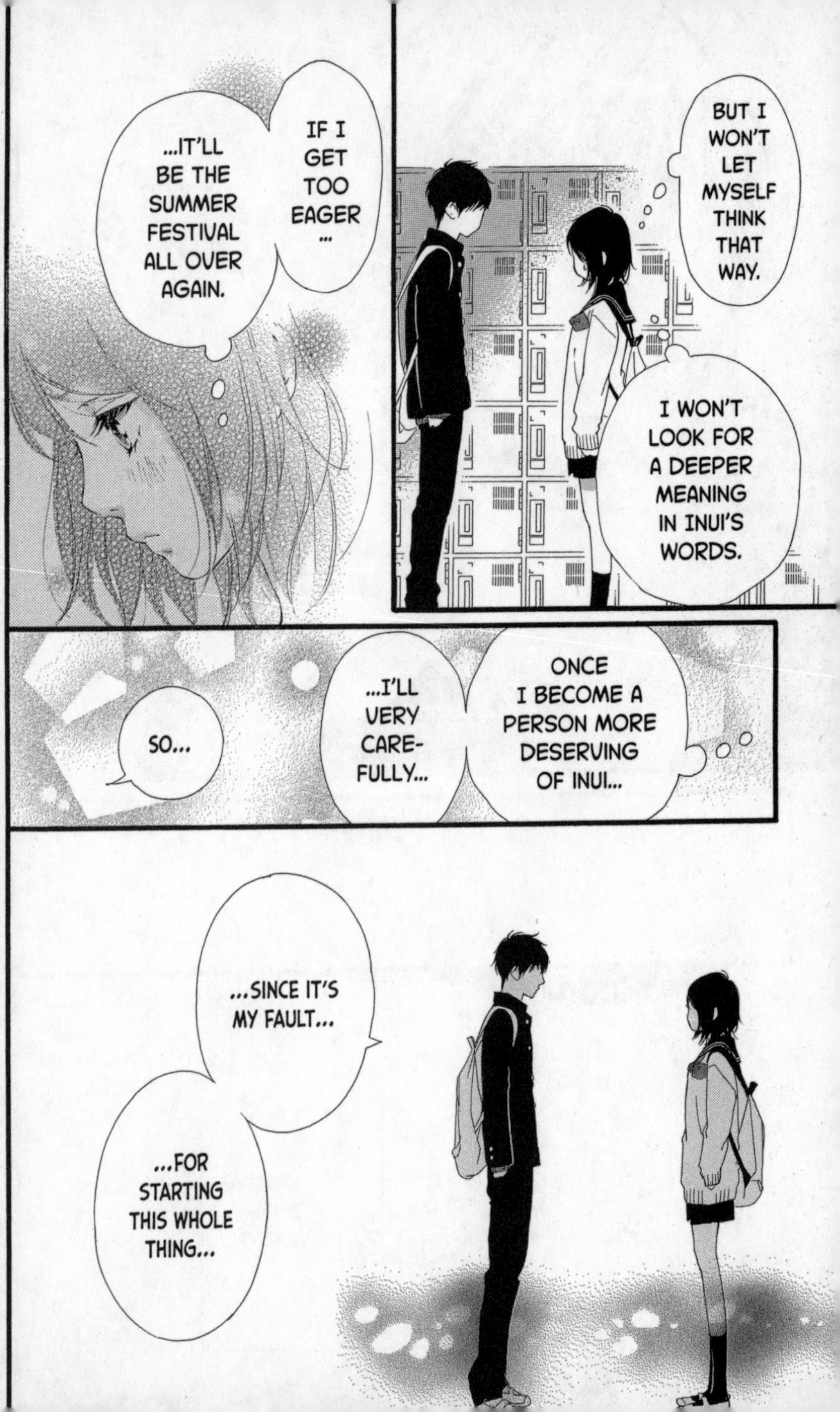
BUT I WON'T LET MYSELF THINK THAT WAY.
I WON'T LOOK FOR A DEEPER MEANING IN INUI'S WORDS.
IF I GET TOO EAGER...
...IT'LL BE THE SUMMER FESTIVAL ALL OVER AGAIN.
ONCE I BECOME A PERSON MORE DESERVING OF INUI...
...I'LL VERY CARE-FULLY...
SO...
...SINCE IT'S MY FAULT...
...FOR STARTING THIS WHOLE THING...

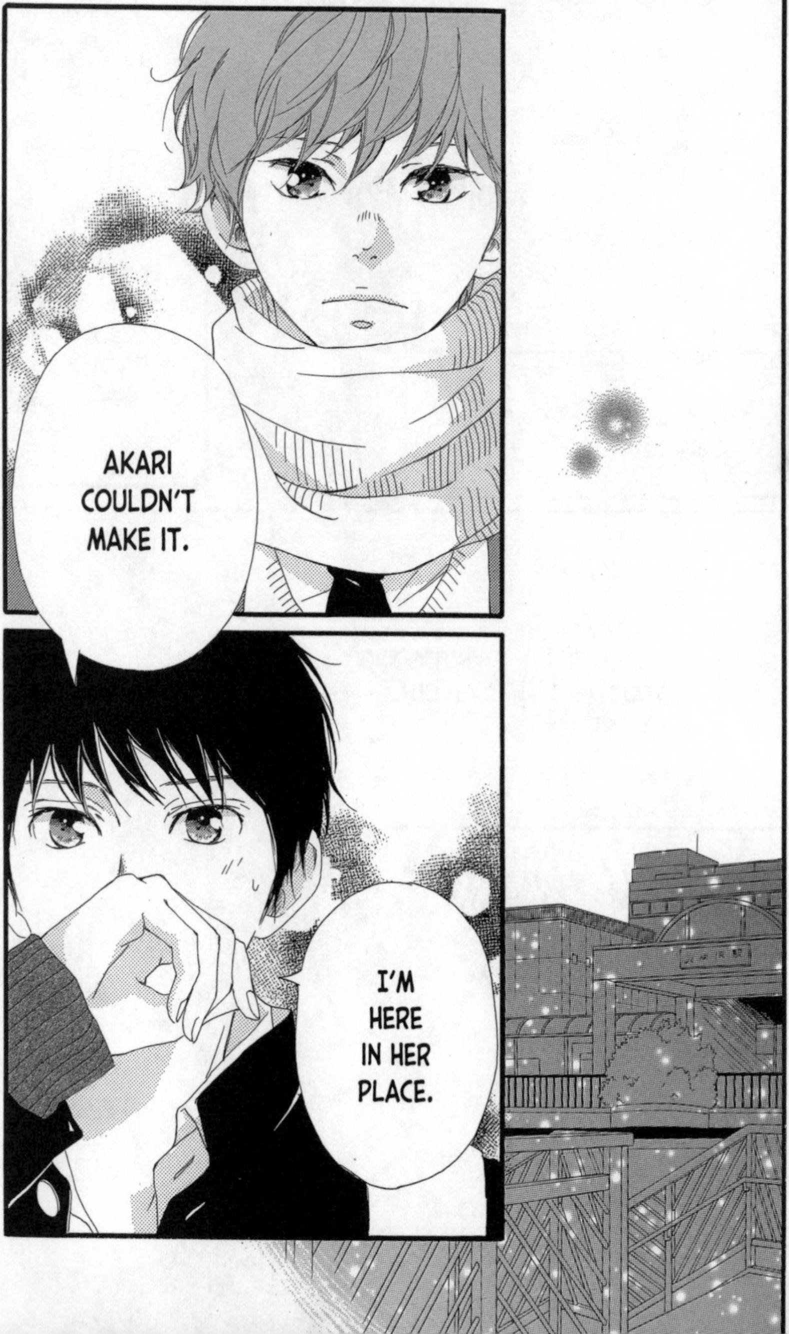
AKARI COULDN'T MAKE IT.
I'M HERE IN HER PLACE.

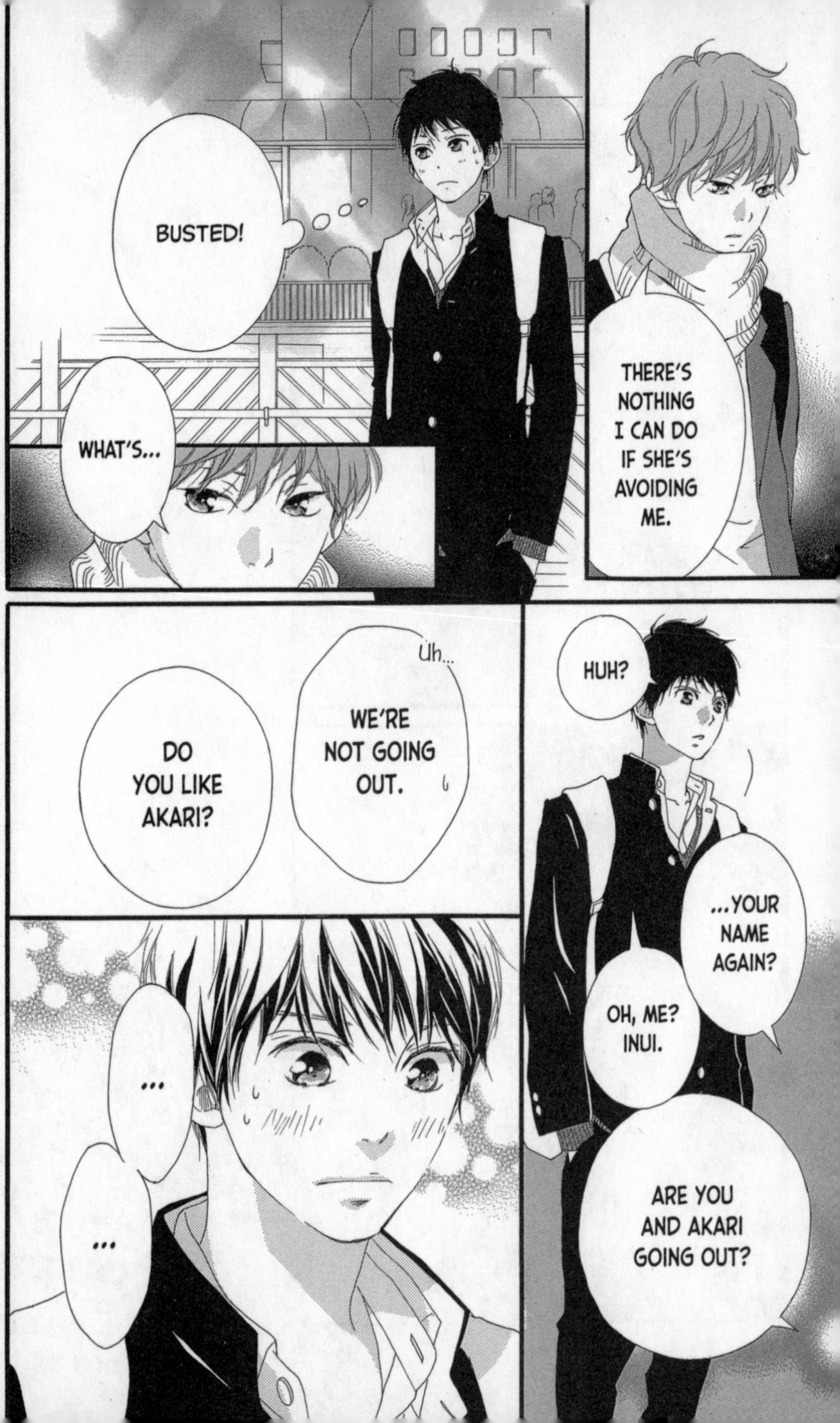

THERE'S NOTHING I CAN DO IF SHE'S AVOIDING ME.
BUSTED!
WHAT'S...
HUH?
...YOUR NAME AGAIN?
OH, ME? INUI.
ARE YOU AND AKARI GOING OUT?
Uh...
WE'RE NOT GOING OUT.
DO YOU LIKE AKARI?
...
...

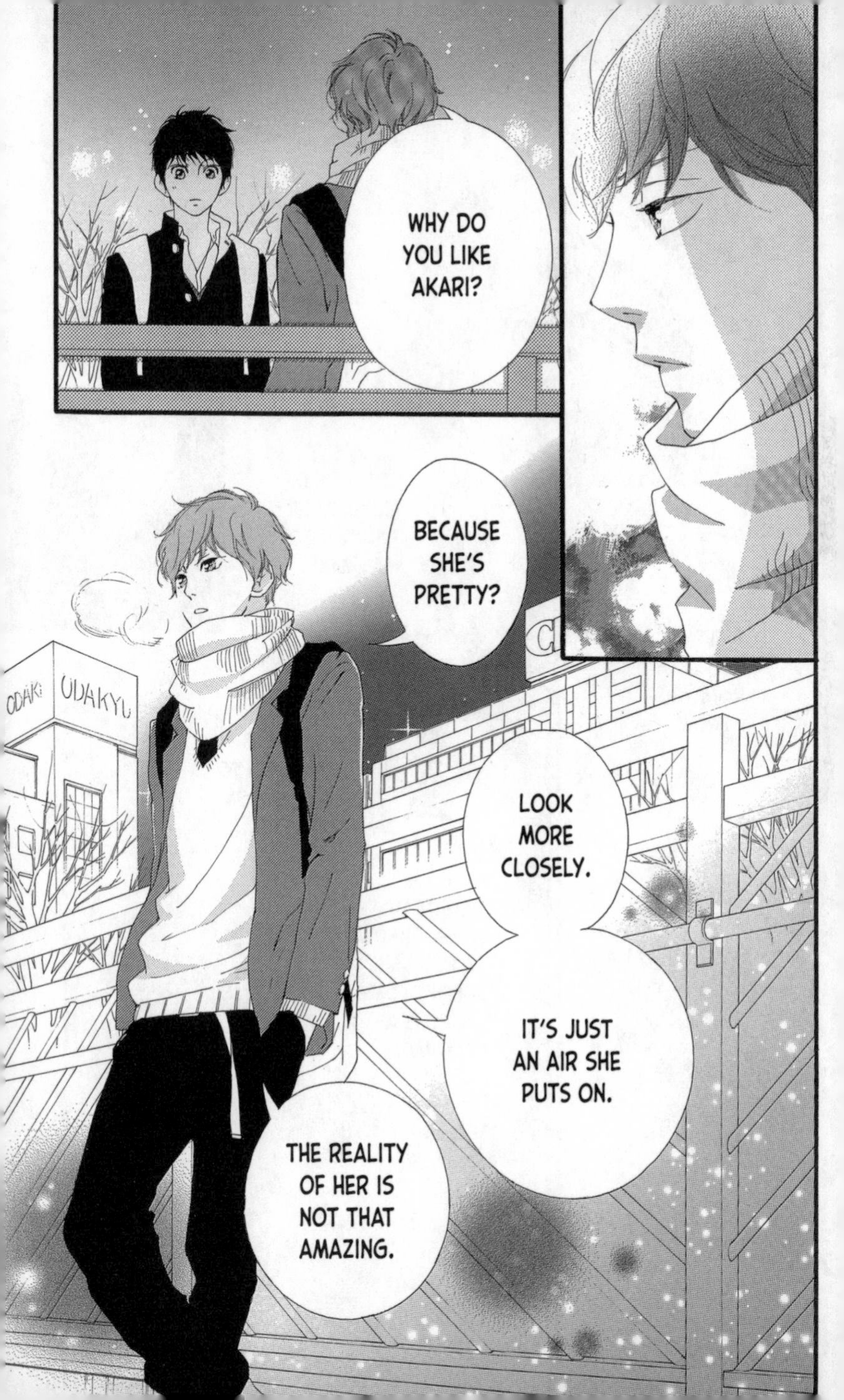
WHY DO YOU LIKE AKARI?
BECAUSE SHE'S PRETTY?
ODAKYU
LOOK MORE CLOSELY.
IT'S JUST AN AIR SHE PUTS ON.
THE REALITY OF HER IS NOT THAT AMAZING.

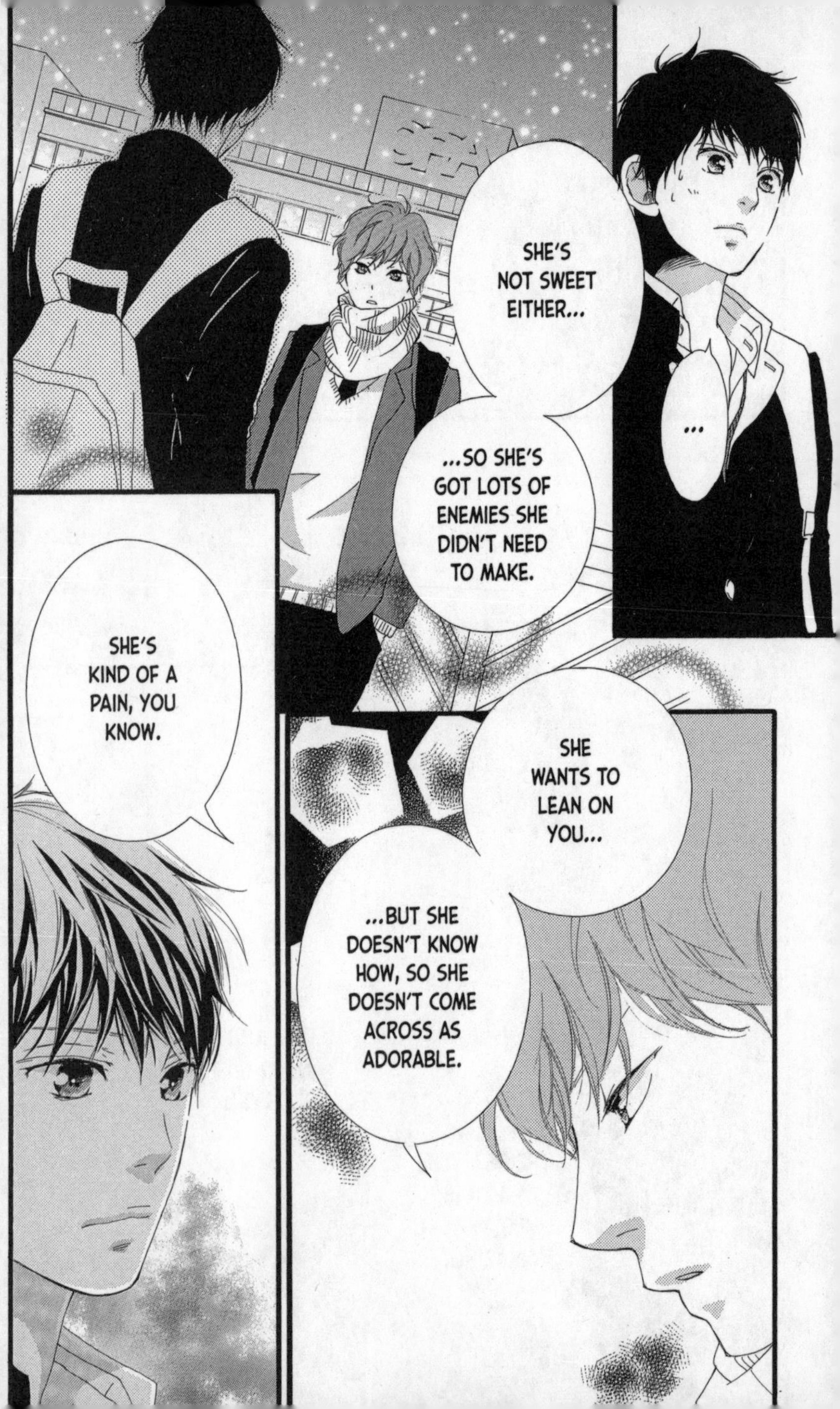
SHE'S NOT SWEET EITHER...
...SO SHE'S GOT LOTS OF ENEMIES SHE DIDN'T NEED TO MAKE.
...
SHE'S KIND OF A PAIN, YOU KNOW.
SHE WANTS TO LEAN ON YOU...
...BUT SHE DOESN'T KNOW HOW, SO SHE DOESN'T COME ACROSS AS ADORABLE.

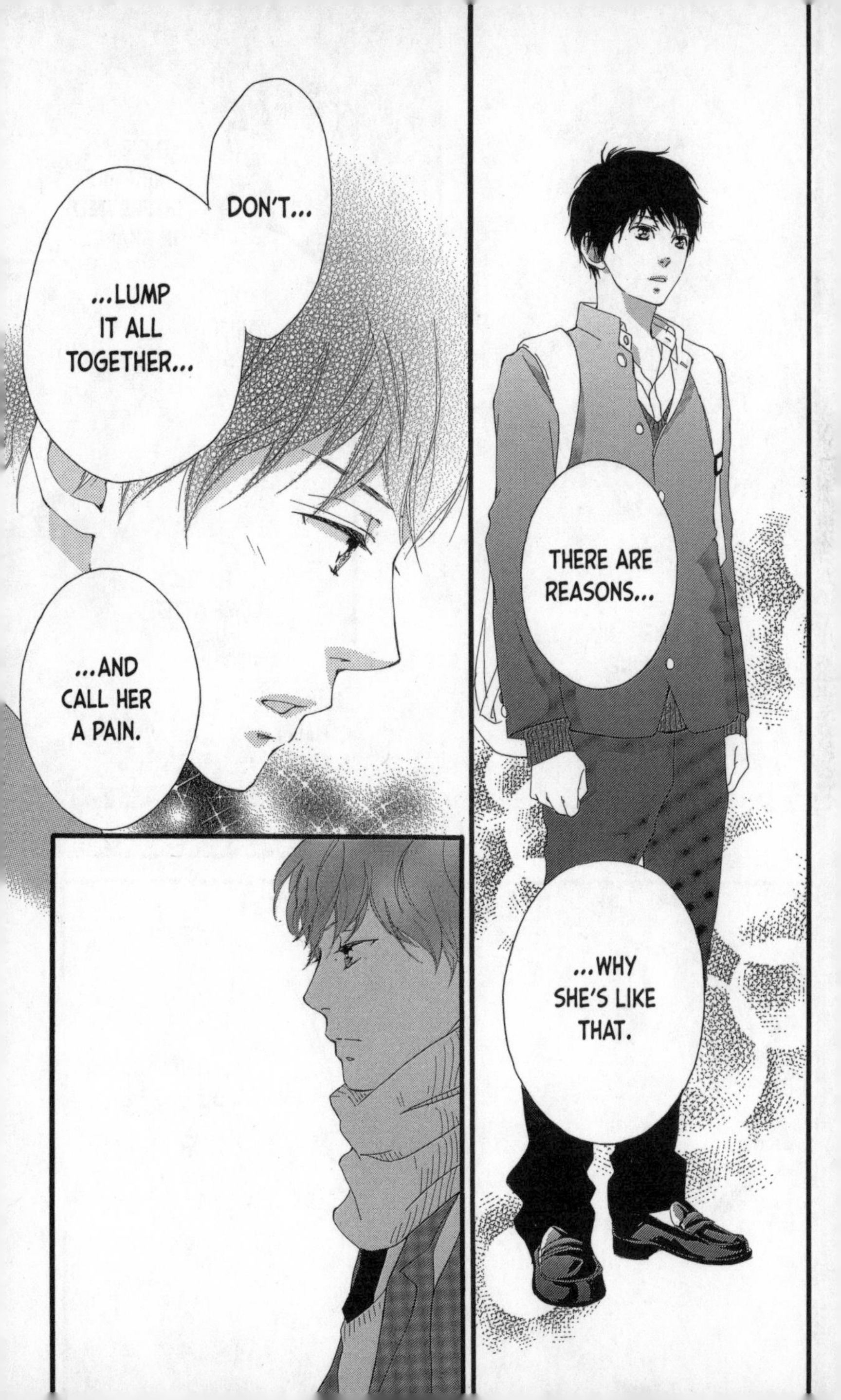
THERE ARE REASONS...
...WHY SHE'S LIKE THAT.
DON'T...
...LUMP IT ALL TOGETHER...
...AND CALL HER A PAIN.

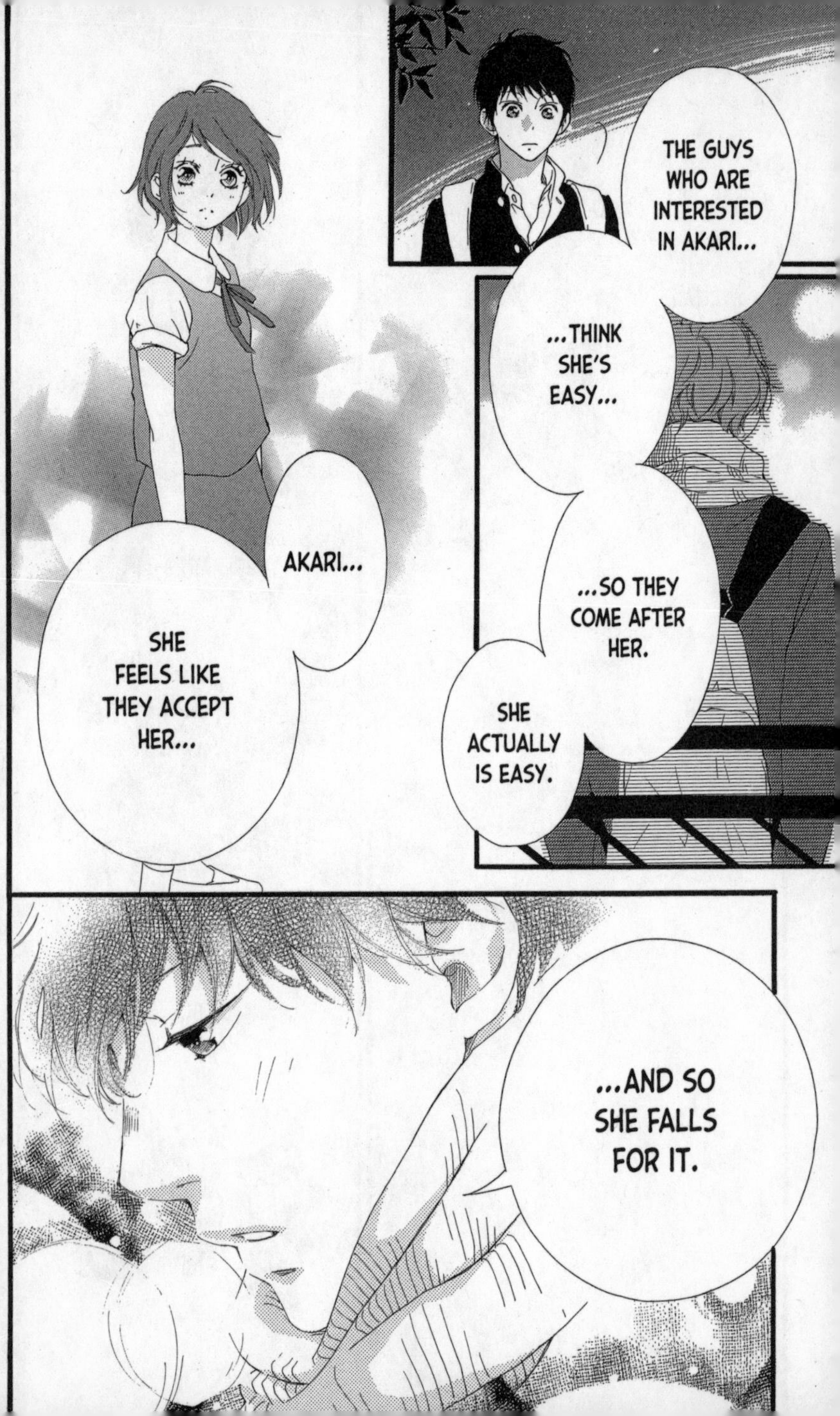
THE GUYS WHO ARE INTERESTED IN AKARI...
...THINK SHE'S EASY...
...SO THEY COME AFTER HER.
SHE ACTUALLY IS EASY.
AKARI...
SHE FEELS LIKE THEY ACCEPT HER...
...AND SO SHE FALLS FOR IT.

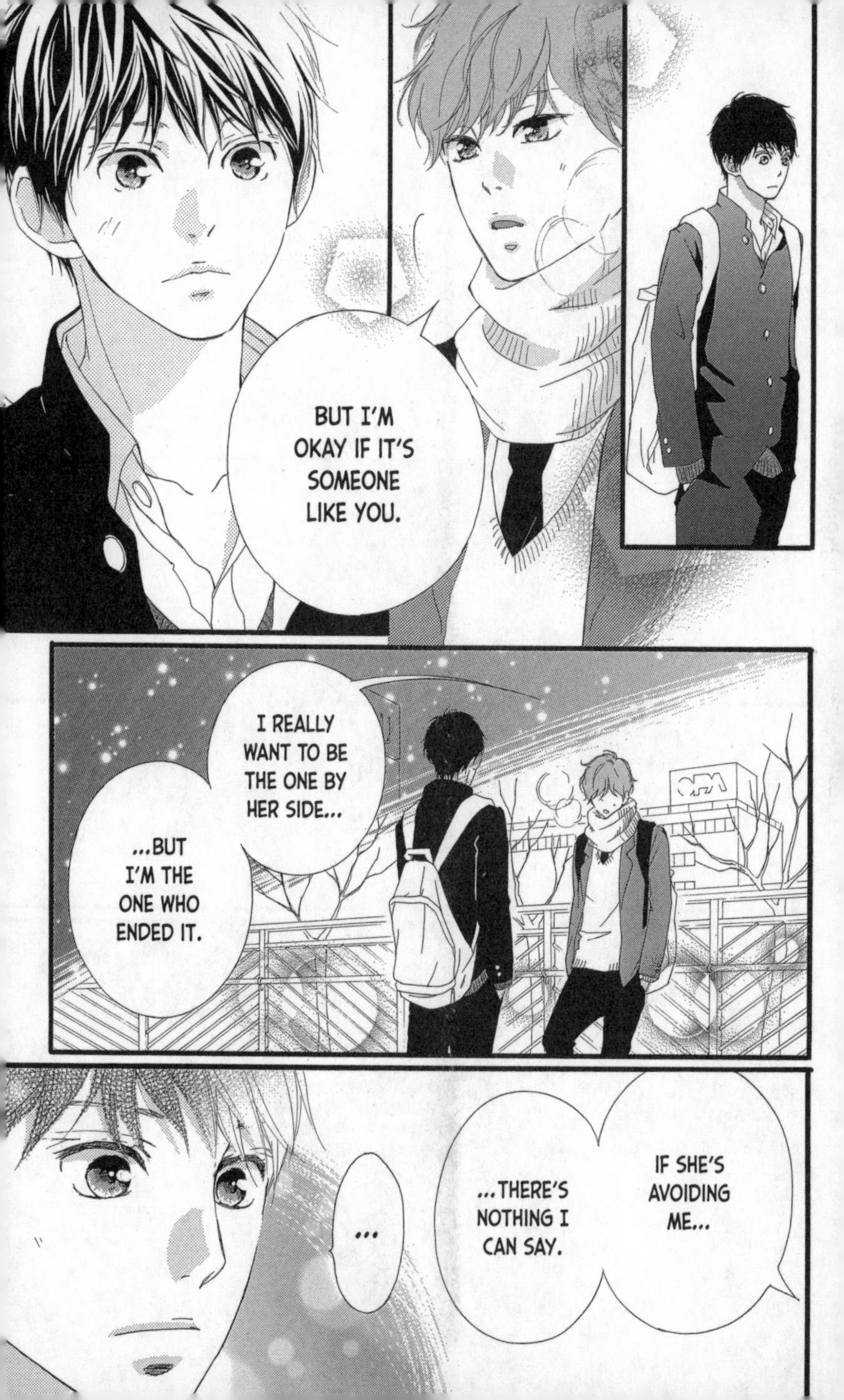
BUT I'M OKAY IF IT'S SOMEONE LIKE YOU.
I REALLY WANT TO BE THE ONE BY HER SIDE...
...BUT I'M THE ONE WHO ENDED IT.
IF SHE'S AVOIDING ME...
...THERE'S NOTHING I CAN SAY.
...

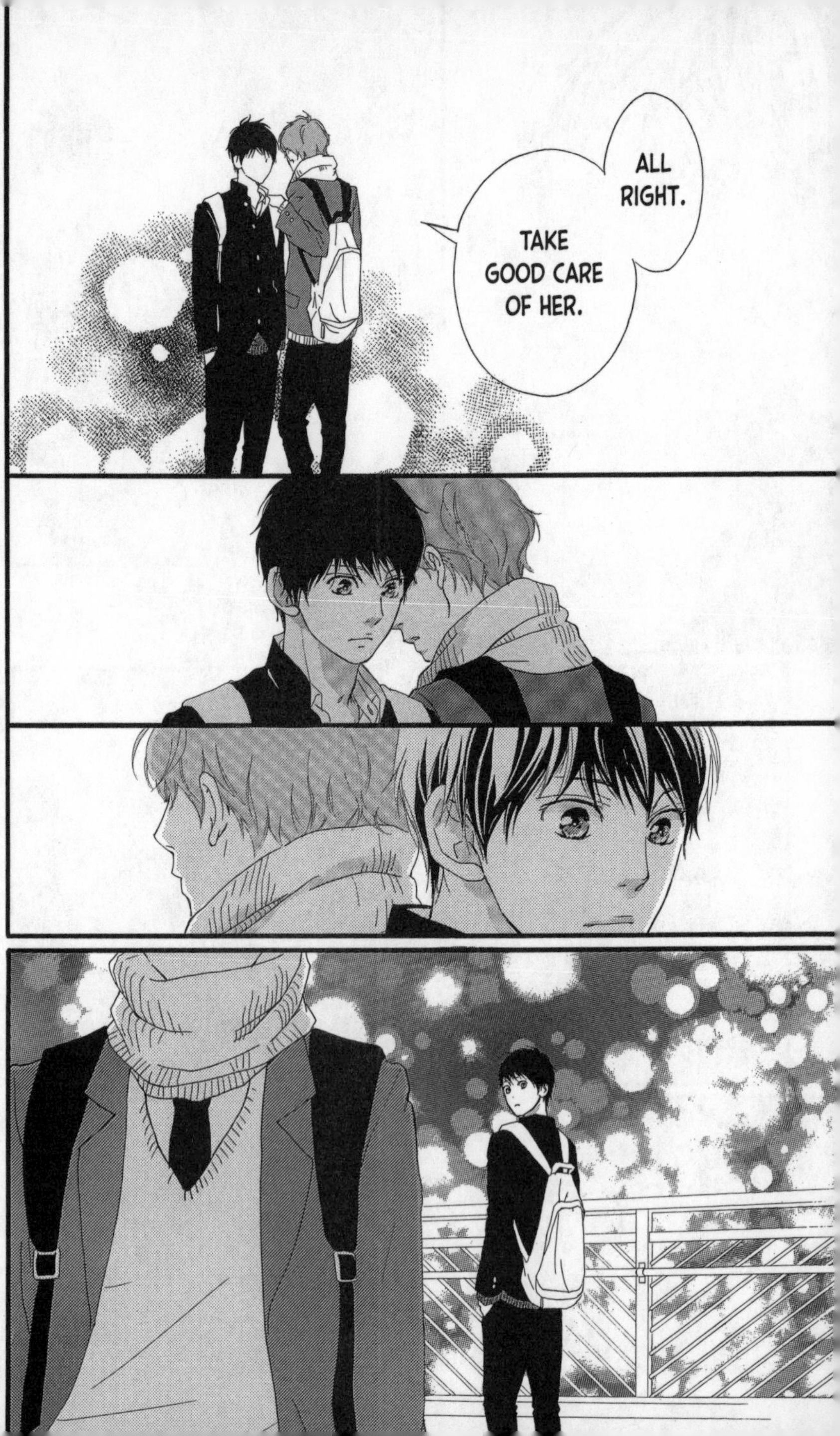
ALL RIGHT.
TAKE GOOD CARE OF HER.

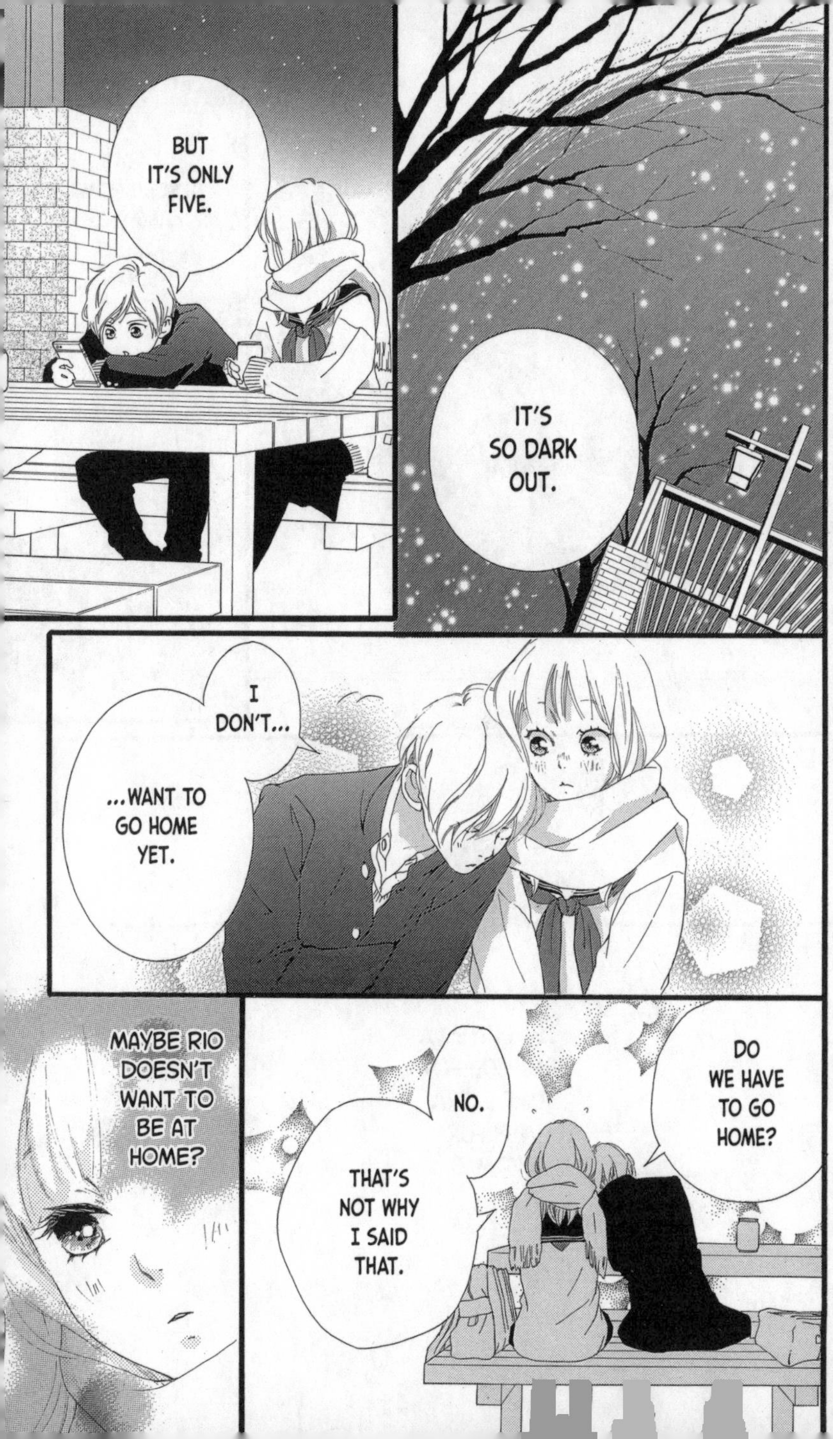
IT'S SO DARK OUT.
BUT IT'S ONLY FIVE.
I DON'T...
...WANT TO GO HOME YET.
DO WE HAVE TO GO HOME?
NO.
THAT'S NOT WHY I SAID THAT.
MAYBE RIO DOESN'T WANT TO BE AT HOME?

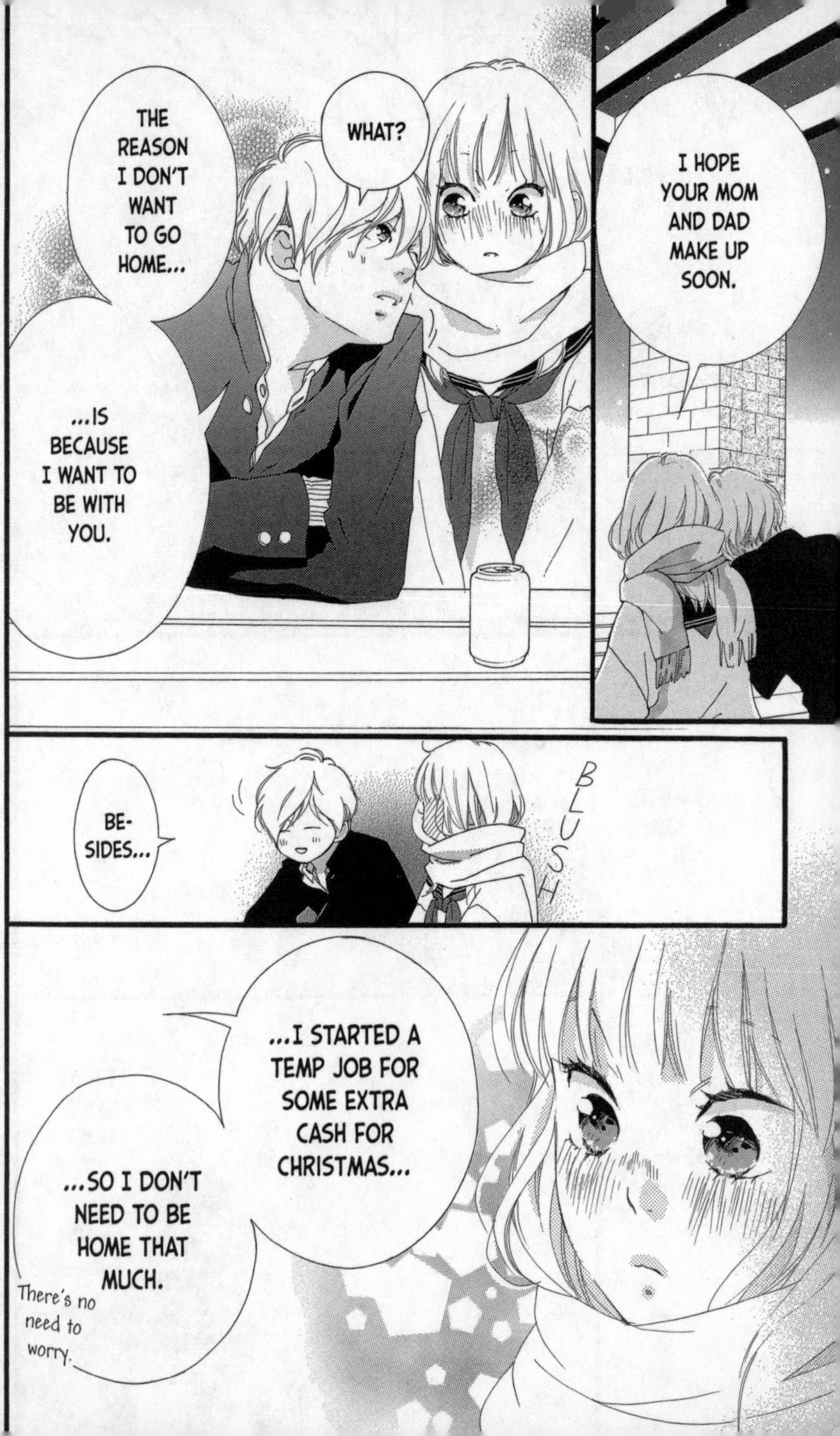
I HOPE YOUR MOM AND DAD MAKE UP SOON.
WHAT?
THE REASON I DON'T WANT TO GO HOME...
...IS BECAUSE I WANT TO BE WITH YOU.
BLUSH
BE-SIDES...
...I STARTED A TEMP JOB FOR SOME EXTRA CASH FOR CHRISTMAS...
...SO I DON'T NEED TO BE HOME THAT MUCH.
There's no need to worry.

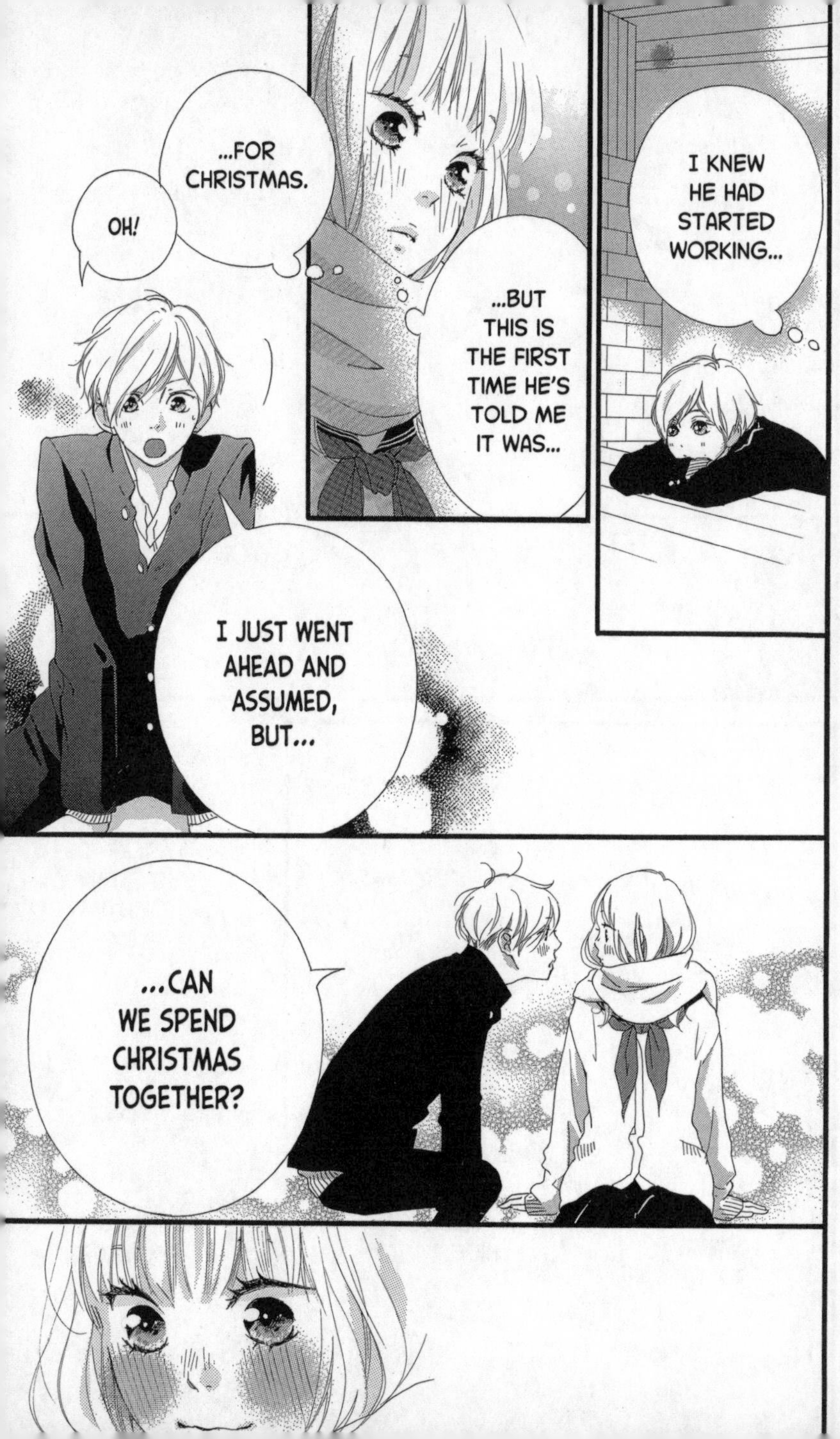
I KNEW HE HAD STARTED WORKING...
...BUT THIS IS THE FIRST TIME HE'S TOLD ME IT WAS...
...FOR CHRISTMAS.
OH!
I JUST WENT AHEAD AND ASSUMED, BUT...
...CAN WE SPEND CHRISTMAS TOGETHER?

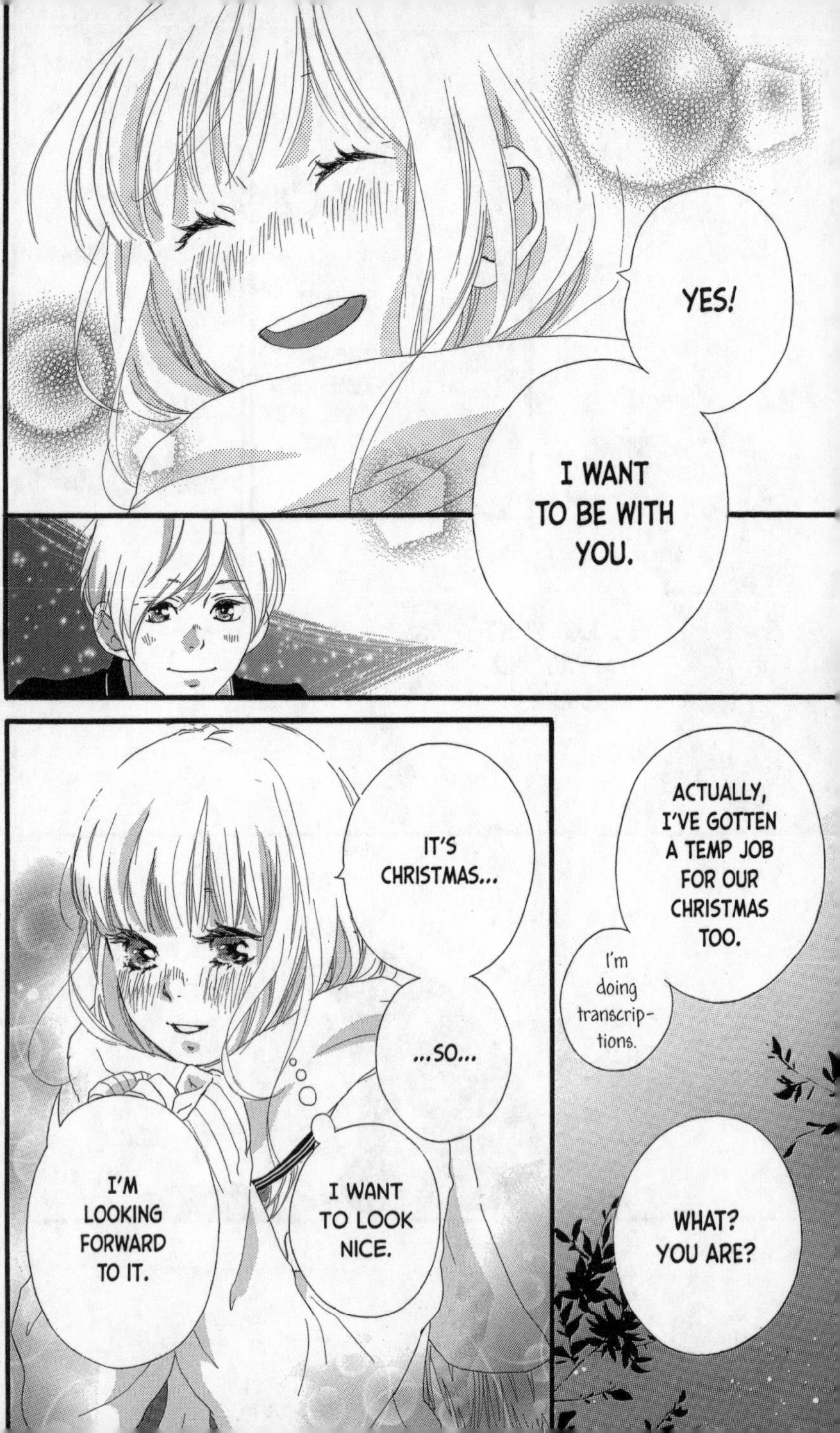
YES!
I WANT TO BE WITH YOU.
ACTUALLY, I'VE GOTTEN A TEMP JOB FOR OUR CHRISTMAS TOO.
I'm doing transcrip-tions.
WHAT? YOU ARE?
IT'S CHRISTMAS...
...SO...
I WANT TO LOOK NICE.
I'M LOOKING FORWARD TO IT.

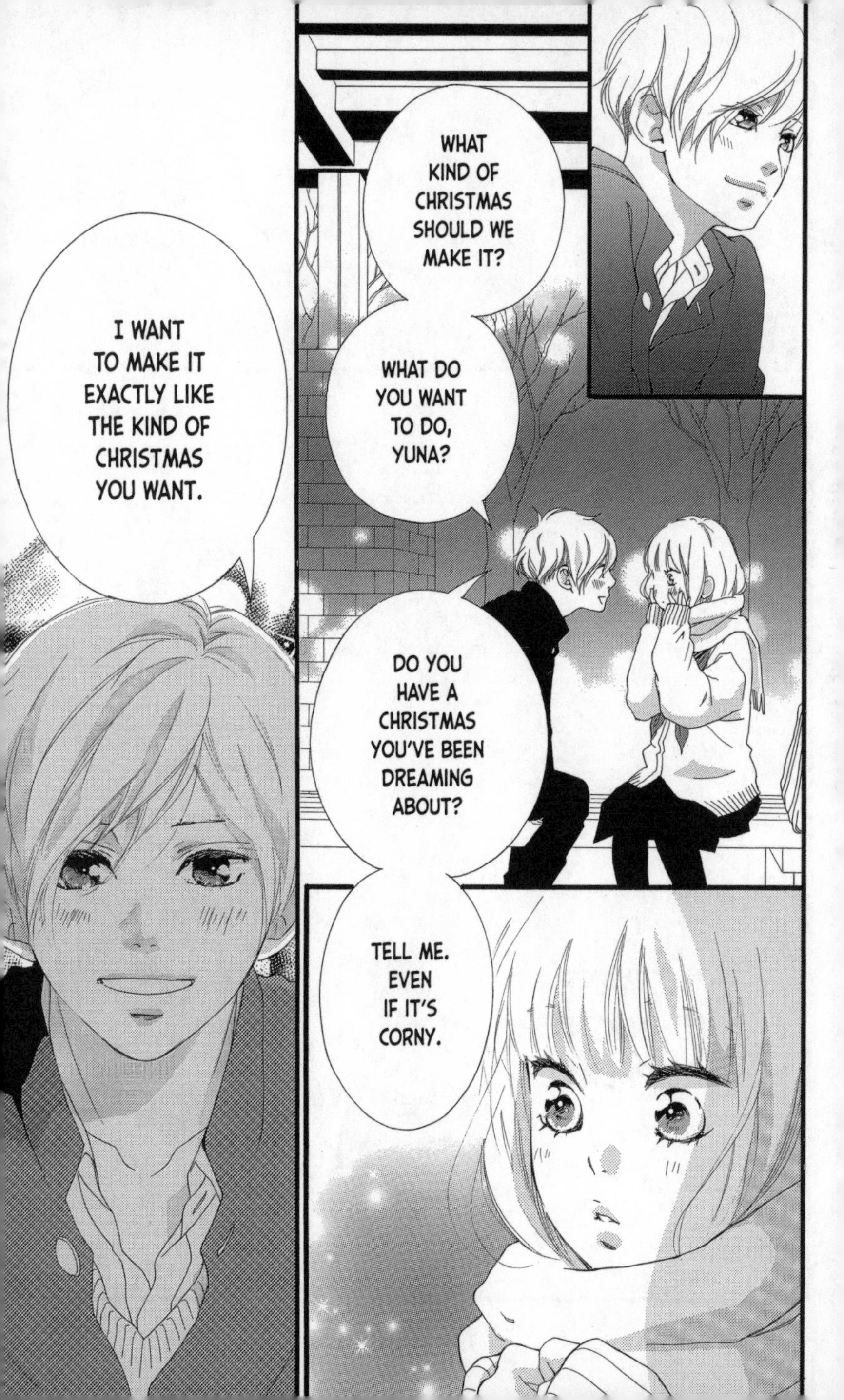
WHAT KIND OF CHRISTMAS SHOULD WE MAKE IT?
WHAT DO YOU WANT TO DO, YUNA?
DO YOU HAVE A CHRISTMAS YOU'VE BEEN DREAMING ABOUT?
TELL ME. EVEN IF IT'S CORNY.
I WANT TO MAKE IT EXACTLY LIKE THE KIND OF CHRISTMAS YOU WANT.

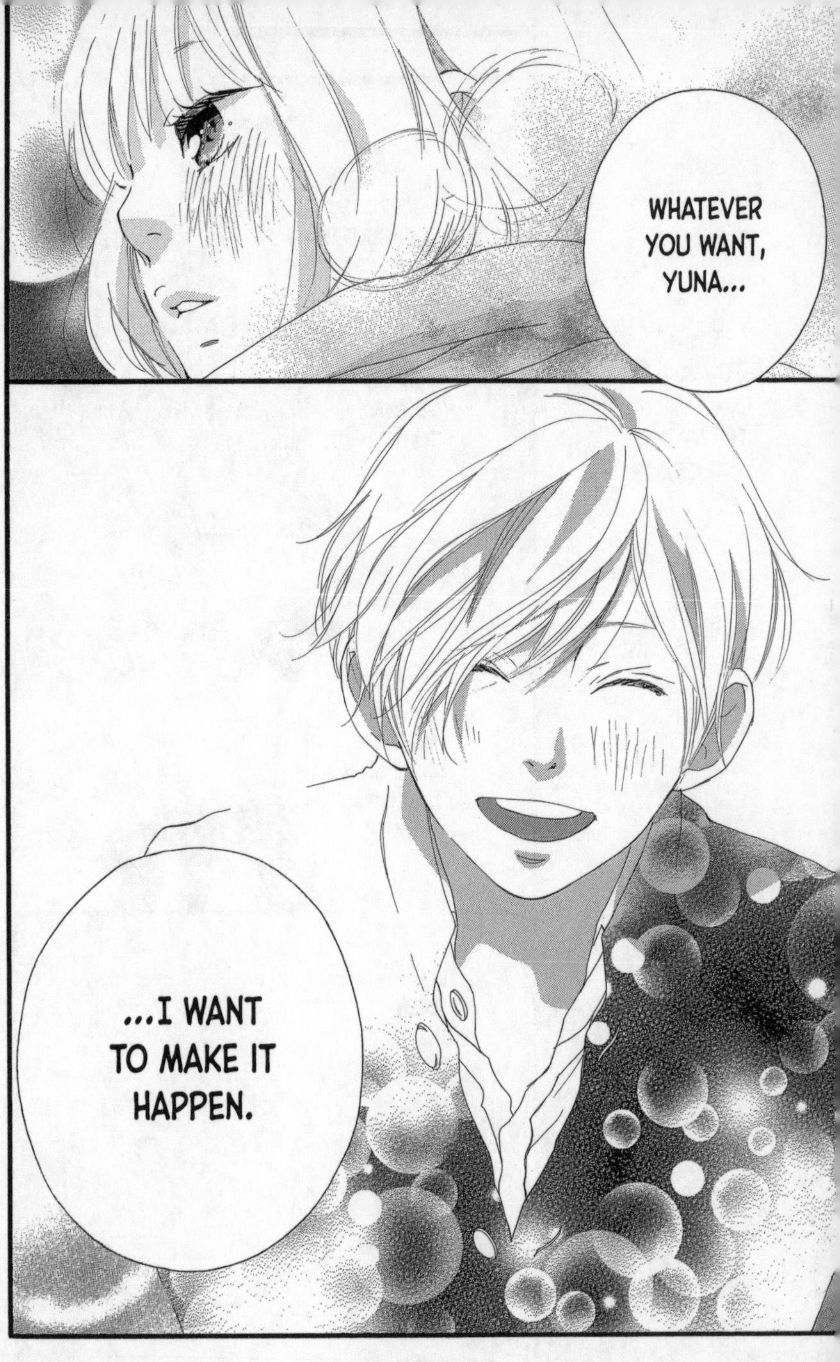
WHATEVER YOU WANT, YUNA...
...I WANT TO MAKE IT HAPPEN.

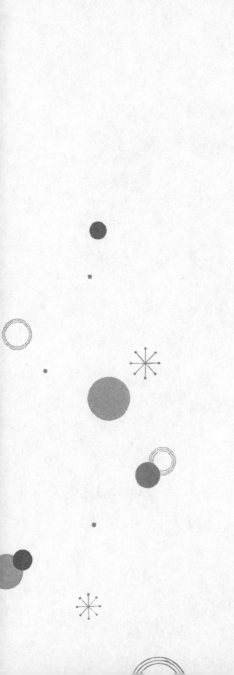

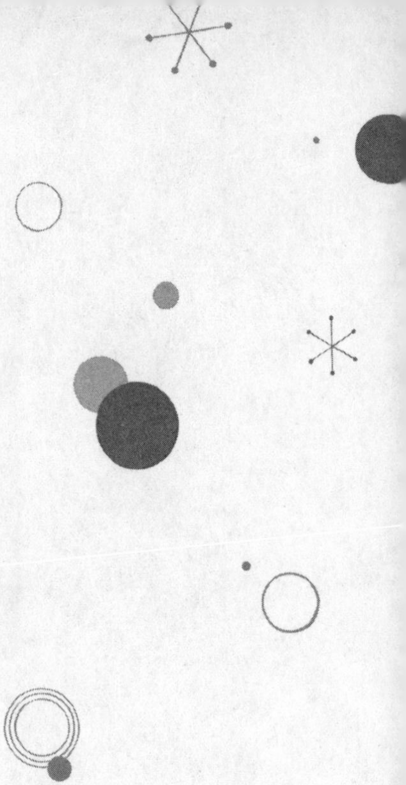

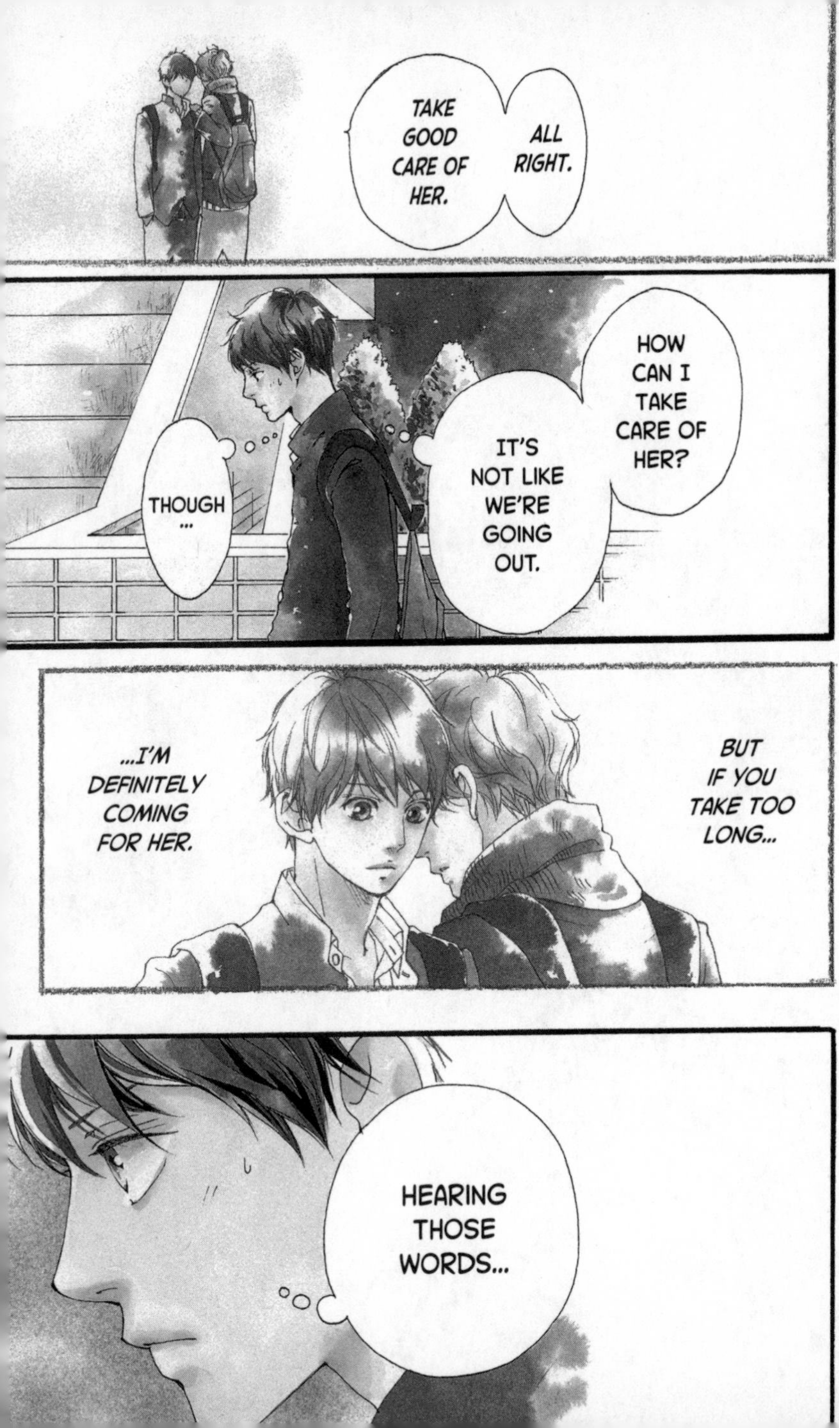
ALL RIGHT.
TAKE GOOD CARE OF HER.
HOW CAN I TAKE CARE OF HER?
IT'S NOT LIKE WE'RE GOING OUT.
THOUGH...
BUT IF YOU TAKE TOO LONG...
...I'M DEFINITELY COMING FOR HER.
HEARING THOSE WORDS...

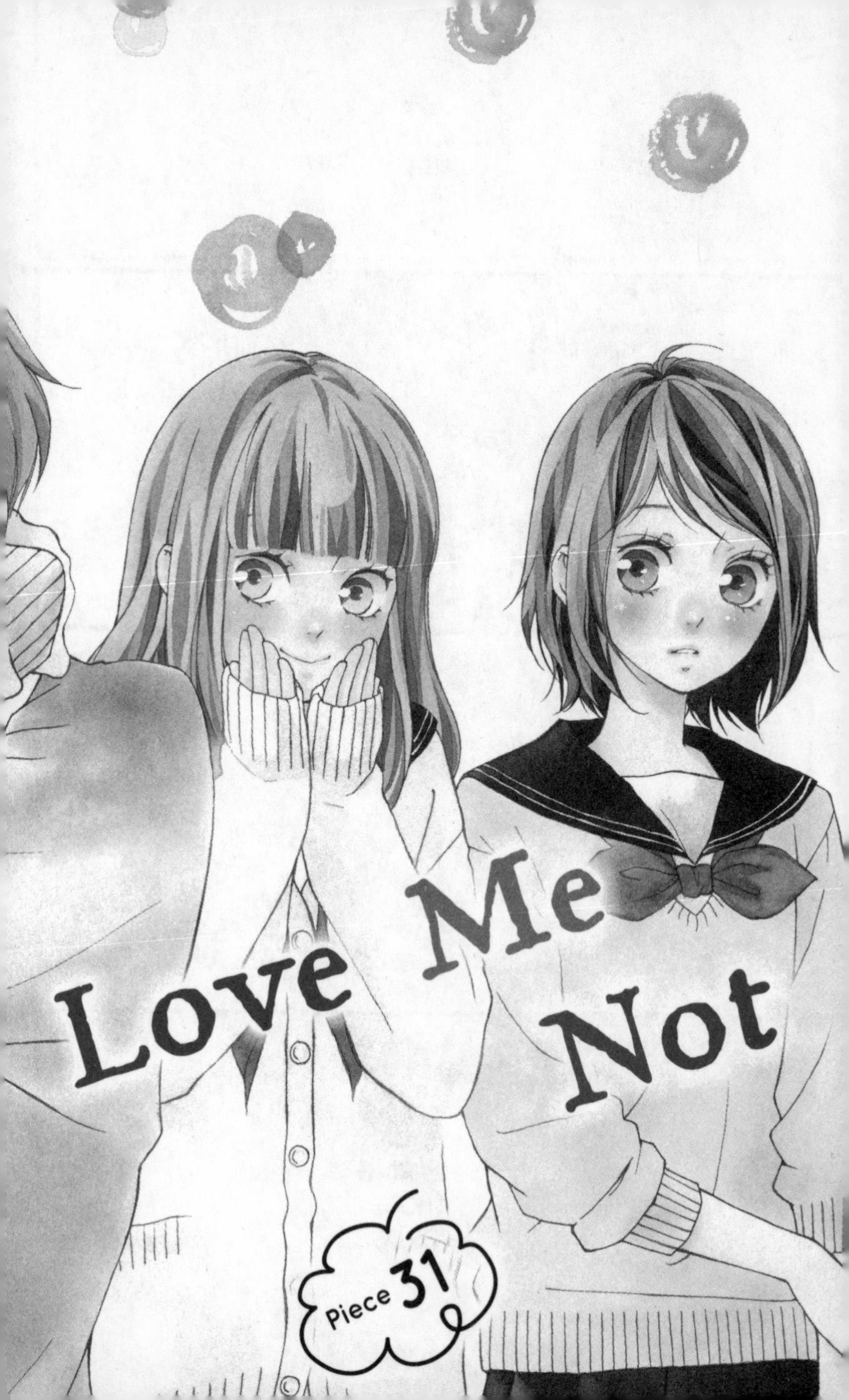
Love Me Not
Piece 31

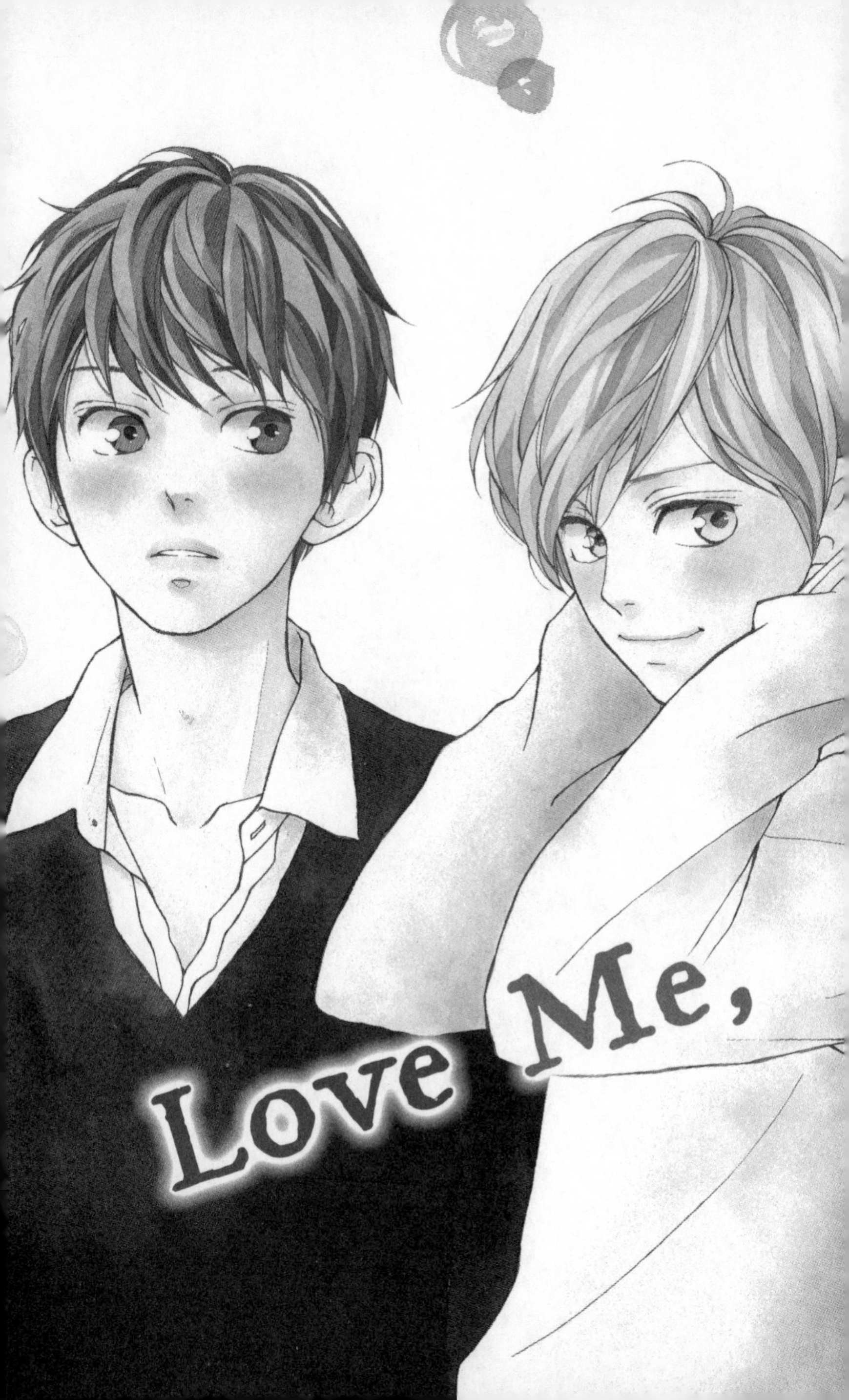
Love Me,

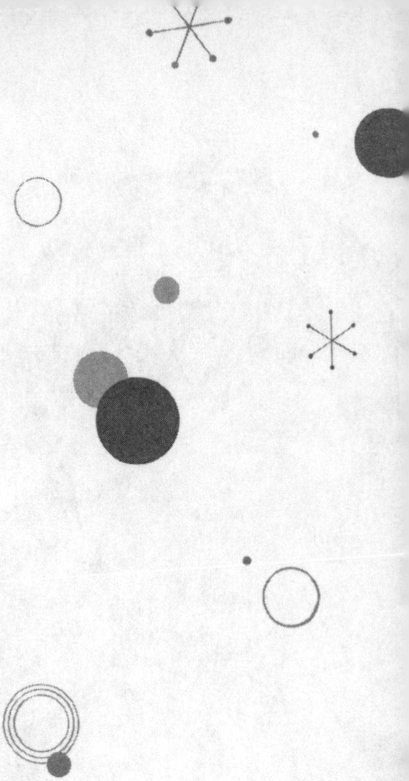

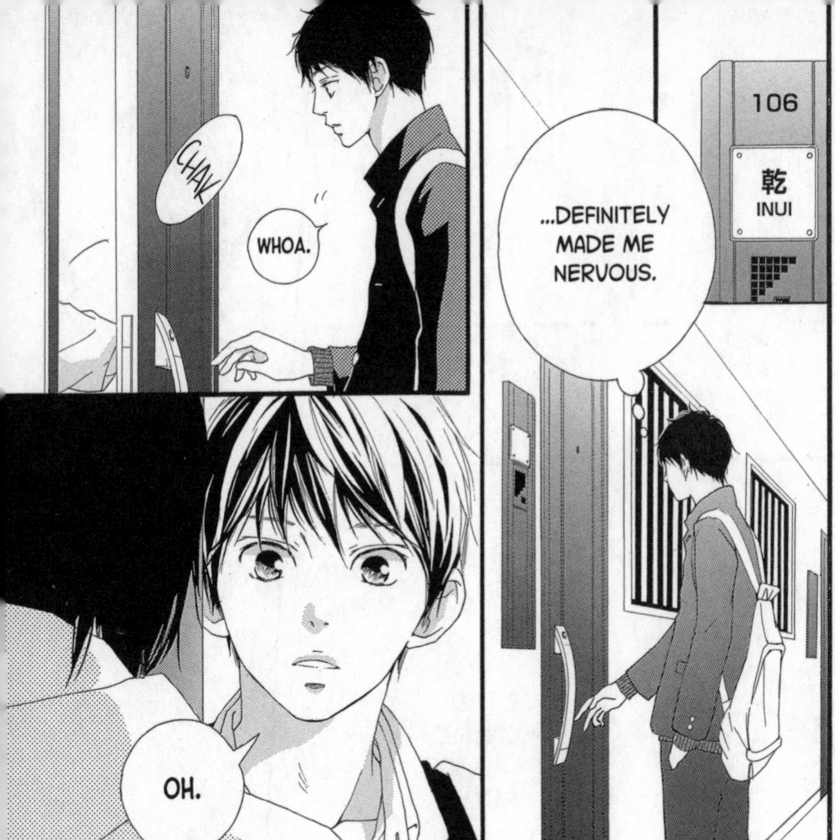
106
乾
INUI
...DEFINITELY MADE ME NERVOUS.
CHAK
WHOA.
OH.

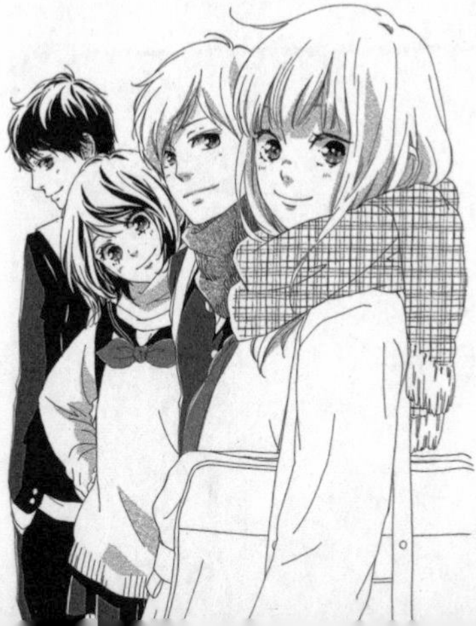

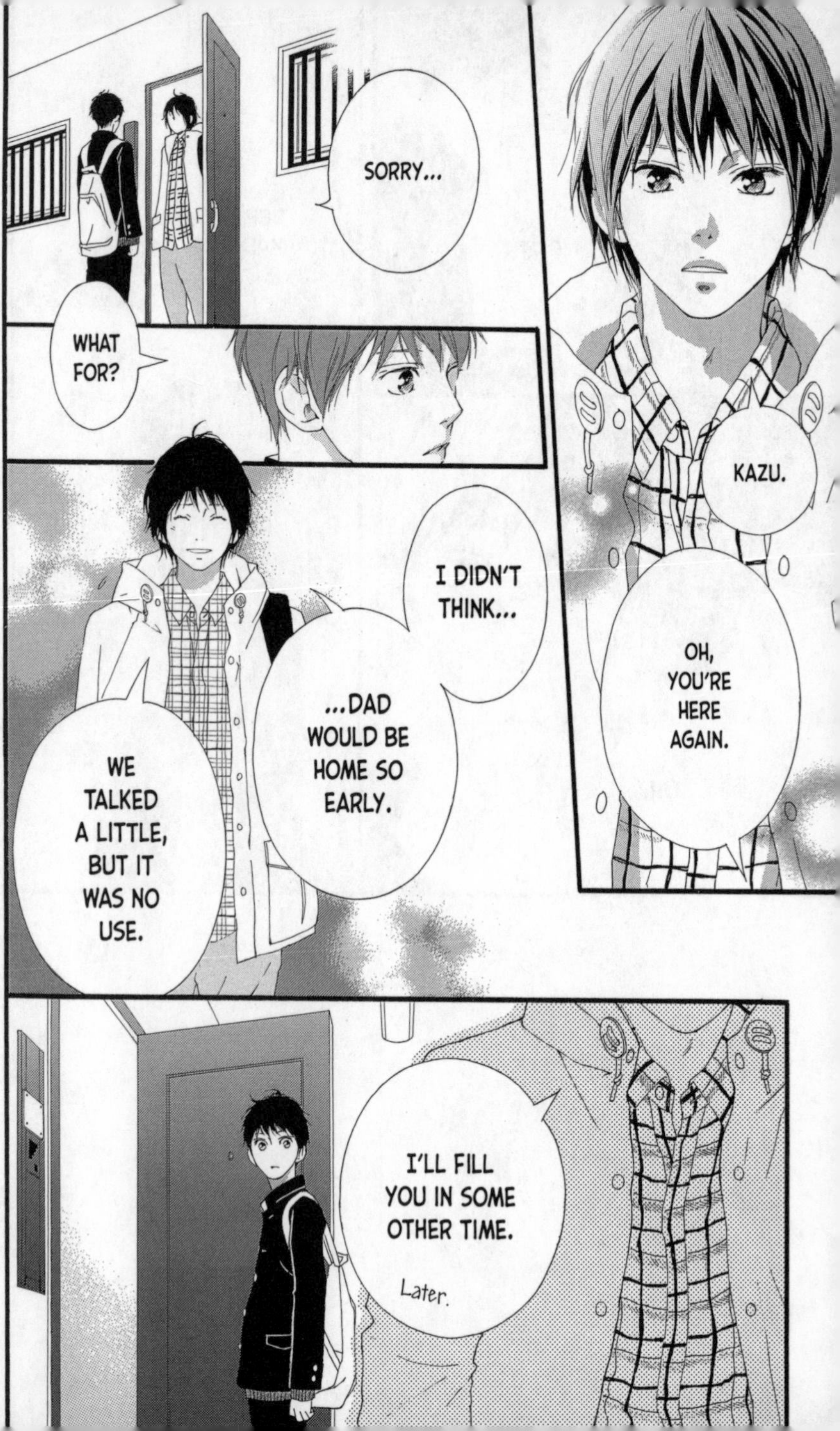
KAZU.
OH, YOU'RE HERE AGAIN.
SORRY...
WHAT FOR?
I DIDN'T THINK...
...DAD WOULD BE HOME SO EARLY.
WE TALKED A LITTLE, BUT IT WAS NO USE.
I'LL FILL YOU IN SOME OTHER TIME.
Later.

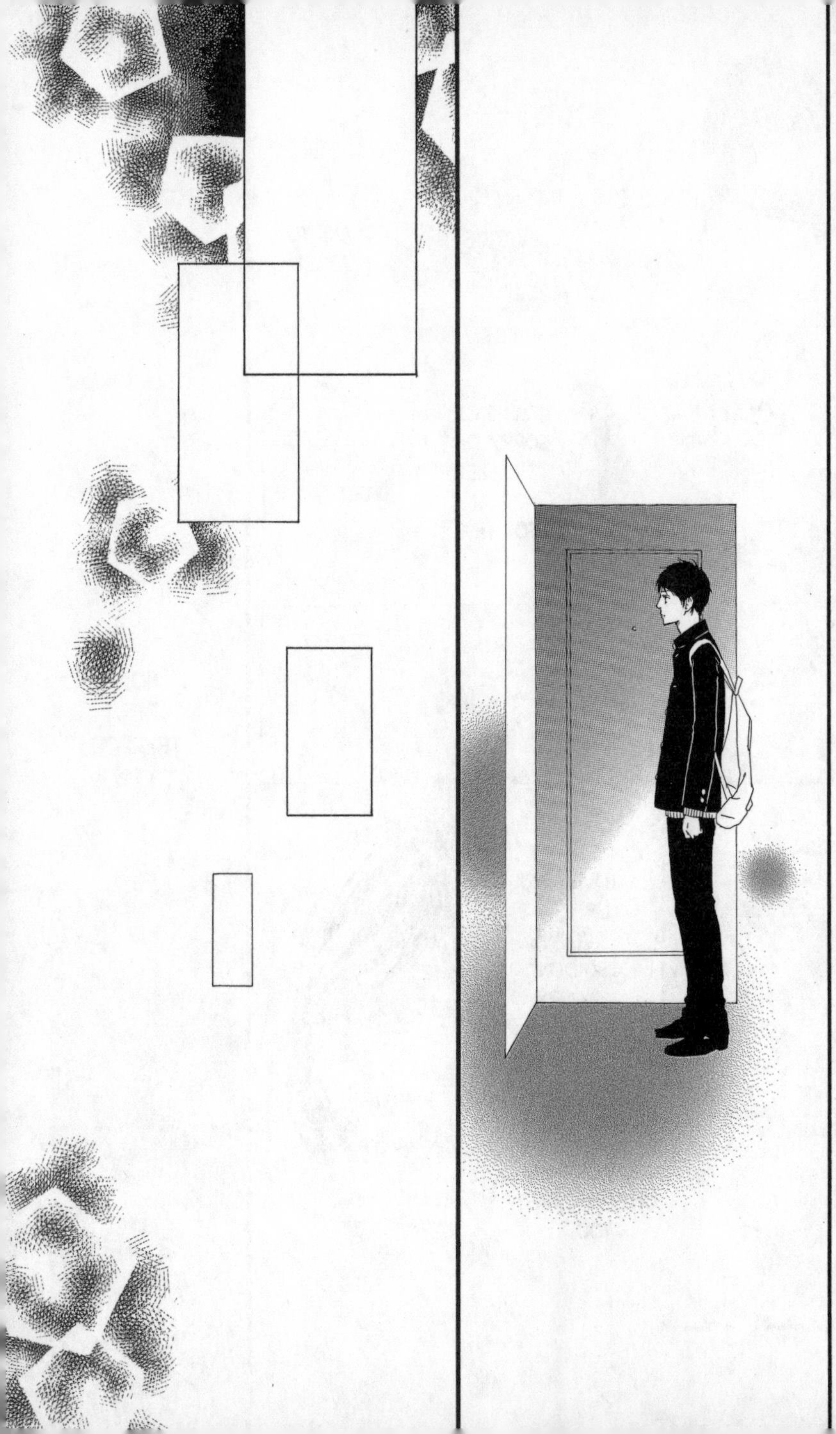

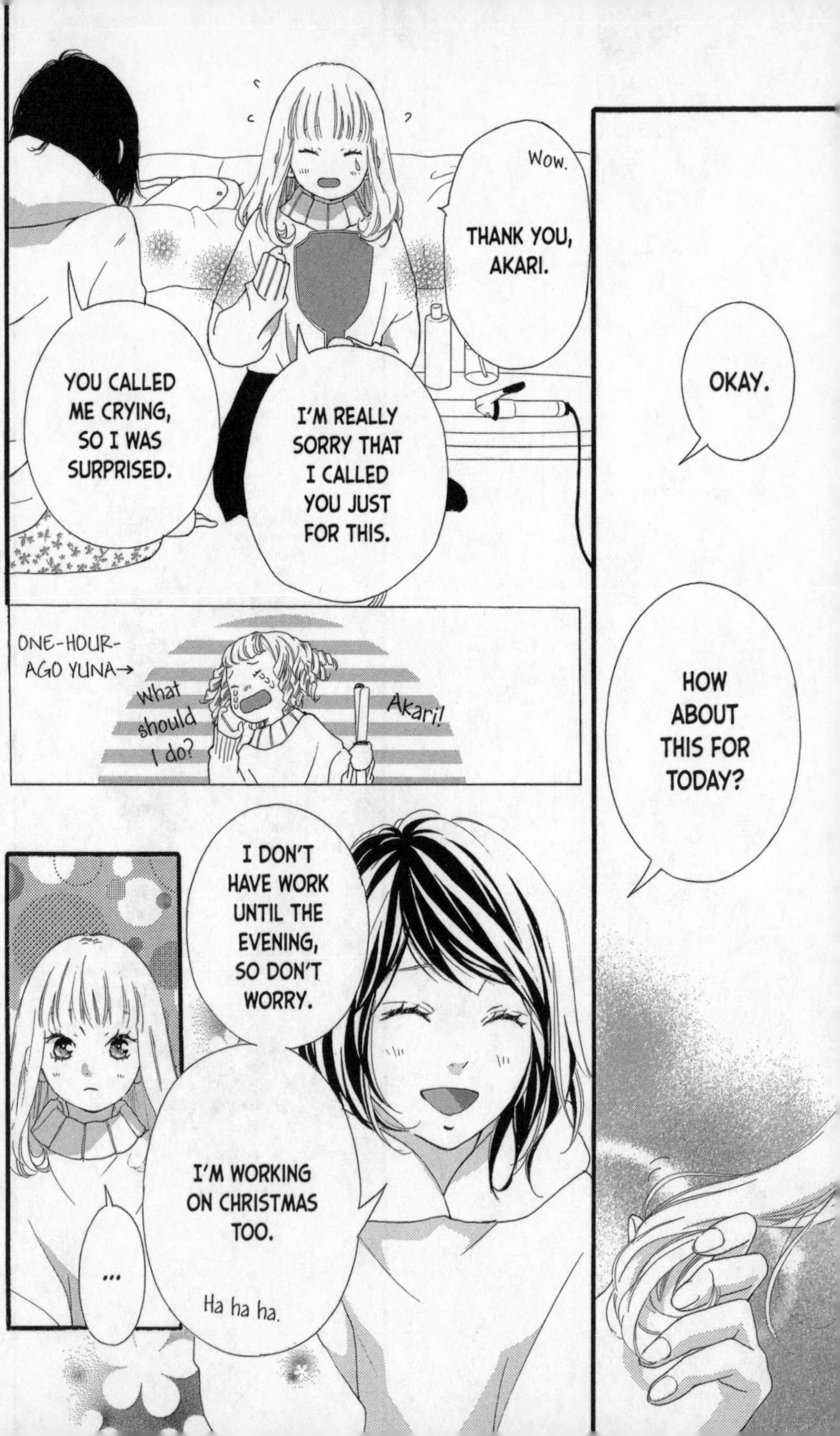

OKAY.
HOW ABOUT THIS FOR TODAY?
Wow.
THANK YOU, AKARI.
I'M REALLY SORRY THAT I CALLED YOU JUST FOR THIS.
YOU CALLED ME CRYING, SO I WAS SURPRISED.
ONE-HOUR-AGO YUNA→
Akari!
What should I do?
I DON'T HAVE WORK UNTIL THE EVENING, SO DON'T WORRY.
I'M WORKING ON CHRISTMAS TOO.
Ha ha ha.
...

Insects come calling. Green lacewings turn up from time to time in my house. They are little and are a pretty color. I don't have any problem with insects, so I usually leave them alone when I see one. But during the peak of the season, I see so many of them I wonder where they've come from. It's not like I have anything good to eat to attract them. And I notice they've given up the ghost here and there, so I assume that once they mature, their lives are very short. I saw an insect that was the same shape as the others, but a different color. I looked it up and discovered it was the winter version of the green lacewing. I was so surprised they live through the winter! They seem so fragile, but they're a lot tougher than they look. But they do drop dead a lot. Maybe because I don't have anything good to eat? Even still, I don't plan on extending my hospitality to them.

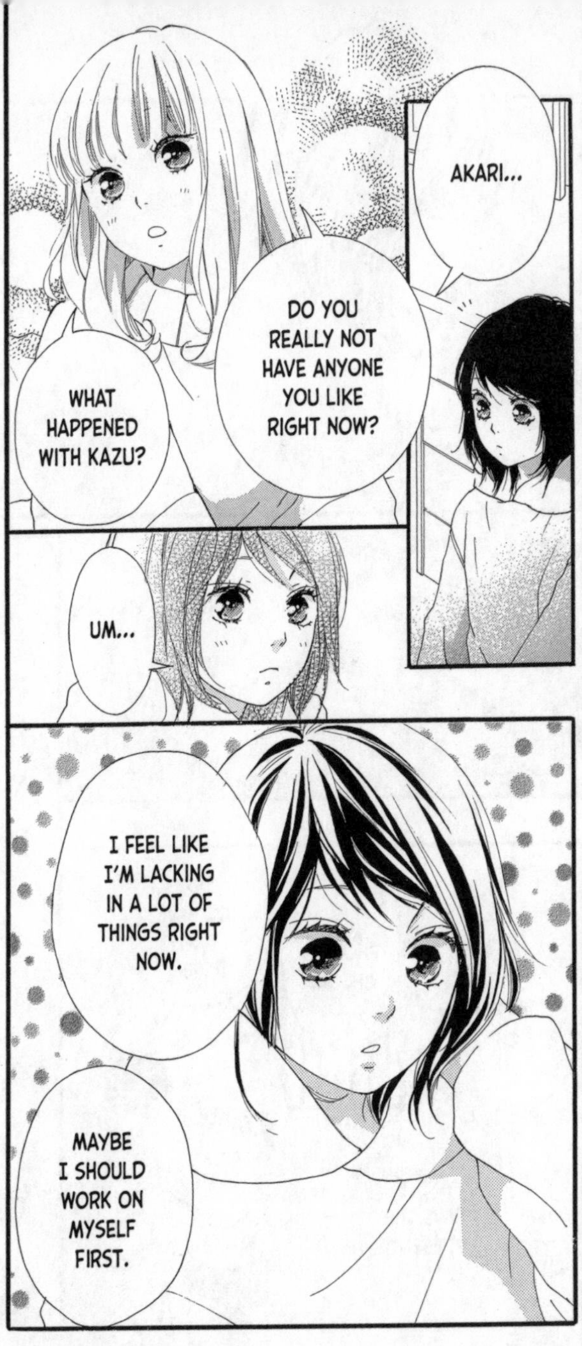
AKARI...
DO YOU REALLY NOT HAVE ANYONE YOU LIKE RIGHT NOW?
WHAT HAPPENED WITH KAZU?
UM...
I FEEL LIKE I'M LACKING IN A LOT OF THINGS RIGHT NOW.
MAYBE I SHOULD WORK ON MYSELF FIRST.

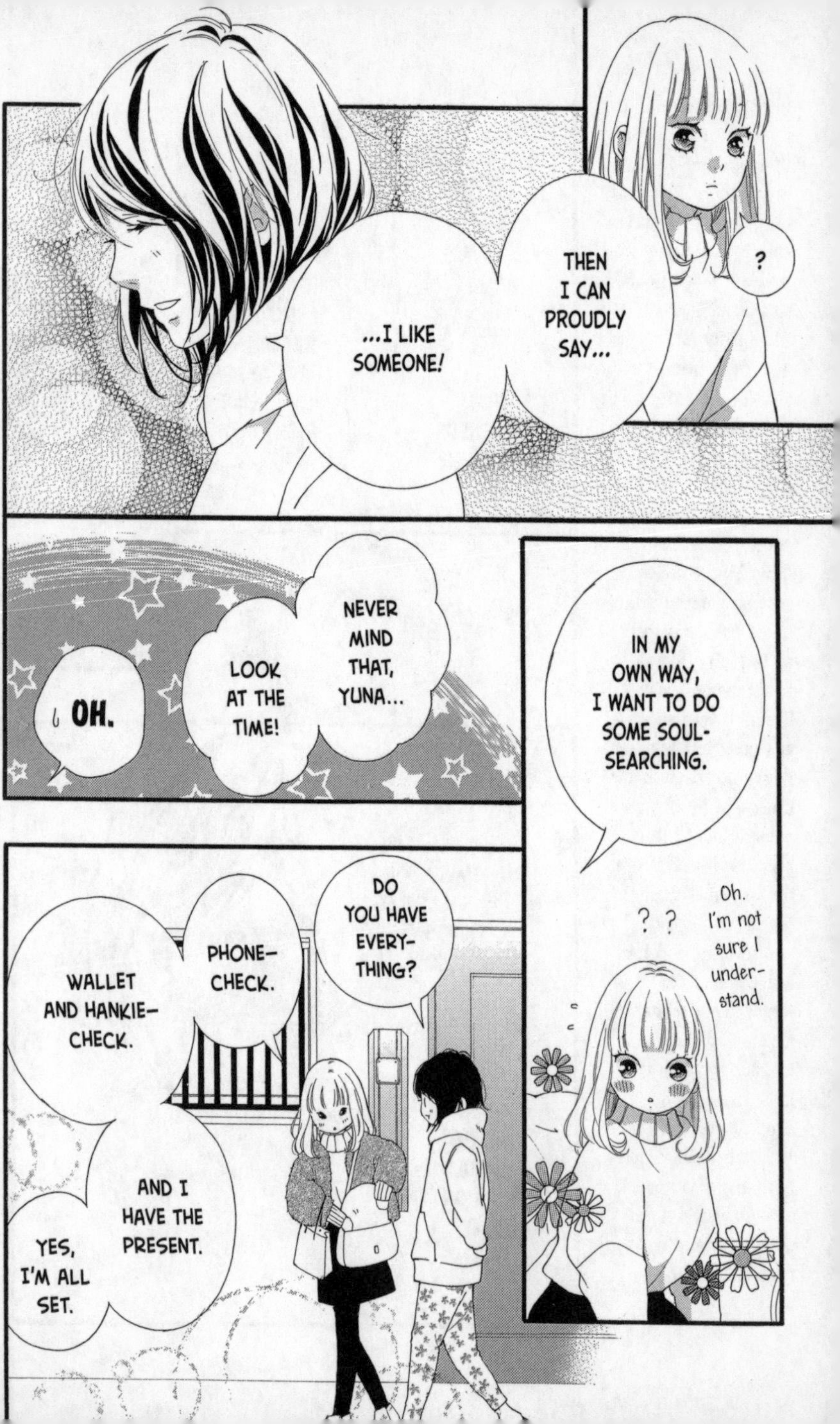
THEN I CAN PROUDLY SAY...
...I LIKE SOMEONE!
?
IN MY OWN WAY, I WANT TO DO SOME SOUL-SEARCHING.
? ?
Oh. I'm not sure I under-stand.
NEVER MIND THAT, YUNA...
LOOK AT THE TIME!
OH.
DO YOU HAVE EVERY-THING?
PHONE—CHECK.
WALLET AND HANKIE—CHECK.
AND I HAVE THE PRESENT.
YES, I'M ALL SET.

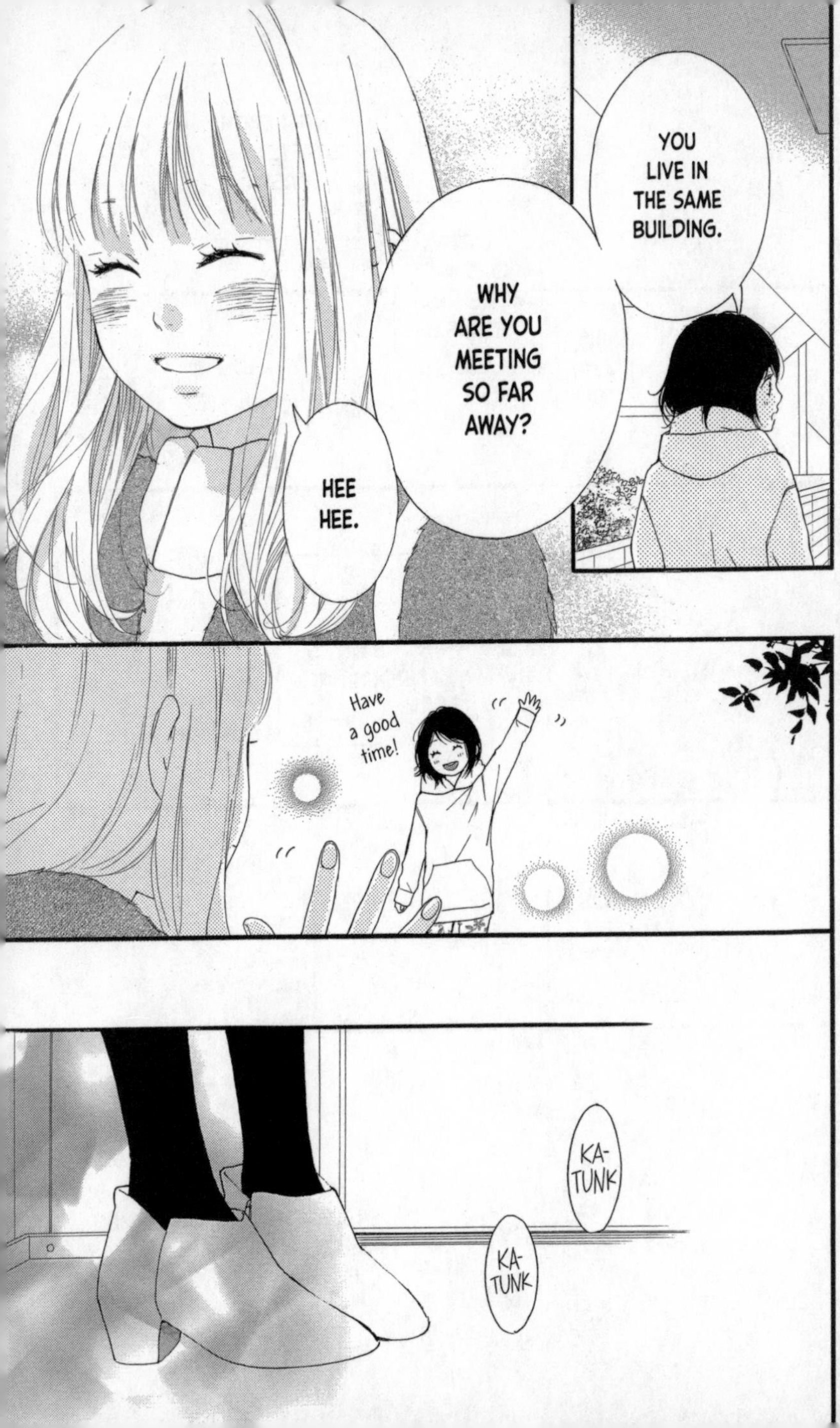
YOU LIVE IN THE SAME BUILDING.
WHY ARE YOU MEETING SO FAR AWAY?
HEE HEE.
Have a good time!
KA-TUNK
KA-TUNK

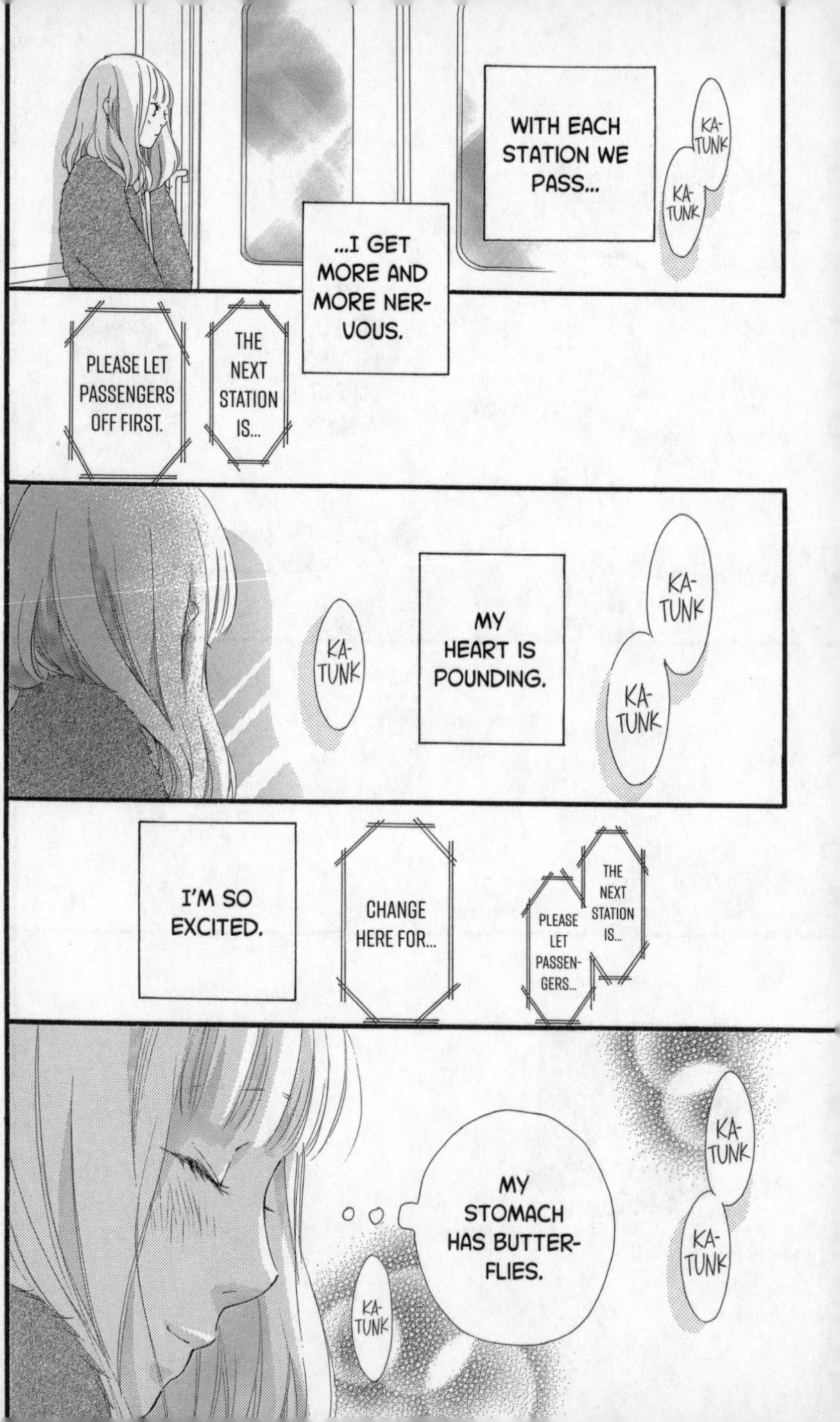
KA-TUNK
KA-TUNK
WITH EACH STATION WE PASS...
...I GET MORE AND MORE NER-VOUS.
THE NEXT STATION IS...
PLEASE LET PASSENGERS OFF FIRST.
KA-TUNK
KA-TUNK
MY HEART IS POUNDING.
KA-TUNK
THE NEXT STATION IS...
PLEASE LET PASSEN-GERS...
CHANGE HERE FOR...
I'M SO EXCITED.
KA-TUNK
KA-TUNK
MY STOMACH HAS BUTTER-FLIES.
KA-TUNK

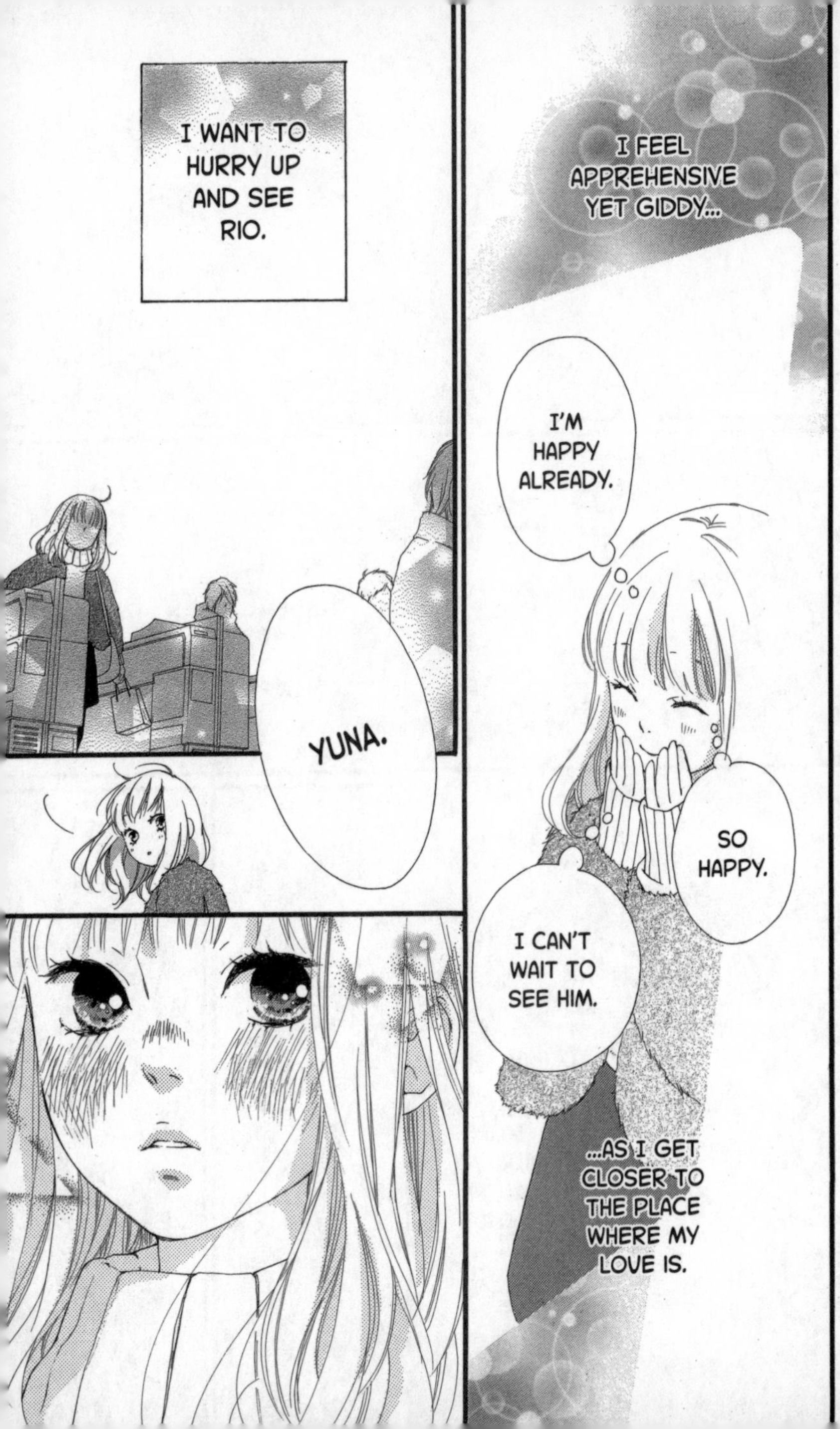
I FEEL APPREHENSIVE YET GIDDY...
I'M HAPPY ALREADY.
SO HAPPY.
I CAN'T WAIT TO SEE HIM.
...AS I GET CLOSER TO THE PLACE WHERE MY LOVE IS.
I WANT TO HURRY UP AND SEE RIO.
YUNA.

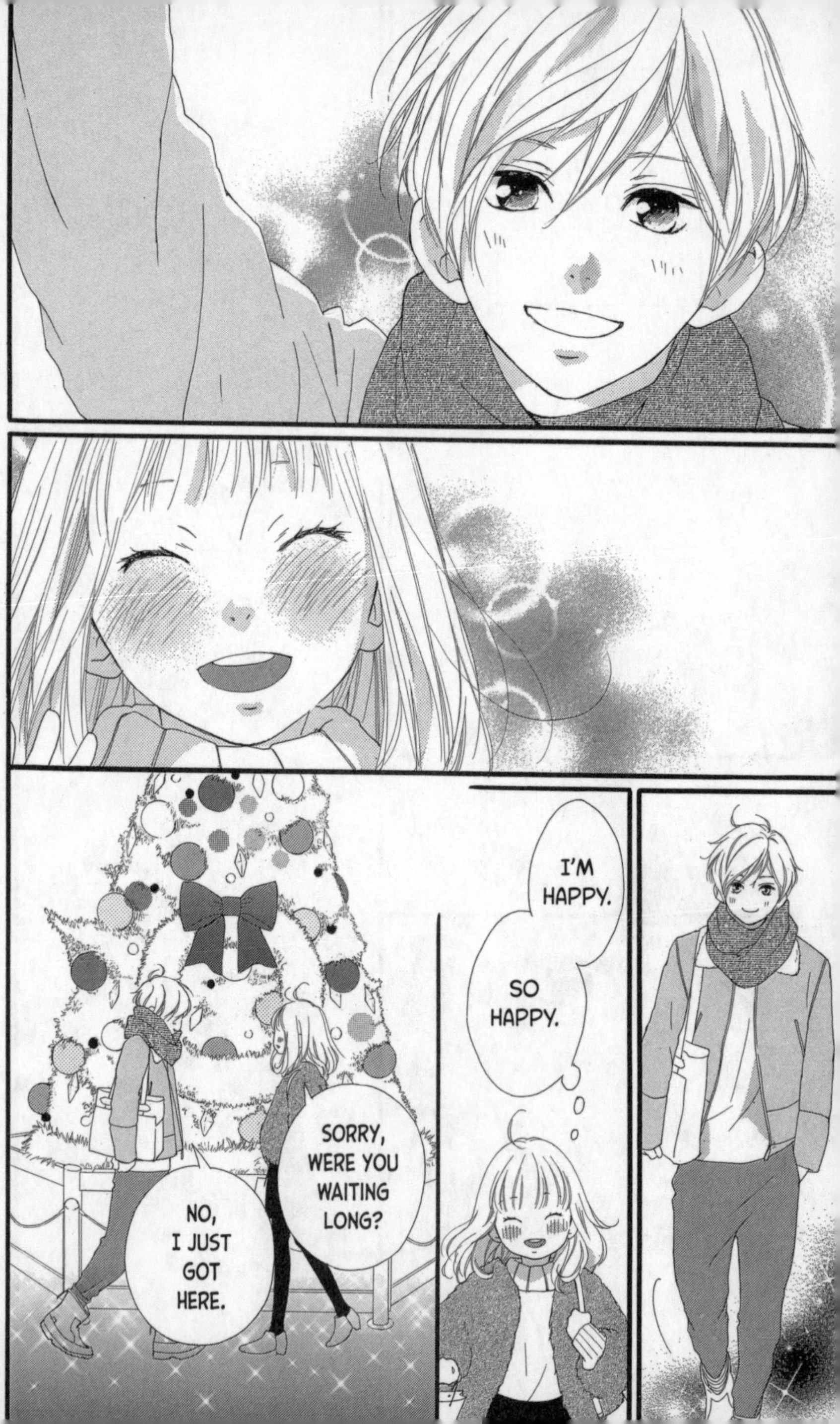
I'M HAPPY.
SO HAPPY.
SORRY, WERE YOU WAITING LONG?
NO, I JUST GOT HERE.

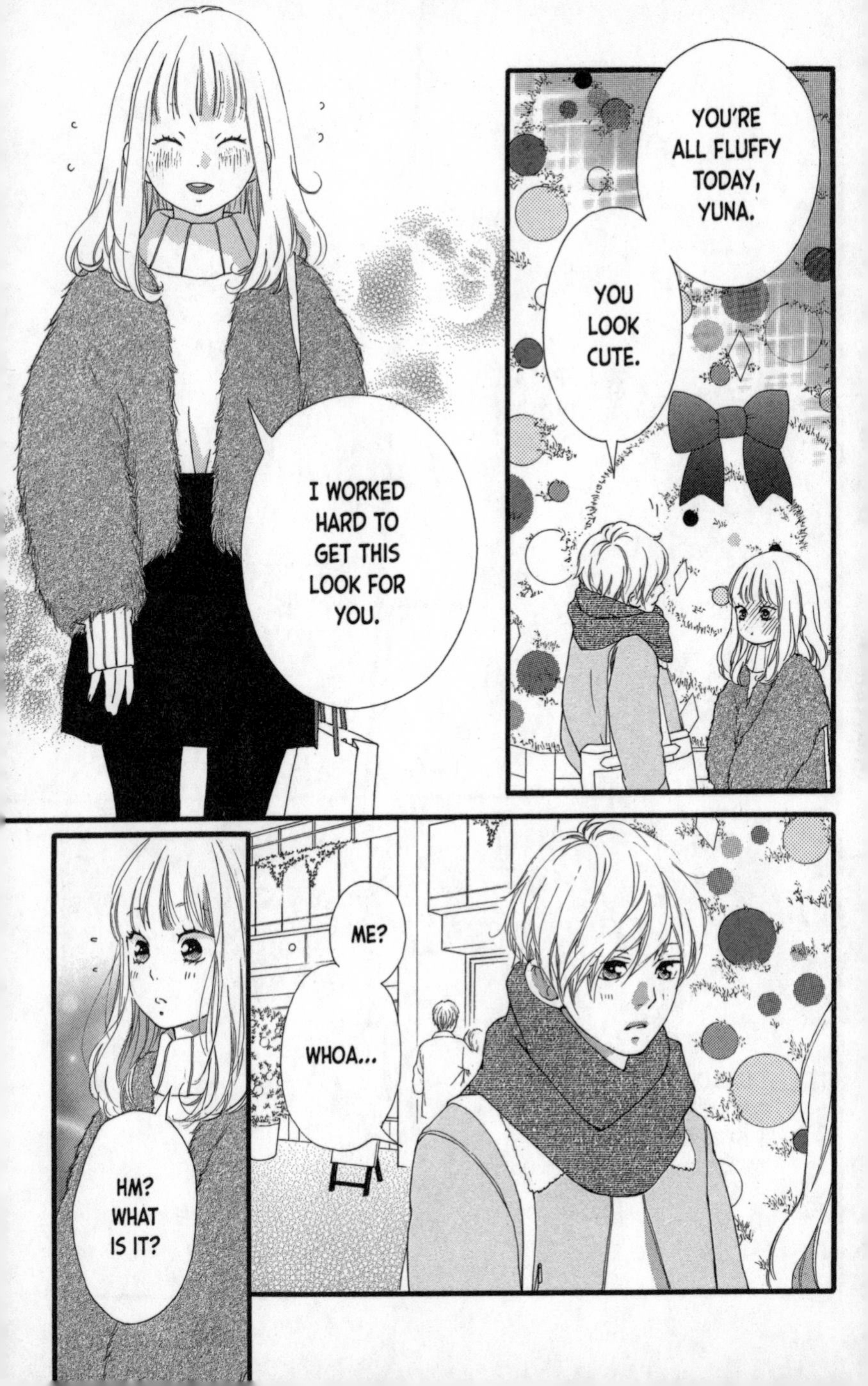
YOU'RE ALL FLUFFY TODAY, YUNA.
YOU LOOK CUTE.
I WORKED HARD TO GET THIS LOOK FOR YOU.
ME?
WHOA...
HM? WHAT IS IT?

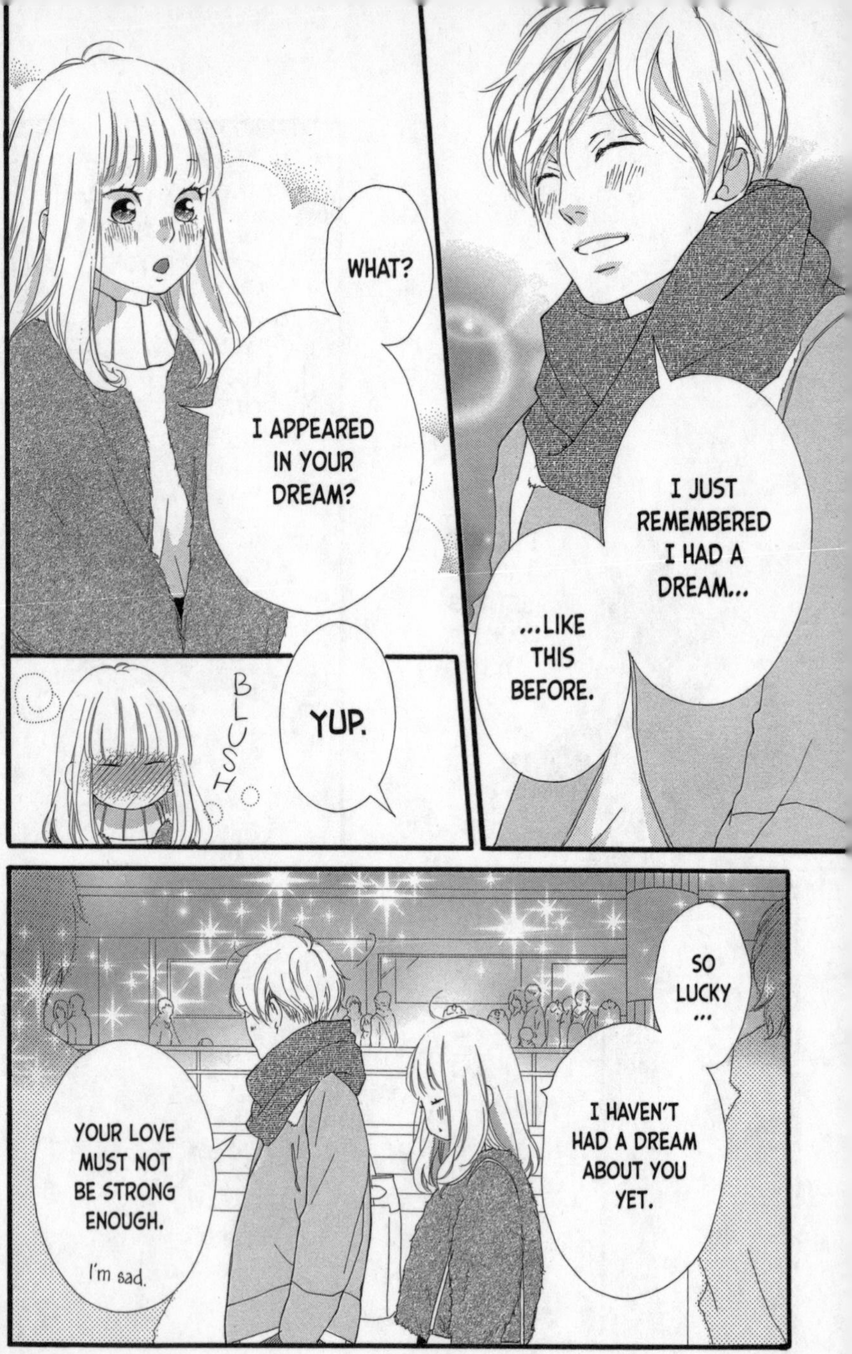
I JUST REMEMBERED I HAD A DREAM...
...LIKE THIS BEFORE.
WHAT?
I APPEARED IN YOUR DREAM?
YUP.
BLUSH
SO LUCKY ...
I HAVEN'T HAD A DREAM ABOUT YOU YET.
YOUR LOVE MUST NOT BE STRONG ENOUGH.
I'm sad.

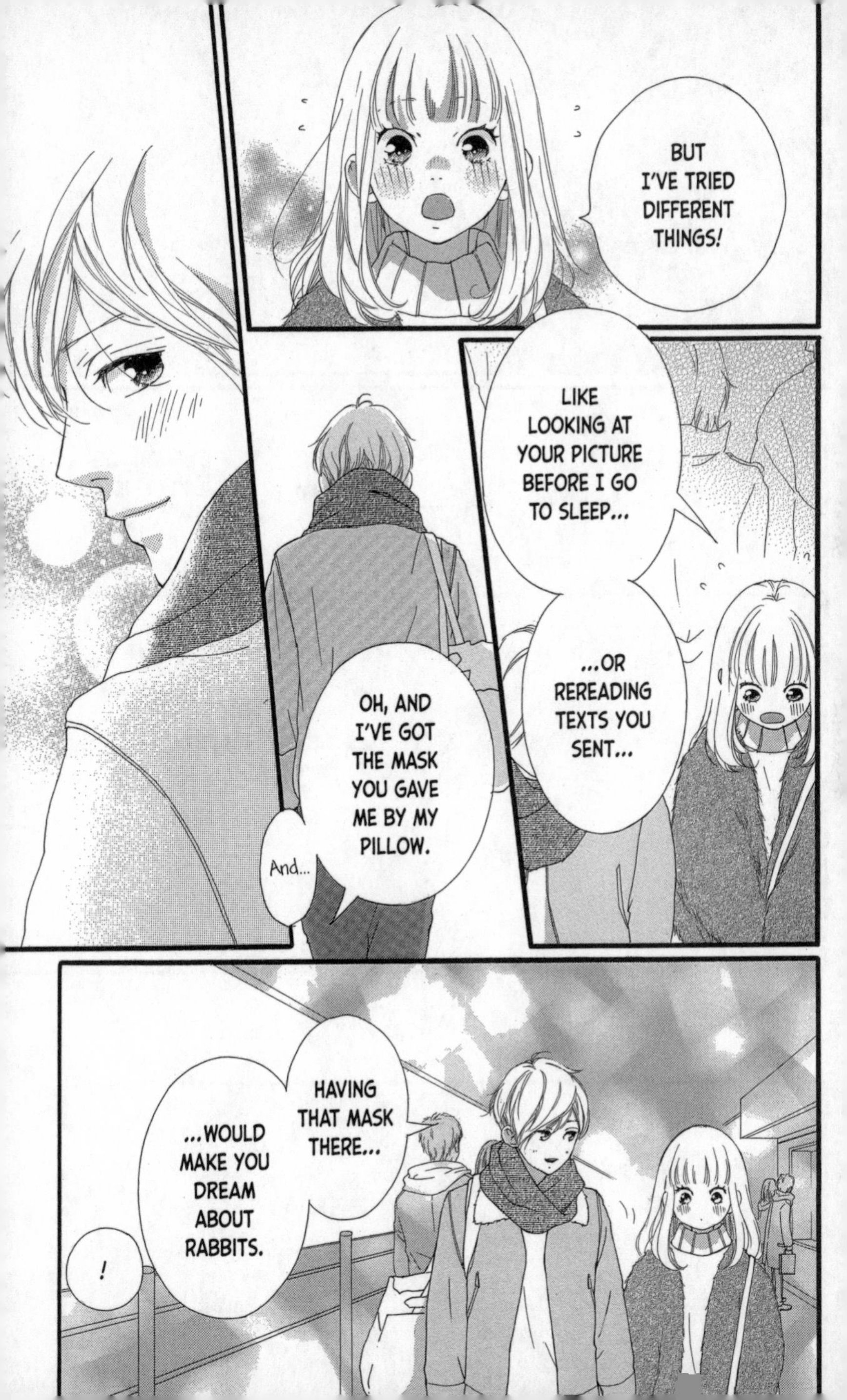
BUT I'VE TRIED DIFFERENT THINGS!
LIKE LOOKING AT YOUR PICTURE BEFORE I GO TO SLEEP...
...OR REREADING TEXTS YOU SENT...
OH, AND I'VE GOT THE MASK YOU GAVE ME BY MY PILLOW.
And...
HAVING THAT MASK THERE...
...WOULD MAKE YOU DREAM ABOUT RABBITS.
!

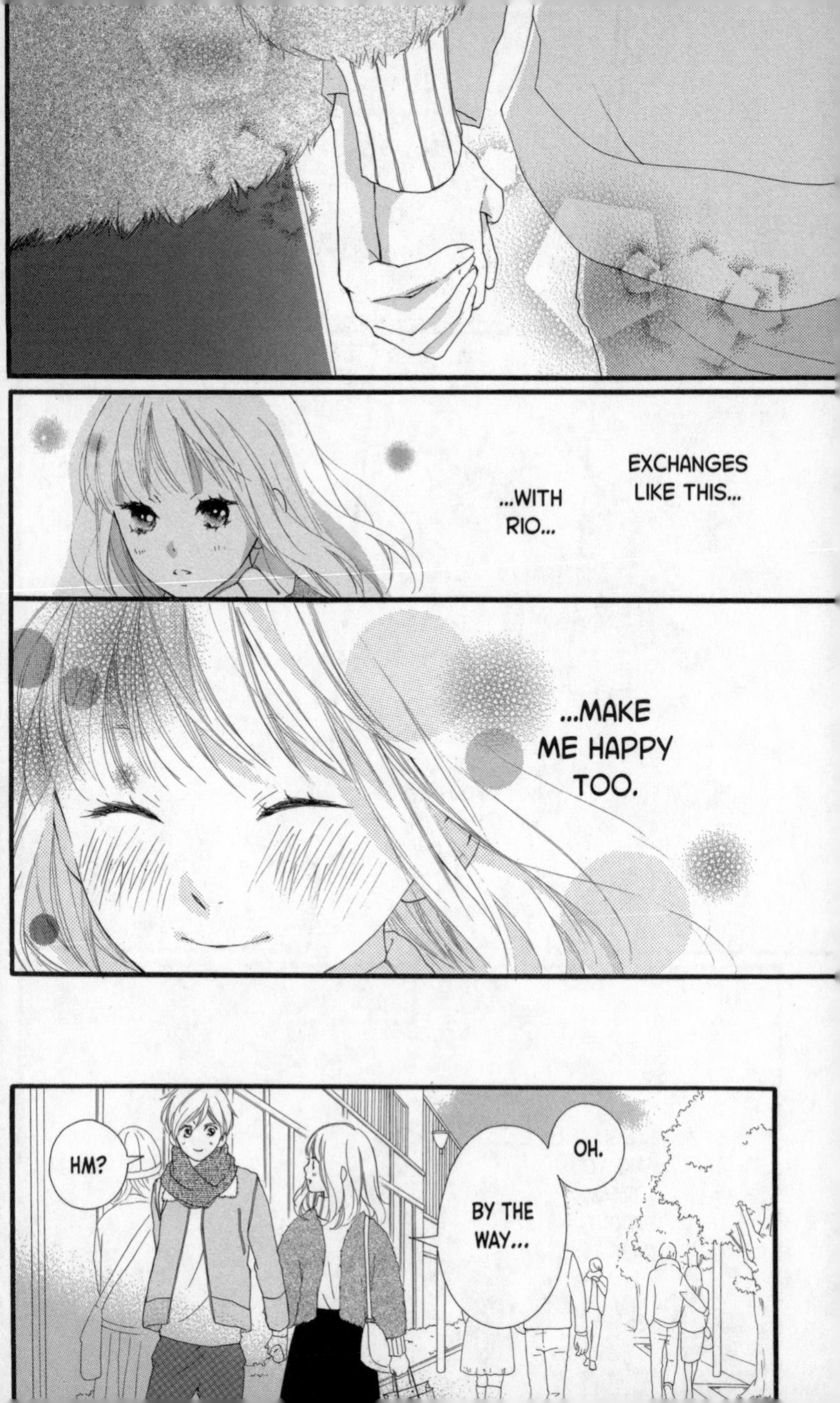
EXCHANGES LIKE THIS...
...WITH RIO...
...MAKE ME HAPPY TOO.
OH.
BY THE WAY...
HM?

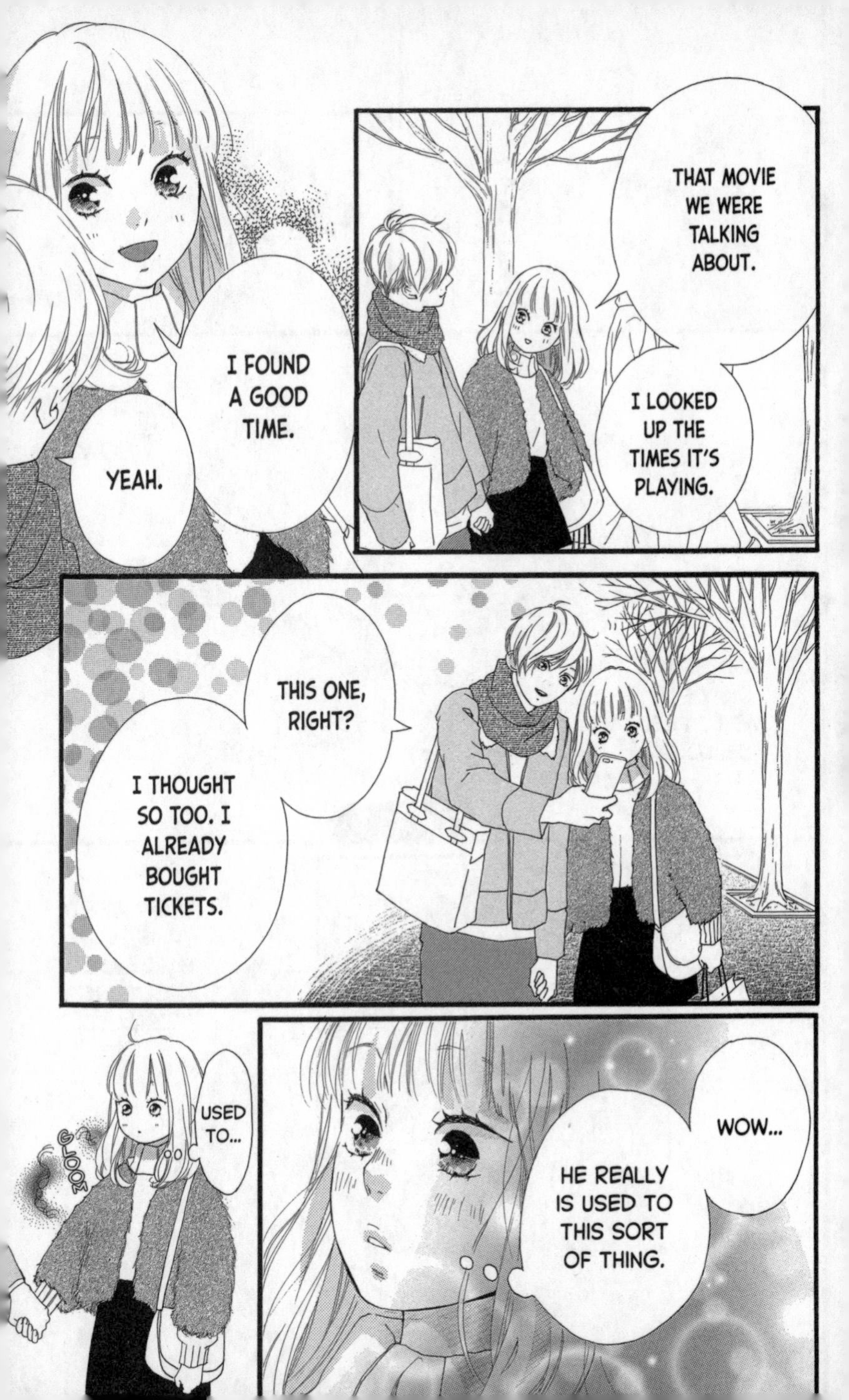
THAT MOVIE WE WERE TALKING ABOUT.
I LOOKED UP THE TIMES IT'S PLAYING.
I FOUND A GOOD TIME.
YEAH.
THIS ONE, RIGHT?
I THOUGHT SO TOO. I ALREADY BOUGHT TICKETS.
WOW...
HE REALLY IS USED TO THIS SORT OF THING.
USED TO...
GLOOM

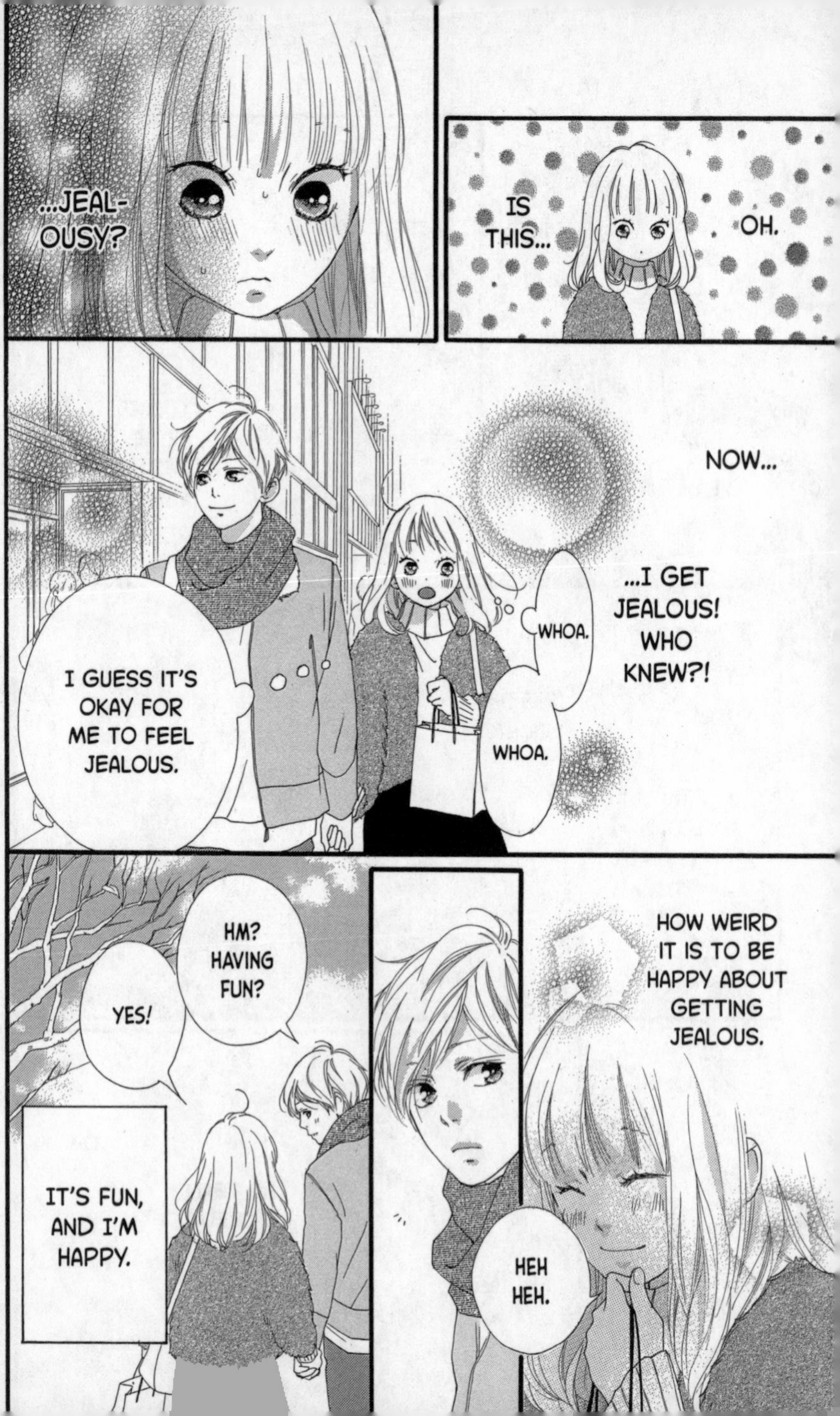
OH.
IS THIS...
...JEAL-OUSY?
NOW...
...I GET JEALOUS! WHO KNEW?!
WHOA.
WHOA.
I GUESS IT'S OKAY FOR ME TO FEEL JEALOUS.
HOW WEIRD IT IS TO BE HAPPY ABOUT GETTING JEALOUS.
HEH HEH.
HM? HAVING FUN?
YES!
IT'S FUN, AND I'M HAPPY.

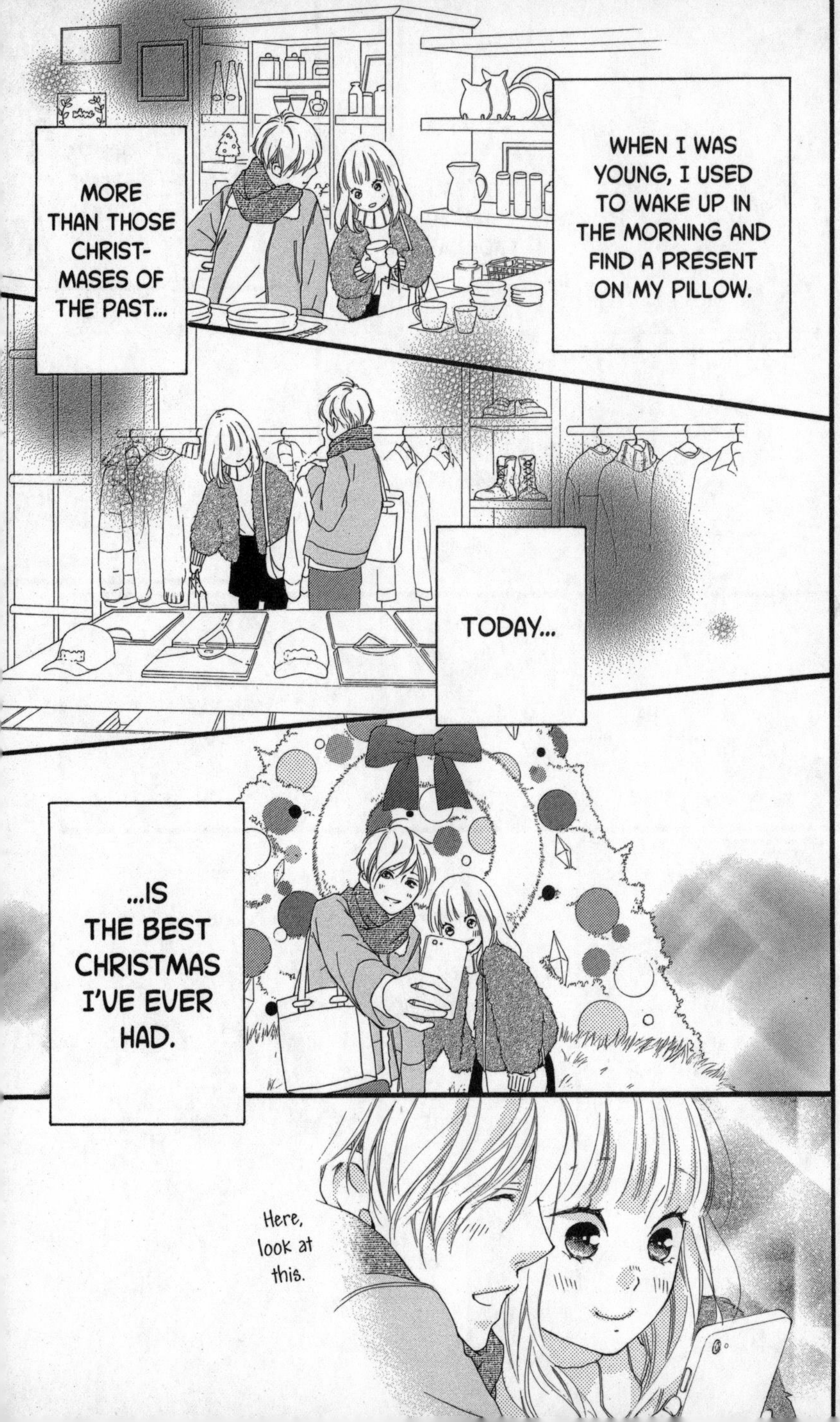
WHEN I WAS YOUNG, I USED TO WAKE UP IN THE MORNING AND FIND A PRESENT ON MY PILLOW.
MORE THAN THOSE CHRIST-MASES OF THE PAST...
TODAY...
...IS THE BEST CHRISTMAS I'VE EVER HAD.
Here, look at this.

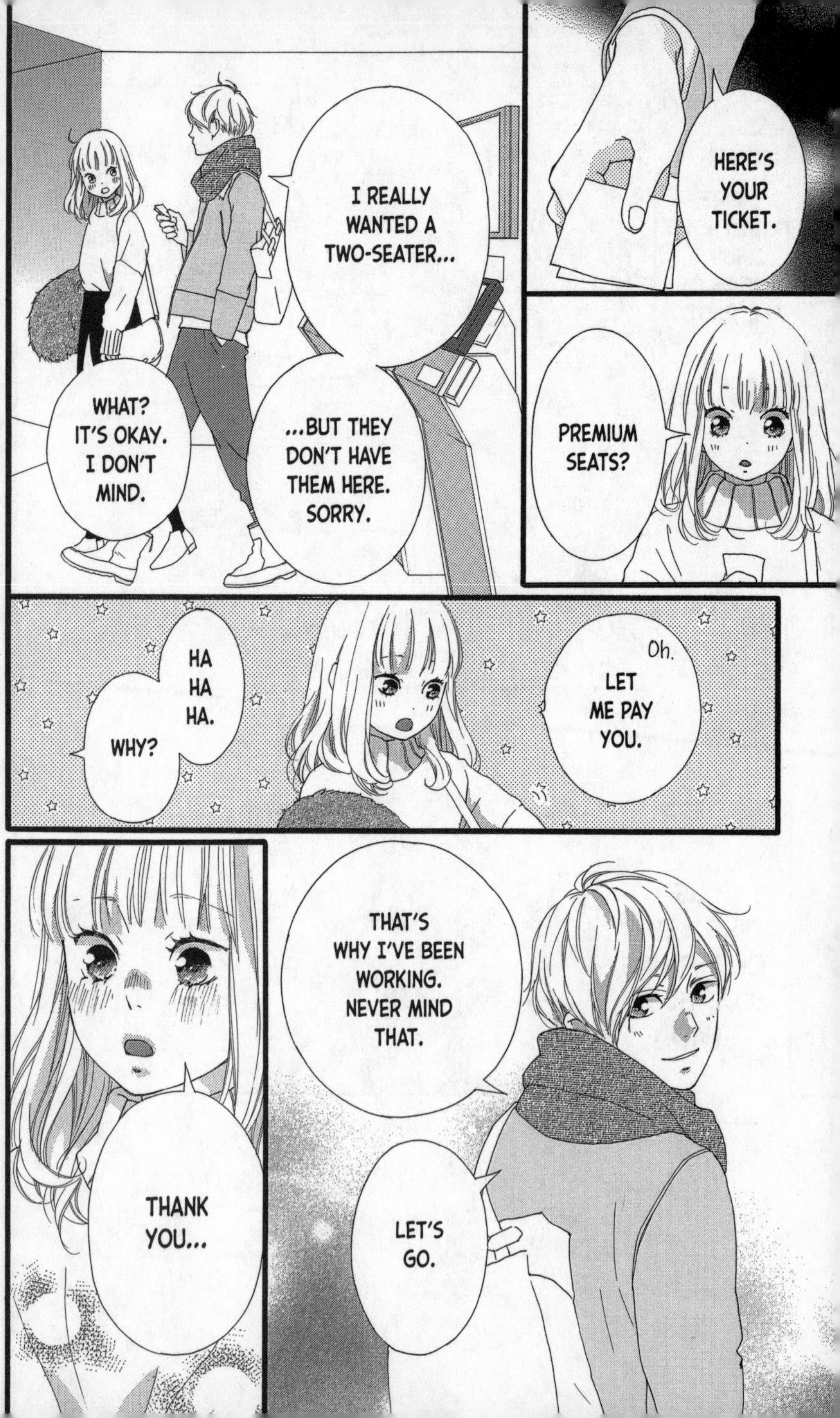
HERE'S YOUR TICKET.
PREMIUM SEATS?
I REALLY WANTED A TWO-SEATER...
...BUT THEY DON'T HAVE THEM HERE. SORRY.
WHAT? IT'S OKAY. I DON'T MIND.
Oh.
LET ME PAY YOU.
HA HA HA.
WHY?
THAT'S WHY I'VE BEEN WORKING. NEVER MIND THAT.
LET'S GO.
THANK YOU...

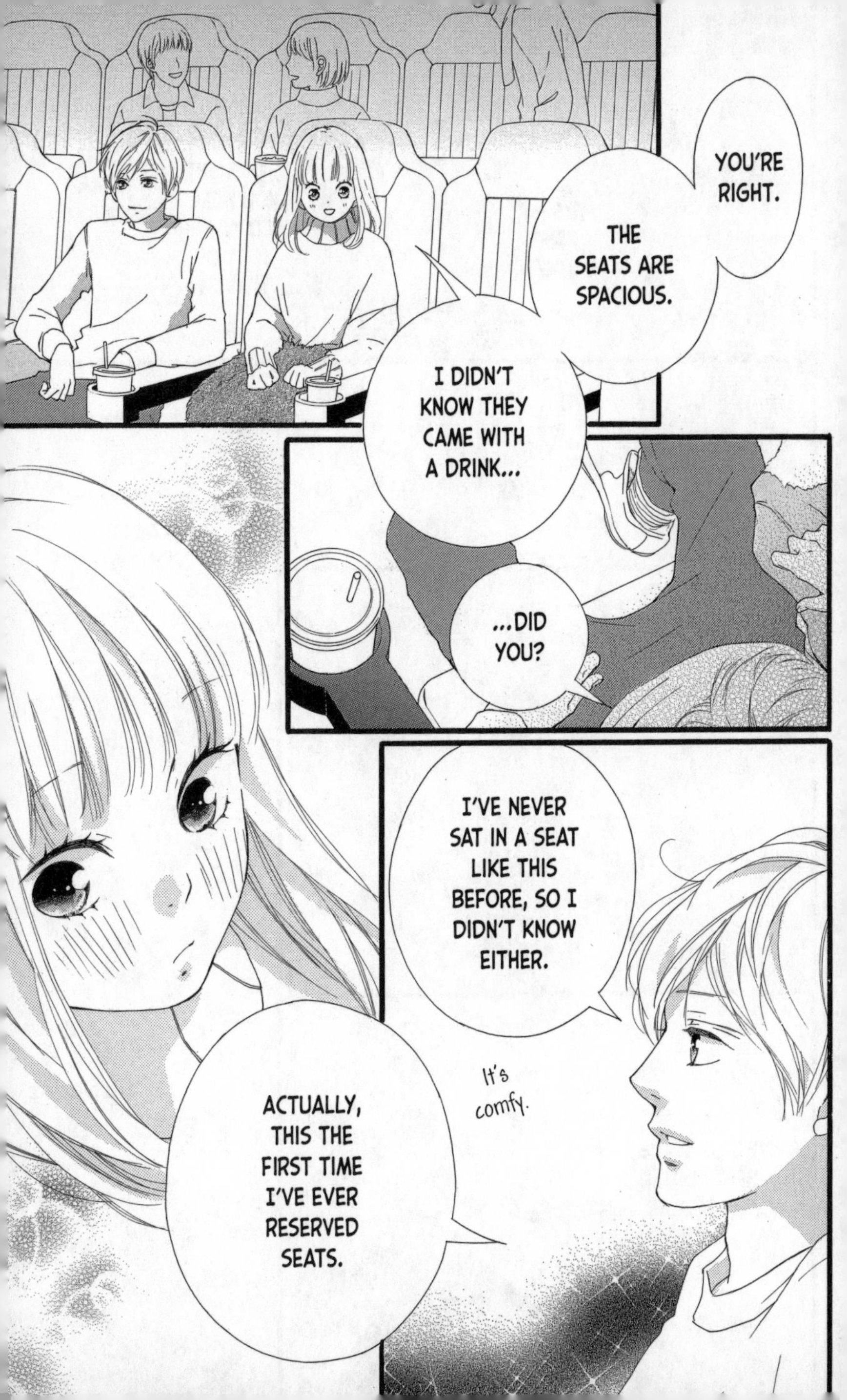

YOU'RE RIGHT.
THE SEATS ARE SPACIOUS.
I DIDN'T KNOW THEY CAME WITH A DRINK...
...DID YOU?
I'VE NEVER SAT IN A SEAT LIKE THIS BEFORE, SO I DIDN'T KNOW EITHER.
It's comfy.
ACTUALLY, THIS THE FIRST TIME I'VE EVER RESERVED SEATS.

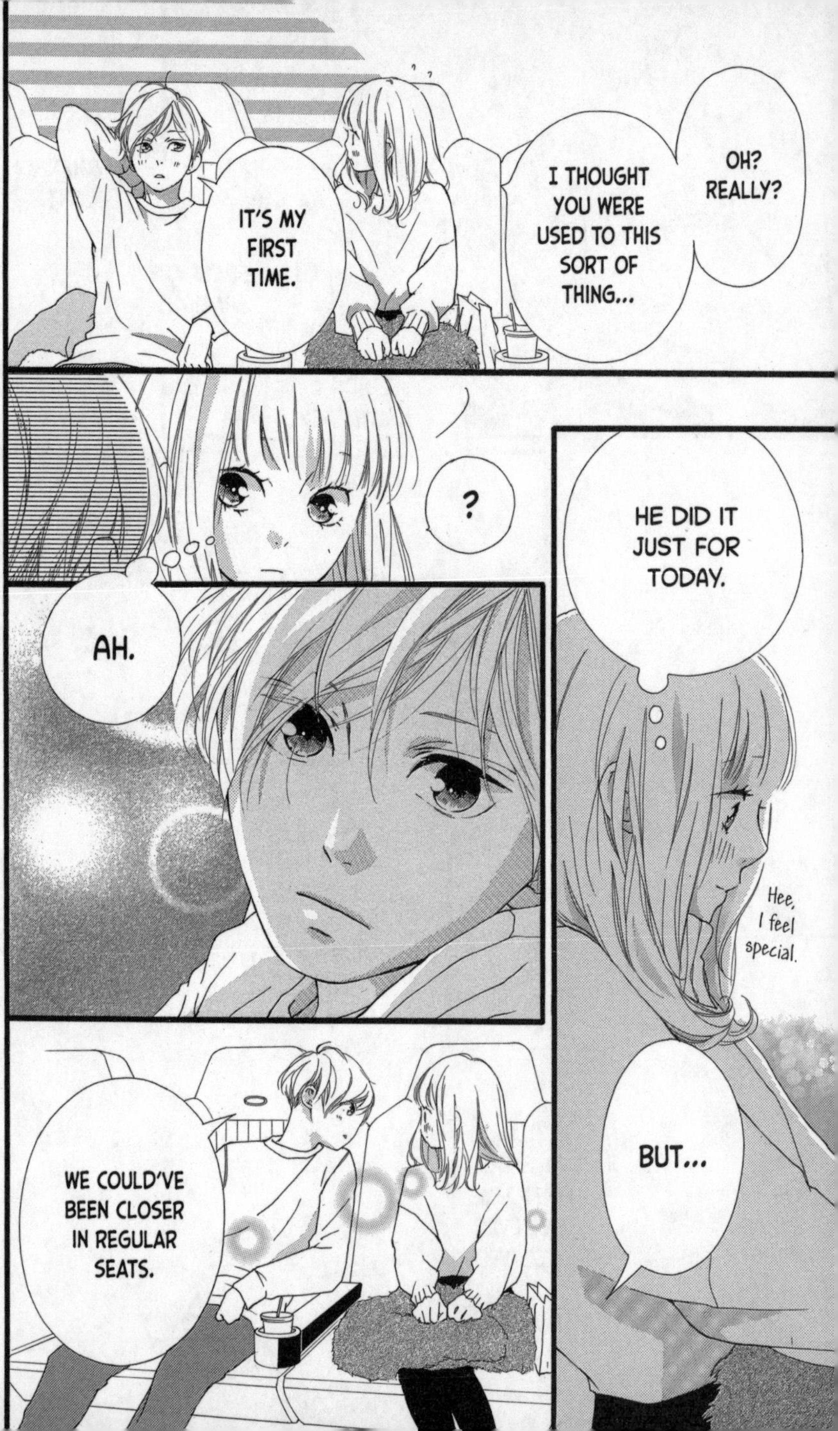
OH? REALLY?
I THOUGHT YOU WERE USED TO THIS SORT OF THING...
IT'S MY FIRST TIME.
HE DID IT JUST FOR TODAY.
Hee, I feel special.
BUT...
?
AH.
WE COULD'VE BEEN CLOSER IN REGULAR SEATS.

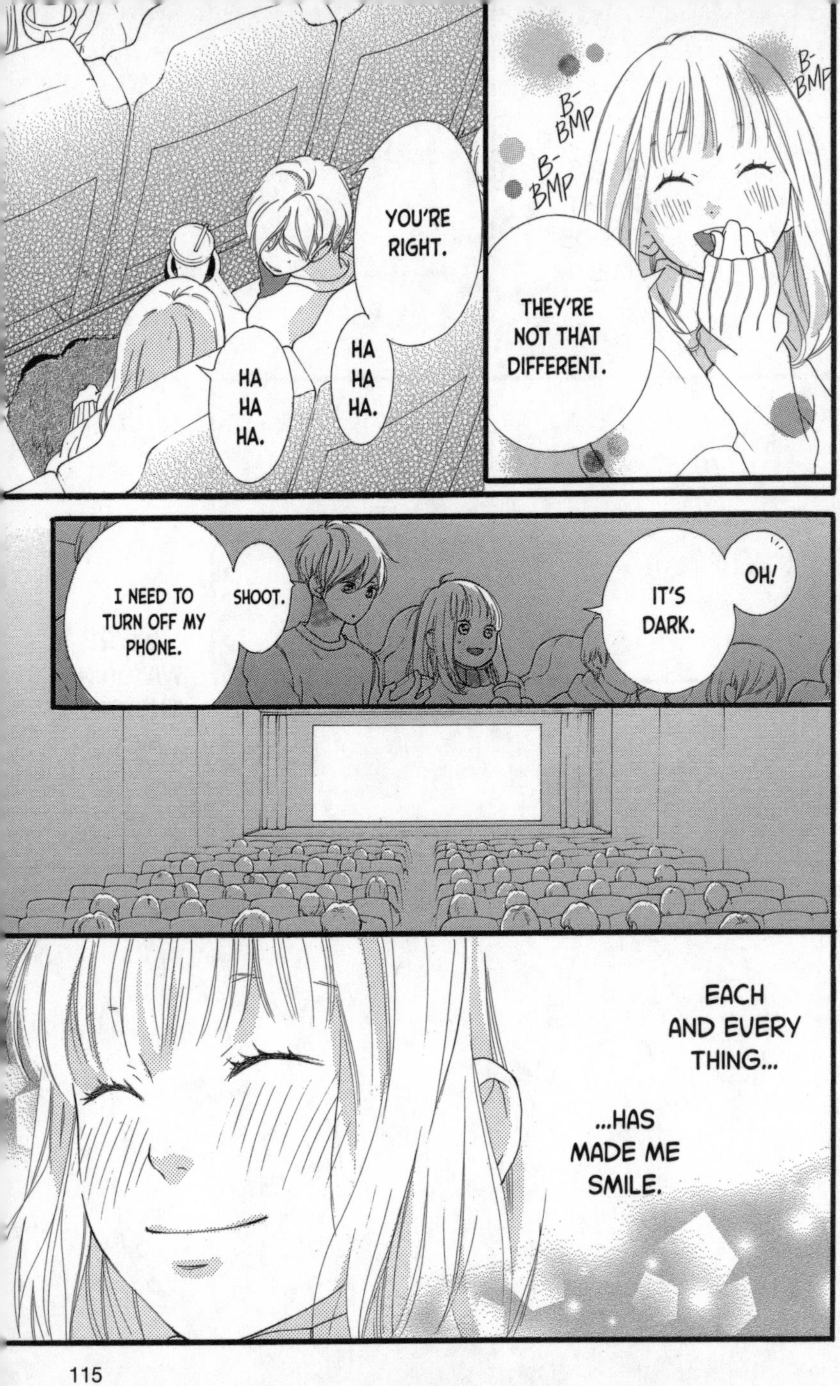
B-BMP
B-BMP
B-BMP
THEY'RE NOT THAT DIFFERENT.
YOU'RE RIGHT.
HA HA HA.
HA HA HA.
OH!
IT'S DARK.
SHOOT.
I NEED TO TURN OFF MY PHONE.
EACH AND EVERY THING...
...HAS MADE ME SMILE.

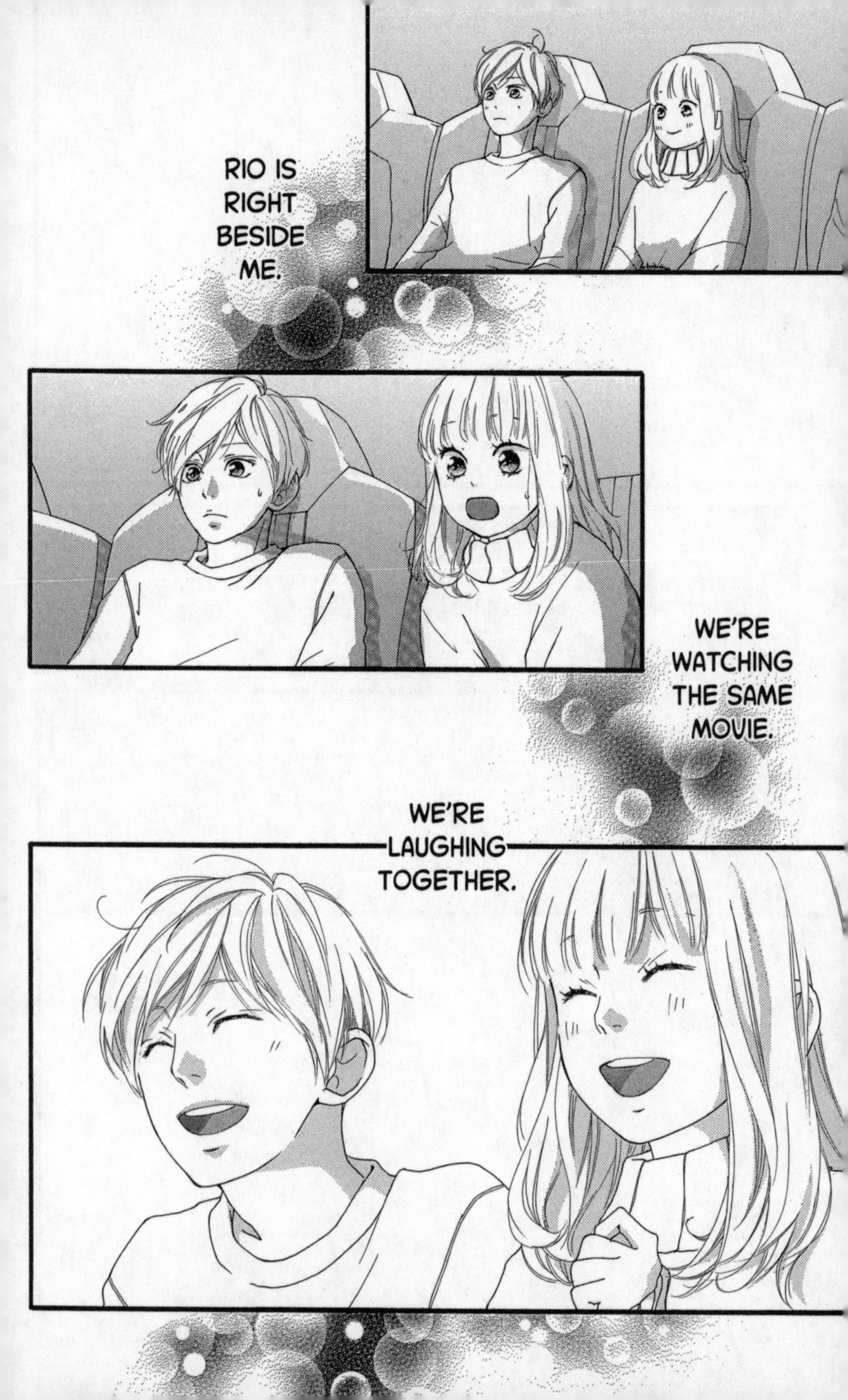
RIO IS RIGHT BESIDE ME.
WE'RE WATCHING THE SAME MOVIE.
WE'RE LAUGHING TOGETHER.

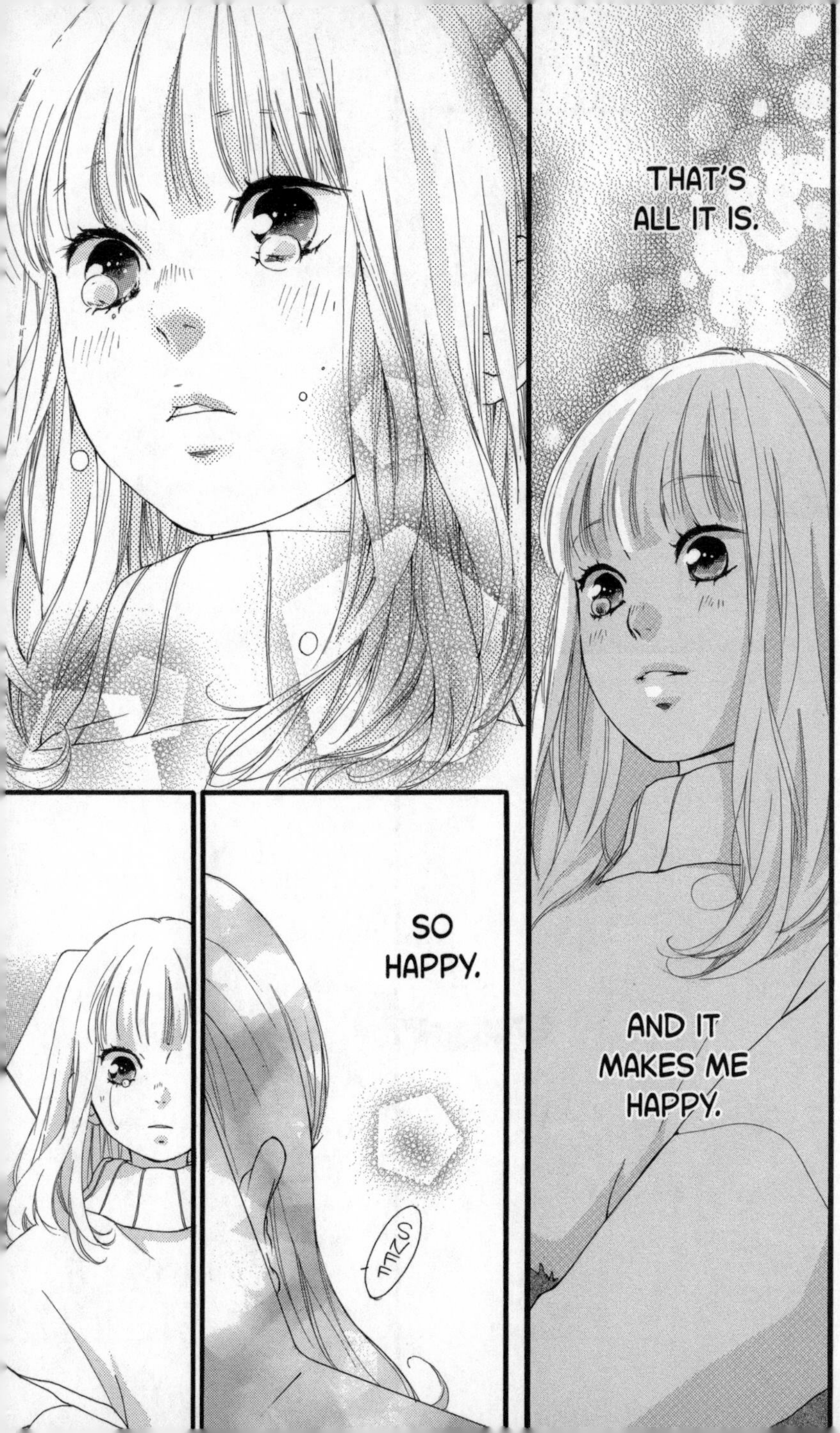
THAT'S ALL IT IS.
AND IT MAKES ME HAPPY.
SO HAPPY.
SNIFF

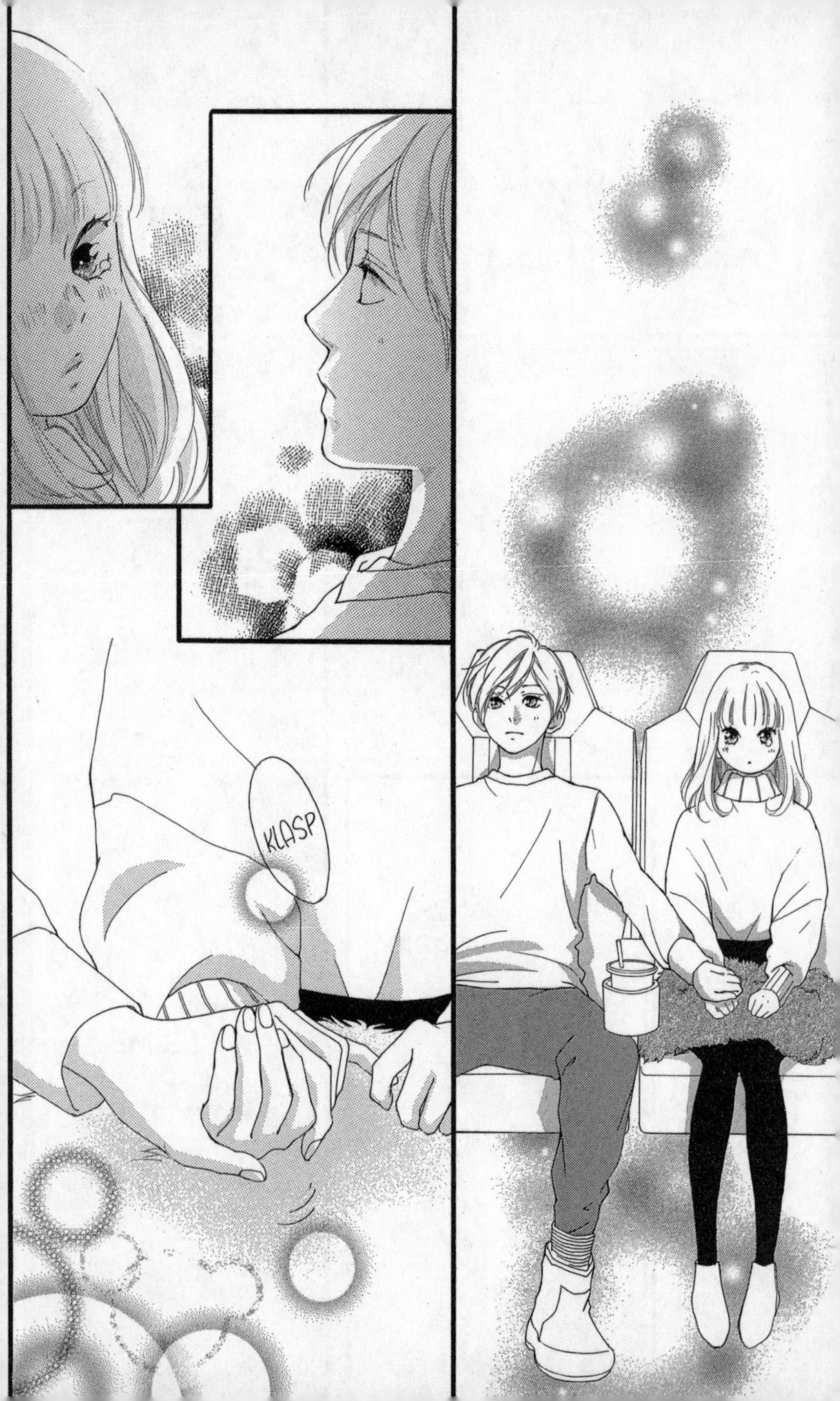
KLASP

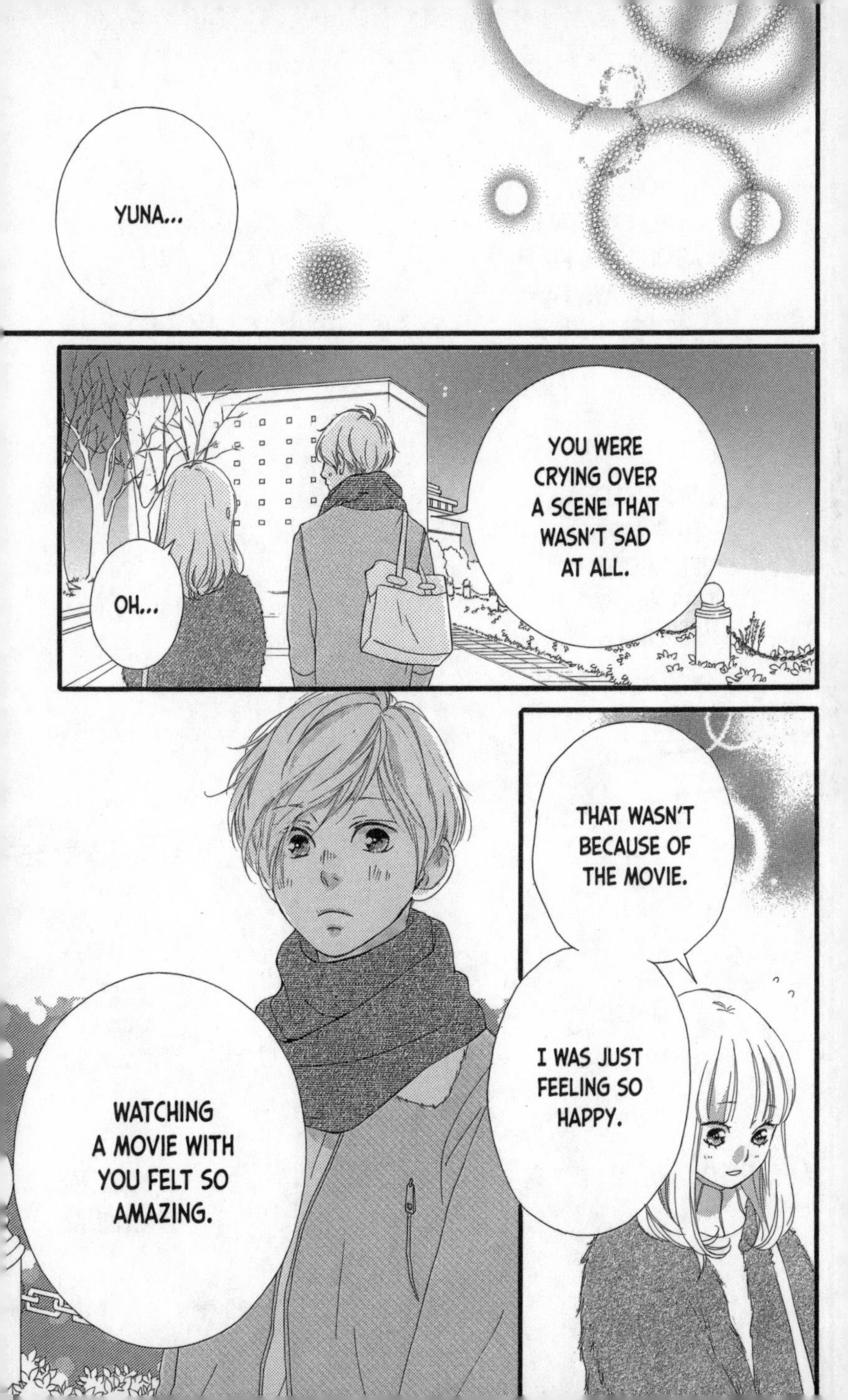
YUNA...
YOU WERE CRYING OVER A SCENE THAT WASN'T SAD AT ALL.
OH...
THAT WASN'T BECAUSE OF THE MOVIE.
I WAS JUST FEELING SO HAPPY.
WATCHING A MOVIE WITH YOU FELT SO AMAZING.

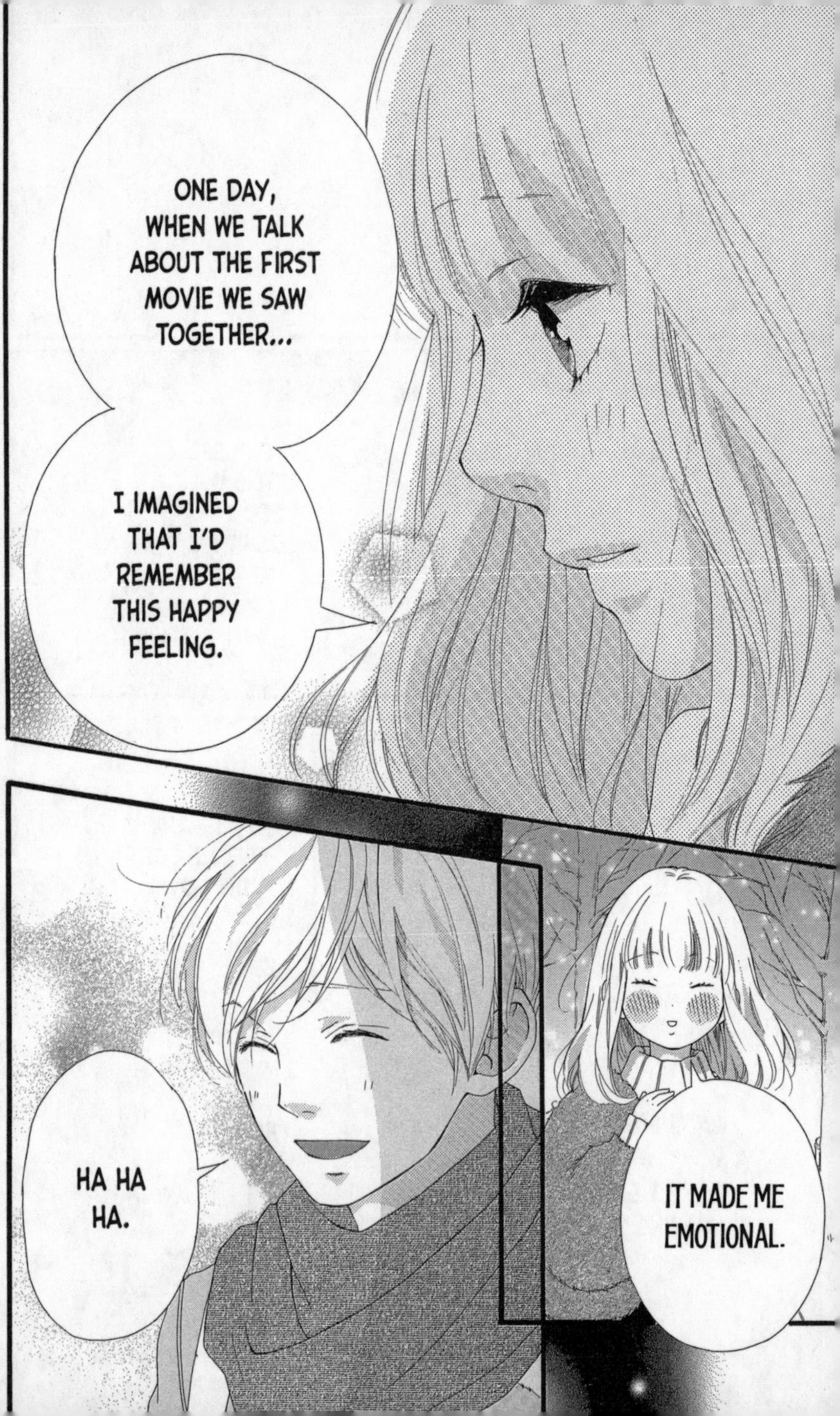
ONE DAY, WHEN WE TALK ABOUT THE FIRST MOVIE WE SAW TOGETHER...
I IMAGINED THAT I'D REMEMBER THIS HAPPY FEELING.
IT MADE ME EMOTIONAL.
HA HA HA.

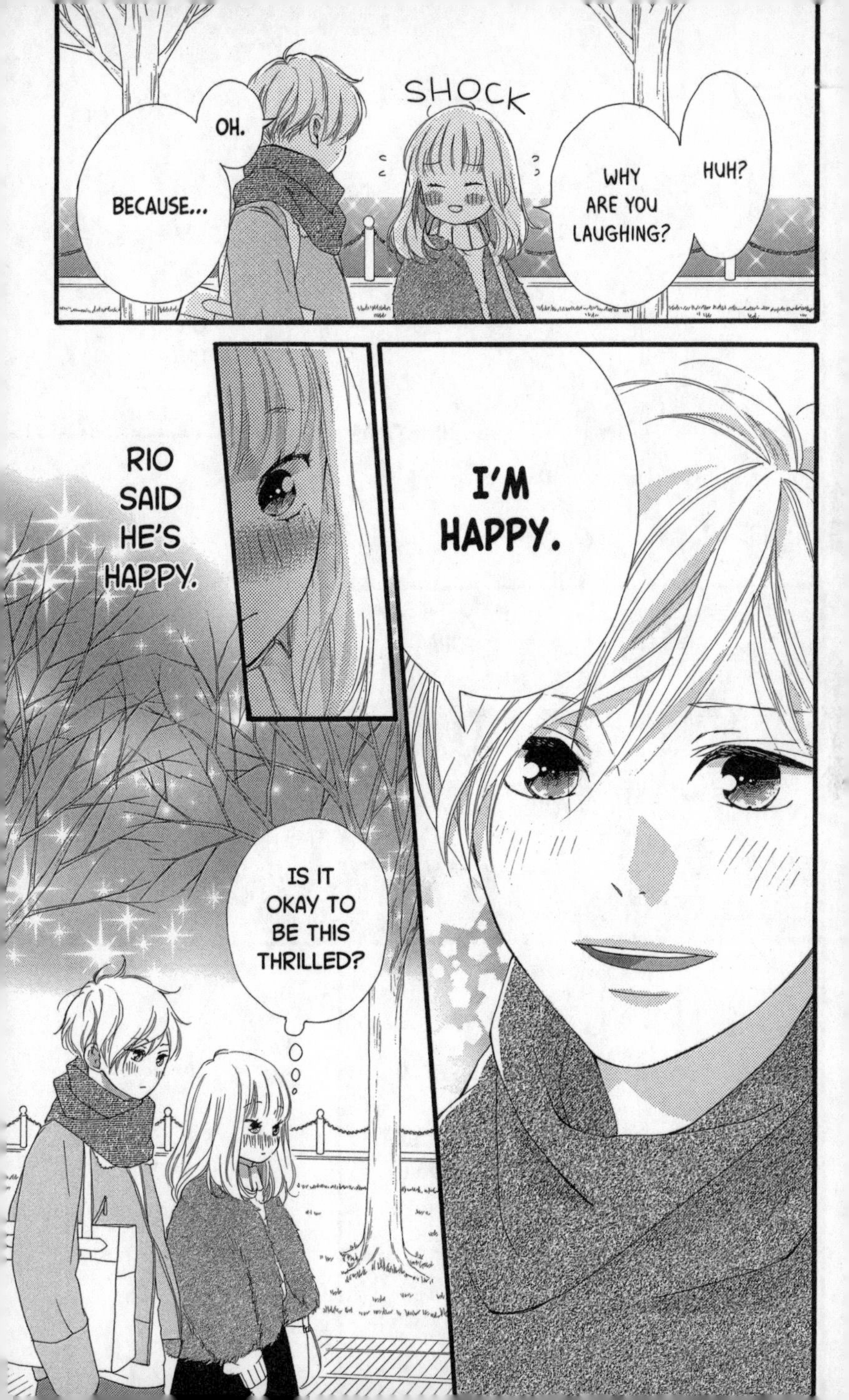
HUH?
WHY ARE YOU LAUGHING?
SHOCK
OH.
BECAUSE...
I'M HAPPY.
RIO SAID HE'S HAPPY.
IS IT OKAY TO BE THIS THRILLED?

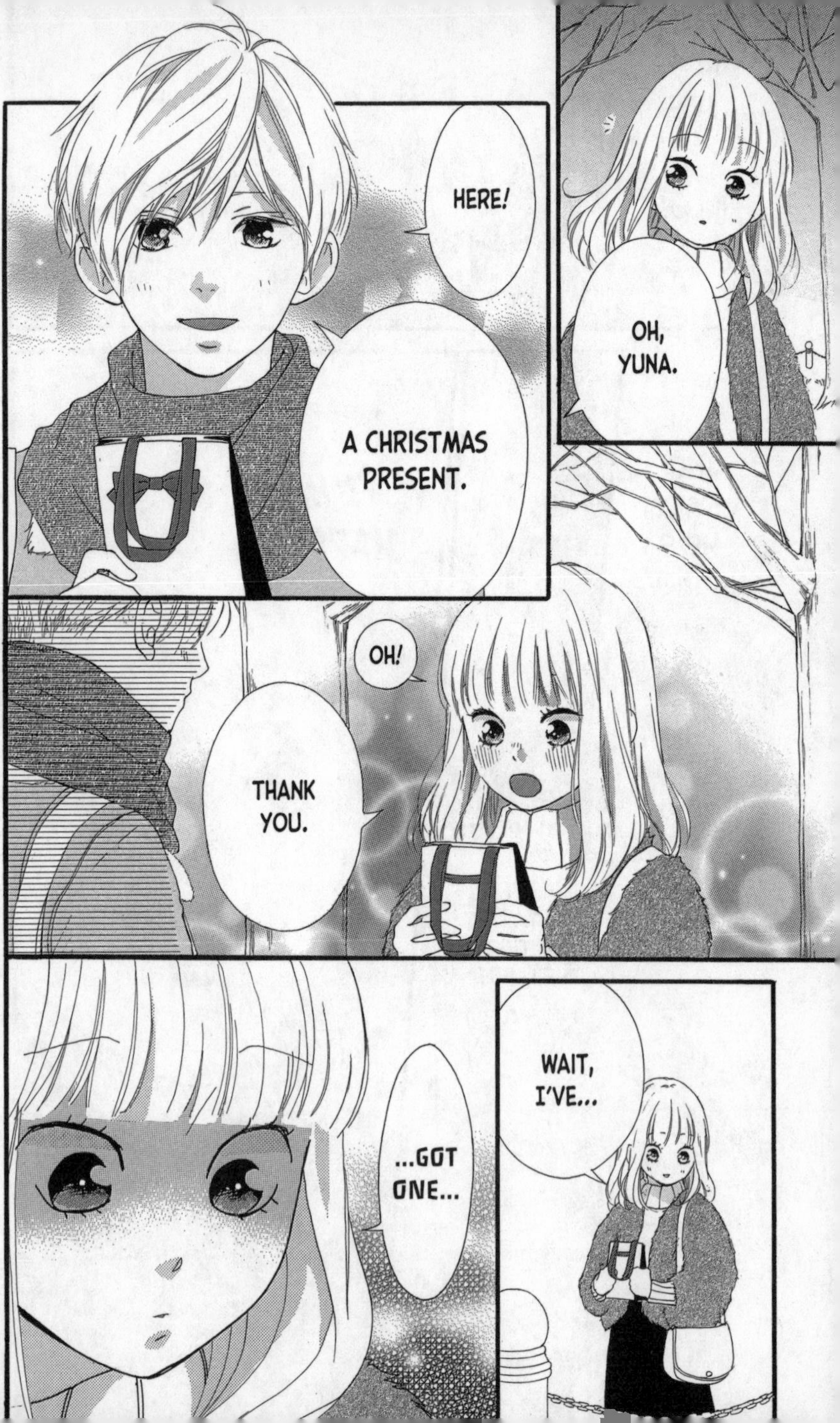
OH, YUNA.
HERE!
A CHRISTMAS PRESENT.
OH!
THANK YOU.
WAIT, I'VE...
...GOT ONE...

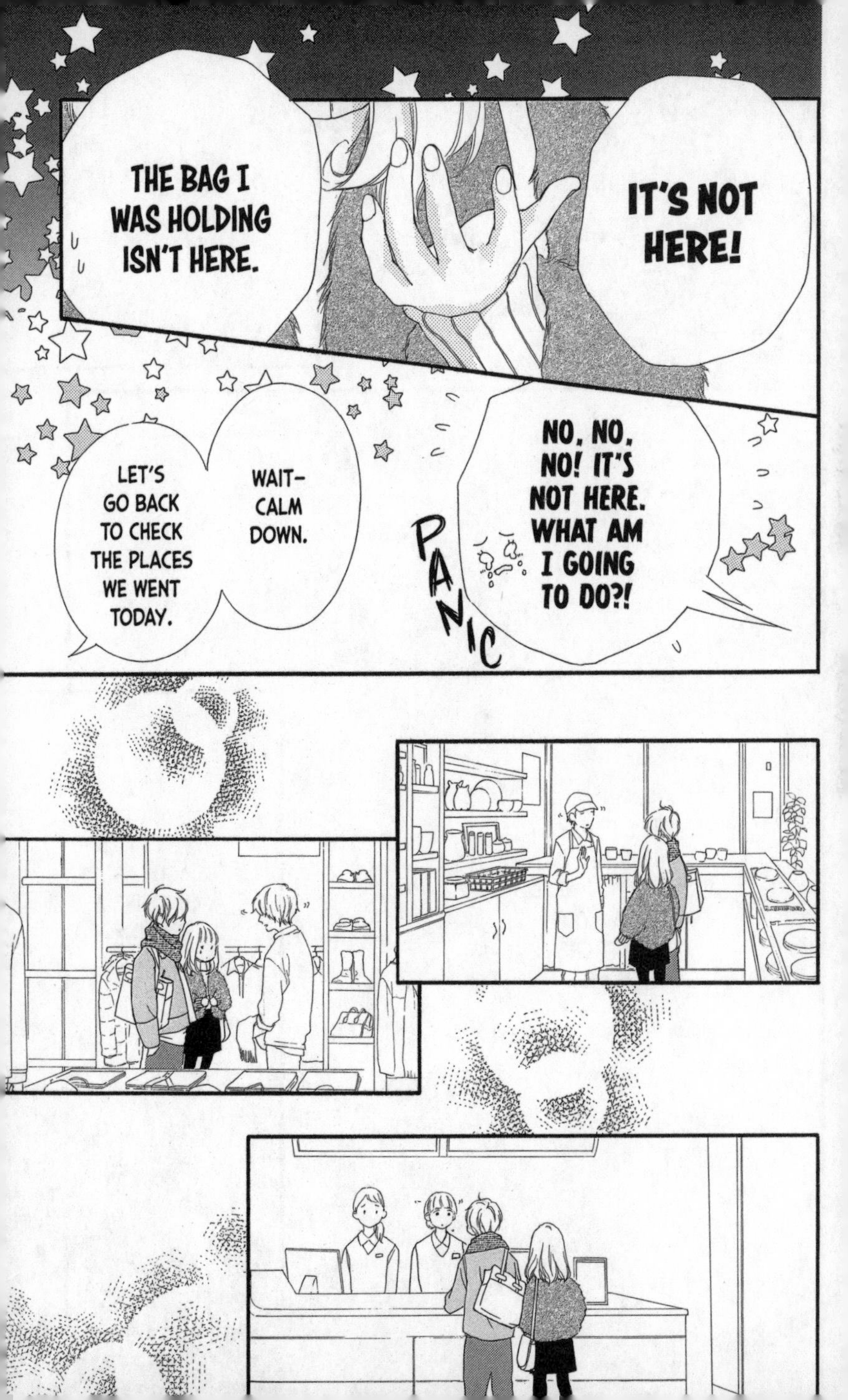
IT'S NOT HERE!
THE BAG I WAS HOLDING ISN'T HERE.
NO, NO, NO! IT'S NOT HERE. WHAT AM I GOING TO DO?!
PANIC
WAIT— CALM DOWN.
LET'S GO BACK TO CHECK THE PLACES WE WENT TODAY.

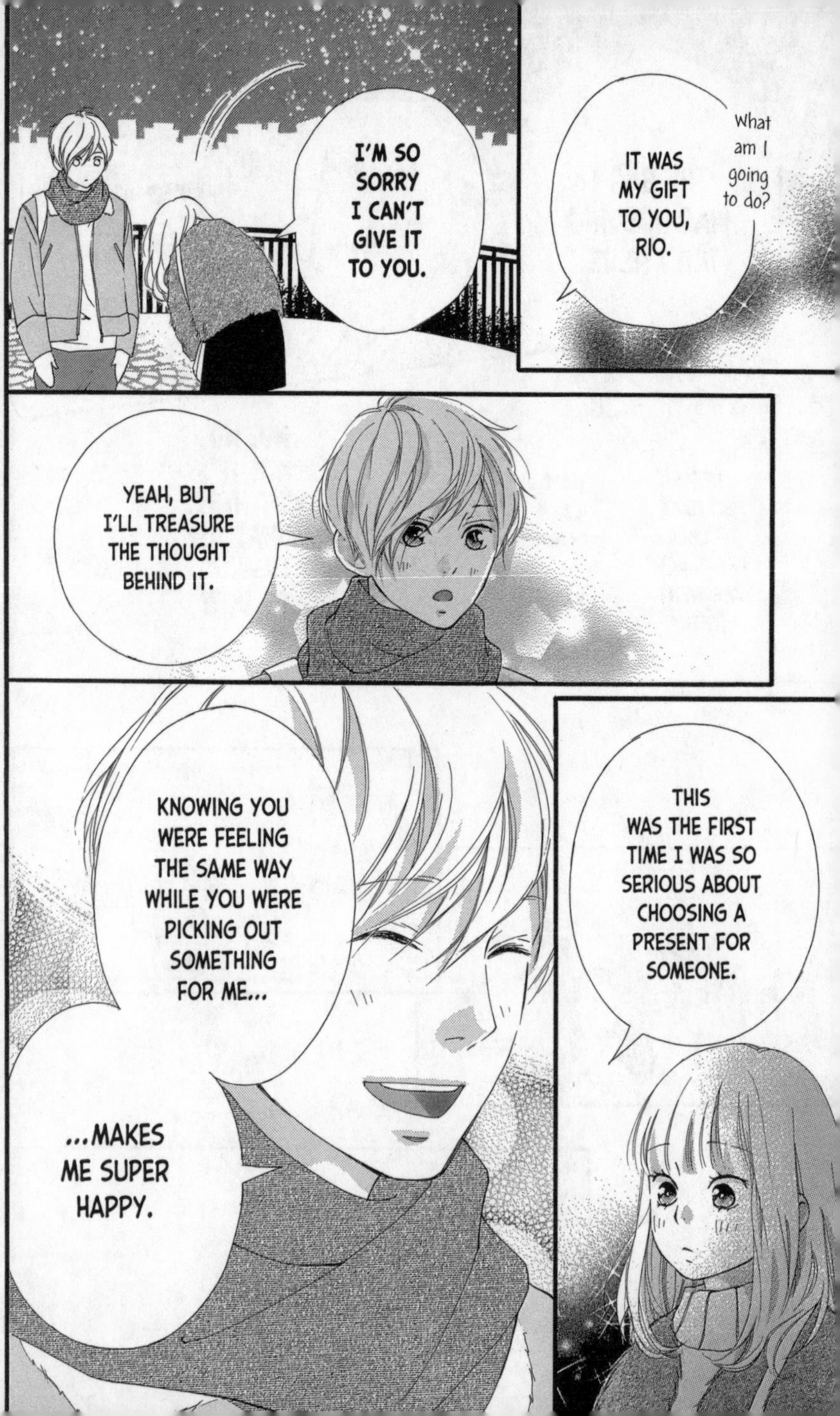
What am I going to do?
IT WAS MY GIFT TO YOU, RIO.
I'M SO SORRY I CAN'T GIVE IT TO YOU.
YEAH, BUT I'LL TREASURE THE THOUGHT BEHIND IT.
THIS WAS THE FIRST TIME I WAS SO SERIOUS ABOUT CHOOSING A PRESENT FOR SOMEONE.
KNOWING YOU WERE FEELING THE SAME WAY WHILE YOU WERE PICKING OUT SOMETHING FOR ME...
...MAKES ME SUPER HAPPY.

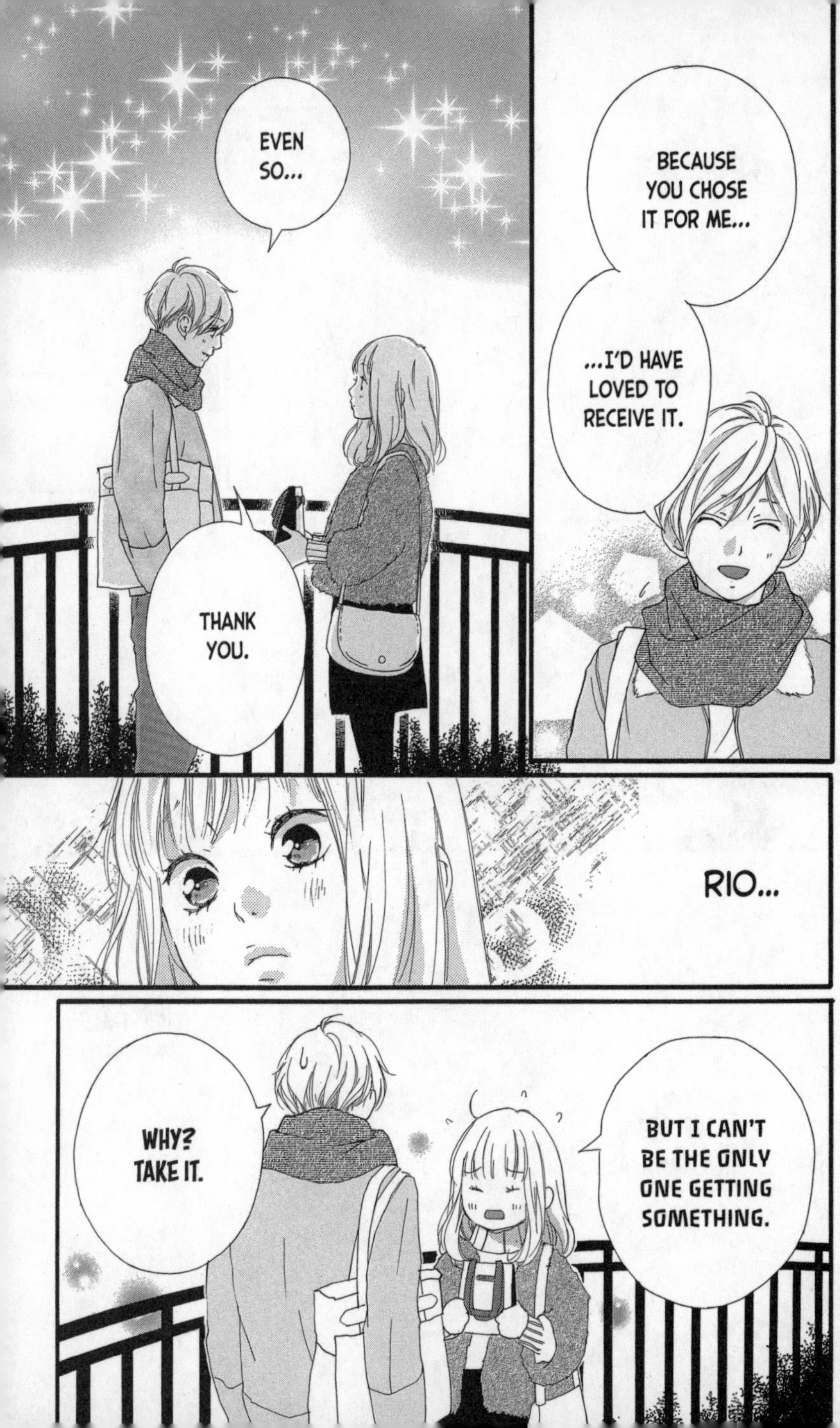
BECAUSE YOU CHOSE IT FOR ME...
...I'D HAVE LOVED TO RECEIVE IT.
EVEN SO...
THANK YOU.
RIO...
BUT I CAN'T BE THE ONLY ONE GETTING SOMETHING.
WHY? TAKE IT.

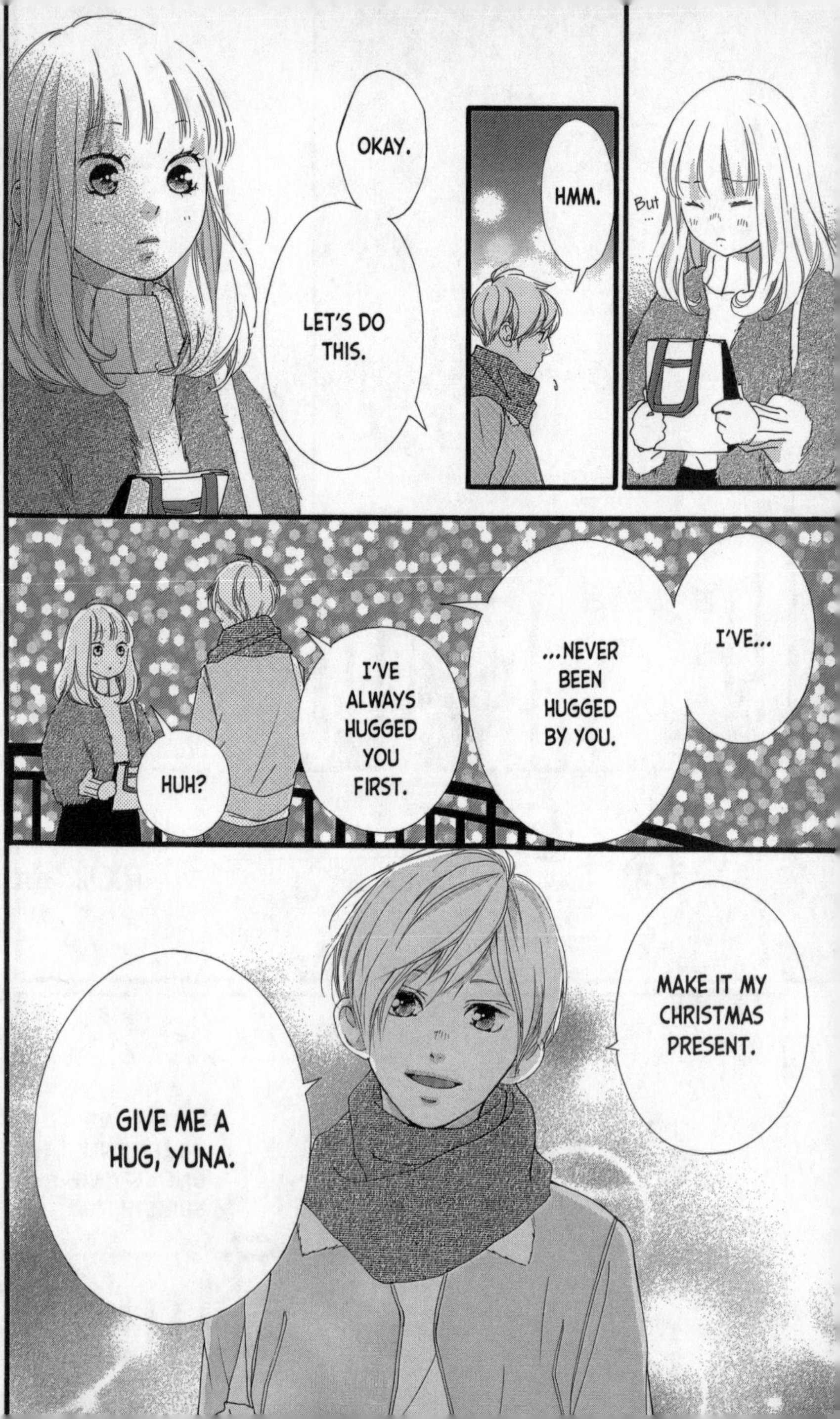
But...
HMM.
OKAY.
LET'S DO THIS.
I'VE...
...NEVER BEEN HUGGED BY YOU.
I'VE ALWAYS HUGGED YOU FIRST.
HUH?
MAKE IT MY CHRISTMAS PRESENT.
GIVE ME A HUG, YUNA.

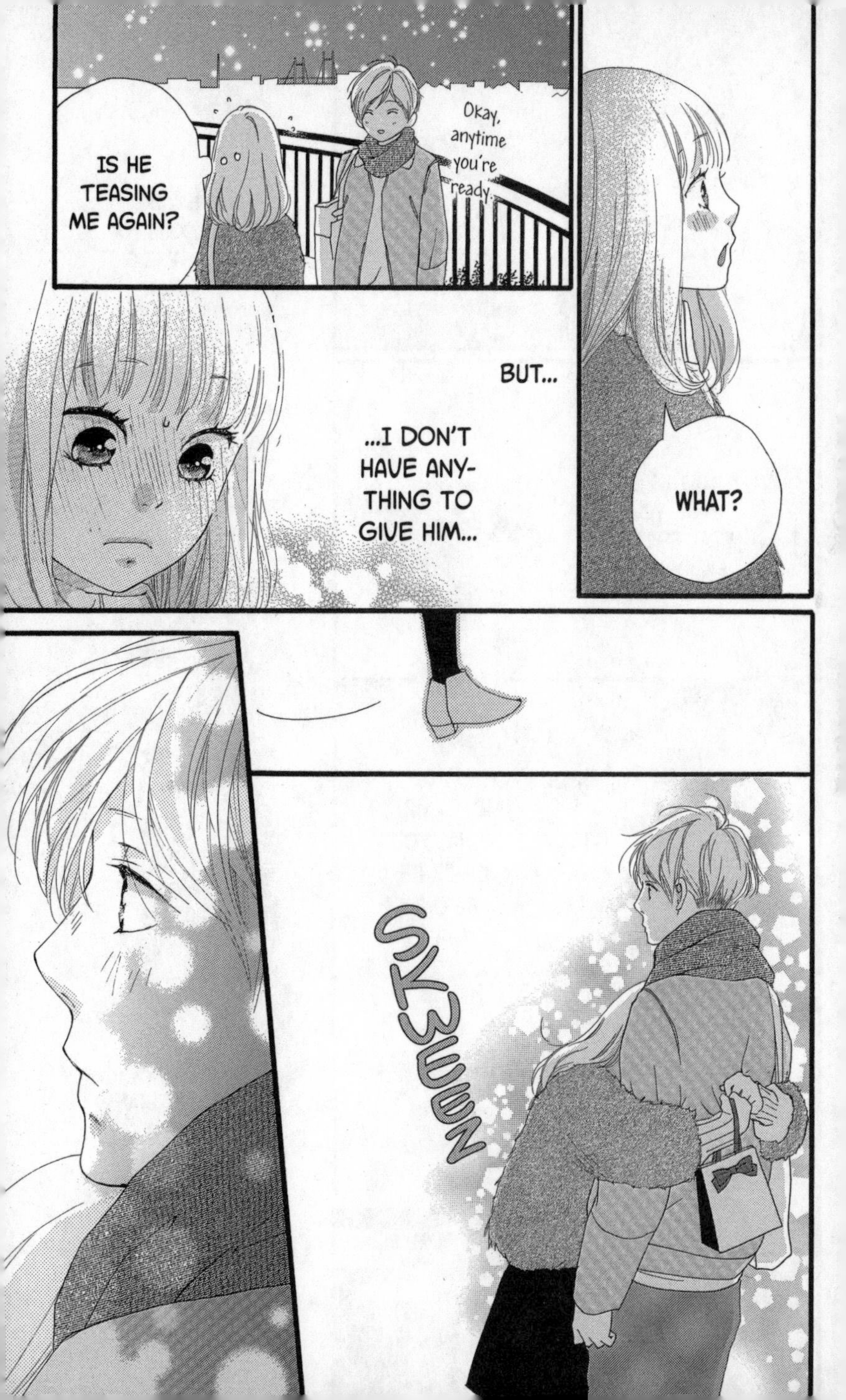
WHAT?
Okay, anytime you're ready.
IS HE TEASING ME AGAIN?
BUT...
...I DON'T HAVE ANY-THING TO GIVE HIM...
SKWEEN

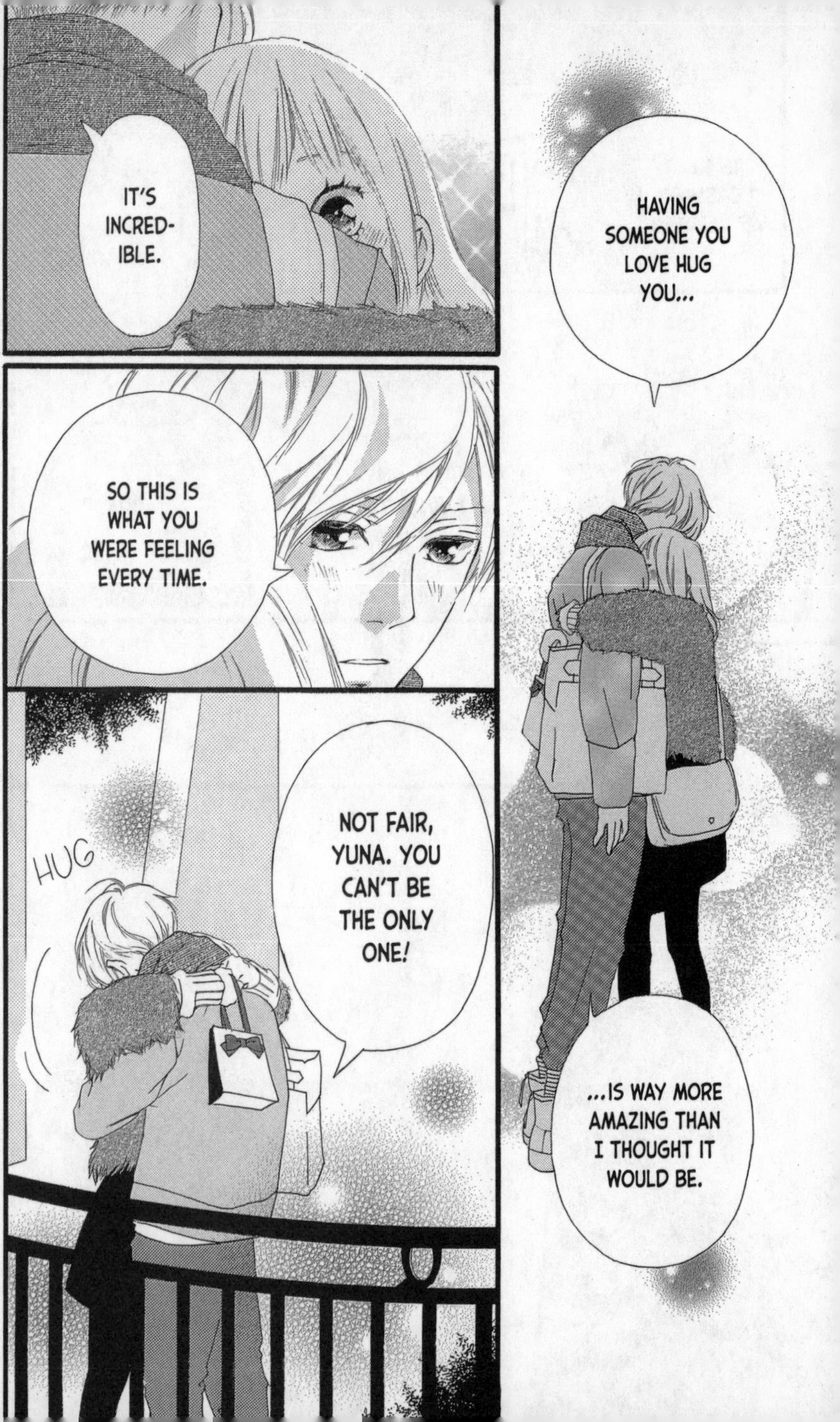
HAVING SOMEONE YOU LOVE HUG YOU...
...IS WAY MORE AMAZING THAN I THOUGHT IT WOULD BE.
IT'S INCRED-IBLE.
SO THIS IS WHAT YOU WERE FEELING EVERY TIME.
NOT FAIR, YUNA. YOU CAN'T BE THE ONLY ONE!
HUG

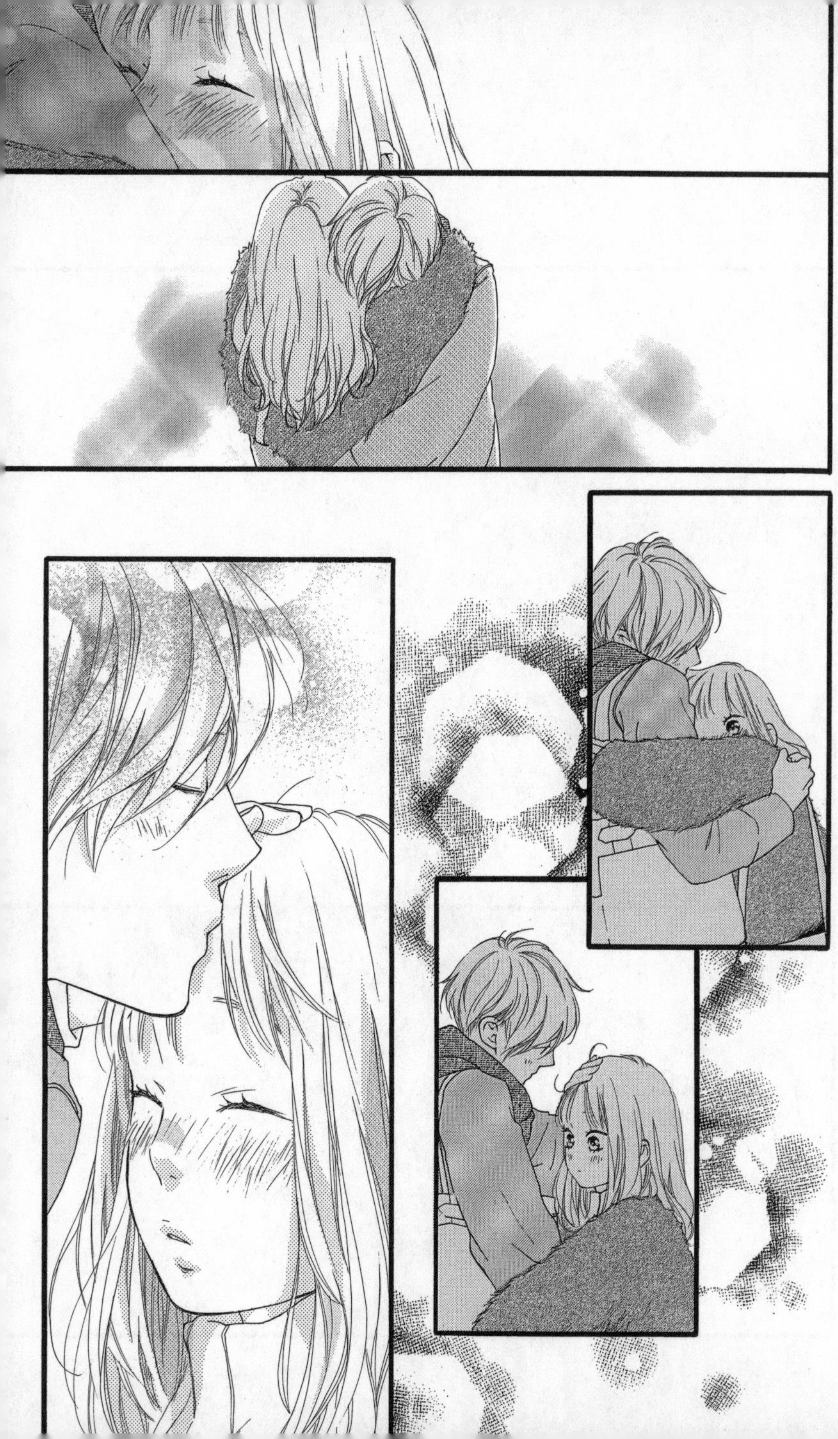

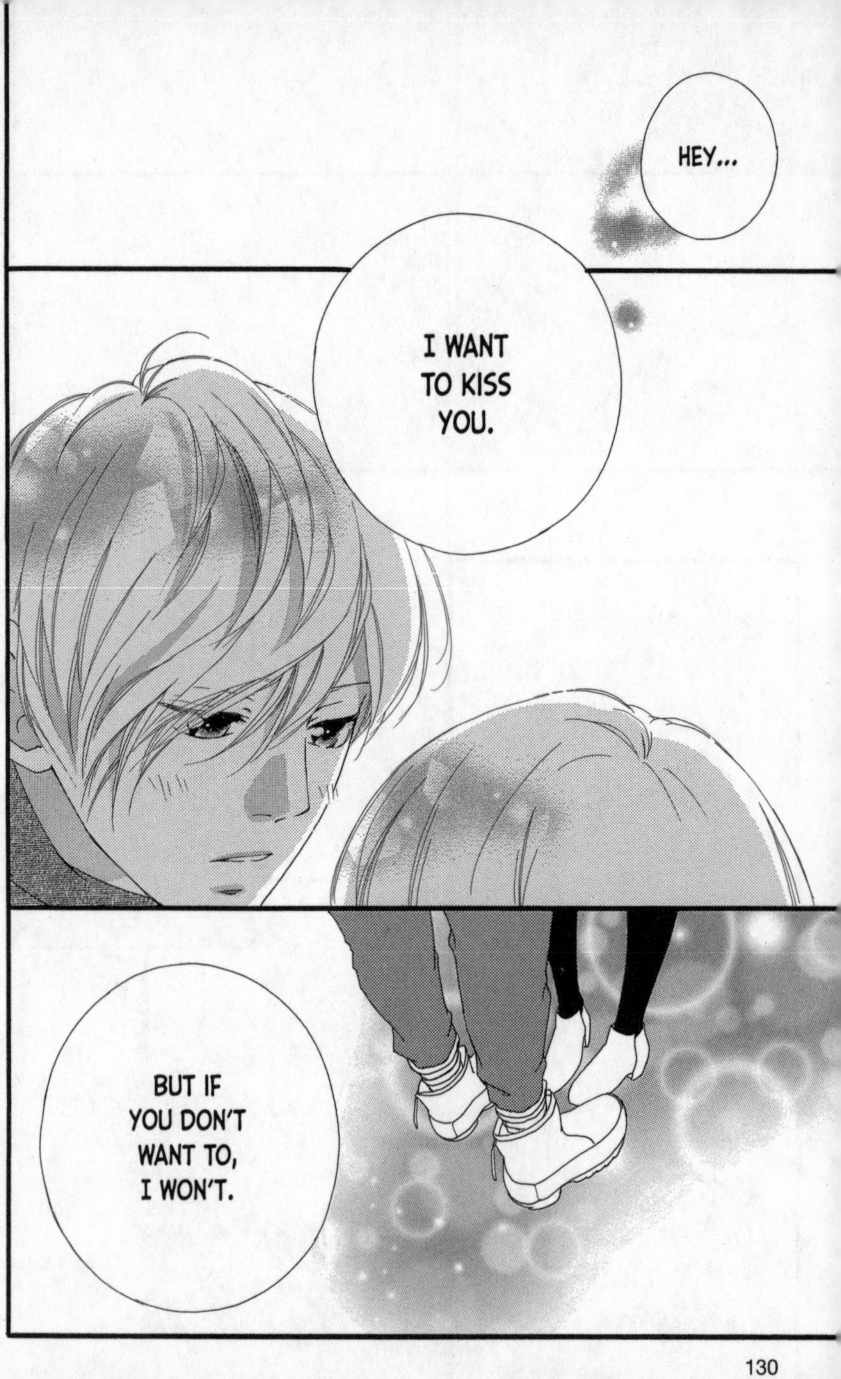
HEY...
I WANT TO KISS YOU.
BUT IF YOU DON'T WANT TO, I WON'T.

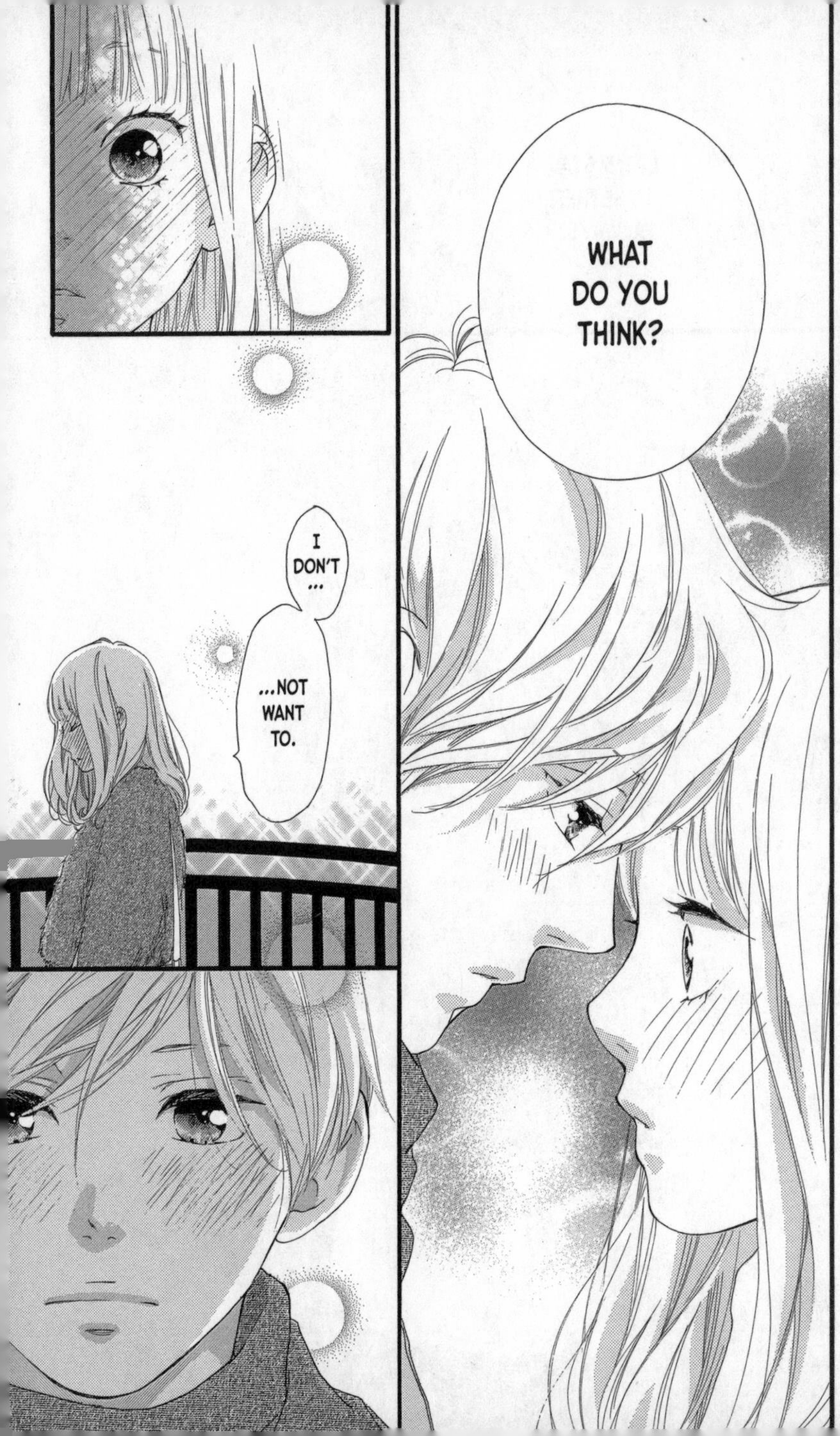
WHAT DO YOU THINK?
I DON'T ...
...NOT WANT TO.

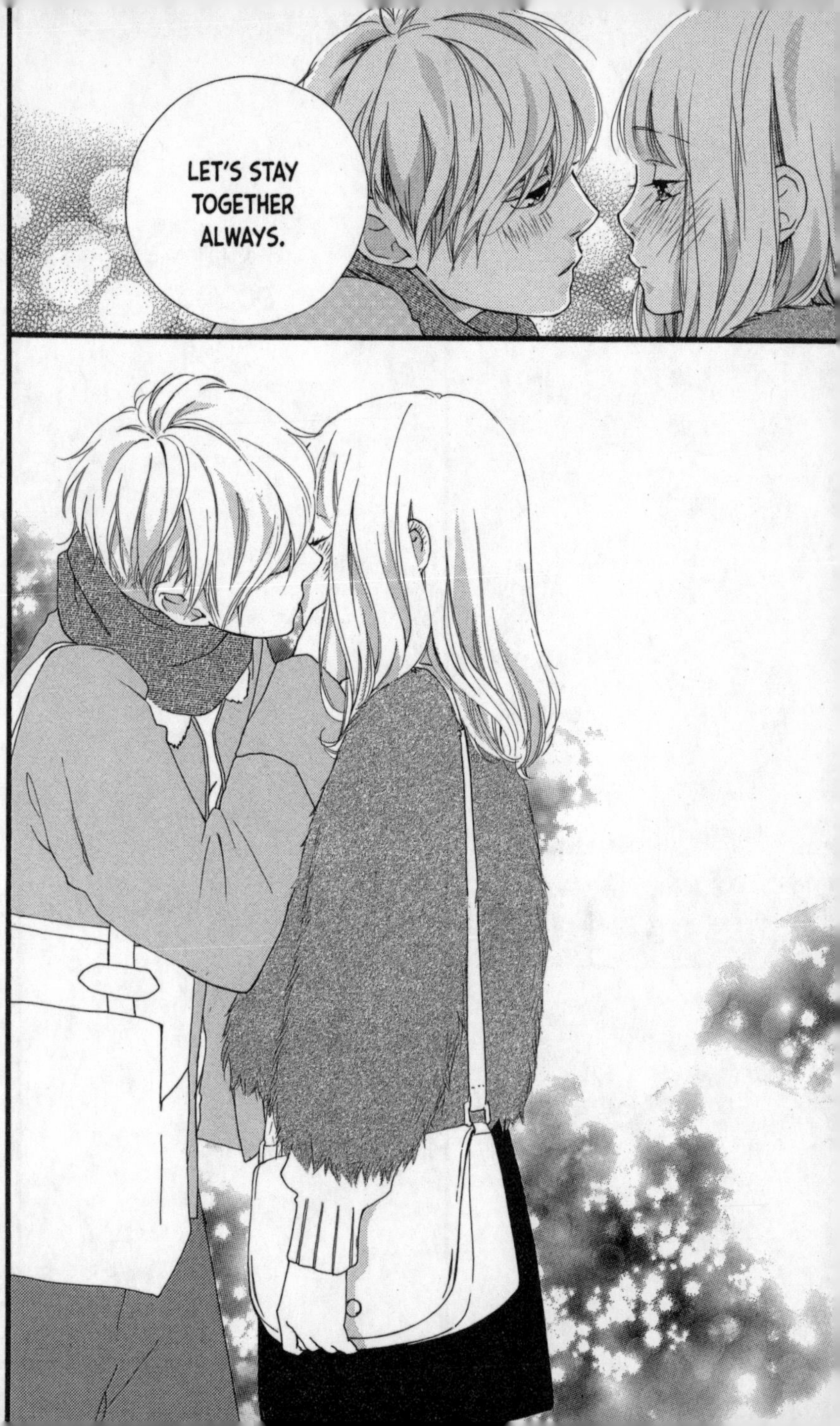
LET'S STAY TOGETHER ALWAYS.

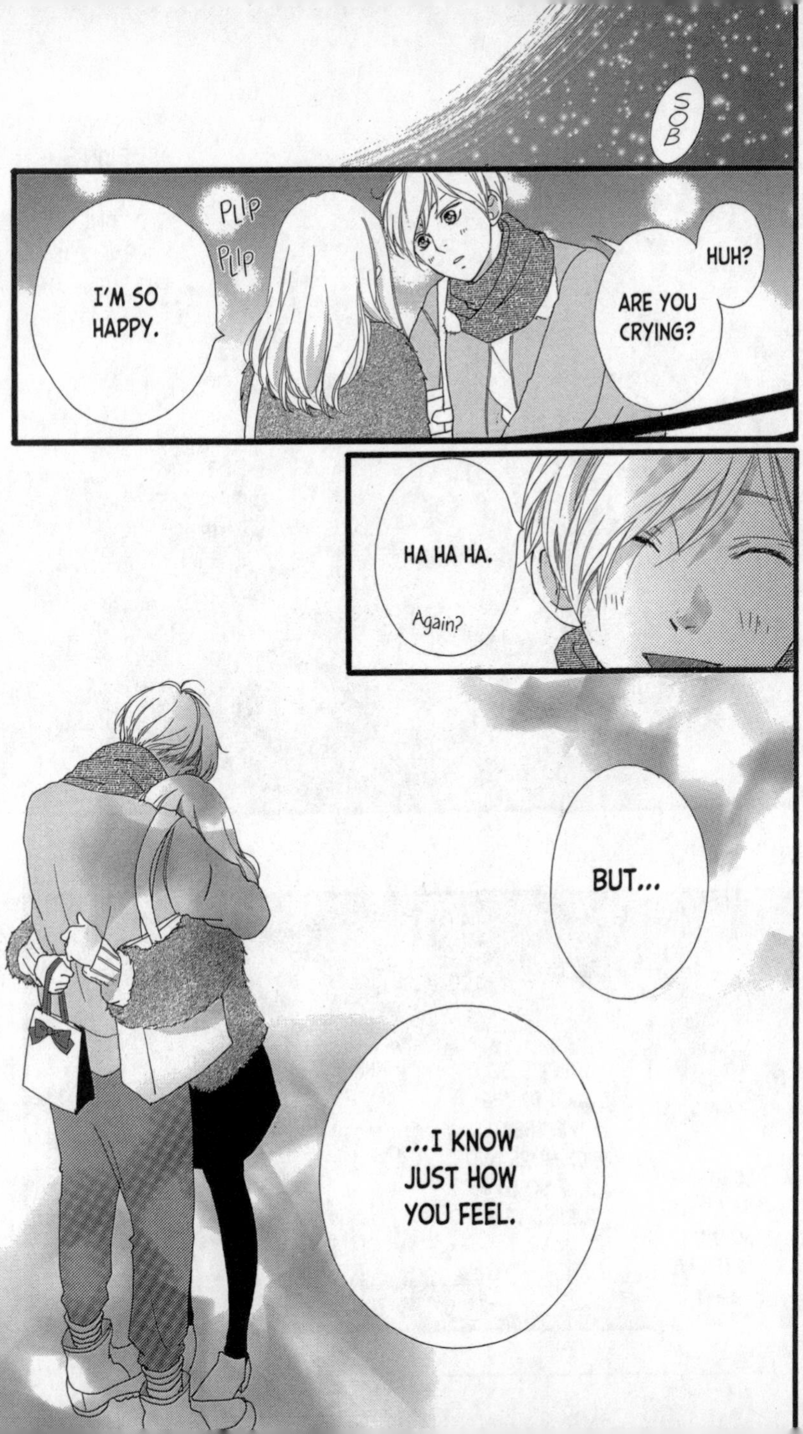
SOB
HUH?
ARE YOU CRYING?
PLIP
PLIP
I'M SO HAPPY.
HA HA HA.
Again?
BUT...
...I KNOW JUST HOW YOU FEEL.

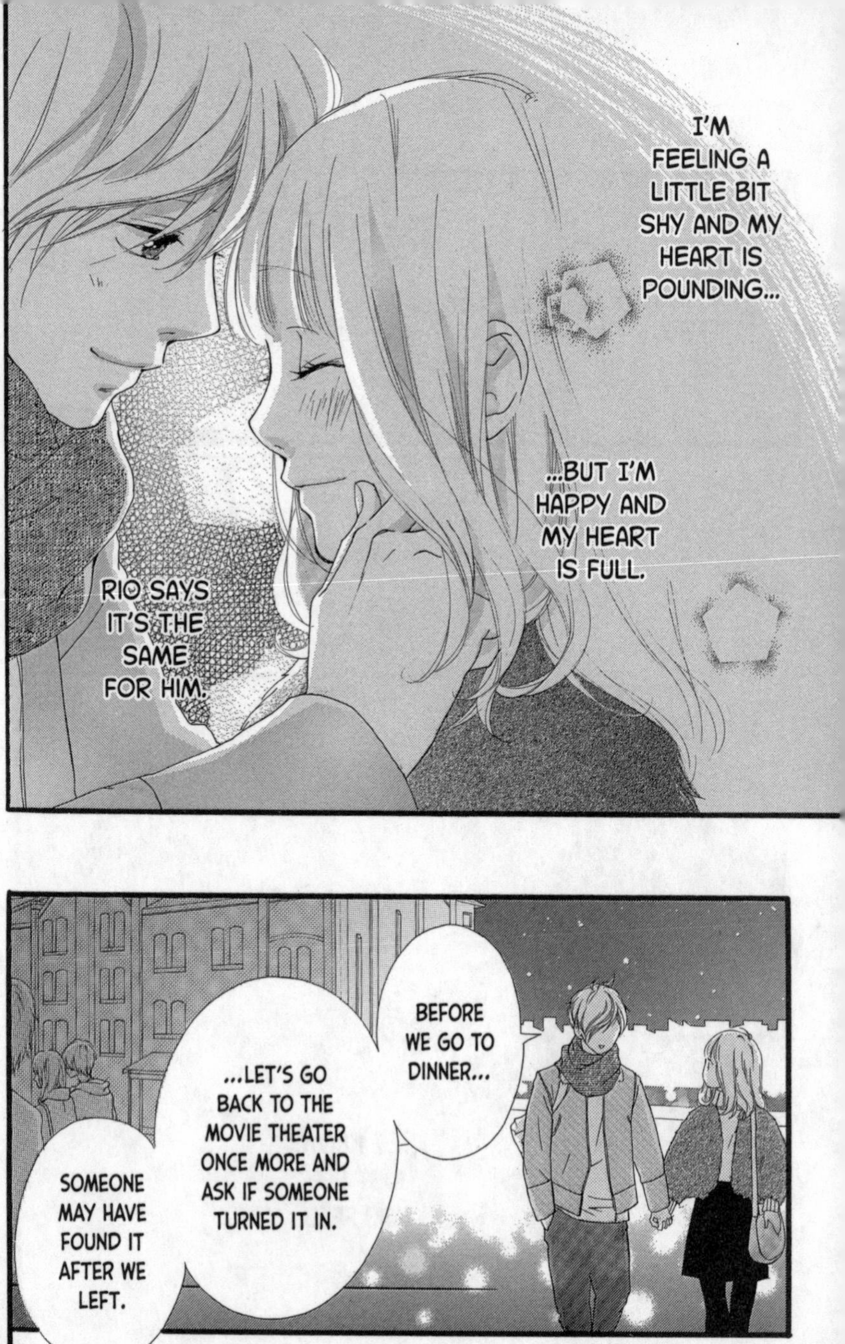
I'M FEELING A LITTLE BIT SHY AND MY HEART IS POUNDING...
...BUT I'M HAPPY AND MY HEART IS FULL.
RIO SAYS IT'S THE SAME FOR HIM.
BEFORE WE GO TO DINNER...
...LET'S GO BACK TO THE MOVIE THEATER ONCE MORE AND ASK IF SOMEONE TURNED IT IN.
SOMEONE MAY HAVE FOUND IT AFTER WE LEFT.

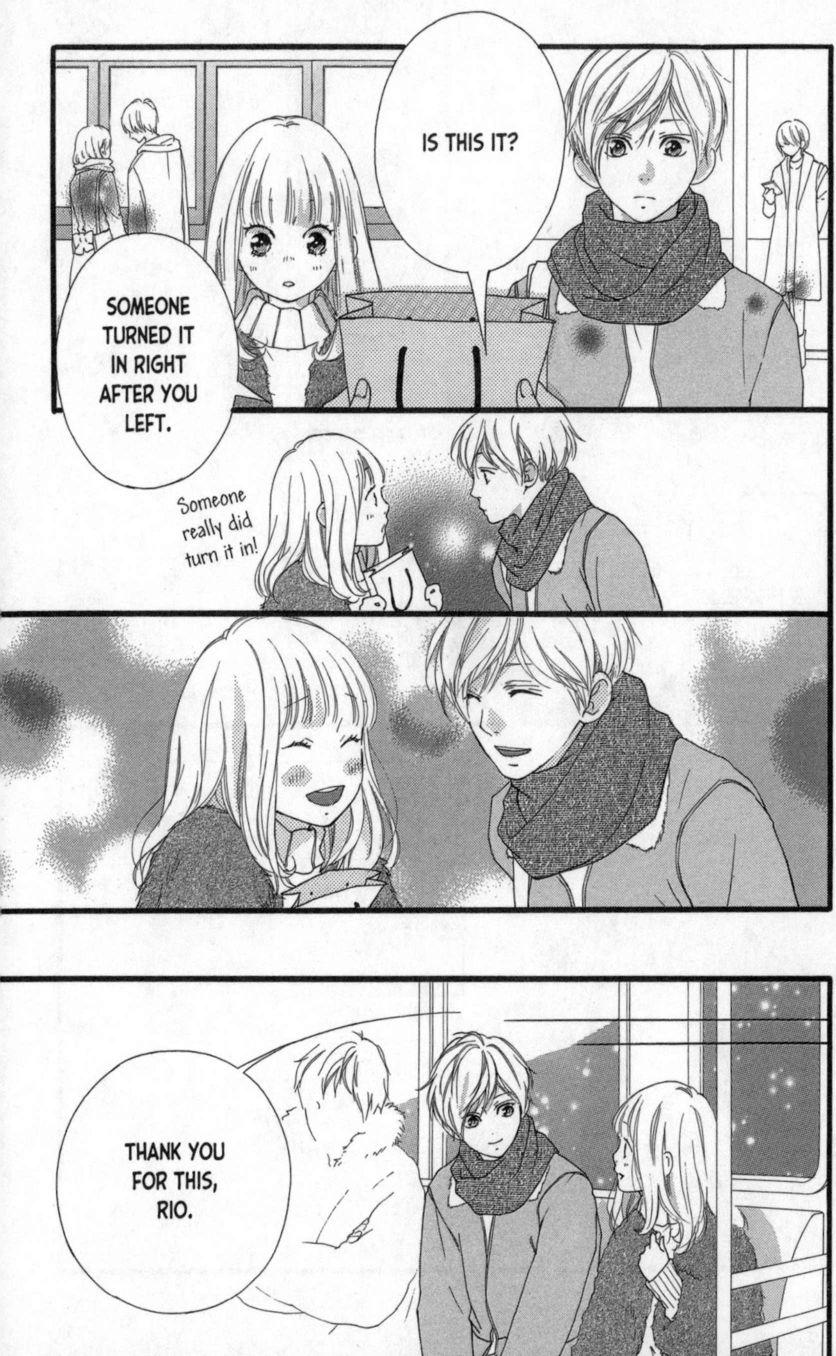
IS THIS IT?
SOMEONE TURNED IT IN RIGHT AFTER YOU LEFT.
Someone really did turn it in!
THANK YOU FOR THIS, RIO.

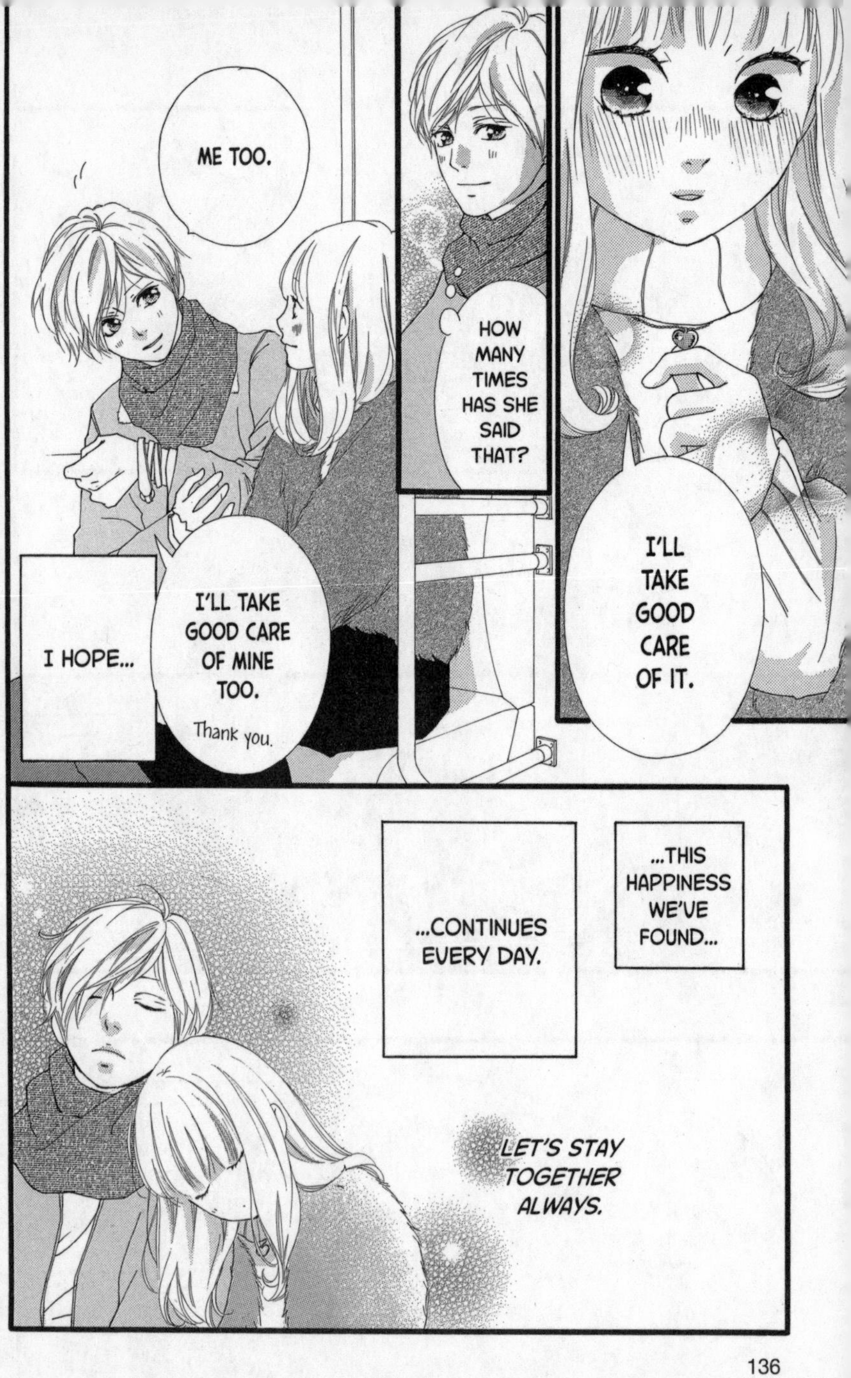
I'LL TAKE GOOD CARE OF IT.
HOW MANY TIMES HAS SHE SAID THAT?
ME TOO.
I'LL TAKE GOOD CARE OF MINE TOO.
Thank you.
I HOPE...
...THIS HAPPINESS WE'VE FOUND...
...CONTINUES EVERY DAY.
LET'S STAY TOGETHER ALWAYS.

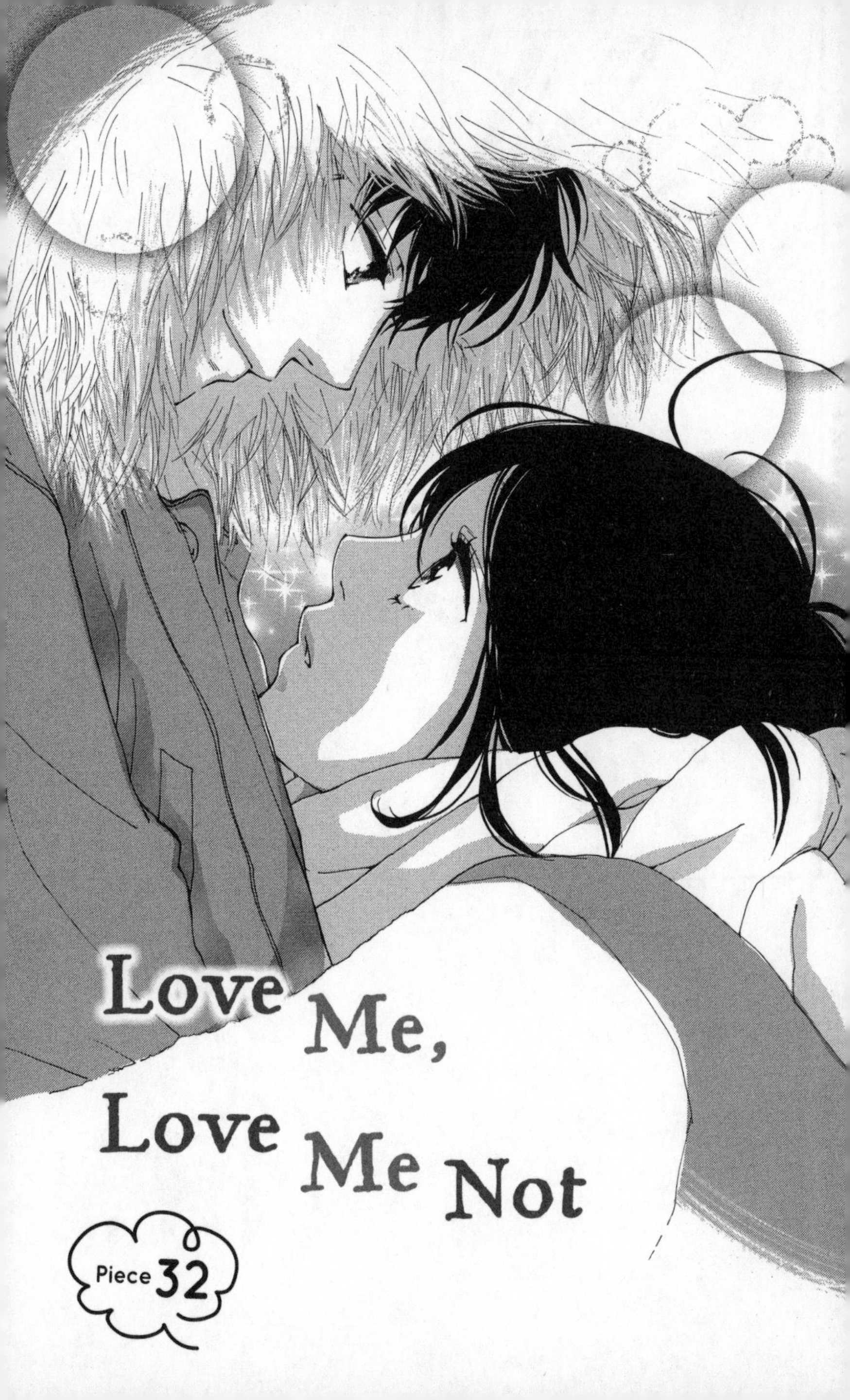
Love Me, Love Me Not
Piece 32

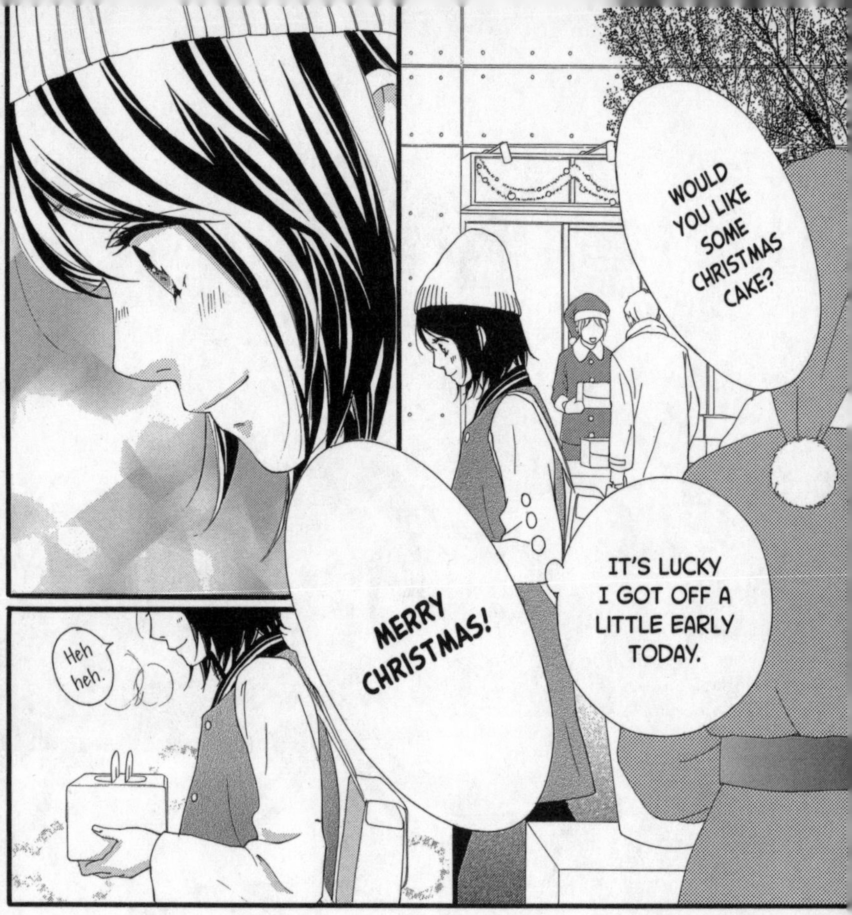
WOULD YOU LIKE SOME CHRISTMAS CAKE?
IT'S LUCKY I GOT OFF A LITTLE EARLY TODAY.
MERRY CHRISTMAS!
Heh heh.

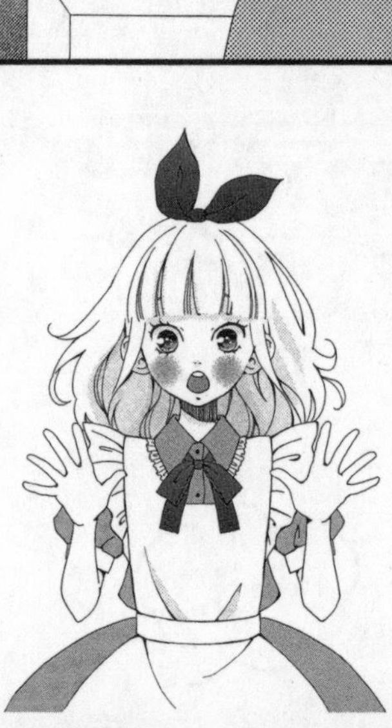

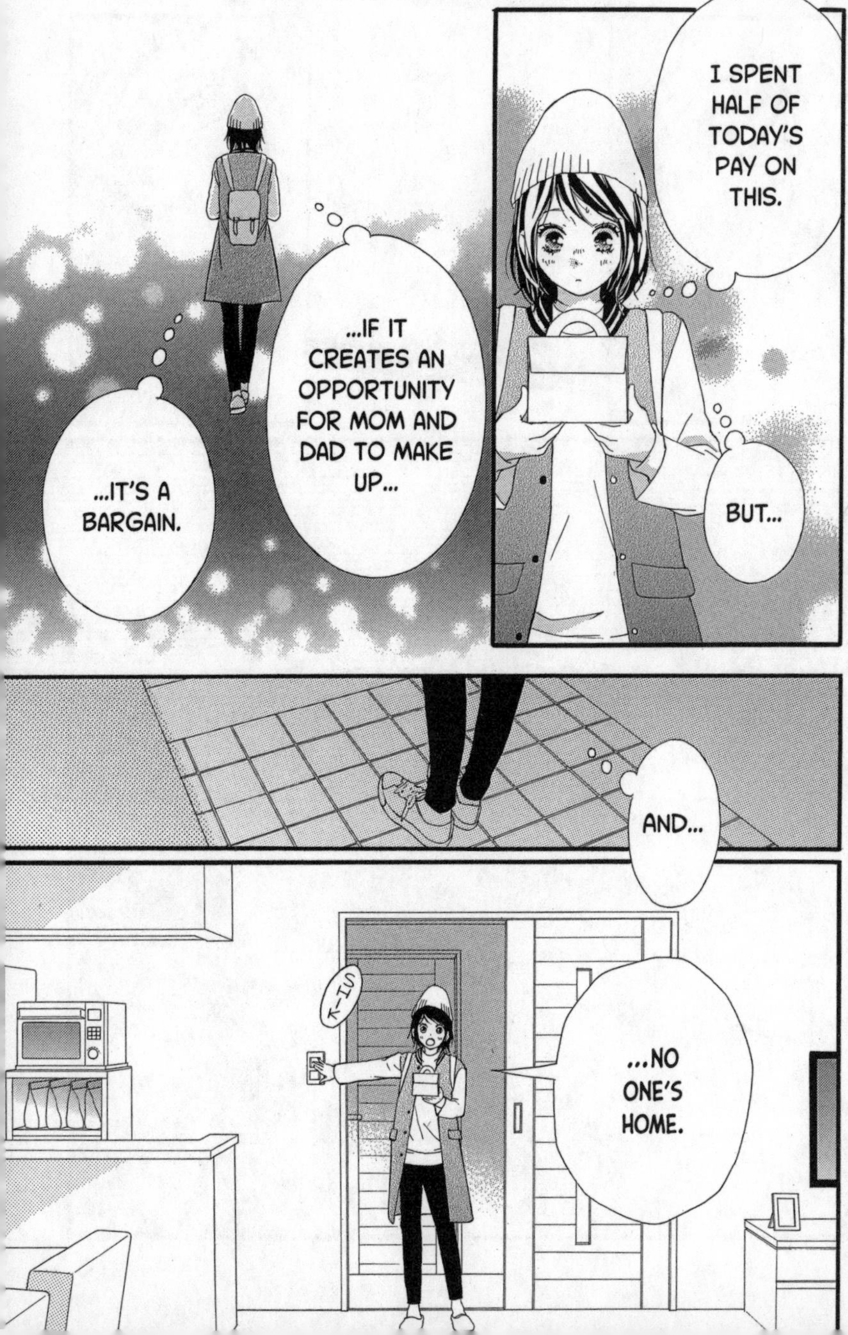
I SPENT HALF OF TODAY'S PAY ON THIS.
BUT...
...IF IT CREATES AN OPPORTUNITY FOR MOM AND DAD TO MAKE UP...
...IT'S A BARGAIN.
AND...
SHK
...NO ONE'S HOME.

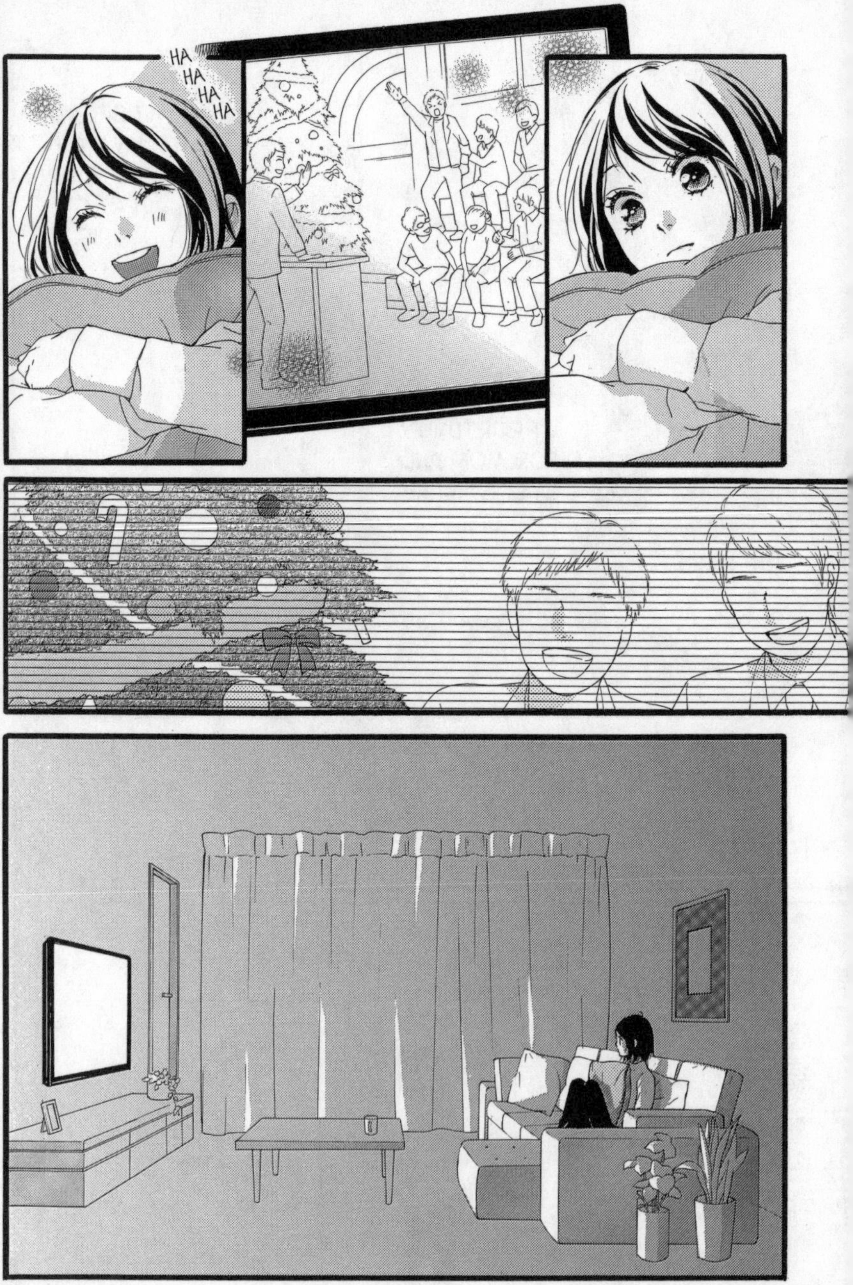
HA
HA
HA
HA

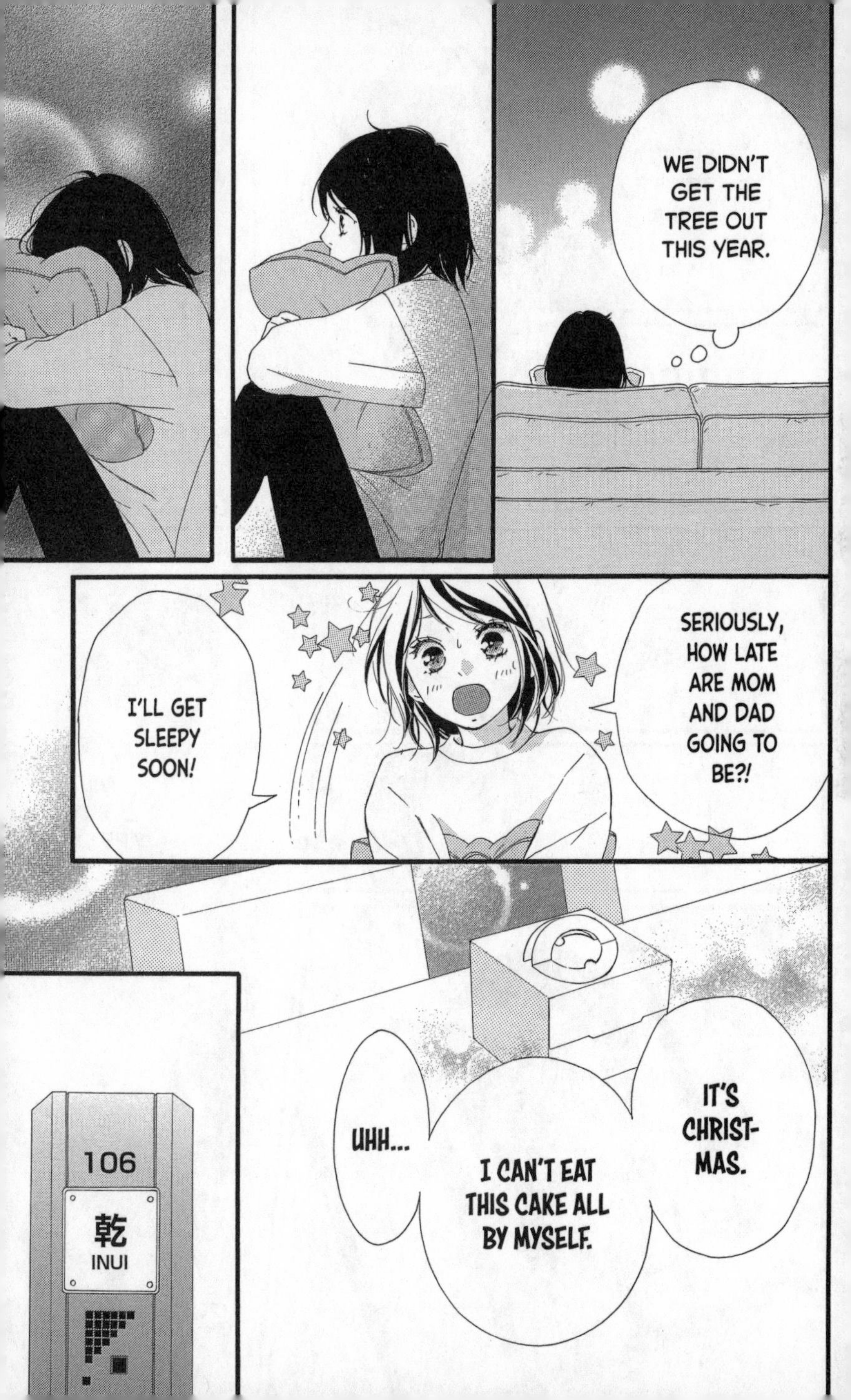

WE DIDN'T GET THE TREE OUT THIS YEAR.
SERIOUSLY, HOW LATE ARE MOM AND DAD GOING TO BE?!
I'LL GET SLEEPY SOON!
IT'S CHRIST-MAS.
I CAN'T EAT THIS CAKE ALL BY MYSELF.
UHH...
106
乾
INUI

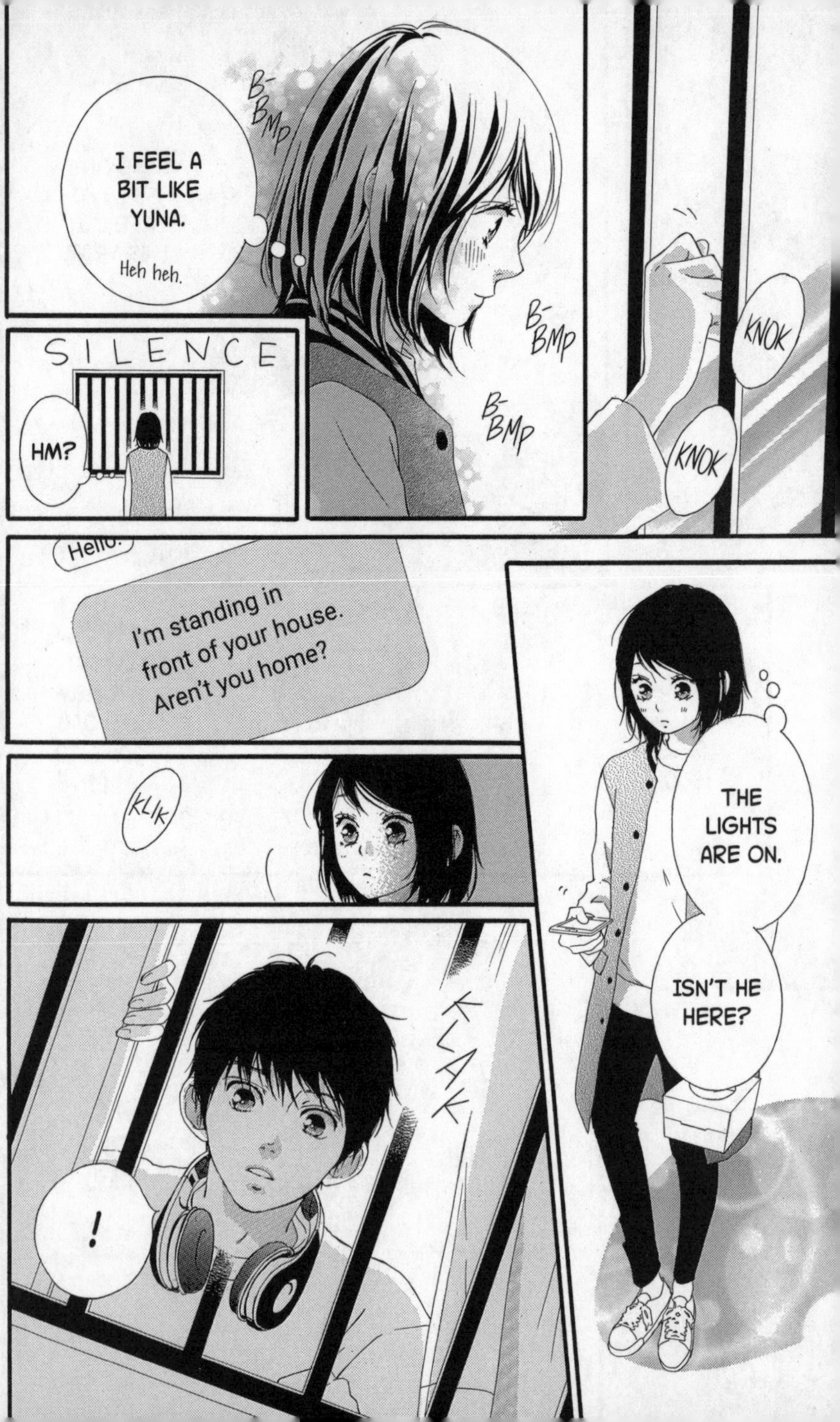
B-BMP
I FEEL A BIT LIKE YUNA.
Heh heh.
B-BMP
B-BMP
KNOK
KNOK
SILENCE
HM?
THE LIGHTS ARE ON.
ISN'T HE HERE?
Hello.
I'm standing in front of your house. Aren't you home?
KLIK
KLAK
!

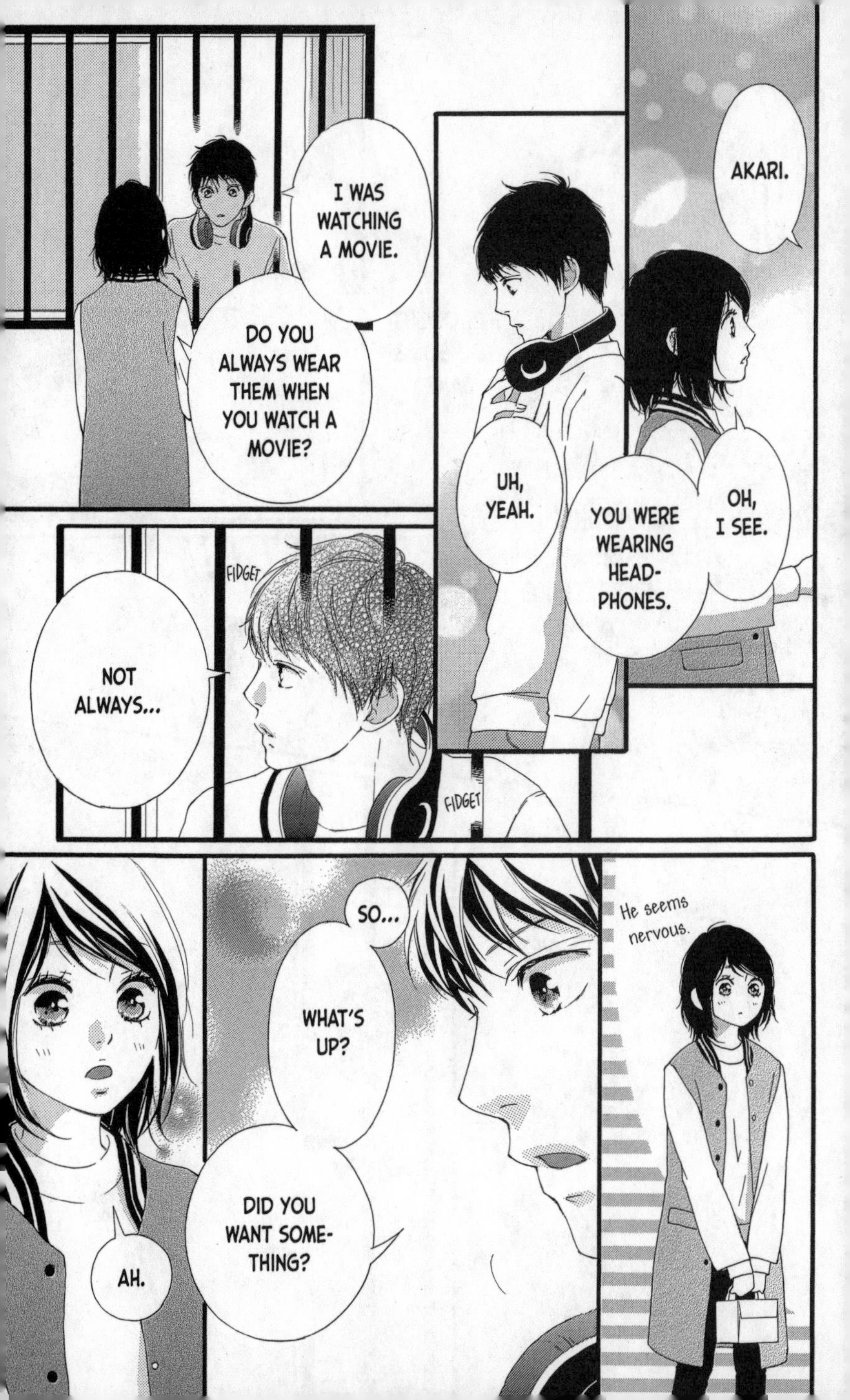
AKARI.
OH, I SEE.
YOU WERE WEARING HEAD-PHONES.
UH, YEAH.
I WAS WATCHING A MOVIE.
DO YOU ALWAYS WEAR THEM WHEN YOU WATCH A MOVIE?
FIDGET
FIDGET
NOT ALWAYS...
He seems nervous.
SO...
WHAT'S UP?
DID YOU WANT SOME-THING?
AH.

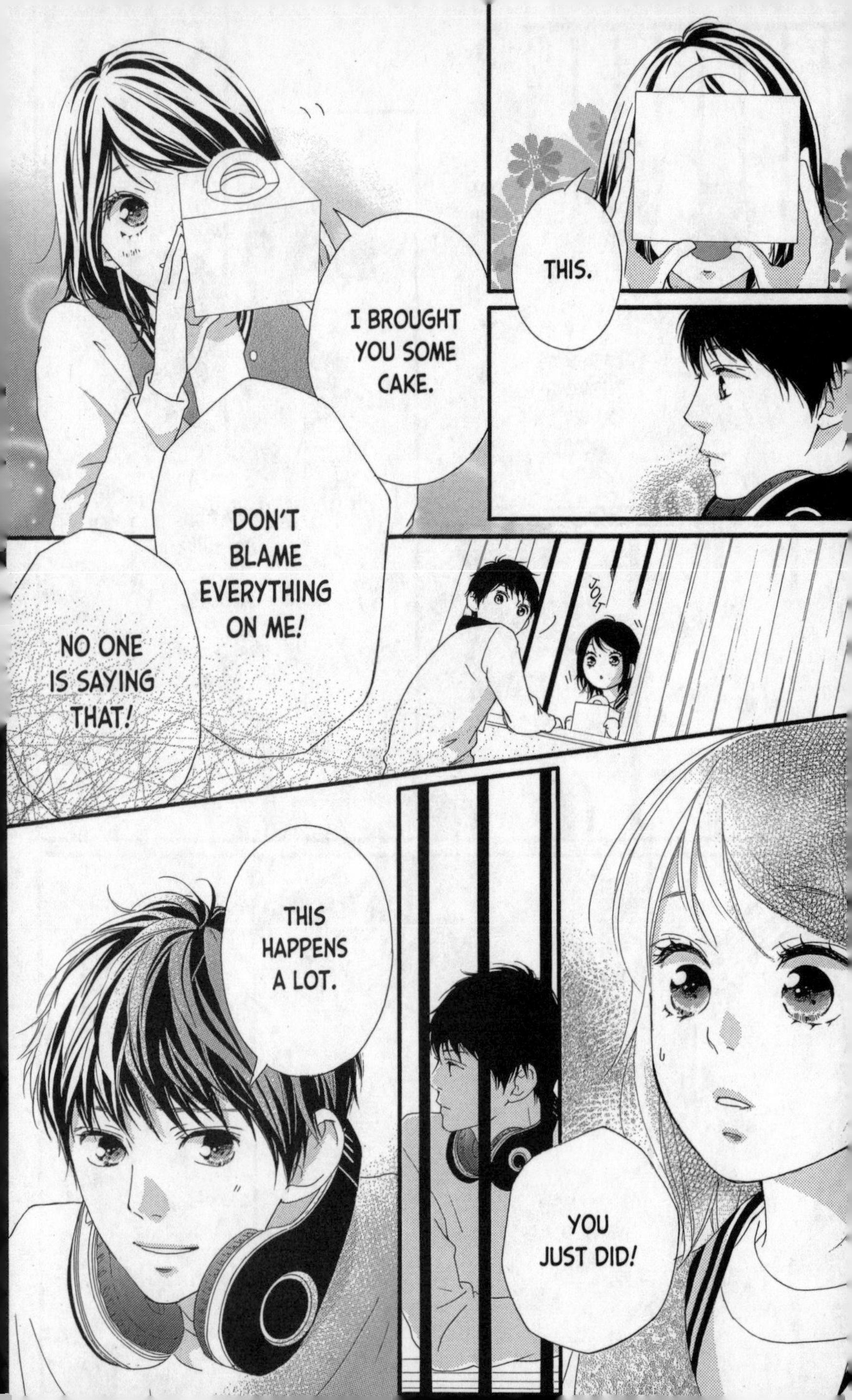
THIS.
I BROUGHT YOU SOME CAKE.
JOLT
DON'T BLAME EVERYTHING ON ME!
NO ONE IS SAYING THAT!
YOU JUST DID!
THIS HAPPENS A LOT.

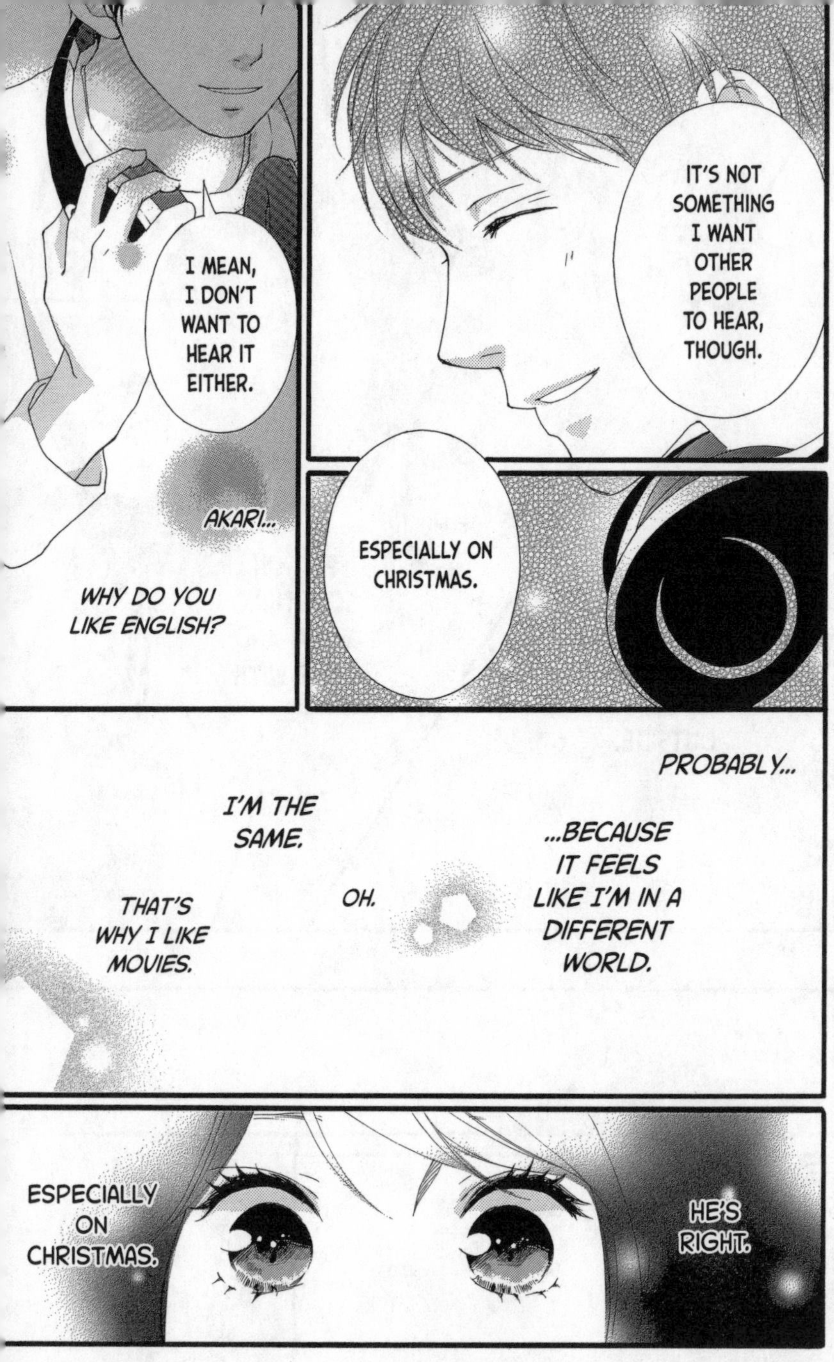
IT'S NOT SOMETHING I WANT OTHER PEOPLE TO HEAR, THOUGH.
ESPECIALLY ON CHRISTMAS.
I MEAN, I DON'T WANT TO HEAR IT EITHER.
AKARI...
WHY DO YOU LIKE ENGLISH?
PROBABLY...
...BECAUSE IT FEELS LIKE I'M IN A DIFFERENT WORLD.
OH.
I'M THE SAME.
THAT'S WHY I LIKE MOVIES.
HE'S RIGHT.
ESPECIALLY ON CHRISTMAS.

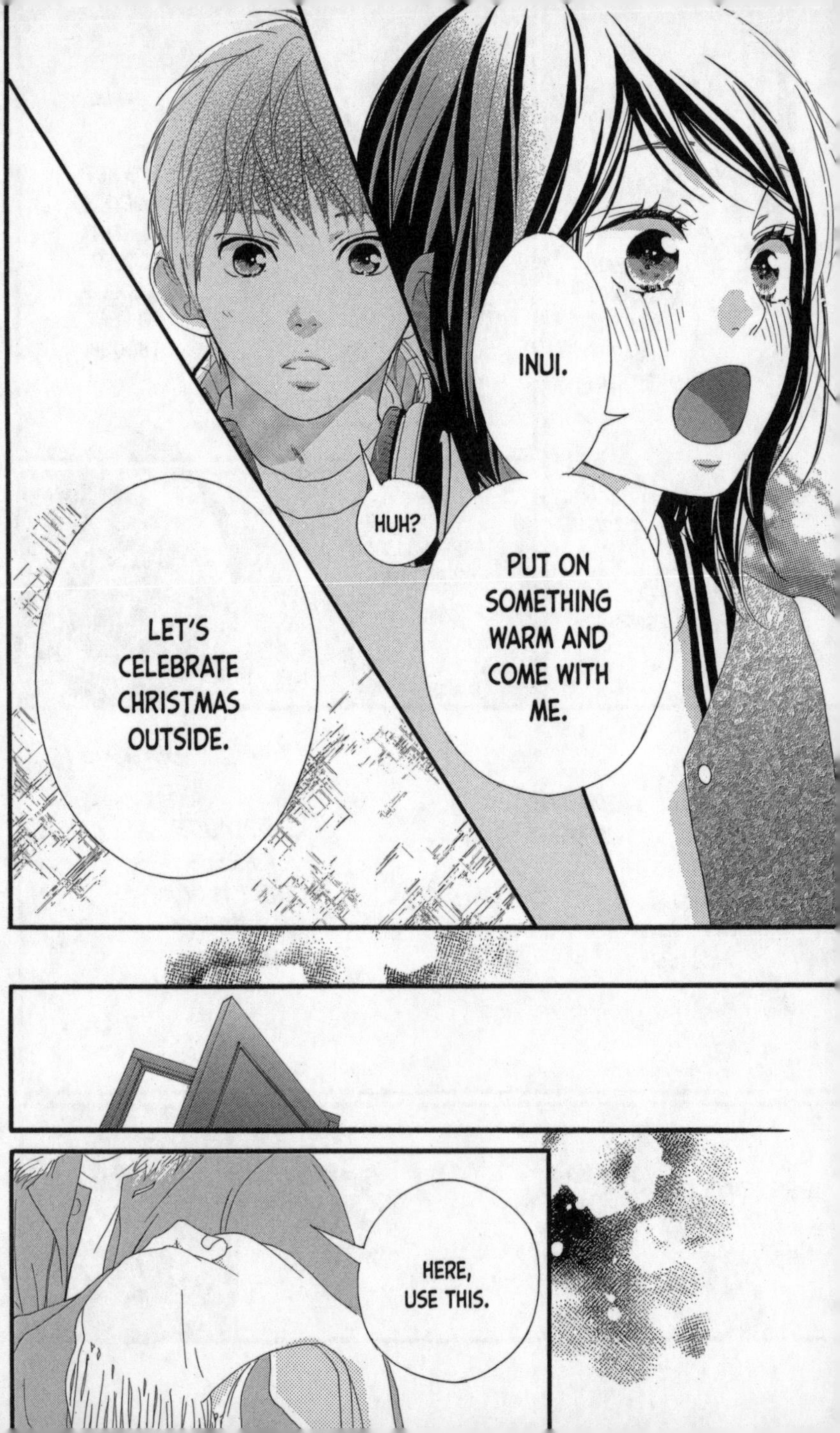
INUI.
PUT ON SOMETHING WARM AND COME WITH ME.
HUH?
LET'S CELEBRATE CHRISTMAS OUTSIDE.
HERE, USE THIS.

I was awarded the 63rd Shogakukan Manga Award (shojo manga category). Thank you so much for your many congratulatory messages. My assistants threw me a surprise party! First off, when I opened my front door, one assistant was there wearing a mask of Taemin (handmade by blowing up a photo and pasting it on card-board), whom I love, carrying a huge bouquet with "Congratulations lo" on it. Another assistant (laughing hysterically) filmed the whole thing while another narrated what was happening. And me? I was so happy, but I was caught between feelings of being moved, surprised, and shocked, so I wasn't able to react the way I wanted. I still regret that. They got me a present, and I thought, "When did you do all this?" I was so blown away. Thank you, everyone! I love you.

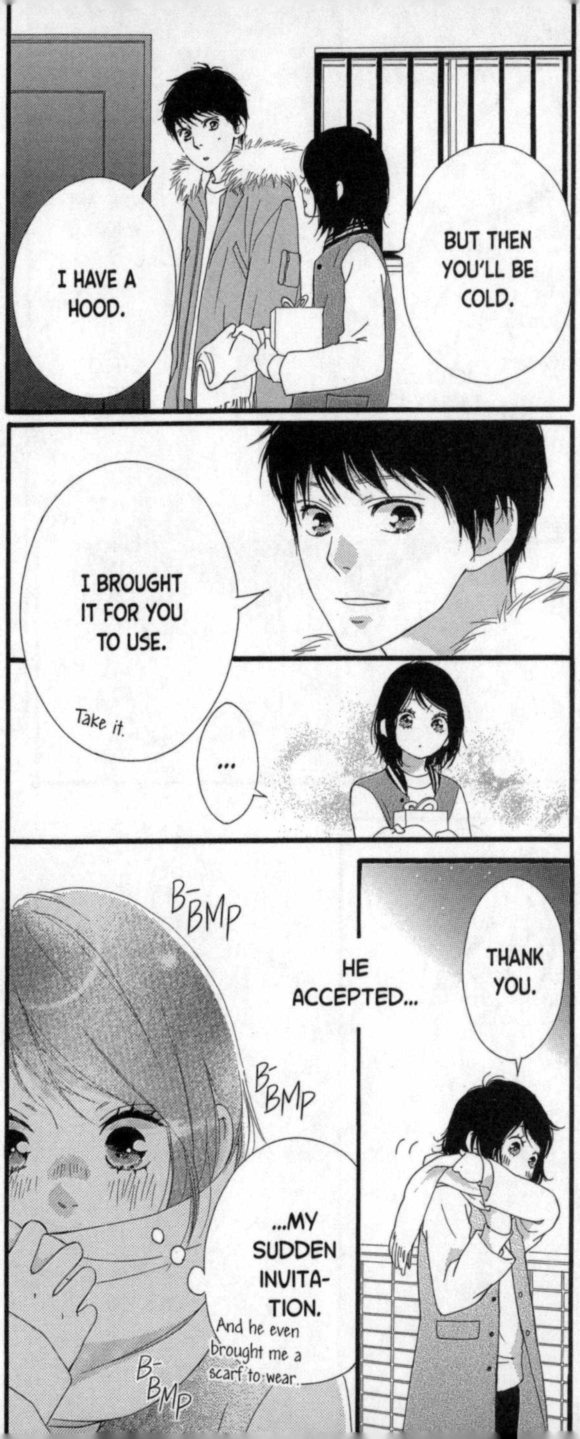
BUT THEN YOU'LL BE COLD.
I HAVE A HOOD.
I BROUGHT IT FOR YOU TO USE.
Take it.
...
THANK YOU.
HE ACCEPTED...
B-BMP
B-BMP
...MY SUDDEN INVITA-TION.
And he even brought me a scarf to wear.
B-BMP

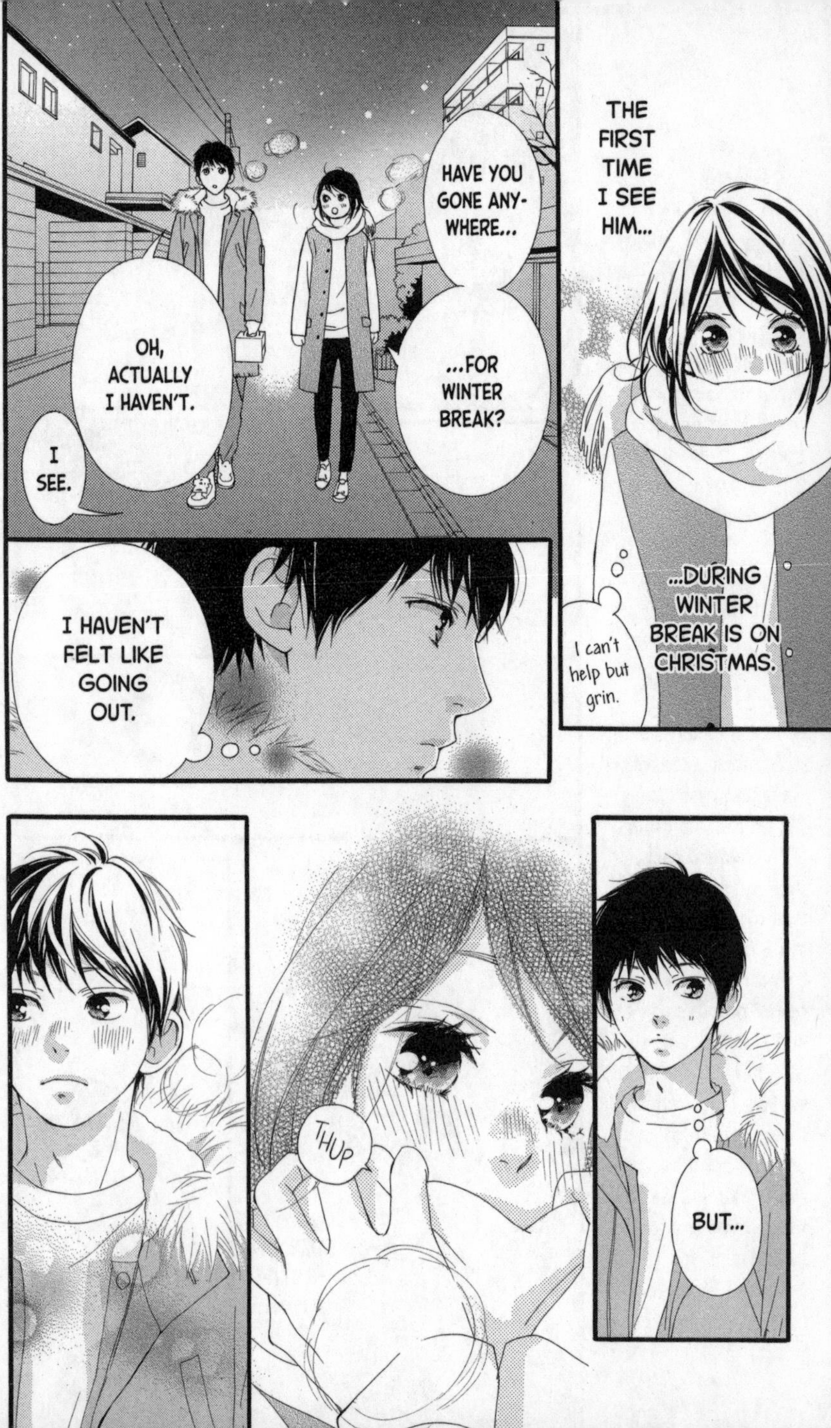
THE FIRST TIME I SEE HIM...
...DURING WINTER BREAK IS ON CHRISTMAS.
I can't help but grin.
HAVE YOU GONE ANYWHERE...
...FOR WINTER BREAK?
OH, ACTUALLY I HAVEN'T.
I SEE.
I HAVEN'T FELT LIKE GOING OUT.
BUT...
THUP

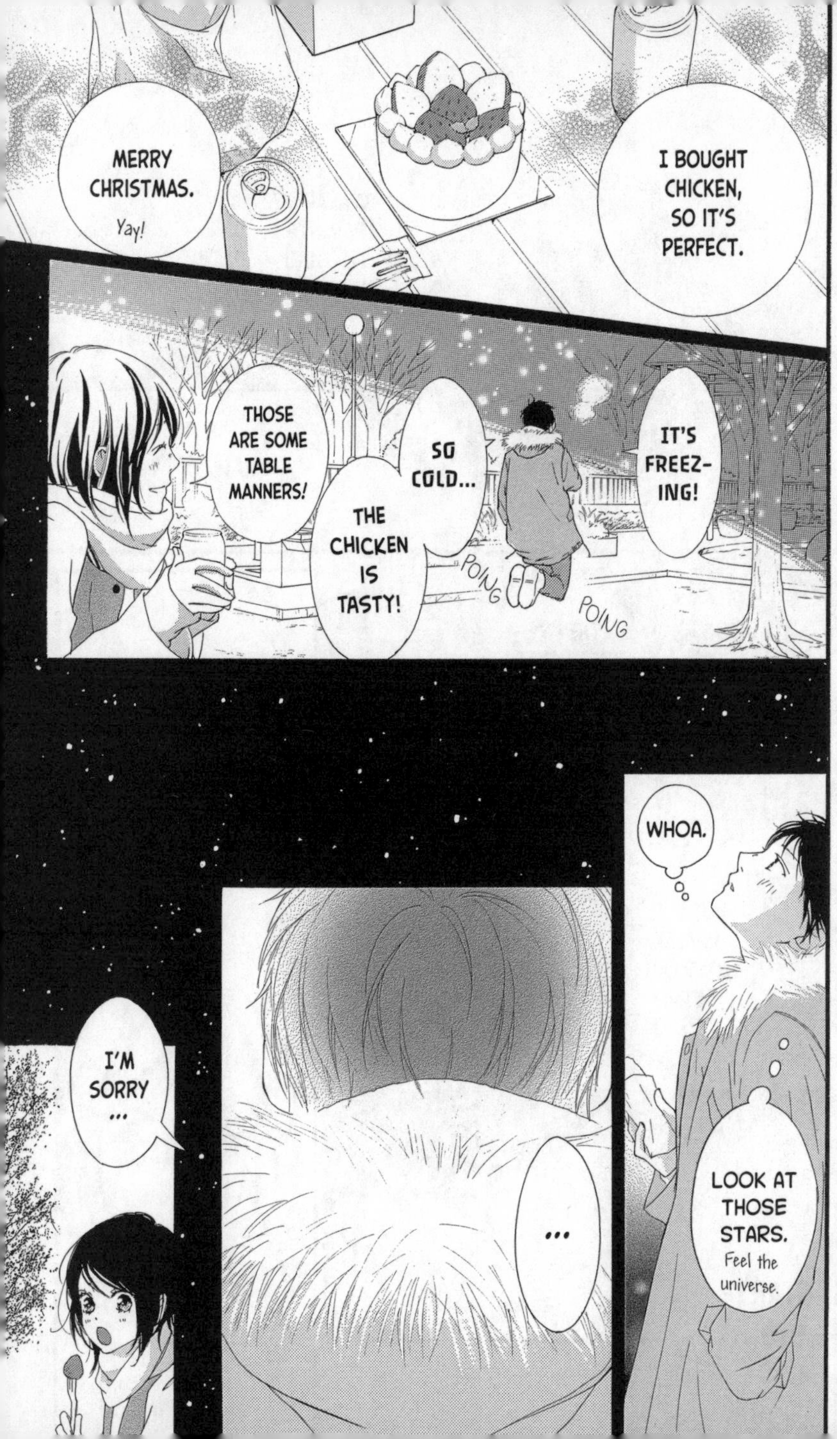
I BOUGHT CHICKEN, SO IT'S PERFECT.
MERRY CHRISTMAS.
Yay!
IT'S FREEZ-ING!
SO COLD...
POING
POING
THE CHICKEN IS TASTY!
THOSE ARE SOME TABLE MANNERS!
WHOA.
LOOK AT THOSE STARS.
Feel the universe.
...
I'M SORRY ...

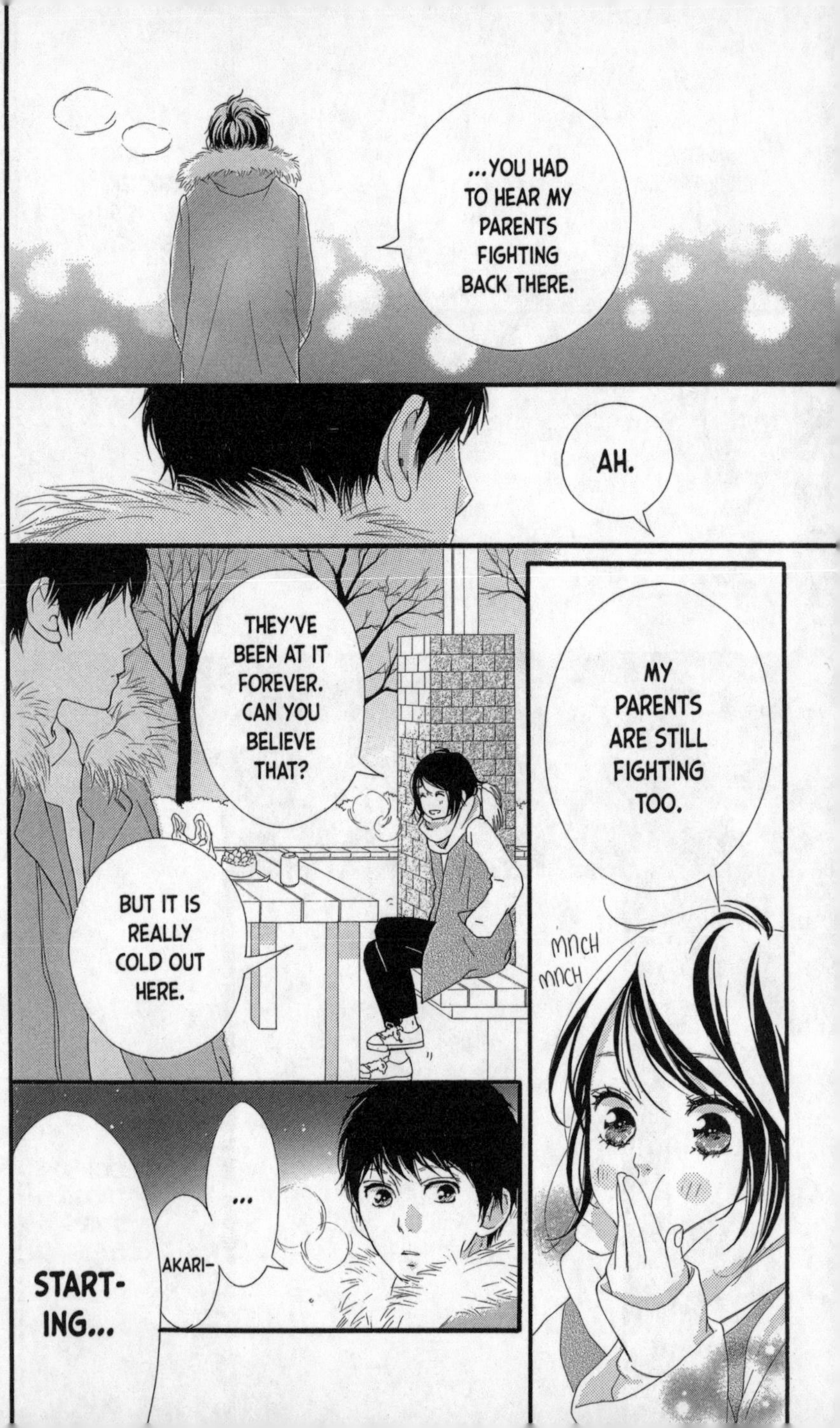
...YOU HAD TO HEAR MY PARENTS FIGHTING BACK THERE.
AH.
MY PARENTS ARE STILL FIGHTING TOO.
MNCH MNCH
THEY'VE BEEN AT IT FOREVER. CAN YOU BELIEVE THAT?
BUT IT IS REALLY COLD OUT HERE.
...
AKARI—
START-ING...

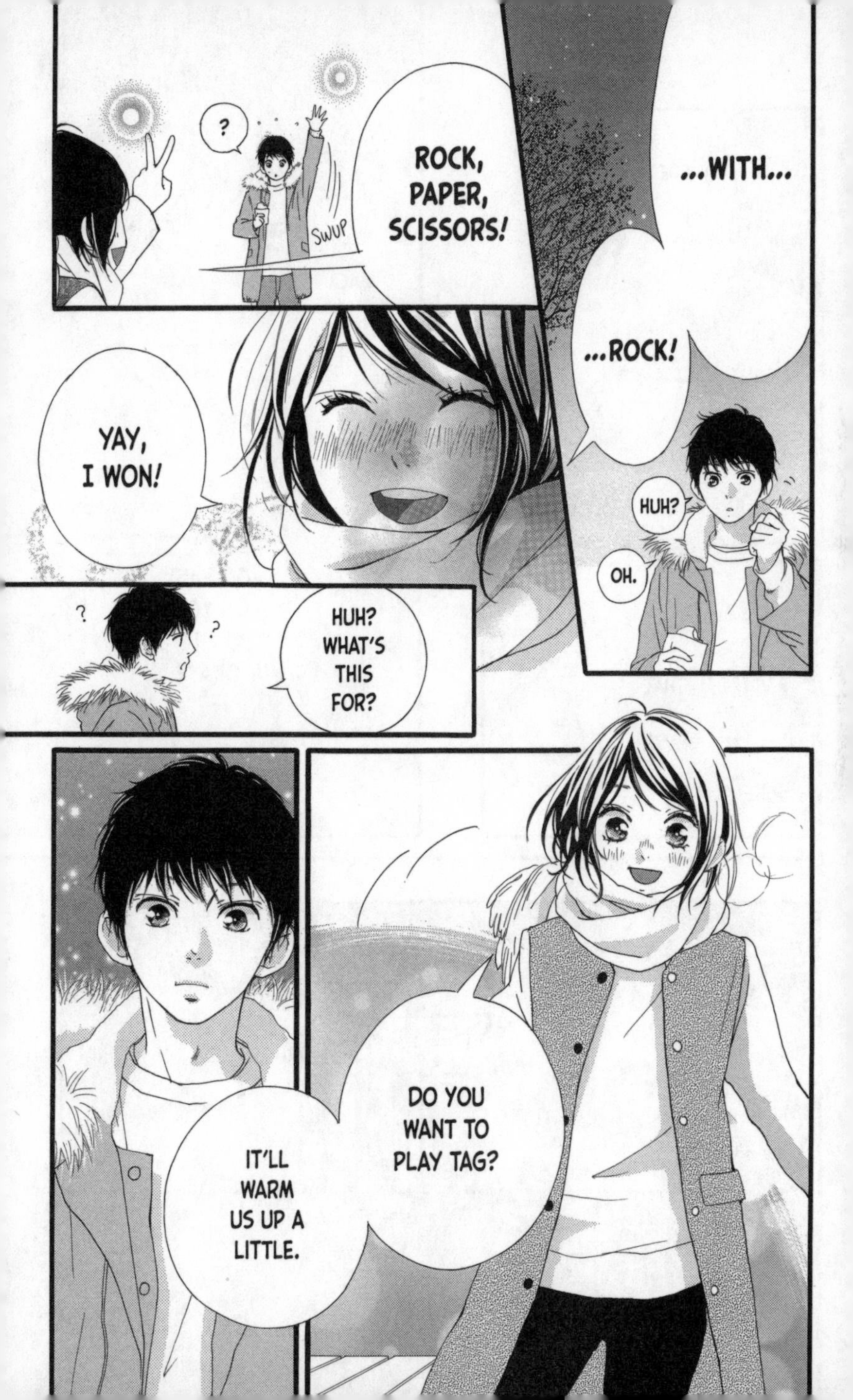
...WITH...
...ROCK!
HUH?
OH.
ROCK, PAPER, SCISSORS!
?
SWUP
YAY, I WON!
HUH? WHAT'S THIS FOR?
?
?
DO YOU WANT TO PLAY TAG?
IT'LL WARM US UP A LITTLE.

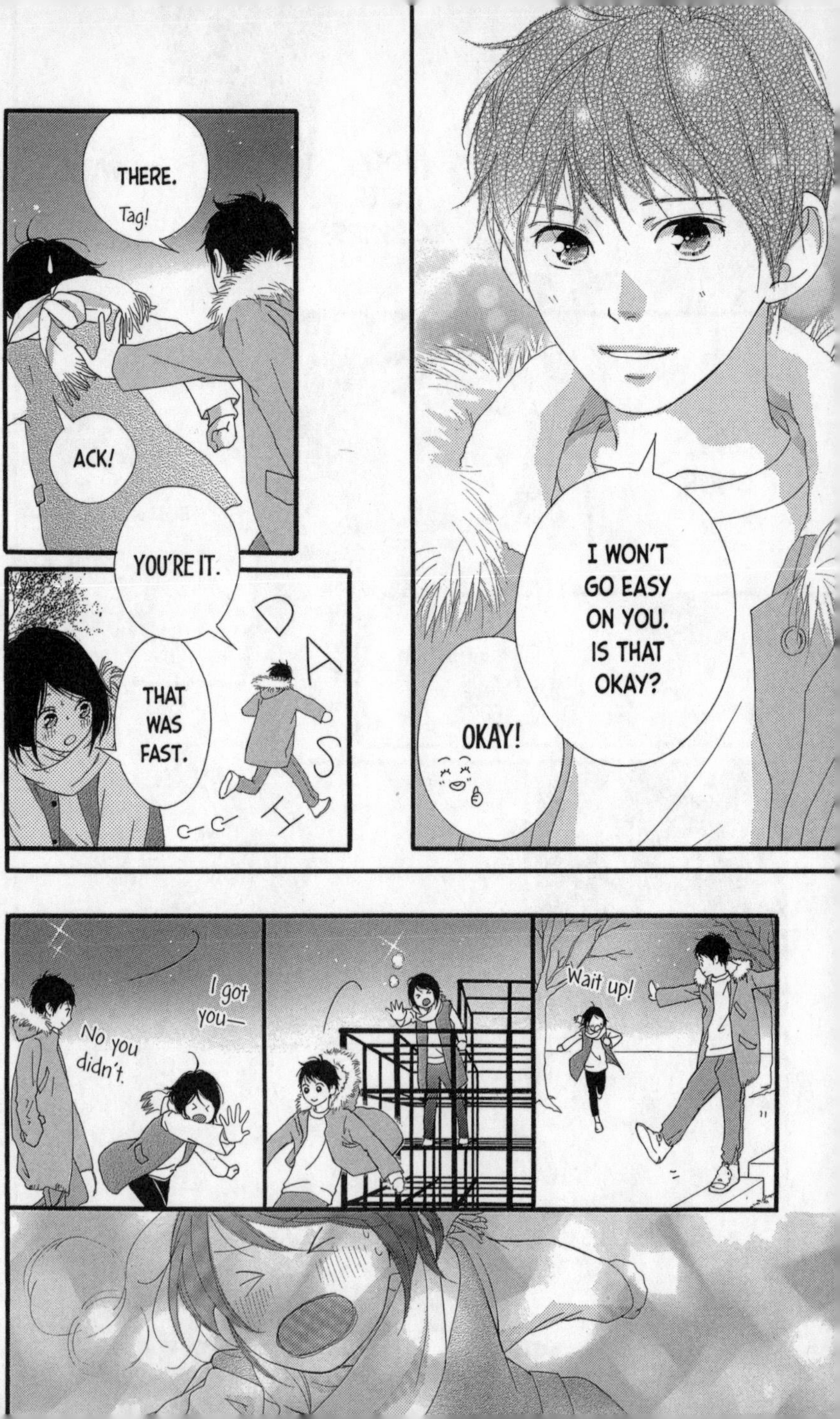
I WON'T GO EASY ON YOU. IS THAT OKAY?
OKAY!
THERE.
Tag!
ACK!
YOU'RE IT.
THAT WAS FAST.
DASH
Wait up!
I got you—
No you didn't.

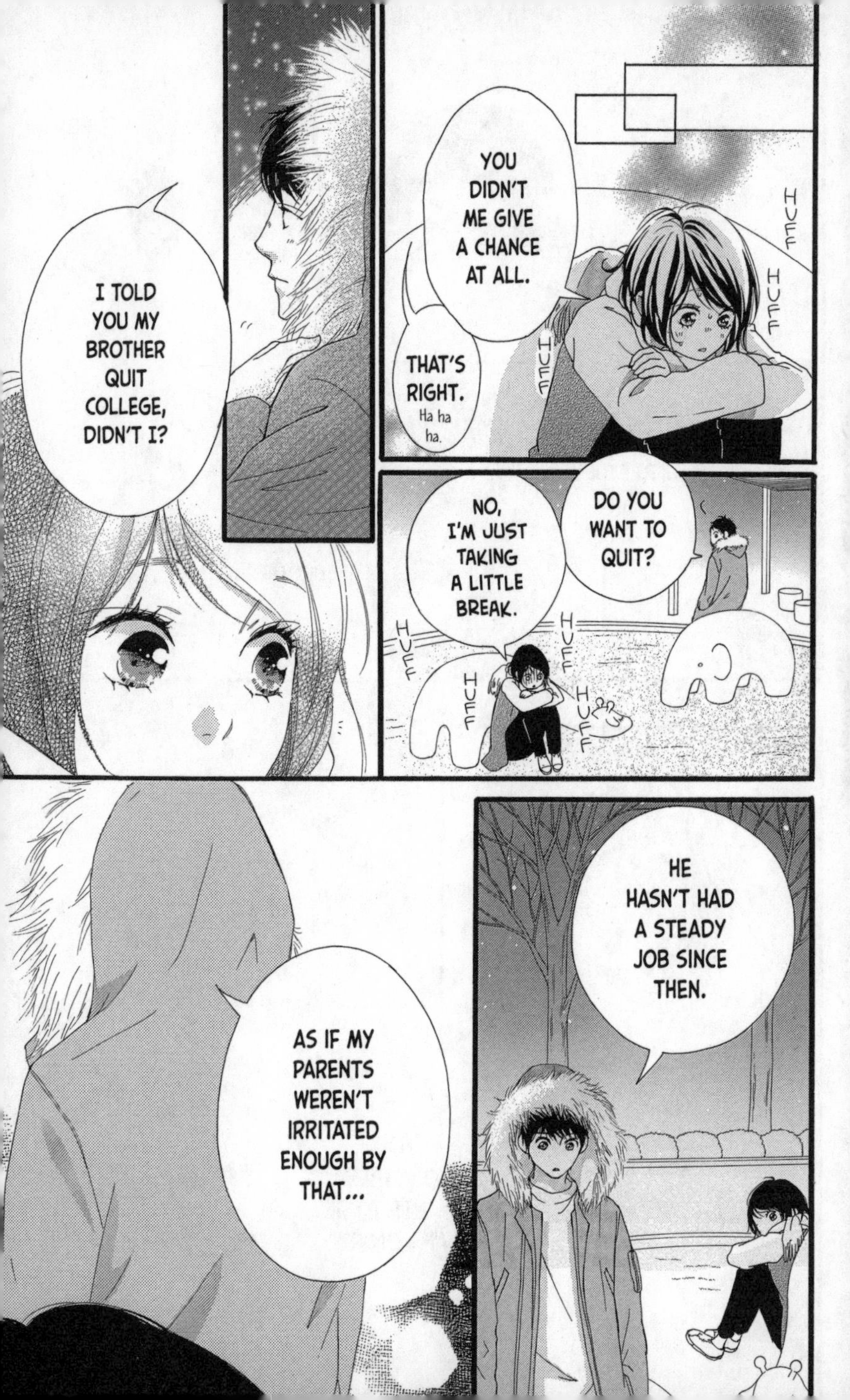
YOU DIDN'T ME GIVE A CHANCE AT ALL.
HUFF
HUFF
HUFF
THAT'S RIGHT.
Ha ha ha.
DO YOU WANT TO QUIT?
NO, I'M JUST TAKING A LITTLE BREAK.
HUFF
HUFF
HUFF
HUFF
HUFF
I TOLD YOU MY BROTHER QUIT COLLEGE, DIDN'T I?
HE HASN'T HAD A STEADY JOB SINCE THEN.
AS IF MY PARENTS WEREN'T IRRITATED ENOUGH BY THAT...

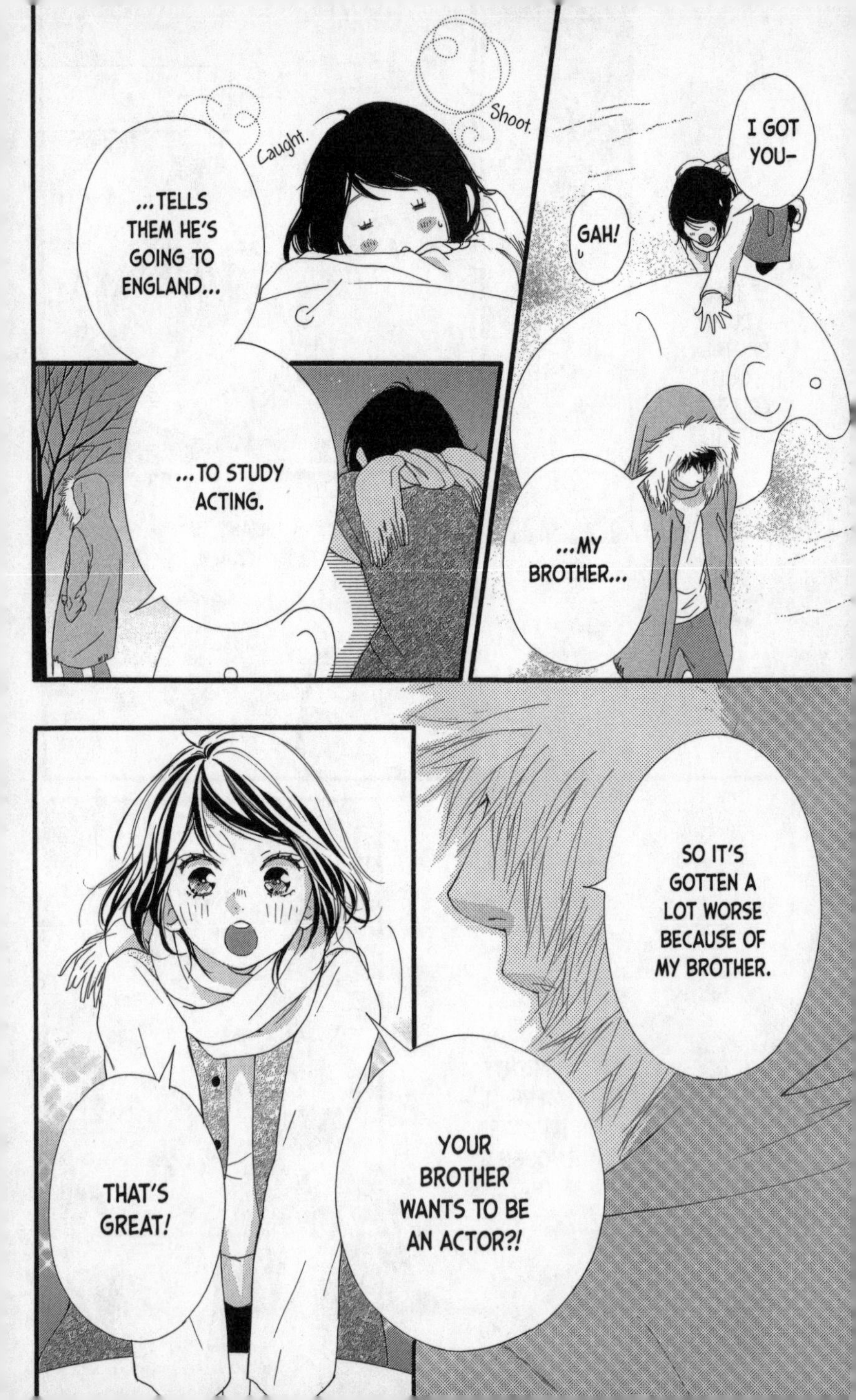
I GOT YOU–
GAH!
...MY BROTHER...
Shoot.
Caught.
...TELLS THEM HE'S GOING TO ENGLAND...
...TO STUDY ACTING.
SO IT'S GOTTEN A LOT WORSE BECAUSE OF MY BROTHER.
YOUR BROTHER WANTS TO BE AN ACTOR?!
THAT'S GREAT!

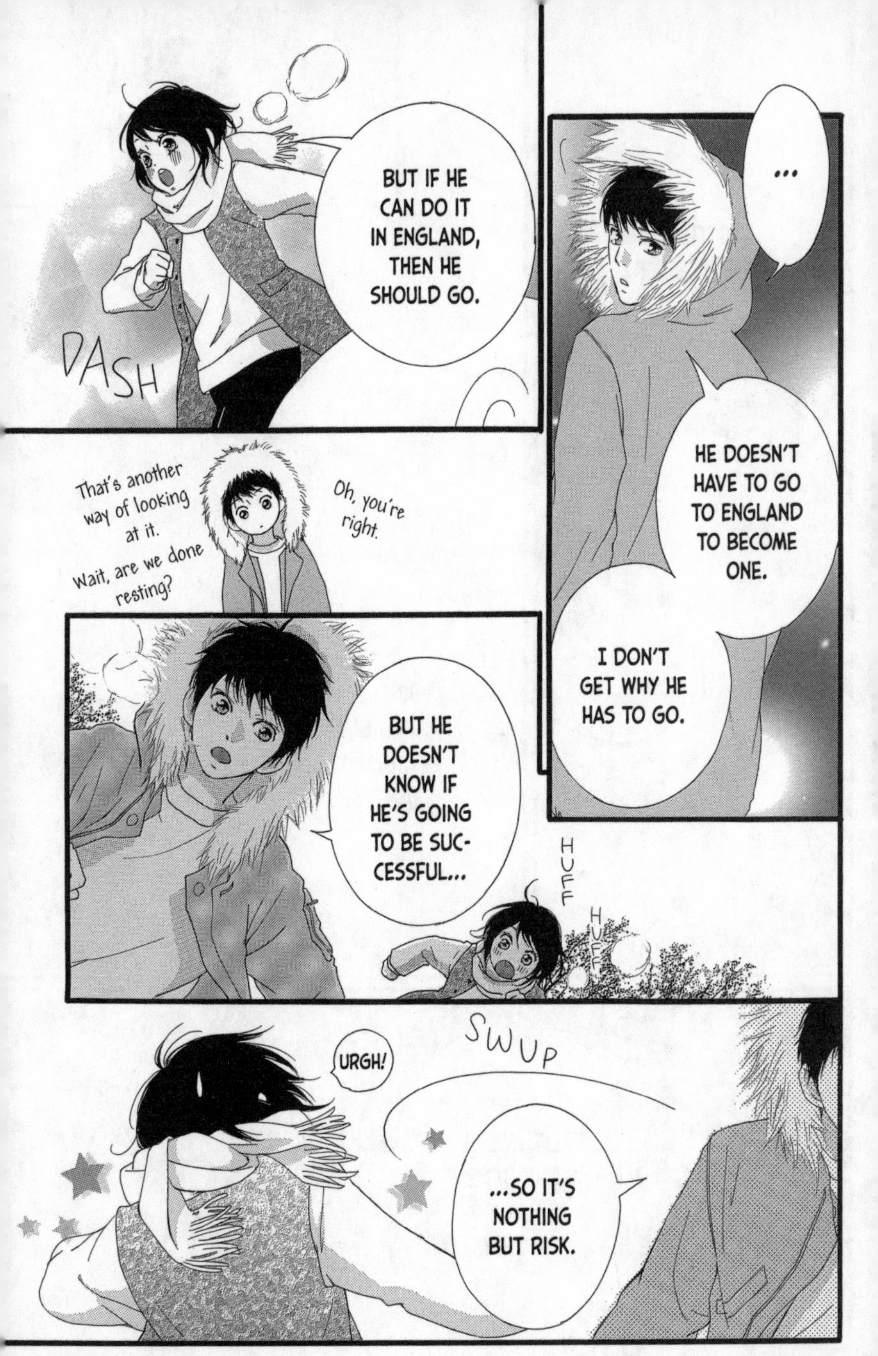
...
HE DOESN'T HAVE TO GO TO ENGLAND TO BECOME ONE.
I DON'T GET WHY HE HAS TO GO.
BUT IF HE CAN DO IT IN ENGLAND, THEN HE SHOULD GO.
DASH
Oh, you're right.
That's another way of looking at it.
Wait, are we done resting?
HUFF HUFF
BUT HE DOESN'T KNOW IF HE'S GOING TO BE SUC-CESSFUL...
SWUP
...SO IT'S NOTHING BUT RISK.
URGH!

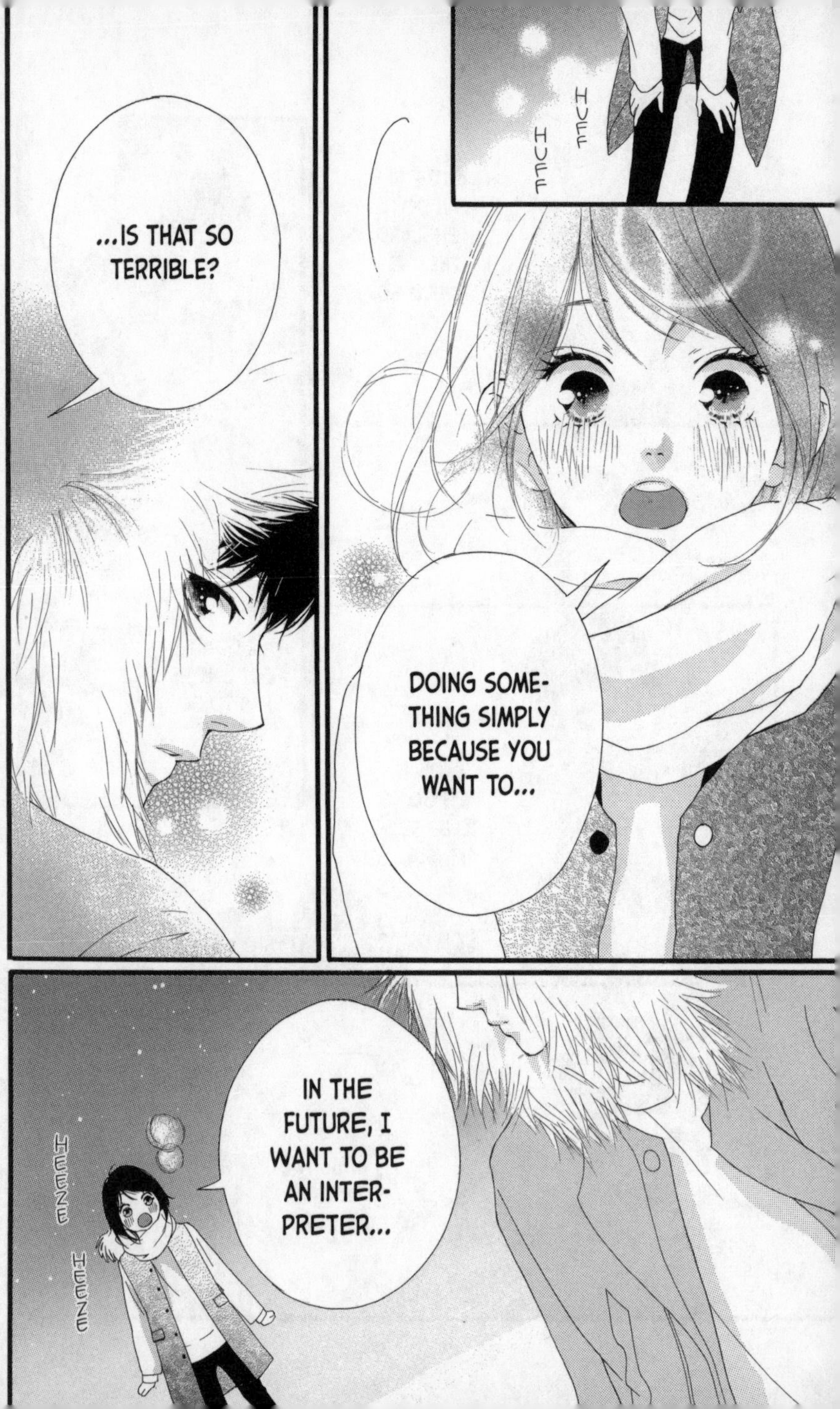
HUFF
HUFF
DOING SOME-THING SIMPLY BECAUSE YOU WANT TO...
...IS THAT SO TERRIBLE?
IN THE FUTURE, I WANT TO BE AN INTER-PRETER...

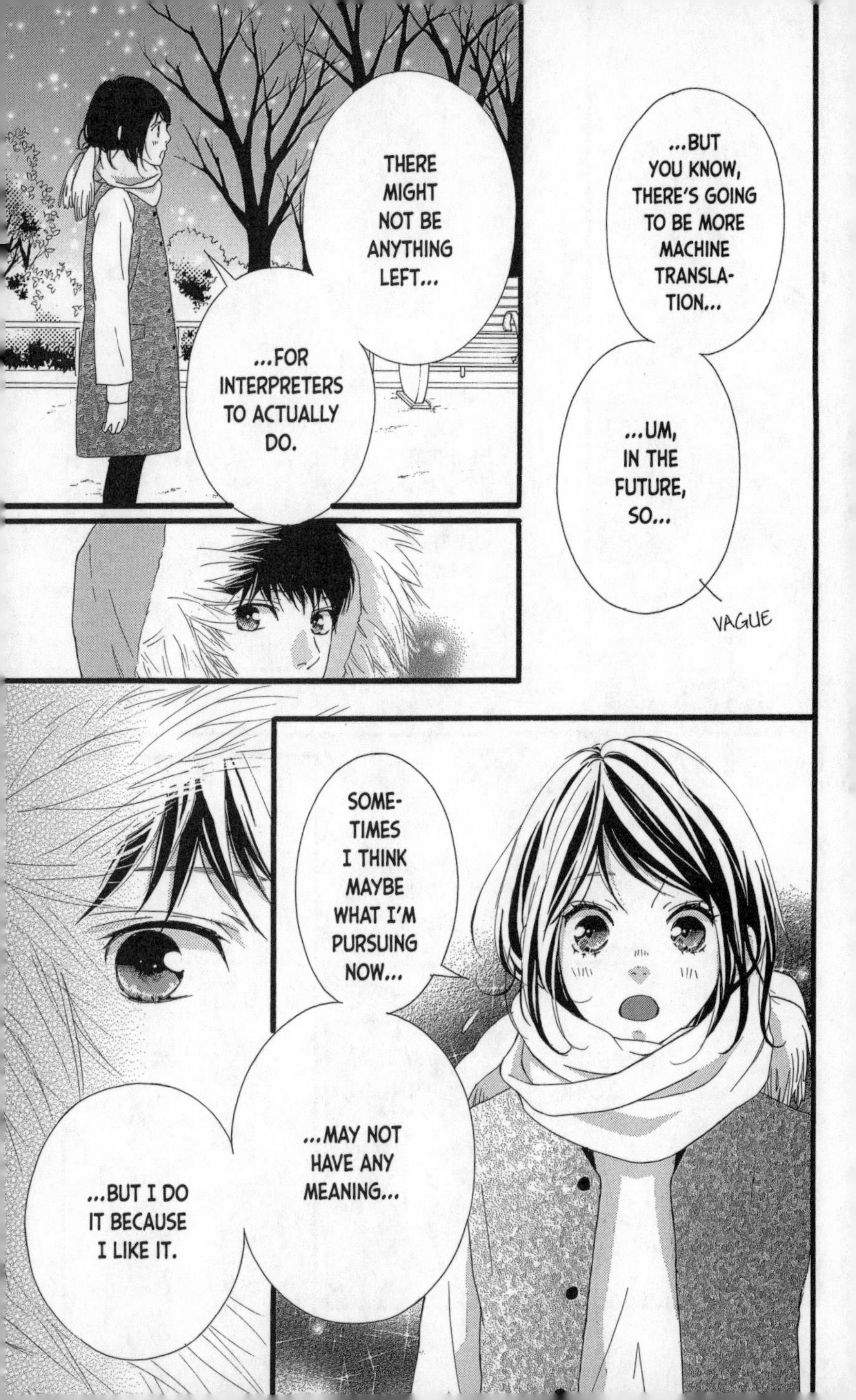
...BUT YOU KNOW, THERE'S GOING TO BE MORE MACHINE TRANSLA-TION...
...UM, IN THE FUTURE, SO...
VAGUE
THERE MIGHT NOT BE ANYTHING LEFT...
...FOR INTERPRETERS TO ACTUALLY DO.
SOME-TIMES I THINK MAYBE WHAT I'M PURSUING NOW...
...MAY NOT HAVE ANY MEANING...
...BUT I DO IT BECAUSE I LIKE IT.

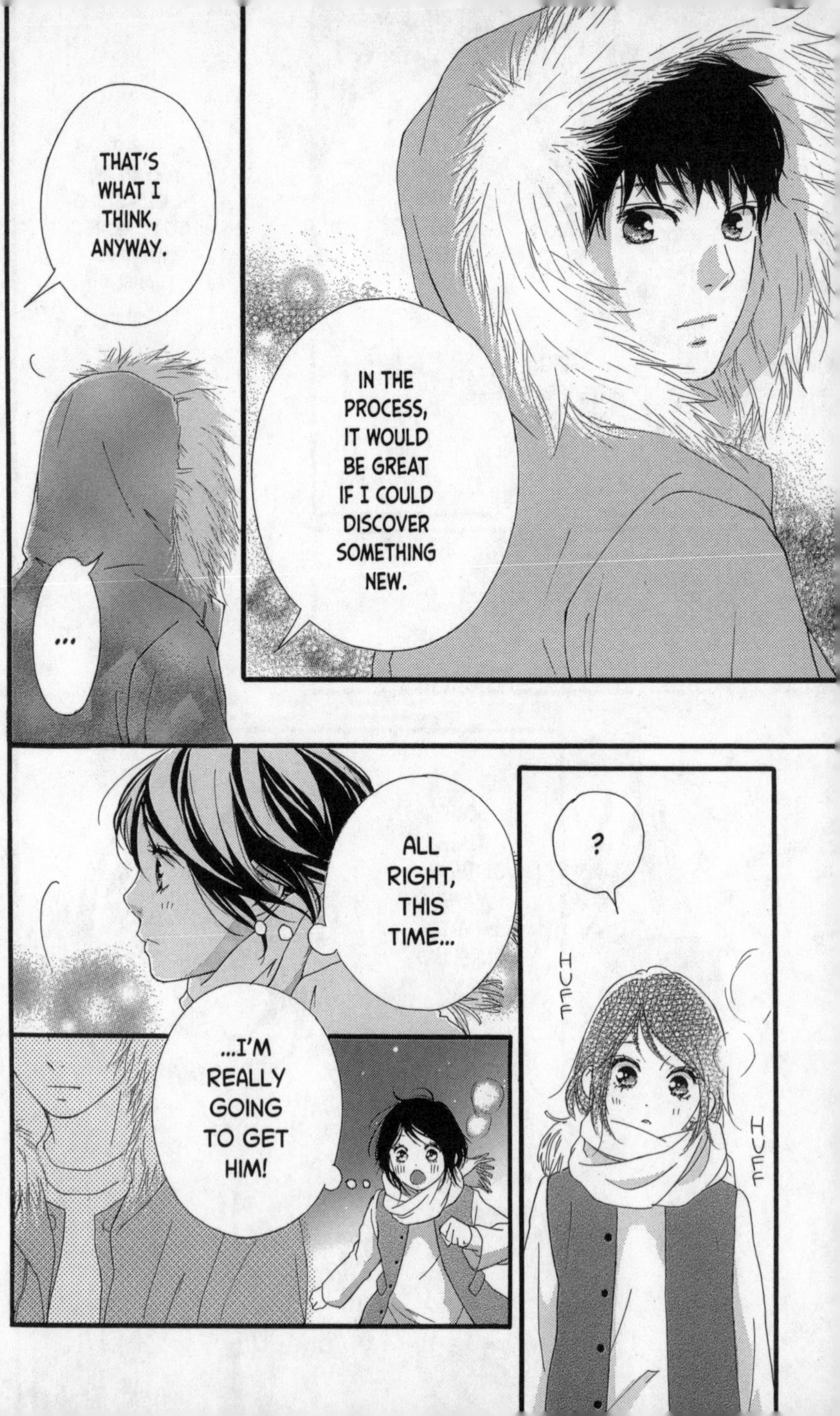
IN THE PROCESS, IT WOULD BE GREAT IF I COULD DISCOVER SOMETHING NEW.
THAT'S WHAT I THINK, ANYWAY.
...
?
HUFF
HUFF
ALL RIGHT, THIS TIME...
...I'M REALLY GOING TO GET HIM!

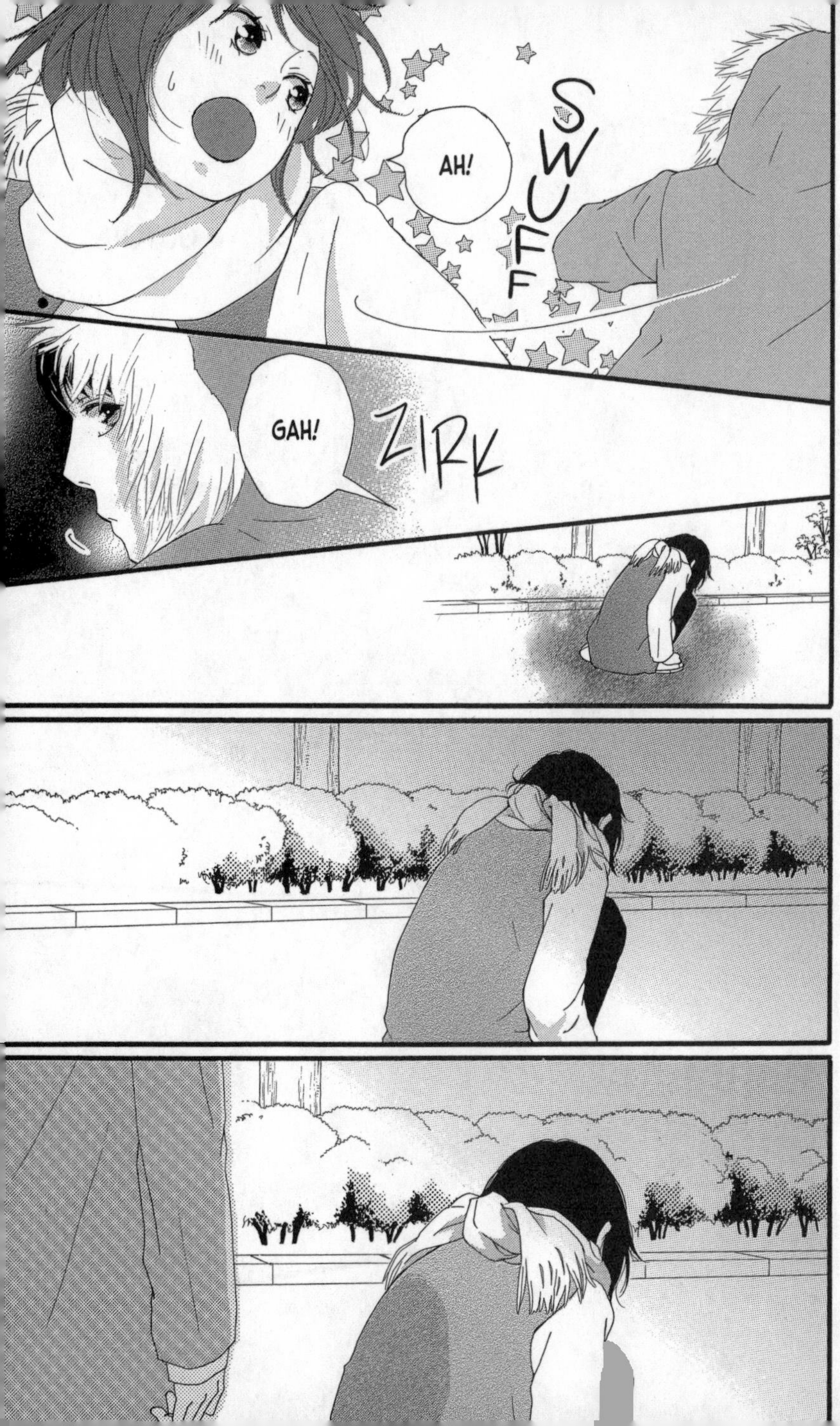
SWUFF
AH!
ZIRK
GAH!

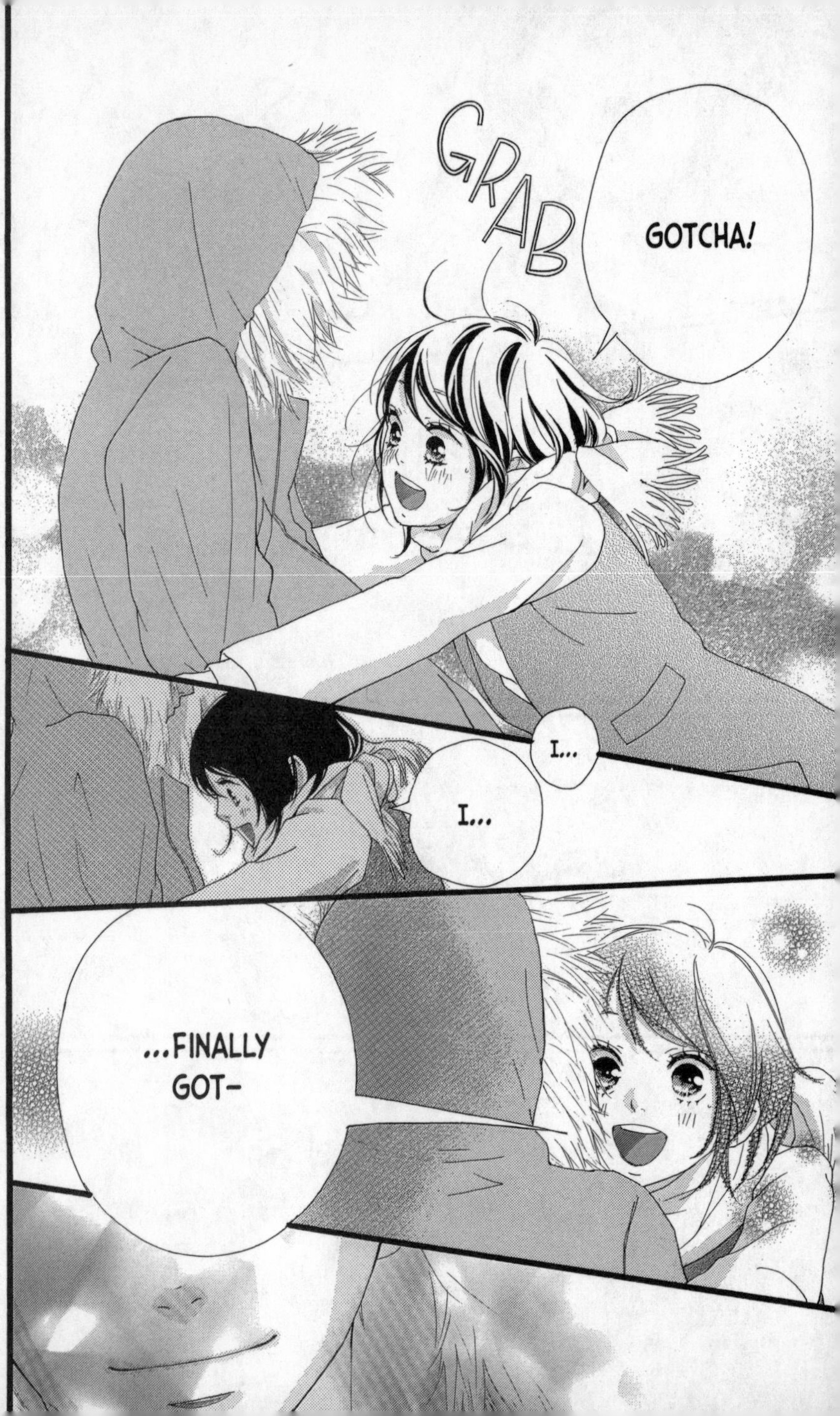
GOTCHA!
GRAB
I...
I...
...FINALLY GOT-

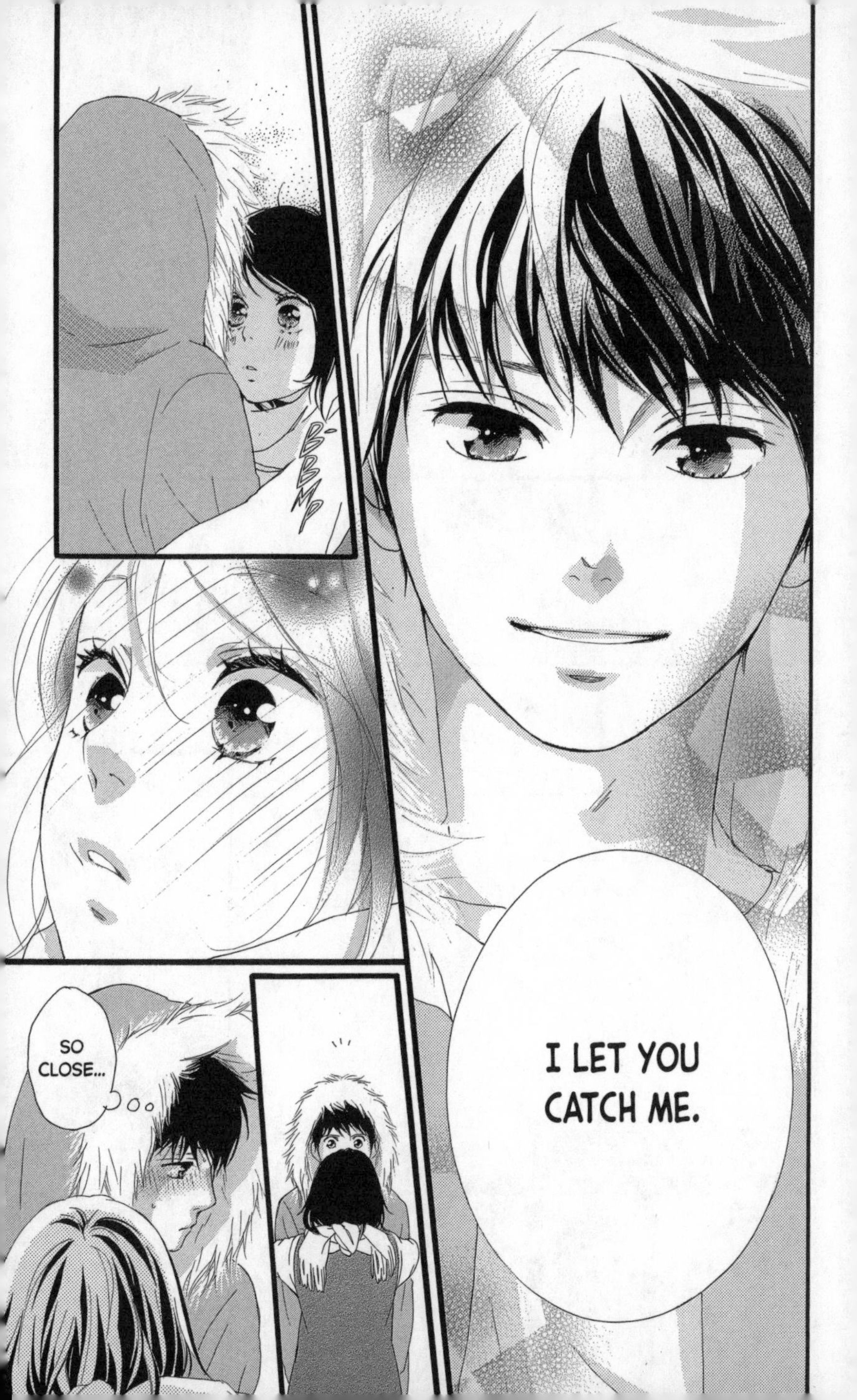
I LET YOU CATCH ME.
B-BUMP
SO CLOSE...

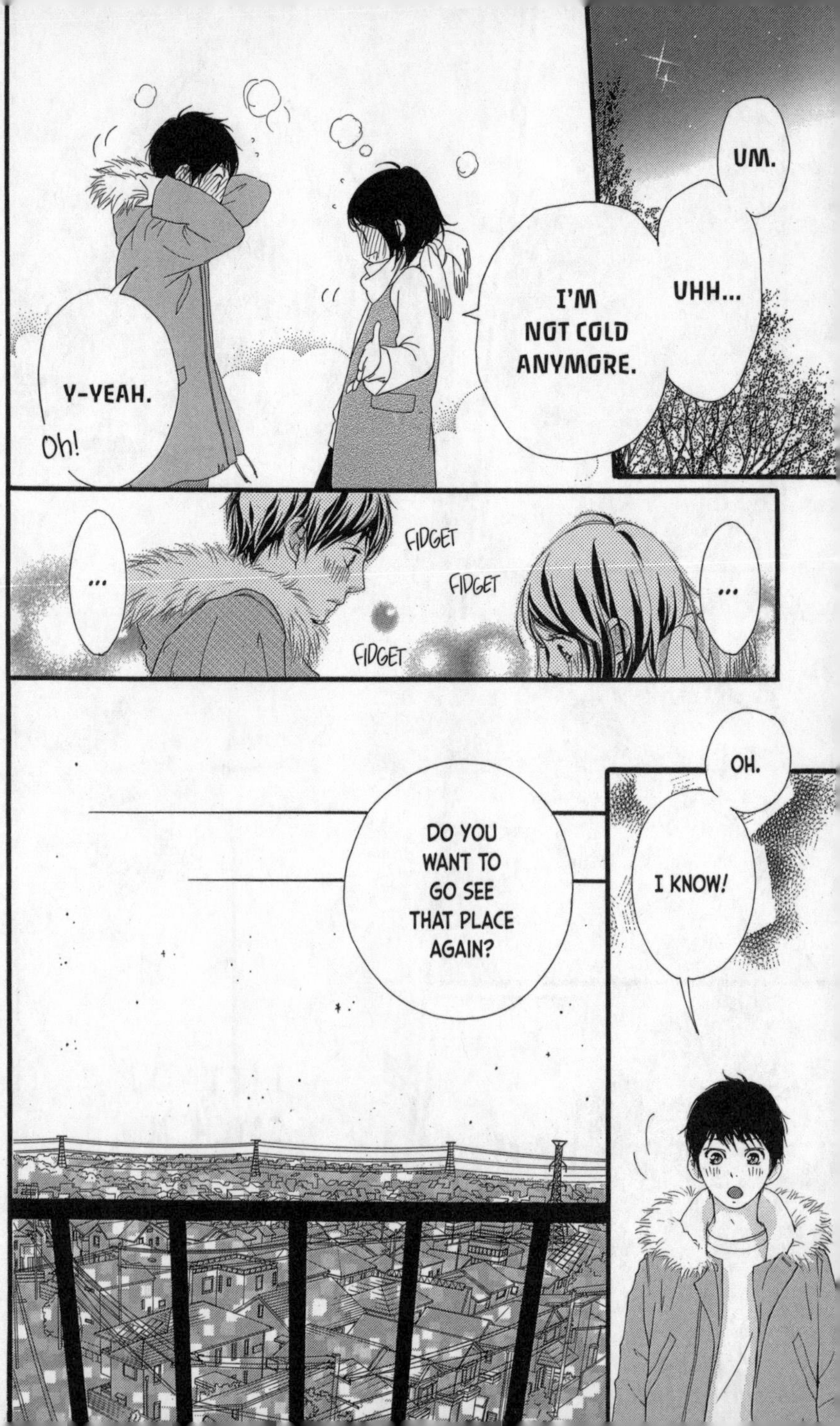
UM.
UHH...
I'M NOT COLD ANYMORE.
Y-YEAH.
Oh!
...
FIDGET
FIDGET
FIDGET
...
OH.
I KNOW!
DO YOU WANT TO GO SEE THAT PLACE AGAIN?

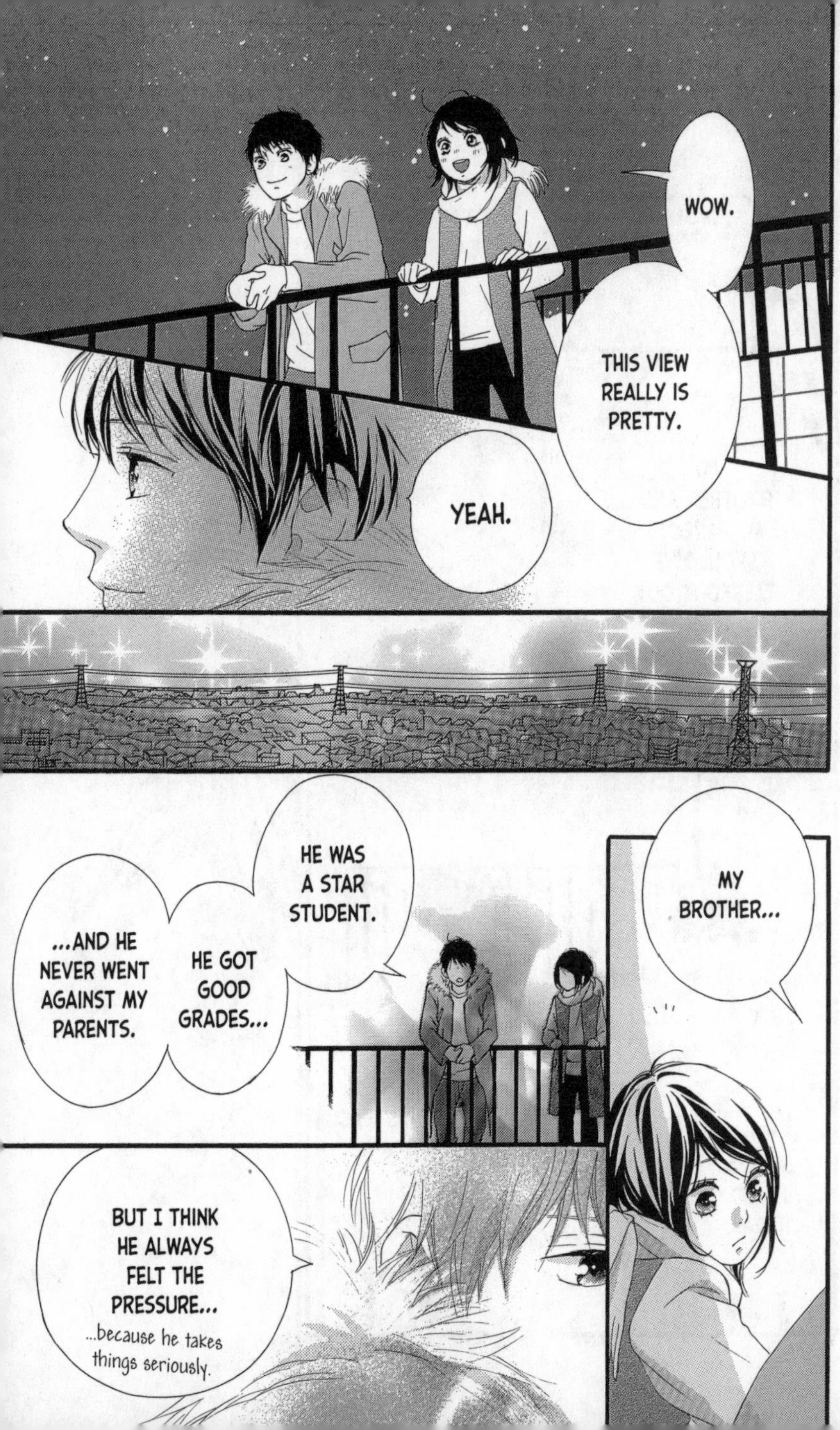
WOW.
THIS VIEW REALLY IS PRETTY.
YEAH.
MY BROTHER...
HE WAS A STAR STUDENT.
HE GOT GOOD GRADES...
...AND HE NEVER WENT AGAINST MY PARENTS.
BUT I THINK HE ALWAYS FELT THE PRESSURE...
...because he takes things seriously.

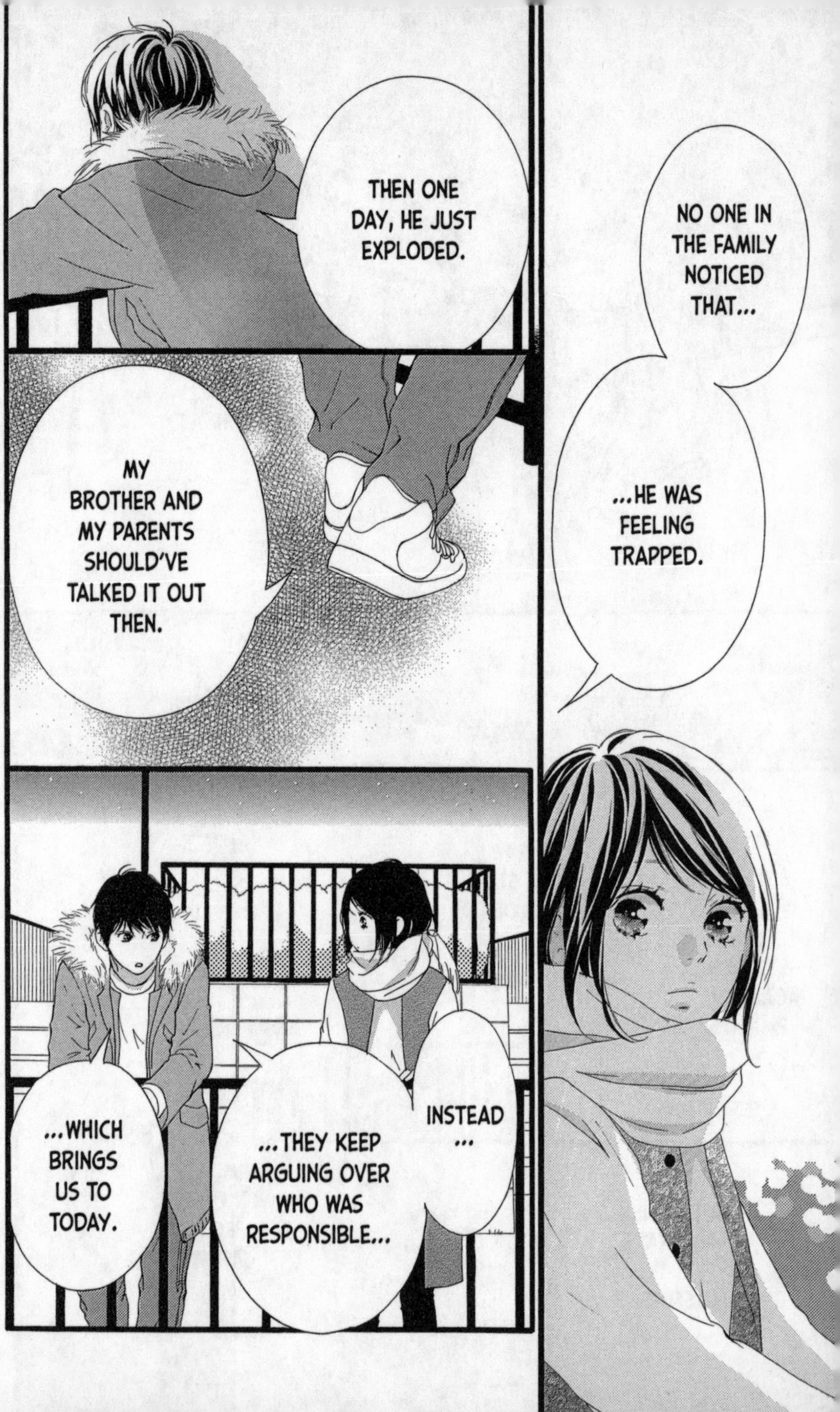
NO ONE IN THE FAMILY NOTICED THAT...
...HE WAS FEELING TRAPPED.
THEN ONE DAY, HE JUST EXPLODED.
MY BROTHER AND MY PARENTS SHOULD'VE TALKED IT OUT THEN.
INSTEAD...
...THEY KEEP ARGUING OVER WHO WAS RESPONSIBLE...
...WHICH BRINGS US TO TODAY.

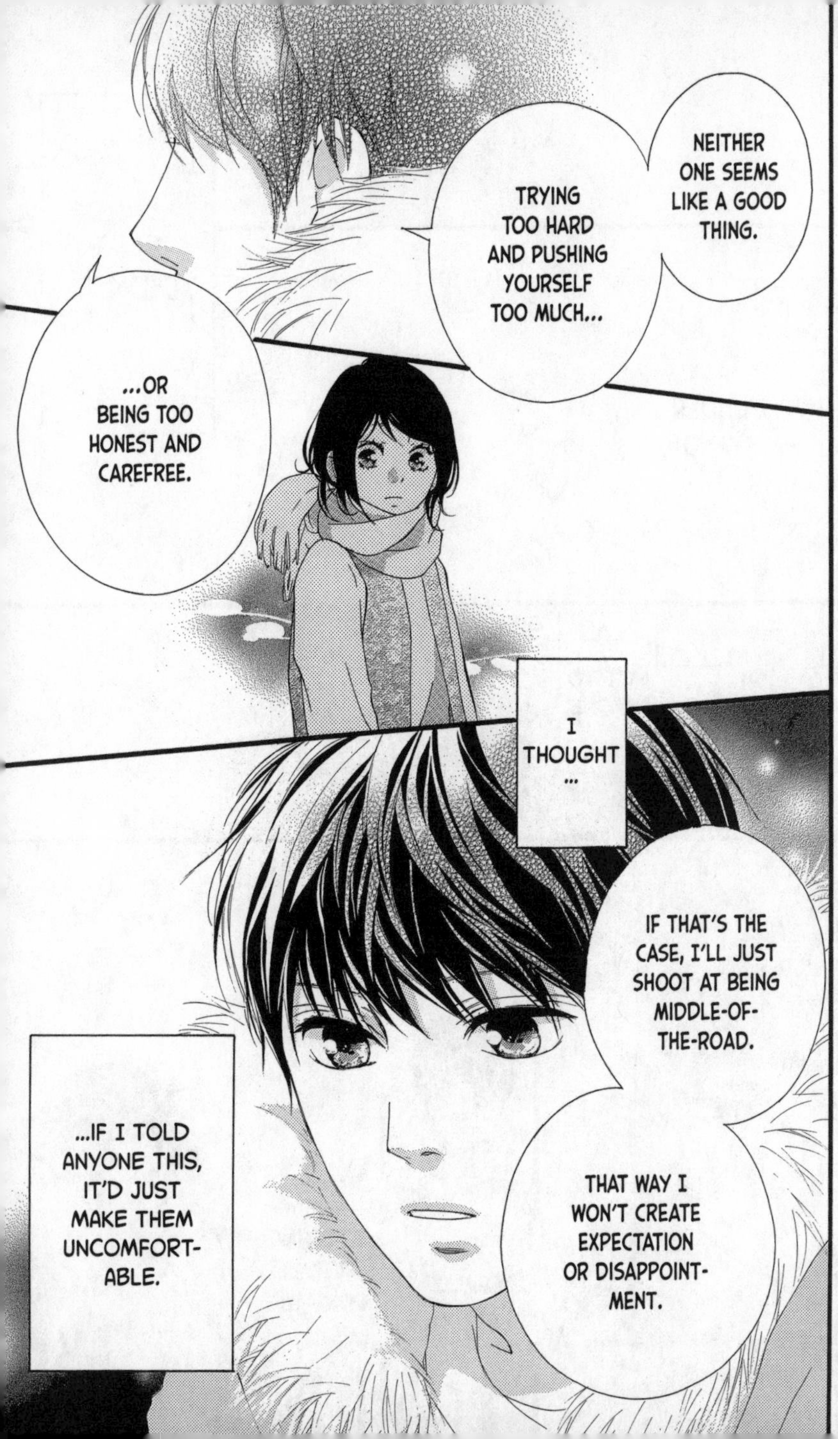
NEITHER ONE SEEMS LIKE A GOOD THING.
TRYING TOO HARD AND PUSHING YOURSELF TOO MUCH...
...OR BEING TOO HONEST AND CAREFREE.
I THOUGHT...
IF THAT'S THE CASE, I'LL JUST SHOOT AT BEING MIDDLE-OF-THE-ROAD.
THAT WAY I WON'T CREATE EXPECTATION OR DISAPPOINT-MENT.
...IF I TOLD ANYONE THIS, IT'D JUST MAKE THEM UNCOMFORT-ABLE.

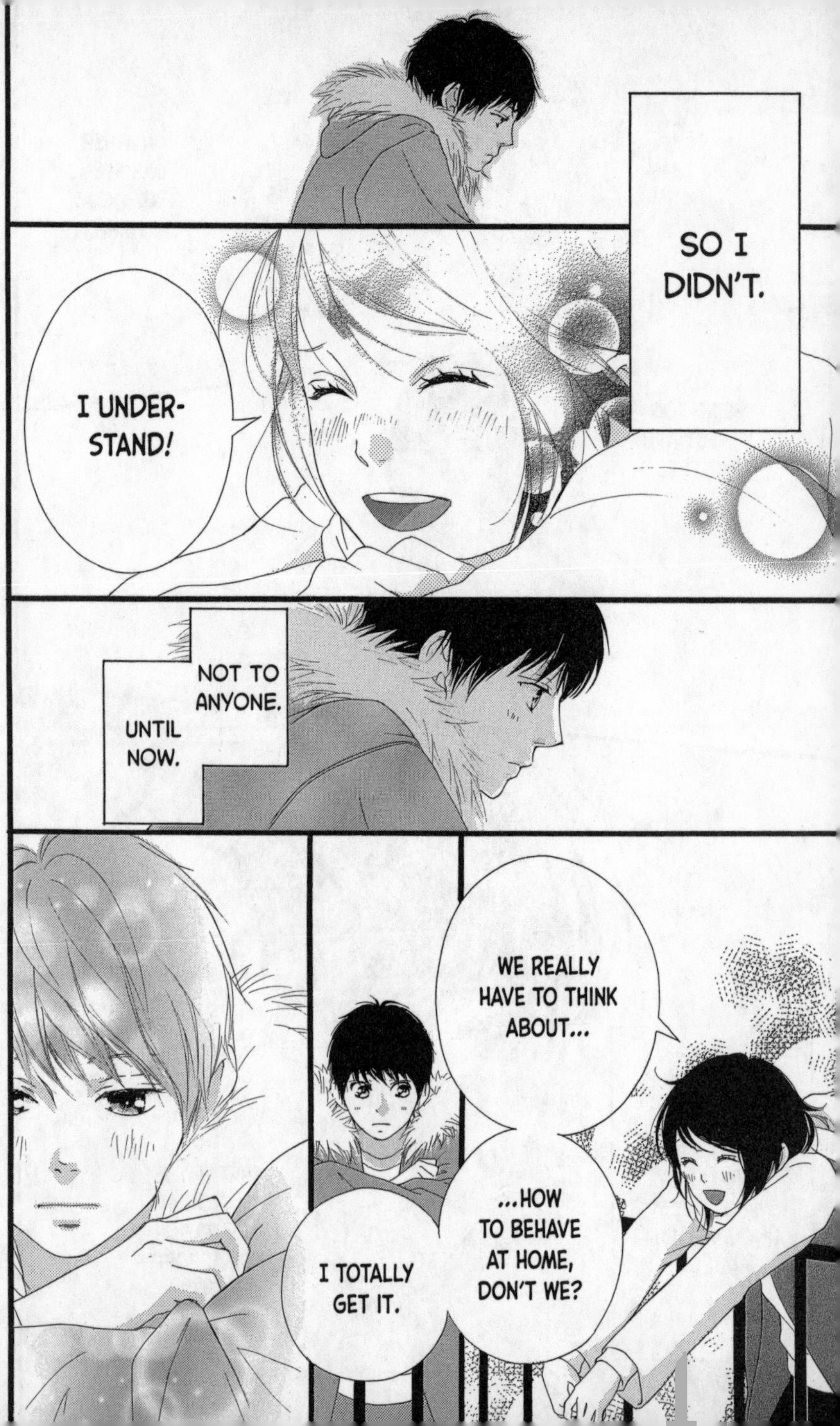
SO I DIDN'T.
I UNDERSTAND!
NOT TO ANYONE.
UNTIL NOW.
WE REALLY HAVE TO THINK ABOUT...
...HOW TO BEHAVE AT HOME, DON'T WE?
I TOTALLY GET IT.

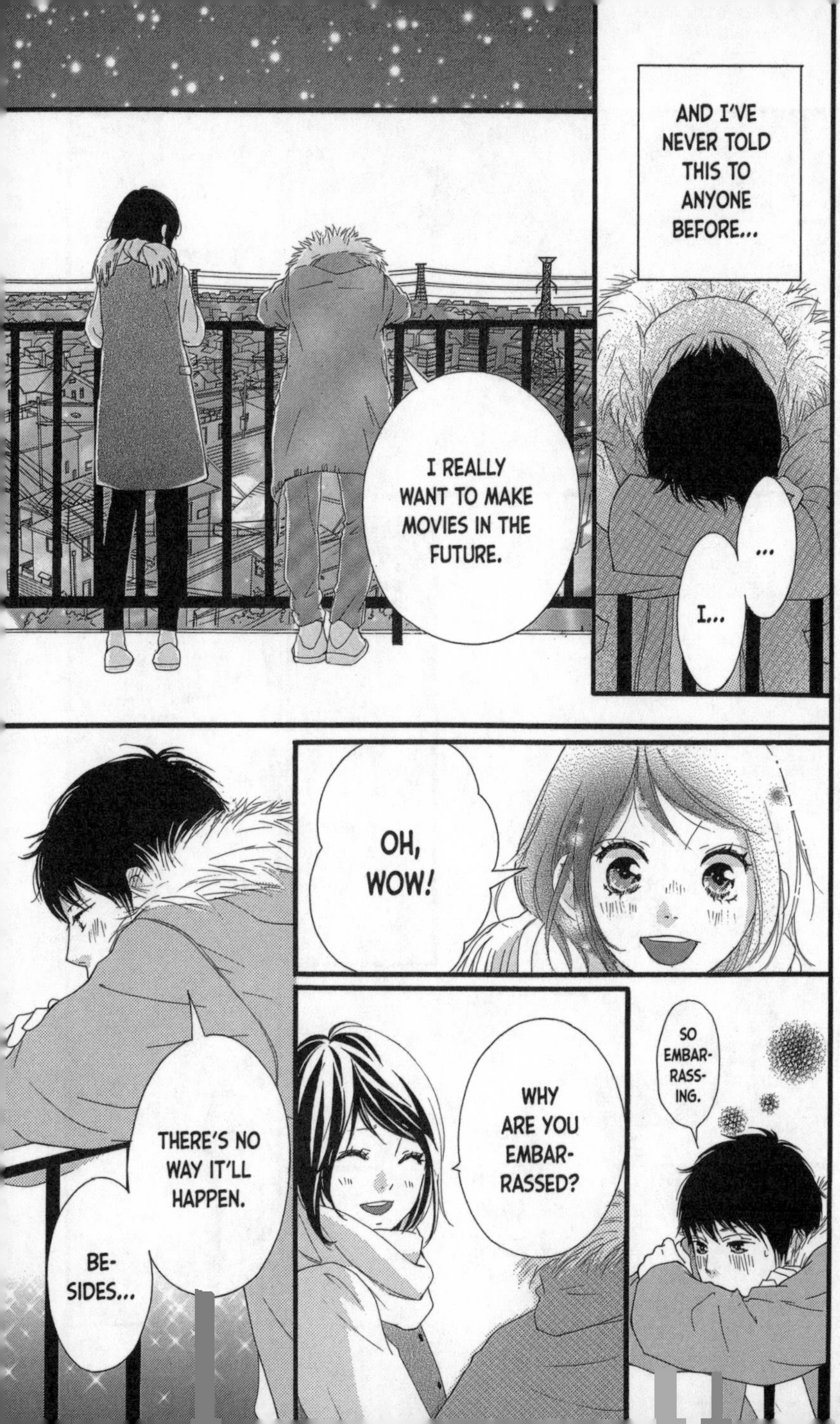
AND I'VE NEVER TOLD THIS TO ANYONE BEFORE...
...
I...
I REALLY WANT TO MAKE MOVIES IN THE FUTURE.
OH, WOW!
SO EMBAR-RASS-ING.
WHY ARE YOU EMBAR-RASSED?
THERE'S NO WAY IT'LL HAPPEN.
BE-SIDES...

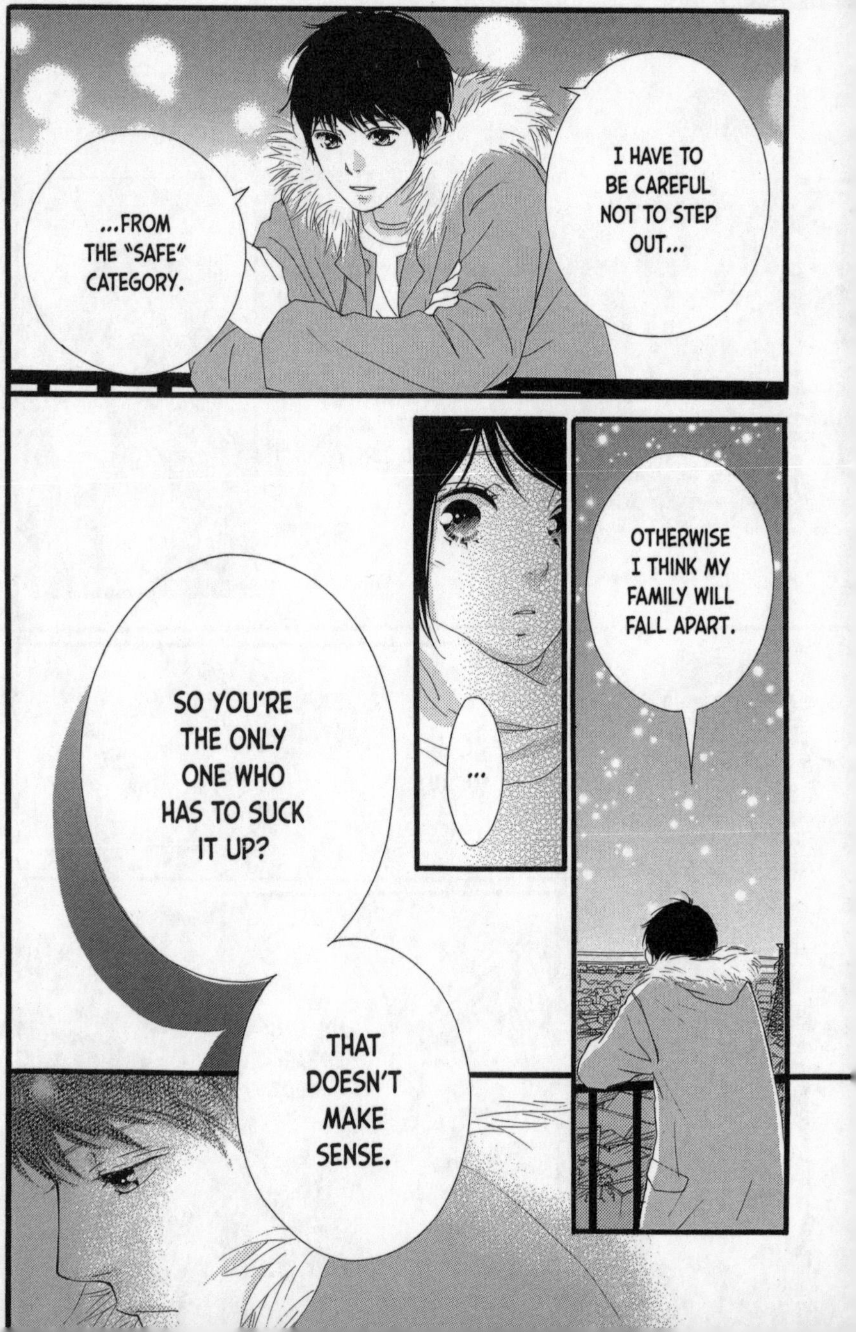
I HAVE TO BE CAREFUL NOT TO STEP OUT...
...FROM THE "SAFE" CATEGORY.
OTHERWISE I THINK MY FAMILY WILL FALL APART.
...
SO YOU'RE THE ONLY ONE WHO HAS TO SUCK IT UP?
THAT DOESN'T MAKE SENSE.

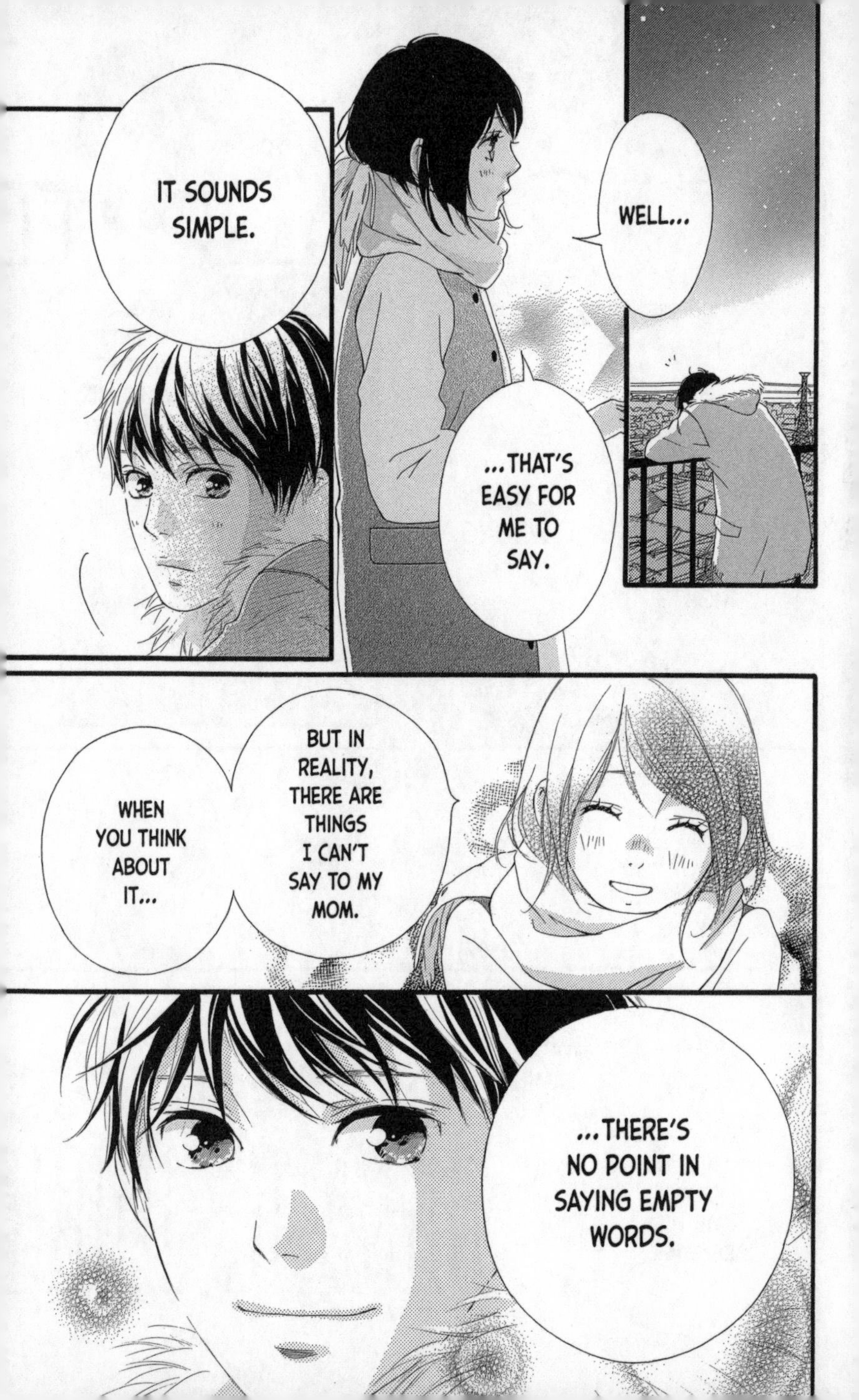
WELL...
...THAT'S EASY FOR ME TO SAY.
IT SOUNDS SIMPLE.
BUT IN REALITY, THERE ARE THINGS I CAN'T SAY TO MY MOM.
WHEN YOU THINK ABOUT IT...
...THERE'S NO POINT IN SAYING EMPTY WORDS.

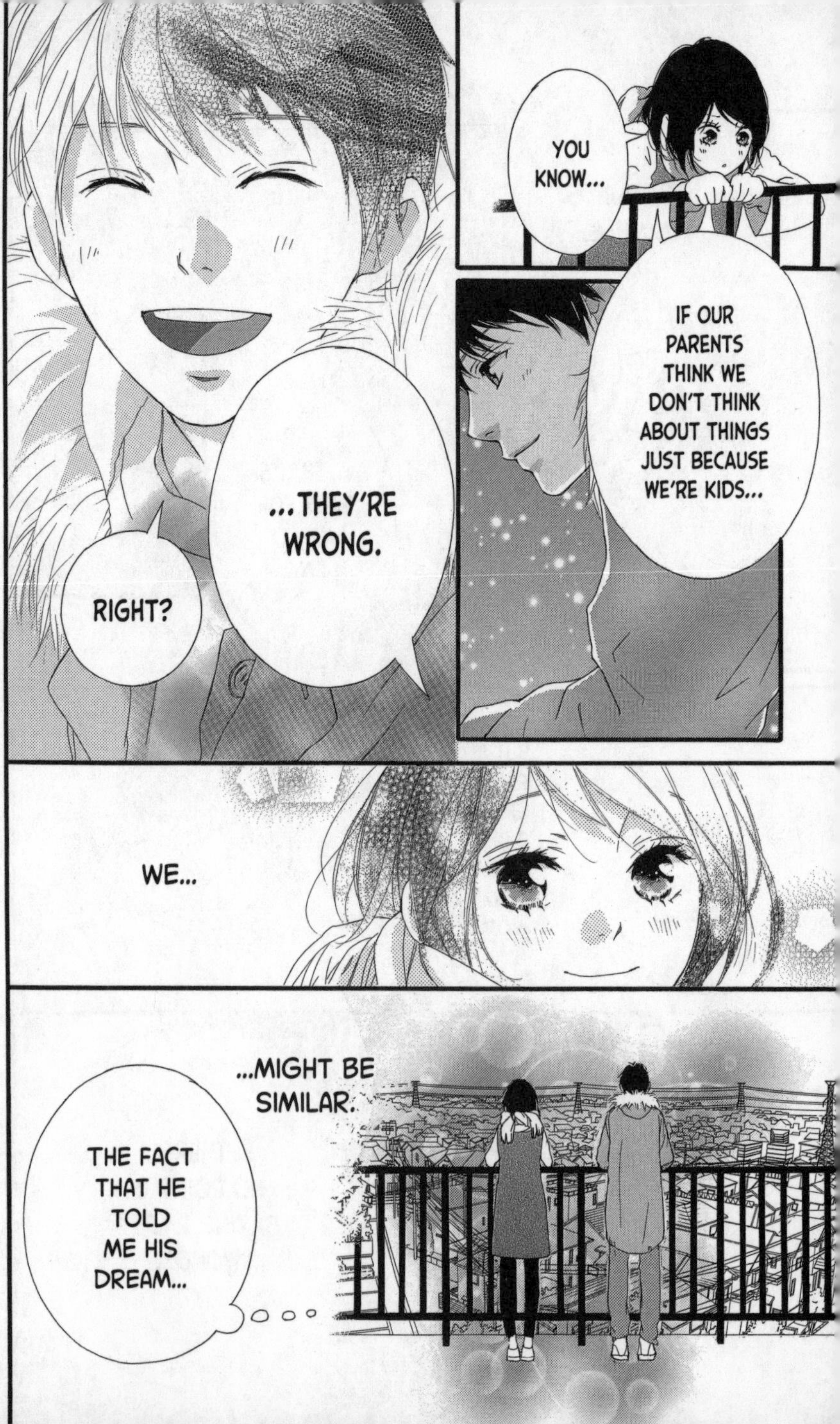
YOU KNOW...
IF OUR PARENTS THINK WE DON'T THINK ABOUT THINGS JUST BECAUSE WE'RE KIDS...
...THEY'RE WRONG.
RIGHT?
WE...
...MIGHT BE SIMILAR.
THE FACT THAT HE TOLD ME HIS DREAM...

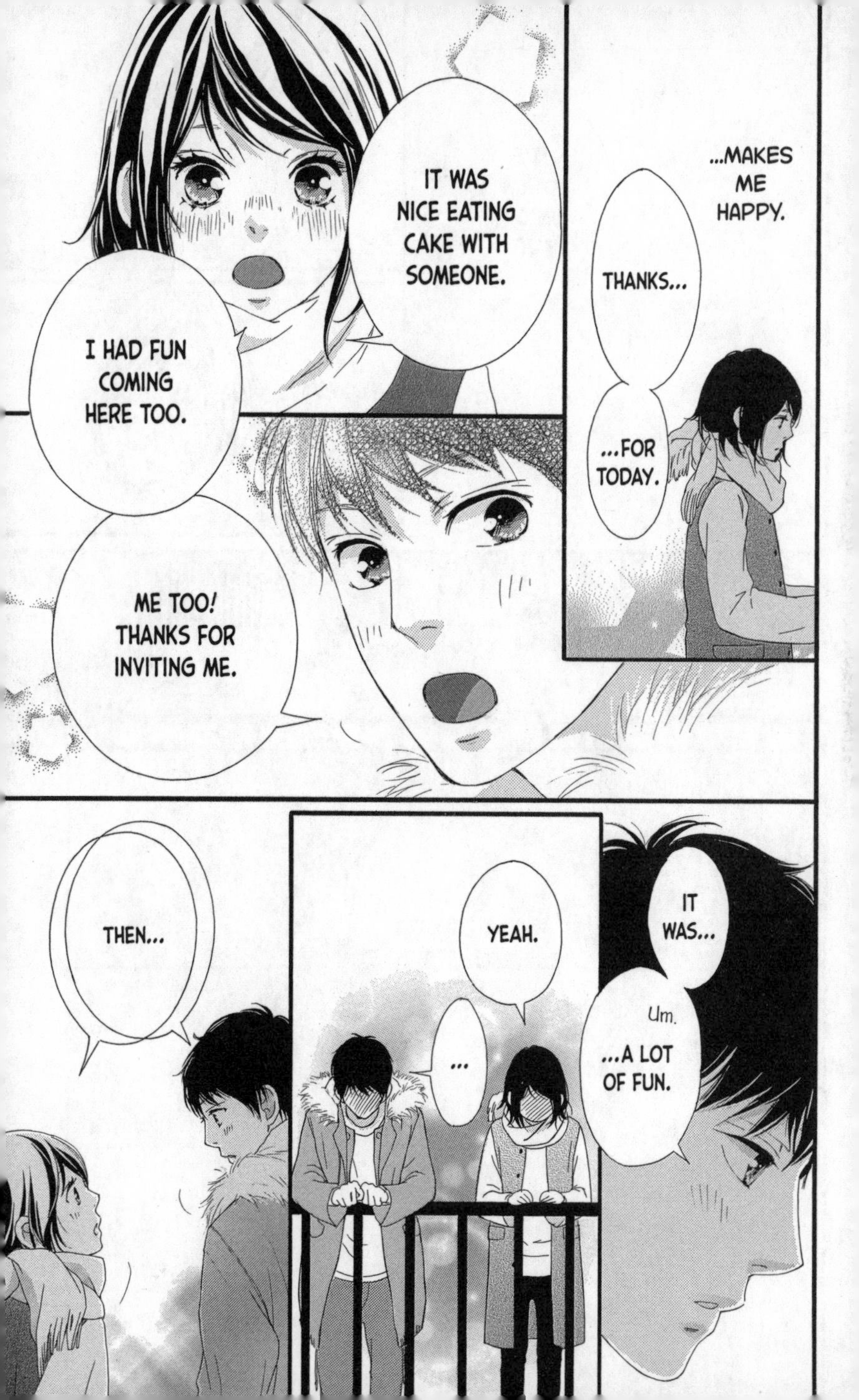
...MAKES ME HAPPY.
THANKS...
...FOR TODAY.
IT WAS NICE EATING CAKE WITH SOMEONE.
I HAD FUN COMING HERE TOO.
ME TOO! THANKS FOR INVITING ME.
IT WAS...
Um.
...A LOT OF FUN.
YEAH.
...
THEN...

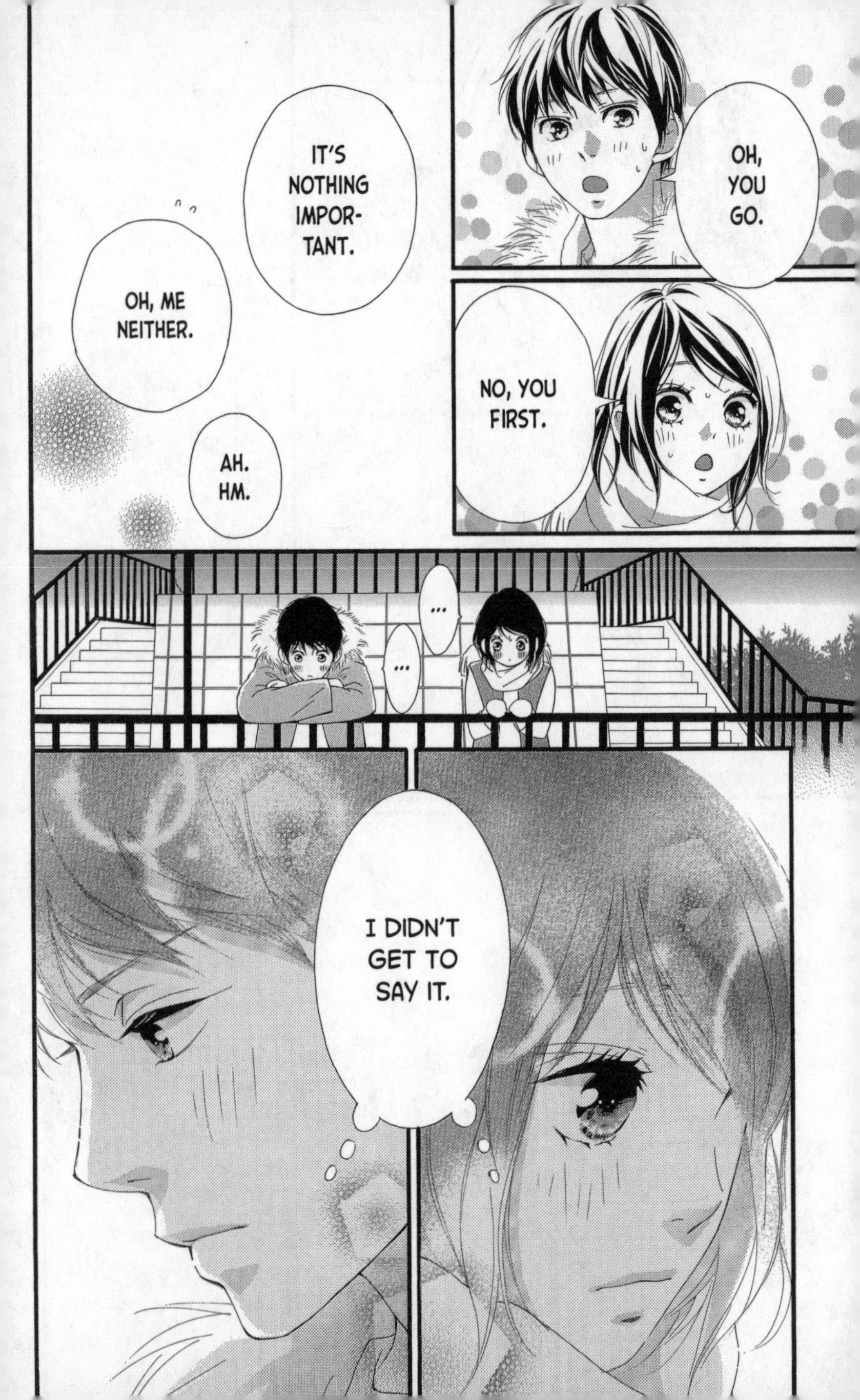
OH, YOU GO.
NO, YOU FIRST.
IT'S NOTHING IMPOR-TANT.
OH, ME NEITHER.
AH. HM.
...
...
I DIDN'T GET TO SAY IT.

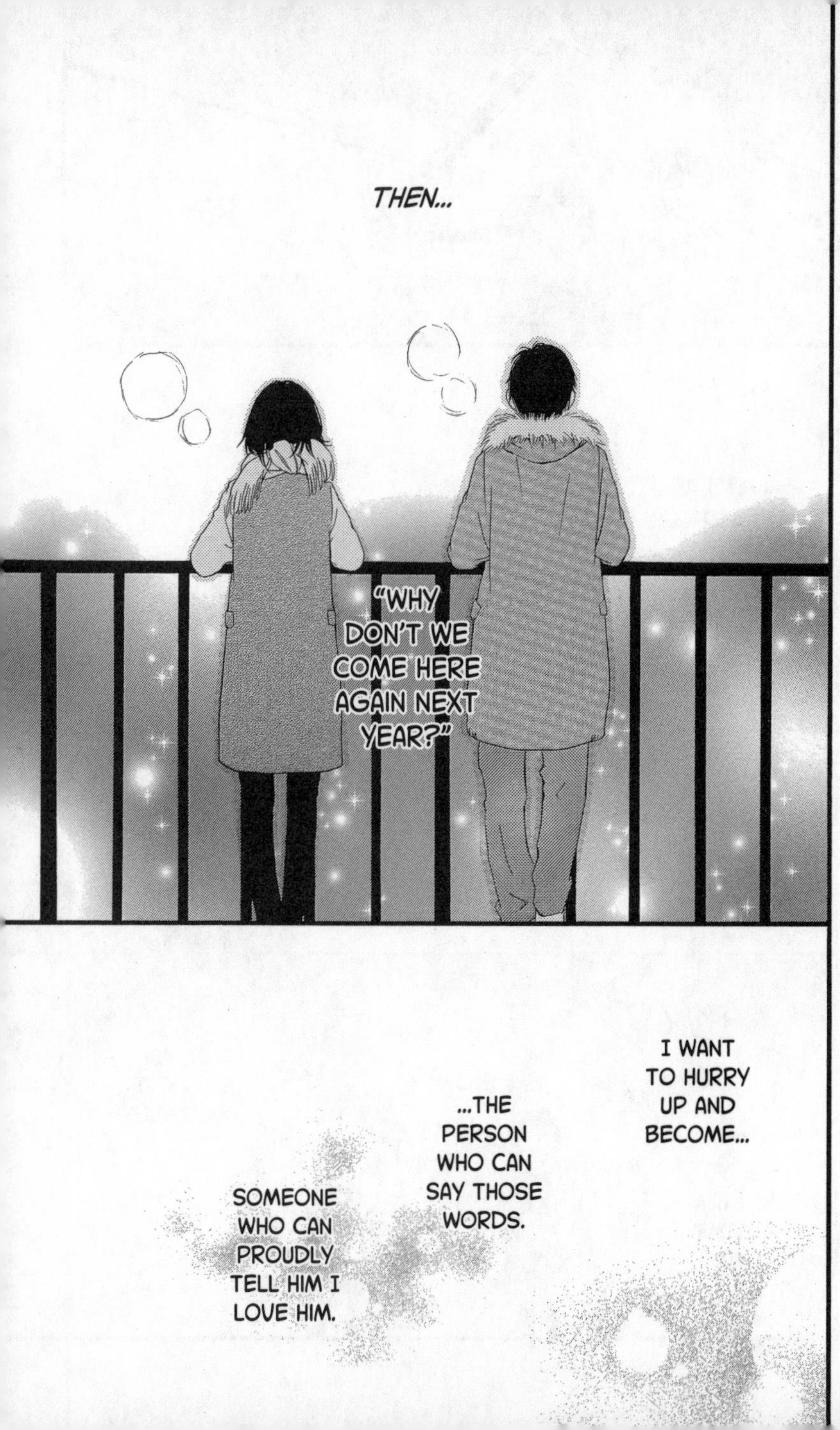
THEN...
"WHY DON'T WE COME HERE AGAIN NEXT YEAR?"
I WANT TO HURRY UP AND BECOME...
...THE PERSON WHO CAN SAY THOSE WORDS.
SOMEONE WHO CAN PROUDLY TELL HIM I LOVE HIM.

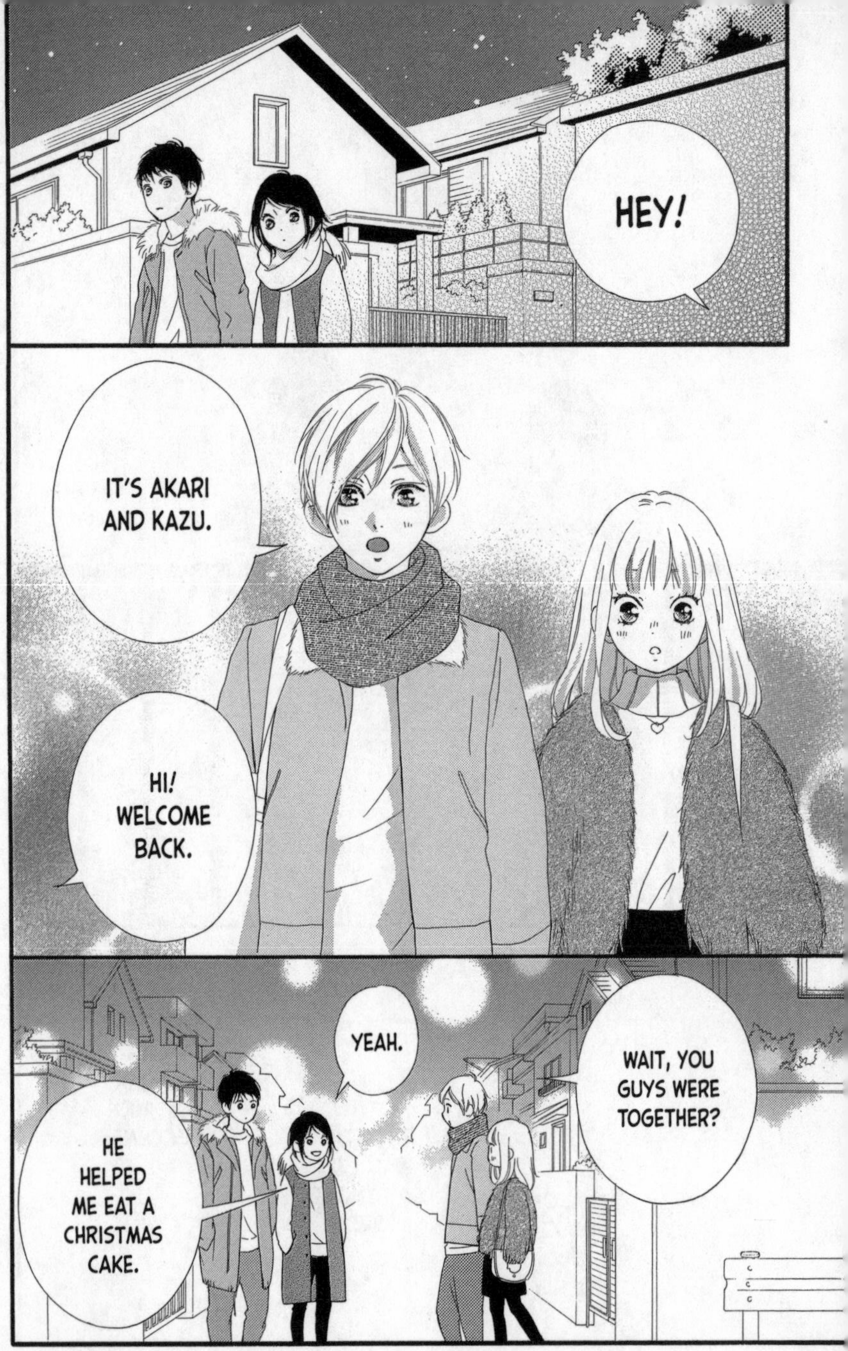
HEY!
IT'S AKARI AND KAZU.
HI! WELCOME BACK.
WAIT, YOU GUYS WERE TOGETHER?
YEAH.
HE HELPED ME EAT A CHRISTMAS CAKE.

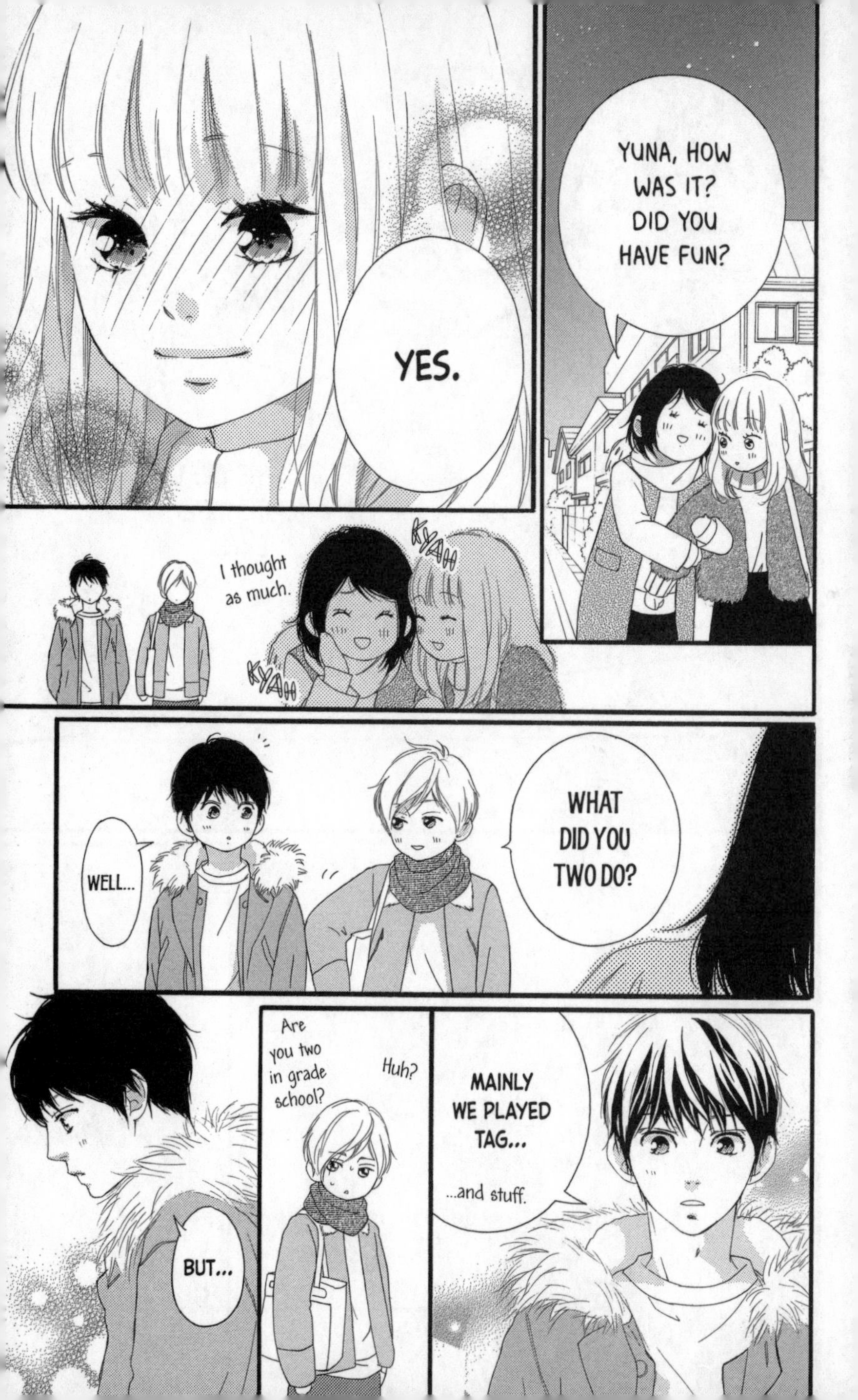
YUNA, HOW WAS IT? DID YOU HAVE FUN?
YES.
KYAH
I thought as much.
KYAH
WHAT DID YOU TWO DO?
WELL...
MAINLY WE PLAYED TAG...
...and stuff.
Are you two in grade school?
Huh?
BUT...

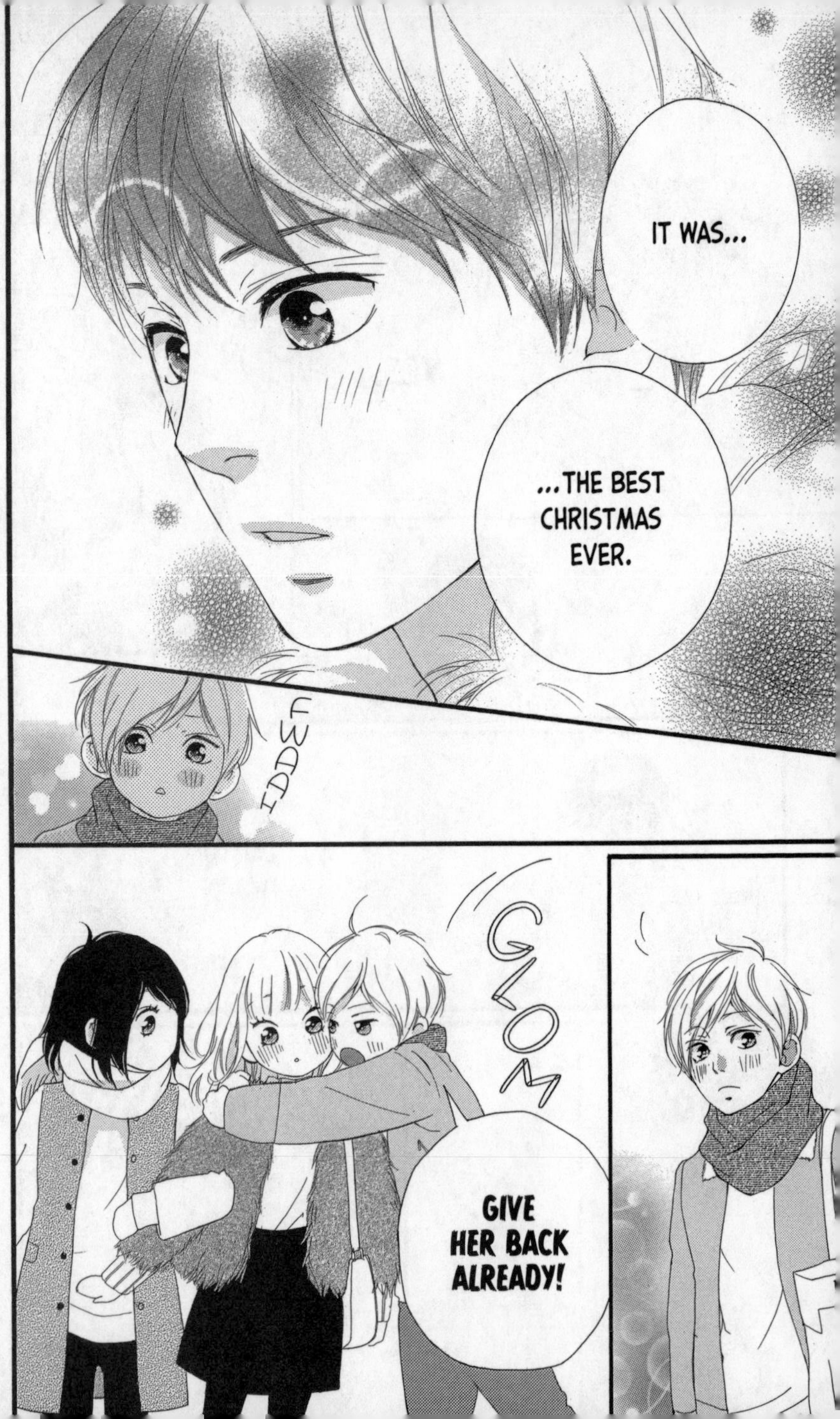
IT WAS...
...THE BEST CHRISTMAS EVER.
FWAAH
GLOMP
GIVE HER BACK ALREADY!

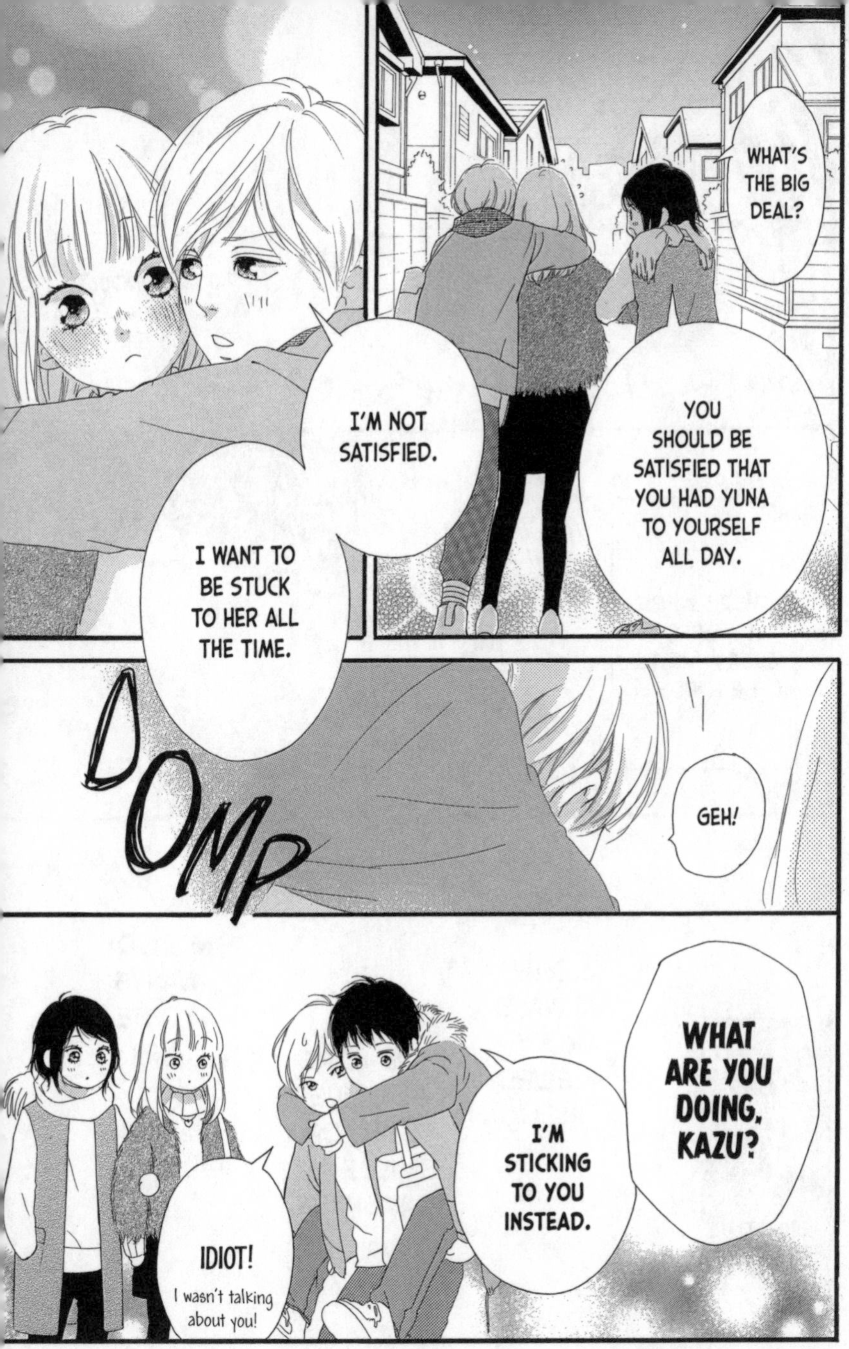
WHAT'S THE BIG DEAL?
YOU SHOULD BE SATISFIED THAT YOU HAD YUNA TO YOURSELF ALL DAY.
I'M NOT SATISFIED.
I WANT TO BE STUCK TO HER ALL THE TIME.
GEH!
DOMP
WHAT ARE YOU DOING, KAZU?
I'M STICKING TO YOU INSTEAD.
IDIOT!
I wasn't talking about you!

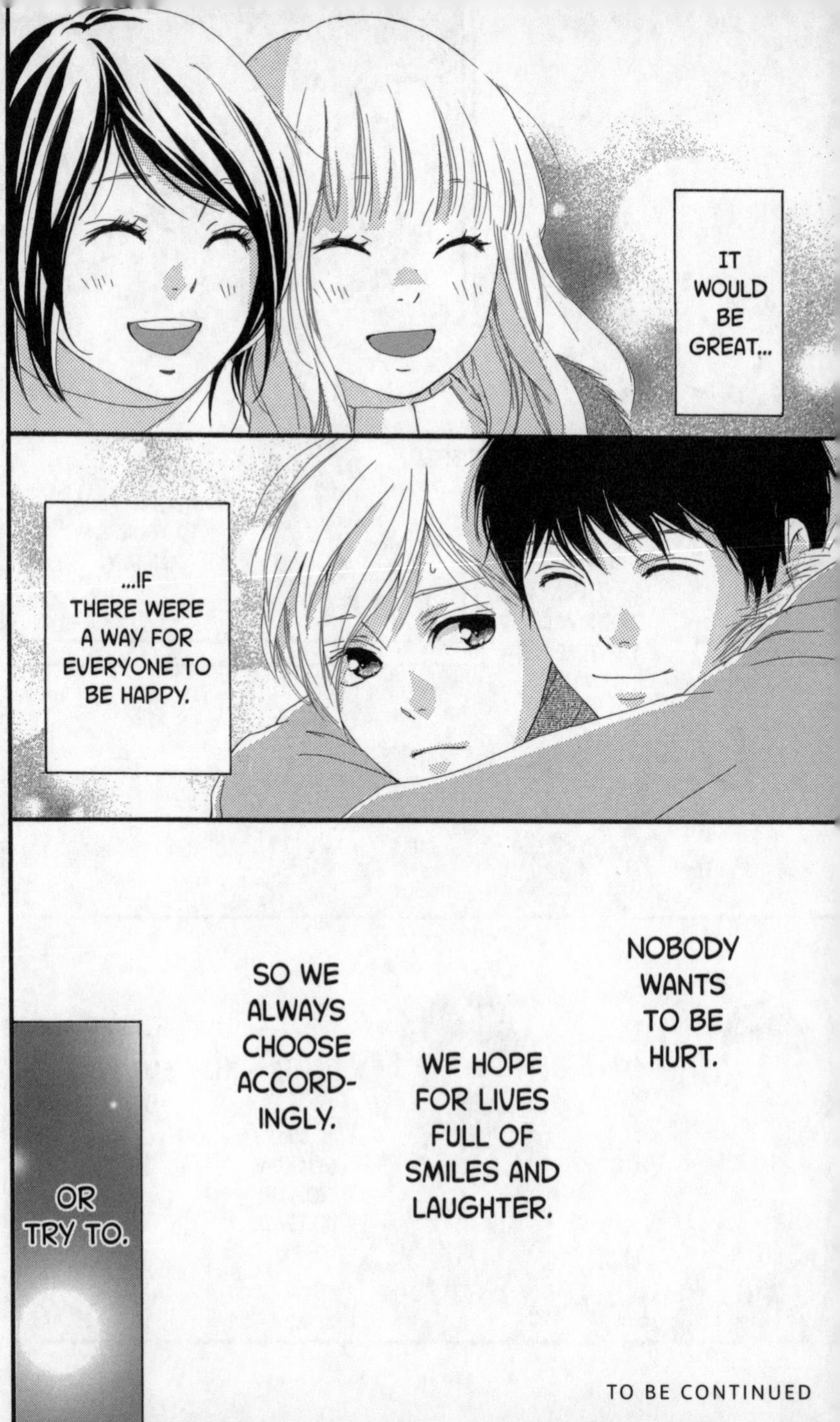
IT WOULD BE GREAT...
...IF THERE WERE A WAY FOR EVERYONE TO BE HAPPY.
NOBODY WANTS TO BE HURT.
WE HOPE FOR LIVES FULL OF SMILES AND LAUGHTER.
SO WE ALWAYS CHOOSE ACCORD-INGLY.
OR TRY TO.
TO BE CONTINUED

AFTERWORD

Thank you so much for reading *Love Me, Love Me Not* vol. 8 to the end.

In this volume, I enjoyed creating Christmas for the two couples. Yuna and Rio's sweet, sweet Christmas, and Akari and Kazuomi's clumsy yet tender Christmas.

The lookout that Akari and Kazuomi hadn't visited since vol. 2 is based on a place in a town where I used to live. (I changed the shape of the clearing.) There was a long gentle hill, and in the evening, the city lights that were just far enough away made the scene feel a little melancholy. Remembering that made me want to visit it all of a sudden. So I went to take photos for my files. But the sunset backlit the view, and I couldn't get the angle I wanted. What was the point of going? The road was not at all gentle, and I was super tired, but seeing two junior high boys up there watching the sunset made me feel better. They were so cute. Feeling re-energized, I made my way home wondering what to have for dinner. See you again in the next volume. I think I may have had noodles with tempura for that dinner.

 Io Sakisaka

I fell spectacularly and got a huge bruise. But when I noticed later that it had completely disappeared, I was struck by how amazing living things are. Getting that bruise hurt a lot, though, so I'd like to live life without falling.

Io Sakisaka

Born on June 8, Io Sakisaka made her debut as a manga creator with *Sakura, Chiru*. Her series *Strobe Edge* and *Ao Haru Ride* are published by VIZ Media's Shojo Beat imprint. *Ao Haru Ride* was adapted into an anime series in 2014, and *Love Me, Love Me Not* will be an animated feature film. In her spare time, Sakisaka likes to paint things and sleep.

Love Me, Love Me Not

Vol. 8

Shojo Beat Edition

STORY AND ART BY

Io Sakisaka

Adaptation/Nancy Thistlethwaite
Translation/JN Productions
Touch-Up Art & Lettering/Sara Linsley
Design/Yukiko Whitley
Editor/Nancy Thistlethwaite

Printed in the U.S.A.

Published by VIZ Media, LLC
P.O. Box 77010
San Francisco, CA 94107

10 9 8 7 6 5 4 3 2 1
First printing, May 2021

ratings.viz.com RATED T TEEN

PARENTAL ADVISORY
LOVE ME, LOVE ME NOT is rated T for Teen and is recommended for ages 13 and up. This story centers around teenage relationships.

VIZ MEDIA
viz.com

Shojo Beat
shojobeat.com

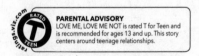

Shojo Beat Romances by IO SAKISAKA

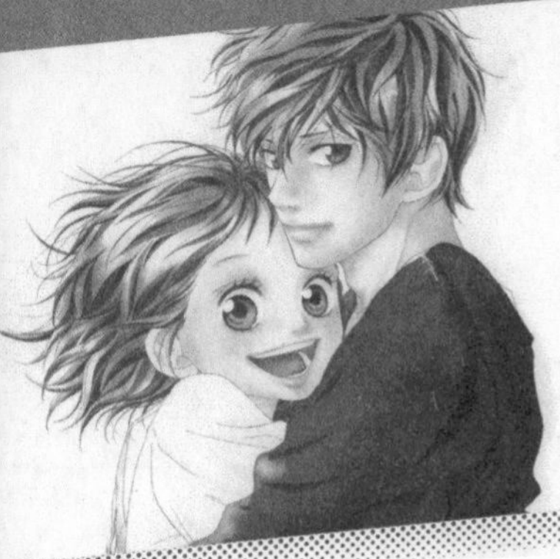

STROBE EDGE

When Ninako meets Ren, the handsome, enigmatic guy that all the girls worship, her life takes an unexpected turn. With just a few words and a smile, he changes her world...

Ao Haru Ride

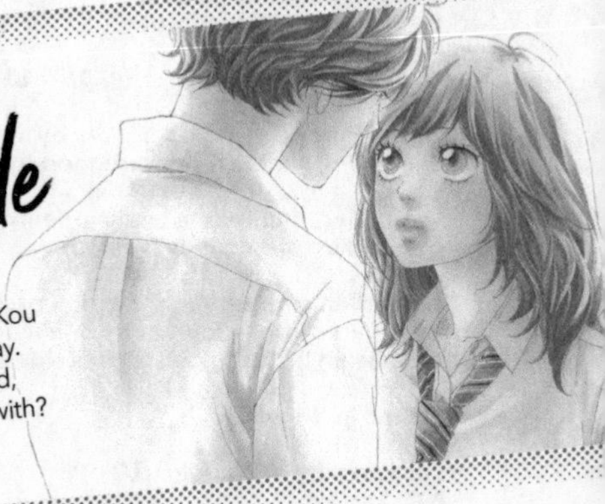

As soon as Futaba realized she really liked Kou in junior high, he had already moved away. Now, in high school, Kou has reappeared, but is he still the same boy she fell in love with?

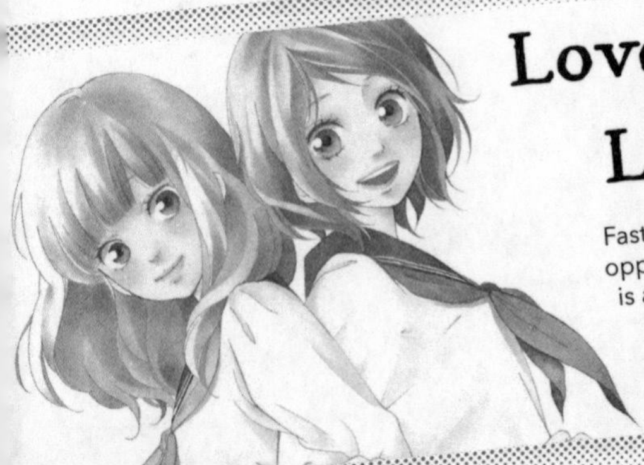

Love Me, Love Me Not

Fast friends Yuna and Akari are complete opposites—Yuna is an idealist, while Akari is a realist. When lady-killer Rio and the oblivious Kazuomi join their ranks, love and friendship become quite complicated!

RATED T TEEN

VIZ

DAYTIME SHOOTING STAR

Story & Art by

Mika Yamamori

Small town girl Suzume moves to Tokyo and finds her heart caught between two men!

After arriving in Tokyo to live with her uncle, Suzume collapses in a nearby park when she remembers once seeing a shooting star during the day. A handsome stranger brings her to her new home and tells her they'll meet again. Suzume starts her first day at her new high school sitting next to a boy who blushes furiously at her touch. And her homeroom teacher is none other than the handsome stranger!

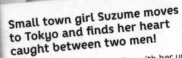

Stop!

You may be reading the wrong way.

In keeping with the original Japanese comic format, this book reads from right to left—so action, sound effects and word balloons are completely reversed to preserve the orientation of the original artwork. Check out the diagram shown here to get the hang of things, and then turn to the other side of the book to get started!

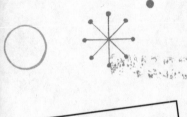

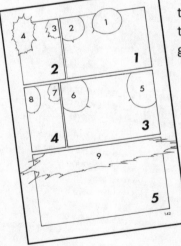